A study of regulatory influences on the quality and variety of products which includes a skillful integration of the theoretical and empirical dimensions of economic science. After attacking the problem of modeling product quality determination the authors offer case studies of self-regulation as a device for controlling product safety, variety, and standardization. Other material includes a consideration of the relationship between regulatory activity and product change through technology and innovation. The editors conclude with a series of papers assessing regulatory impacts on the price and availability of products to different geographic and income groups.

D0065208

rd E. Caves is Professor Economics at rd University. He was born in Akron, n 1931. He received his B.A. degree Oberlin College and his Ph.D. degree Harvard University. From 1957 to e taught at the University of California (Berkeley) before coming to Harvard. At Harvard he teaches in the fields of industrial organization and international trade. He is the author or co-author of numerous books and articles in these areas. His books include: *The Canadian Economy: Prospect and Retrospect, Trade and Economic Structure, Air Transport and Its Regulators, American Industry: Structure, Conduct, Performance, Britain's Economic Prospects, Capital Transfers and Economic Policy: Canada, 1951–1962,* and *World Trade and Payments.*

Marc J. Roberts is an Associate Professor of Economics at Harvard University. He was born in 1943 in Bayonne, New Jersey. He received his B.A. degree from Harvard in 1964 and his Ph.D. degree in 1969. He has taught industrial organization and environmental economics at Harvard. He is the author of a number of articles on the problems of public policy, including, "River Basin Authorities: A National Solution to Water Pollution," *Harvard Law Review;* "On Reforming Economic Growth," *Daedalus;* "Is there an Energy Crisis?" *Public Interest,* as well as a forthcoming book on environmental decision-making by electric utilities.

Regulating the Product

Contributors

Gerald Brock, Assistant Professor of Economics, University of Arizona

Sidney L. Carroll, Associate Professor of Economics, University of Tennessee, Knoxville

Richard E. Caves, Professor of Economics, Harvard University

Michael S. Hunt, Eli-Lili Corporation Inc.

Robert T. Kudrle, Assistant Professor, School of Public Affairs; Assistant Director, Center of International Studies, University of Minnesota

Harvey J. Levin, Augustus B. Weller, Professor of Economics, Hofstra College

Elisha A. Pazner, Lecturer on Economics, Tel-Aviv University

Marc J. Roberts, Associate Professor of Economics, Harvard University

Thomas R. Stauffer, Lecturer in Economics and Research Associate, Middle Eastern Studies, Harvard University

Lawrence J. White, Assistant Professor of Economics, Princeton University

Regulating the Product

Quality and Variety

Edited by Richard E. Caves and Marc J. Roberts

Prepared for
The Brookings Institution

Workshop on the Regulation
of Economic Activity,
Harvard University

Ballinger Publishing Company ● Cambridge, Mass.
A Subsidiary of J.B. Lippincott Company

Published in the United States of America by Ballinger Publishing Company
Cambridge, Mass.

First Printing, 1975

International Standard Book Number: 0-88410-272-6

Library of Congress Catalog Card Number: 74-18123

Printed in the United States of America

Library of Congress Cataloging in Publication Data

Main entry under title:
        Regulating the product: quality and variety.

        "Prepared for the Brookings Institution."
        Papers presented at a workshop on the regulation of economic
activity held at Harvard University.
        Includes bibliographical references.
        1. Industry and state—Case studies—Congresses.
        2. Quality control—Congresses.
        I. Caves, Richard E., ed.
        II. Roberts, Marc J., ed.
        III. Brookings Institution, Washington, D.C.
        IV. Harvard University.
HD3611.R38   338.4   74-18123
ISBN 0-88410-272-6

Contents

HD
3611
R38

List of Tables xi

Acknowledgements xiii

Introduction   *Richard E. Caves and Marc J. Roberts* xv

1. Regulating the Product: A Point of View xv
2. General Issues and Conclusions xvi

Part One
Regulation and the Level of Product Quality 1

Chapter One
Quality Choice and Monopoly Regulation
Elisha A. Pazner 3

1. Introduction 3
2. The Model 3
3. Effects of Regulation 6
   A. Rate-of-Return Regulation 7
   B. Price Regulation 9
   C. Mark-up Regulation 11
   D. Optimal Regulation 13
4. Conclusions 15
   Notes to Chapter One 16

Chapter Two
**Quality, Competition and Regulation: Evidence
from the Airline Industry**   *Lawrence J. White* 17

1. The Assumptions of the Model   18
2. The Model in the Absence of Regulation   19
3. The Model under Price Regulation   21
4. Airline Flight Frequencies: An Application of the Model   24
5. Explaining the Results   31
6. Conclusions   32
   Notes to Chapter Two   33

   Part Two
   Self-Regulation of Product Characteristics   37

   Chapter Three
   Trade Associations and Self-Regulation:
   Major Home Appliances   *Michael S. Hunt*   39

1. The Major Home Appliance Industry   40
2. AHAM: History and Organization   41
3. Self-Regulation   43
   Safety Standards   44
   Product Standards   46
   Product Certification   49
   MACAP   50
4. Conclusions   52
   Notes to Chapter Three   54

   Chapter Four
   Regulation and Self-Regulation in the Farm
   Machinery Industry   *Robert T. Kudrle*   57

1. Product Certification: The Nebraska Tractor Tests   58
2. Self-Regulation through Trade Associations   60
   Cooperative Suppression of Variety   61
   Power Farming and the Growth of the Full-Line Farm   62
   Interfunctional Compatibility   65
   Interchangeable Parts   67
3. Safety, Public Policy and Self-Regulation   69
4. Conclusion   72
   Notes to Chapter Four   72

   Chapter Five
   Competition, Standards and Self-Regulation
   in the Computer Industry   *Gerald Brock*   75

1. The Need for Standards 75
2. The Development of COBOL 81
3. The Development of ASCII 85
4. Conclusions and Recommendations 91
   Notes to Chapter Five 94

Chapter Six
How Should the Content of Entertainment Television
Be Determined? Self-Regulation and the
Alternatives *Marc J. Roberts* 97

1. Introduction 97
2. Welfare Judgments When Tastes are Endogenous 98
3. The Current Situation 103
4. Alternatives 112
   Notes to Chapter Six 116

Part Three
Product Mix, Technological Change and Market 123
Structure under Regulation

Chapter Seven
Market Structure and Embodied Technological
Change *Richard E. Caves* 125

1. Bilateral Market Structure and Progressiveness 126
   Assumptions 126
   Market Behavior 128
2. The Electric Utilities and the Turbine Generator Industry:
   A Case Study 131
   Assumptions of the Model 131
   Seller Concentration and Behavior in the Turbine-Generator Market 134
   Buyer Concentration and Behavior in the Turbine-Generator Market 137
   Notes to Chapter Seven 141

Chapter Eight
The Market for Commercial Airliners *Sidney L. Carroll* 145

1. Introduction 145
2. Airline Structure 145
3. Structure in the Airliner-Producer Industry 147
4. The Recent Record: Behavior 150
5. The Recent Record: Profits Performance 153

6. A More General Analysis of Behavior in the Commercial
   Aircraft Market   156
7. Long-run Structure, Technological Progress and Resource
   Allocation   163
   Notes to Chapter Eight   165

Chapter Nine
Liquefied and Synthetic Natural Gas—Regulation Chooses
The Expensive Solutions   *Thomas R. Stauffer*   171

1. Introduction
2. The Innovative Options   171
   Synthetic Natural Gas (SNG)   175
   Liquefied Natural Gas   177
3. The Conventional Solution: "Natural" Methane   179
   Expanding Domestic Production   179
   Fuel Substitution   181
4. Economic Comparisons: The Four Options   186
5. "The Reason Why"   188
6. Summary and Epilogue   193
   Notes to Chapter Nine   196

Part Four
Regulation, Welfare and the Distribution of Products   199

Chapter Ten
Optimal Pricing and Income Distribution
Elisha A. Pazner   201

1. Introduction   201
2. Methodological Preamble   202
3. The Simplest Pricing Problem   203
4. Optimal Discriminatory Pricing   210
   Uniform Pricing   210
   Discriminatory Pricing   212
   Perfectly Discriminatory Pricing   214
5. Some Extensions   214
   The Multiple-Output Enterprise   215
   Consumption Externalities and Merit Wants   216
   Imposing a Budgetary Constraint   217
6. Conclusions   217
   Notes to Chapter Ten   218

Chapter Eleven
Franchise Values, Merit Programming and Policy
Options in Television Broadcasting   *Harvey J. Levin*   221

1. Introduction and Statement of the Problem   221
2. Origin, Magnitude and Significance of TV Franchise Values   223
3. Policy Options in Broadcasting   233
   Better Performance from the Commercial System   233
   Collecting and Transferring Rents   234
   Subsidy in Kind for Alternate Programming   237
   Cable Television and Cross-Subsidy in the Long Run   240
   Notes to Chapter Eleven   242

Chapter Twelve
Value of Options, Value of Time and Local Airline
Subsidy   *Richard E. Caves and Elisha A. Pazner*   249

1. Consumer Surplus: Problems of Uncertain Benefits   250
2. A Simple Model of Option Value   252
3. Consumer Surplus from Local Air Service   256
4. Estimation of Value of Time Saved   258
5. Conclusions   263
   Notes to Chapter Twelve   265

   About the Authors   269

List of Tables

Tables

1- 1	Conditions for Profit Maximization	5
2- 1	Mean Values of Variables, Analysis of Determinants of Load Factors	26
2- 2	Regressions of Load Factors on Distance and Number of Carriers, All Markets	27
2- 3	Regressions of Load Factor on Distance, by Year and Number of Carriers Per Market	28
2- 4	Regressions of Load Factors on Distance, Number of Carriers, and Aircraft Size, All Markets	29
2- 5	Regressions of Load Factor on Distance and Aircraft Size, by Year and Number of Carriers Per Market	30
8- 1	United States Airline Scheduled Service First Six Months of 1972	146
8- 2	Jet Aircraft in Service on United States Airlines	147
8- 3	Commercial Sales as a Percentage of Total Sales	148
9- 1	Terms of Applications to Import Liquified Natural Gas, 1972	178
9- 2	Estimates of Economic Cost of Producing Domestic Natural Gas Under Alternative Rates of Return and Reservoir Decline Rates	178
9- 3	Estimates of Incremental Transport Cost of Natural Gas	181
9- 4	Conversion Costs per Mcf of Gas Saved, Alternative Fuel-using Facilities	185
9- 5	Economic Costs of Unconventional and Conventional Substitutes for Domestic Natural Gas	186
9- 6	Federal Power Commission Formula Cost and Corrected Cost of Natural Gas per Mcf	191

11-1 TV Station Revenues, Net Income, and Profit Rates, 1971,
in Relation to Number of Stations Per Market   225

11-2 Regression Analysis of Television Station Sales Prices,
1940-1965   226

11-3 Regression Analysis of TV Station Income, Net Revenue,
and Program Diversity in Relation to Rent-yielding Market
Variables   227

11-4 Sensitivity of Station's Share of Viewers, Prime-time Program
Diversity, and Composition of Prime-time Programs to
Changes in Rent-Yielding Market Variables   228

12-1 Distribution of Air Travelers by Income Class and Implied
Cumulative Distribution of Average Values of Time   259

12-2 Minimum Value of Time (Dollars Per Hour) Needed for
Traveler to Choose Air Over Private Automobile, in Relation
to Distance Traveled and Assumptions about Price and Speed
of Travel Modes   260

Acknowledgements

Most of the papers collected in this volume grew from a Workshop in the Regulation of Economic Activity at Harvard University, supported by the Brookings Institution on the basis of a grant from the Ford Foundation. We are grateful to Brookings and Ford for their support. They do not necessarily concur with any opinions expressed in these papers.

Over the course of several years our seminar, run in conjunction with the workshop, benefited from the presence of many participants other than those whose names appear in this volume. In particular we must mention John R. Baldwin and Paul S. Brandon, whose doctoral dissertations produced valuable parallel research that is being published elsewhere.

The editors' task was made easier by the interest and cooperation of Mr. Joseph Pechman, who oversaw the project for the Brookings Institution at an early stage. Ms. Lois Hager, who typed and retyped many of these papers, was invaluable. We are grateful for her efforts and good cheer, and for the substantial amount of typing of chapters done by Ms. Charlene Gay. We also appreciate the efforts of many faculty colleagues and students who participated in the various projects included here. But we have left it to the individual authors to acknowledge their own particular debts. Speaking of the authors, we are also grateful for the good judgement they showed in being willing to accept our suggestions and comments graciously, and for their cooperation with a schedule that fluctuated from the leisurely to the urgent several times. Despite the burden of detail that is the unavoidable lot of editors, we have enjoyed putting this collection together, and hope the other participants found it equally stimulating.

Introduction

1. REGULATING THE PRODUCT: A POINT OF VIEW

Economic studies of regulated industries and the uses of regulation have focused largely on allocative efficiency and, to a lesser extent, on technical efficiency. They have been much less concerned with the quality and variety of the available products. That is, we inquire how the prices of an industry relate to the costs of the output mix it produces and whether that output mix emerges at minimum cost. But we ignore the fact that its output is invariably heterogeneous: that products might be high quality or low, varied or similar, standardized or unstandardized in their specifications, slotted to one submarket or another. We forget that technological innovations may serve some uses and users but not others. The papers collected in this volume try to remedy this neglect of the output mixture of regulated industries.

These questions are important because society cares about which of the multitude of possible product variants are made available and whose preferences they serve—or offend. Control over this dimension of market performance is often partly removed from the hands of individual buyers and sellers. For some regulatory bodies these problems are central—for example, the Federal Communication Commission in its control of broadcasting. Indeed, all regulatory commissions with comprehensive authority maintain some policies intended to affect product qualities, and many more that constrain them indirectly or unintentionally. And in industries not subject to formal public regulation, the producers themselves, sometimes under public prodding, often act in concert to shape the quality and variety of the goods they place before the public.

When does independent behavior in the market fail in this dimension of performance? Are there output variants that should be suppressed? Should others be produced even if commercially unprofitable? If so, how should their costs be covered? In general, what mechanism of collective control holds the greatest promise for improved performance? Economic analysis can attack these questions in two ways: it can identify the conditions and information necessary to define better and worse performance, and it can analyze actual situations to identify the direct and indirect effects of the prevailing devices of collective control on these dimensions of market performance. The papers in this volume make no claim to be major contributions in the former area—a dark and tangled thicket of welfare economics. But they do attempt a theoretical and empirical attack on various neglected questions of how collective control mechanisms affect product quality. They examine a variety of industries and control mechanisms in an attempt to expose the range of performance problems that arise and control techniques that may be effective.

Underlying this emphasis is our belief that the choice of regulatory institutions represents a major strategic decision for the society. No actual policy is ever perfect, costless or fully reversible. As we go down one institutional road or another, certain economic, technological and political outcomes become either more or less likely. The results depend on what we decide about decision-making institutions—and in ways that cannot be settled by deductive reasoning. The choice of social mechanisms for regulating product characteristics—indeed, for controlling all allocative decisions—is further complicated by two considerations. First, the total effect of imposing any system of public control or regulation on an industry is hard to predict because it proceeds through diverse channels. It depends not only on the direct response of regulated enterprises to the threats, penalties and incentives held forth by public authority, but also on how the controls affect the market structures surrounding these enterprises and thereby the setting of any market rivalry that takes place among them. (These subsurface influences are often the more important, as is illustrated by chapters 2, 7, and 8 of this volume). Second, the regulated influence the regulators as well as vice versa. A behavioral analysis of regulatory situations must then recognize that regulatory decisions are themselves endogenous variables in the politicoeconomic mechanism that determines the industry's performance.[1] One's appraisal of different social mechanisms cannot neglect the possibility that the choice of public regulation itself may serve the interest of the industry that is regulated, or of voting majorities or interest groups who grasp the power of regulation to alter the pattern of output in directions they favor.

Let us outline the contents of this volume before drawing together some findings that emerge from it. Part One attacks the problem of integrating the determination of product quality into a formal model in which price, quality and quantity are simultaneously determined in an industry subject to public regulation. It also provides a test for the influence of regulatory decisions on one dimension of quality through determining the number of competitors and thus the extent of rivalry in regulated airline markets. Part Two asks what patterns of joint self-regulation sellers choose to impose on the safety, variety and standardization of their products. Our four case studies show how the occurrence and effects of self-regulation depend on market structure and external pressures impinging on the industry and inquire how fully producers' self-interest serves society's concern with optimal market performance.[2] Part Three takes up the effect of regulation on changes in product characteristics and cost through innovation and technological change. Its viewpoint departs sharply from the preoccupation of previous research on innovation in regulated industries with capital-intensity bias of rate-of-return regulation.[3] The emphasis instead falls on two other channels by which regulation influences product characteristics: (1) the rate and direction of embodied technological change depends on the market structures of the industry that embodies and the industry that buys the change-embodying goods, and one or both structures are sometimes influenced by regulation; (2) regulators may promote innovations not because they are economically efficient but because they avert the need to decide between contending parties. Finally, Part Four recognizes that an industry's output passes to buyers who are heterogeneous in income levels, tastes and geographic location. Regulation affects not only the overall price and quantity in a market but also its price (or availability) in specific forms or to particularly situated groups.

If this book has any distinctive elements, we believe they are the substantial empirical detail of many of the studies and the effort made to juxtapose theory and fact in a directed and unified way. We are certainly not opposed to theorizing, as the substantial amount of abstract work included here attests. Rather we believe that any science—including economics—makes progress only when it asks clear questions and then systematically confronts the proposed answers with data sufficient to make the ensuing encounter instructive. Theoretical and empirical work should be interdependent—with new theoretical formulations provoked by unexplained empirical phenomena and the analysis of those phenomena structured and informed by theoretical arguments. The questions that cry out for reasoned empirical research go far beyond the ones that allow the investigator to exhibit the sort of mathematical virtuosity currently so fashionable. Papers in this collection that launch into new empirical territory seek to gather evidence guided by the best conceptual scheme available, however crude that may be. Indeed, in several respects the essays here have taken the next step as well, suggesting preliminary generalizations and proposing hypotheses to guide further research.

2. GENERAL ISSUES AND CONCLUSIONS

Two sets of analytical issues stand behind much of the discussion in this volume. The first group involves the problem of nonconvexities in the production set of the economy implicitly raised by the possibility of variations in the product mix. As White mentions (chapter 2), under very strong assumptions about the absence of scale economies this problem disappears, and each consumer can have his good tailor-made to his tastes. Otherwise, the marginal conditions so central to the theory of both normative and descriptive economics become an incomplete guide to behavior for both profit-maximizing producers and welfare-maximizing prescribers of public policy. These conditions at best tell how much of any given good should be provided to achieve various ends, and not which (narrowly defined) goods should be produced. In practice we almost always face some economies of scale, and hence a trade-off between the number of distinct commodities and the cost of each—a normative problem that can be resolved only by looking at total as well as marginal conditions. Some useful insights into the problems of regulatory schemes for optimizing product variety can be gained by assuming, as Pazner does (chapter 1), that all firms in the industry produce goods of identical quality. But that specialization admittedly does not deal with all instances of interest here.

Nonconvexities raise problems for producers as well, because they too must look beyond marginal conditions in order to make output decisions. In an oligopoly in which mutual dependence is recognized and the demand for each firm's differentiated product depends on what else is available, it is not clear that there exists an equilibrium set of products for the industry to offer.[4] In television broadcasting, as Roberts discusses (chapter 6), imitation, product cycles and a rapidly changing product mix do suggest a market in continuing disequilibrium with respect to at least some product variables. Indeed the cross-licensing agreements mentioned by Hunt in his study of home appliances (chapter 3) and the product standardization efforts explored both by him and by Kudrle in his study of farm machinery (chapter 4) appear to represent, in part, firms' efforts to cling to the status quo lest such unstable and risky patterns of competition emerge in their own industries.

The second and closely related series of analytical issues is the role of imperfect information and information costs when product variants are numerous and multidimensional. Problems of transferring information arise both among competing producers and between producers and their customers. As the case studies of farm equipment and home appliances make clear, the costs to buyers of making intelligent purchase decisions are hardly independent of regulatory and self-regulatory practices. Collective efforts to define common parameters by which products can be described are not without their competitive implications—both for driving out technically less successful producers and for expanding industry-wide demand by reducing consumers' uncertainty. For these reasons, formal agreements about how to define the parameters to be used in describing product characteristics has often been pursued by firms on their own account, via self-regulation, because of the profits it might produce.

The attractiveness of creating such generally accepted metrics, both to the firms involved and for public policy, depends on how well buyers can use the resulting information. We hypothesize that this process is more likely to develop for costly items, where the expense makes analysis by the buyer—and information to conduct that analysis—more valuable. Indeed, both regulatory agencies (in tractors) and trade-associations (in home appliances) have gone on to perform the testing needed to establish the actual characteristics of various firms' products. Given the economic characteristics of information, if the information itself is worth the costs of obtaining it, such common testing is probably efficient.

The crux of the problem for economic efficiency, however, is whether the costs of obtaining, diffusing and using information about products are in fact worth the benefits. One approach, as Hunt discusses, is to set minimum performance standards. They lessen product variety and impose a loss on those who prefer goods now unavailable, but can save both on the costs of search and appraisal and on the costs incurred by consumers who do not spend enough on decision-making to avoid unintentionally purchasing inferior products. Such constaints are more attractive when the cost to the buyer of a faulty choice are relatively high and when there are relatively fewer customers who prefer the proscribed products. When such measures are taken, rational buyers and sellers can safely devote fewer resources to transmitting and using information about the product dimensions that are controlled. If the buyer knows that all refrigerators meet certain standards of electrical safety, he may save more than he loses by simply ignoring any residual variations in safety while making his choice.

Information is also a major problem in the relationship of producers to each other. An agreement on how to measure a product's quality dimensions can have a feedback effect on product development efforts, as competitive moves become focused on the parameters subject to standardized measurement. Indeed, as Hunt discusses, such agreements can enhance interdependence recognized in oligopoly sectors by giving firms a framework and a mechanism for noticing competitive moves in the realm of product variety.

A lack of information about competitors' products can be crucial to the strategic situation of some firms in an industry. As Brock points out (chapter 5), IBM, as the dominant firm in computers, had an interest in keeping secret the technical specifications for the interface between central processing units and peripheral equipment. This made imitation more difficult for competitive producers specialized in the latter areas. In contrast, competitors might sometimes want to undertake collusive actions but are prevented from doing so by information costs. Television networks, as Roberts describes (chapter 6), have been able to coordinate their behavior on a number of dimensions of the product they offer, including length of season, format and length of news broadcasts and broad programming patterns (e.g., daytime soap operas, culture on Sundays, kid shows on Saturday morning, etc.). Yet they have not been able to keep quality competition from raising production expenses; while the former parameters are easy for each to monitor, production costs are too complex and too difficult to discover for reliable coordination to develop.

On the other hand, even good information will not necessarily sustain cooperative behavior on product characteristics when other conditions will not support such tacit agreements. As White's discussion of airline scheduling makes clear (chapter 2), independent profit-maximizing behavior persists even in two-firm markets with respect to product parameters (schedules) that are essentially costless to observe. Carroll's examination of commercial aircraft (chapter 8) tells the same story. A small number of manufacturers (two or three) with enough information to imitate each other's product closely and match each other's prices may still hold to strategies or objectives divergent enough to prevent joint maximization.

Carroll's study also relects the concern, widely represented in these papers, with the vertical interaction among industries with respect to products, technology and market structure in the context of regulation. Caves' paper (chapter 7) provides a general theoretical review of some of the major propositions in this area, and examines the evidence in the interrelated sectors of electric utilities and the manufacturers of turbine generators. He finds some support for the proposition that the size distribution in each industry has an impact on the size distribution in the other, as well as on the character of the capital goods that one industry supplies to the other. Carroll's paper, too, touches on many of these same issues. Particularly, he argues that the regulation-induced focus on product competition among the airlines tends to increase the number of manufacturers of any generation of aircraft by making airlines most reluctant to accept places far down the delivery queue. White's paper also provides indirect evidence on the same phenomena in his finding that rivalry depresses load factors, one dimension of the product competition hypothesized by Carroll.

The interaction of airframe manufacturers and airlines is also striking because the airlines seem constantly to get the better of the bargaining—despite their greater numbers, which presumably restrict their monopsony power. This finding shows that in any one industry like airlines the degree of collusion or competition on some product variables may be very different from behavior with respect to others (again TV is a parallel). It also exhibits the power of buyers who are large relative to the market to impose their desires as to product characteristics when the individual product variant is produced with important economies of scale. In his essay on computers, Brock urges as a matter of policy that the government, as the largest (indeed the only "large") buyer, should make a greater effort to impose its desire for standardization on the producers. In other words, government departments should act more like the airlines. Note that in computers, like aircraft, the buyers are much less concentrated than sellers, and the largest buyer much smaller than the largest seller. Yet Brock argues that significant market power of buyers over product characteristics remains unexploited—in part, apparently, because of the political effectiveness of IBM in sidetracking government efforts.

The papers show that regulation becomes entangled in vertical market relations in numerous and subtle ways. The government may be in a position to regulate through its posture as a leading customer for an industry's products (as in computers). It may be able to affect the mixture of specific goods a sector produces by manipulating the prices of strategic input goods or services; Levin (chapter 11) reviews the proposals to support public TV broadcasting by price discrimination for interconnection services. When the government controls the number and size distribution of buyers in a market, it inevitably influences their bargaining power. It thereby affects the distribution of rents accruing to the buyers and sellers (between TV stations and networks or program producers; between airlines and airframe manufacturers) and the rate and character of innovation in the product that passes from sellers to the controlled buyers (turbine generators or passenger aircraft).

The ease of public regulation of product characteristics depends in some measure on whether producers can agree on self-regulation. There is thus a public interest in the features of market structure that govern whether agreements among producers are more or less likely. Brock urges the imposition of standards from outside because, as he shows, the computer makers' interests in standardization systematically diverge. This outcome is in striking contrast to the effective self-regulation program of standardization and certification Hunt reviews in home appliances. Hunt's main hypothesis is that such self-regulation will be undertaken whenever either the lure of profit or the fear of more adverse government action is sufficiently strong. Brock advances the additional qualification that cooperative efforts require all industry participants to have similar enough interests. In view of its dominant position, IBM had every competitive reason to oppose self-regulatory ventures and by and large did so successfully.

On the basis of the home appliances case, Hunt also theorizes that the existence of a trade association with a strong professional staff would significantly increase the likelihood of self-regulation. This follows, he argues, because, even considering its costs, such a staff could so lower the transaction costs of reaching agreements that cooperation becomes more attractive to each participant. The available net gains become sufficient to facilitiate finding at least one outcome that everyone sees as an improvement. However, Roberts's study of network television shows that, in small-numbers markets with homogeneous firms, an independent staff is not necessary for self-regulation of the product because the negotiation costs are already quite low. In contrast, Kudrle's study of farm equipment found that even an apparently well-organized professional society could not bring about standardization of tractor parts, because the action would tend to lower entry barriers. And the airline non-cooperation found by White also occurs in the context of a strongly organized trade association. Thus it appears that the presence of an organization that can lower bargaining costs is not sufficient to produce self-regulation, because no bargain may exist that would both be perceived as mutually profitable and be consistent with the overall business strategies of the firms involved.

Self-regulation is generally insufficient to accomplish social goals when those involve complex distributive questions, "merit wants," or demands that the market fails to serve. Pazner's paper on pricing (chapter 10) demonstrates how prices should diverge from marginal costs when the income distribution is imperfect. Even a traditionally "free good" like a crossing on an uncrowded bridge should not necessarily be free if we can use the price to affect a desired redistribution—which is possible if different income groups differ in their use of the bridge.

A related circumstance that may require public intervention is the presence of "option value," the willingness of the public to pay for the guaranteed availability of a specific service that they may wish to purchase. Lacking a perfect equilibrium in an Arrow-Debreu market for contingent claims, we may expect the market provision of various kinds of uncertain goods to be imperfect. This issue is important politically for the regulation of product variety because it has supported the subsidized provision of certain transportation services on the grounds that option demand for them is not reflected in market demand. Caves and Pazner (chapter 12) explore the theoretical relation between option demand and expected consumer surplus. Their results are indecisive but support the relevance of a comparison of consumer-surplus benefits of subsidy to local-service airlines with the cost of that subsidy. The comparison, which values the travelers' net benefits from time saved well below the subsidy cost, shows the pervasive political risks of invoking non-economic motives in regulatory matters. Absent good measures of costs and benefits, the pressure to provide benefits leads to programs whose costs far outweigh the benefits.

Finally, "merit goods" create a case for some regulation, although actual regulation may fail to effect the appropriate redistribution toward merit goods. In his study of television franchise values, Levin concludes that this has indeed been the case, and recommends the diversion of some rents due to the scarce broadcasting spectrum to provide support for such programming. This study relates to Roberts's consideration of network program product quality from the perspective of its impact on viewers. A normative analysis leads Roberts to the conclusion that decentralization and structural variety in the organizations that provide entertainment programs is of major importance. The current system of joint self-regulation is "too effective," that is, too confining of program content and too subject to political and social pressures. The type of arrangements Levin explores could help to provide the variety Roberts urges.

Certain broad themes run through the volume as a whole. The first is the interconnection of economic and political processes. Firms foiled in the market not infrequently resort to the political sphere to gain their ends—with highly varying success. We need a better understanding of why some economic units are able to mobilize different pieces of the political system more effectively than others. We also need a better understanding of how regulatory and other government agencies behave in the face of various pressures.

Second, we need to increase the resolving power of our theory of the firm to account for more of the short- to medium-run details of its decision-making. Otherwise, oligopolistic interaction in the area of product quality and variety cannot be sufficiently disentangled. In the presence of substantial information costs, product and factor market constraints may be loose enough to leave the firm with many viable product strategies, and equilibrium in product variety may be indeterminate. Several chapters invoke firms' strategies, rules of thumb, and conventional behavior patterns to explain market outcomes. Indeed such a methodology, focused on the decision problems of the organization's members, also promises help in explaining the behavior of producers in the public sector.[5]

Finally, time and again the studies in this collection reveal the endogenous nature of forces we usually count as exogenous—whether the structure of markets or the direction of public policy. In particular, market conduct clearly has had a significant cumulative effect on market structure over time. The classic Bain-Mason view of industrial organization really does not account for these phenomena. But there is no question, to pick a flagrant example, that IBM's current market share is not independent of its previous product and pricing decisions. Similarly, barriers to entry via product differentiation have been lowered in home appliances via cooperative standardization and certification programs. The list of examples is a long one. Now that we do have a quarter century of "normal" industrial history in the United States to draw on, these interactions can be explored in a way that would not have been possible in 1955. This constitutes a major frontier not only in cases where regulating the product is a major concern, but for the study of industrial organization more generally.

Notes to Introduction

1. See, for example, George J. Stigler, "The Theory of Economic Regulation," *Bell Journal of Economics and Management Science,* 2 (Spring 1971), pp. 3-21. For a closely reasoned analysis of the endogenous behavior of public enterprises and regulatory agencies see John R. Baldwin, *Regulation and the Public Corporation: the Canadian Air Transportation Industry* (Cambridge: Ballinger, 1975).

2. For a broader comparative analysis of industries' voluntary product standards, see David Hemenway, "Industrywide Voluntary Product Standards" (Ph.D. thesis, Harvard University, 1973).

3. See William M. Capron (ed.), *Technological Change in Regulated Industries,* (Washington, D.C.: Brookings Institution, 1971).

4. For some discussion of such problems of non-equilibrium in a market with various products (insurance policies) see J. Stiglitz and M. Rothchild, "Equilibrium in Competitive Insurance Markets; The Economics of Markets with Imperfect Information." Presented at the Oslo Meetings of the Econometric Society, September, 1973.

5. See Marc J. Roberts, "A Framework for Analyzing the Behavior of Resource Allocating Organizations" (Harvard Institute of Economic Research, Discussion Paper no. 264, 1972).

Part One

Regulation and the Level of Product Quality

Chapter One

Quality Choice and Monopoly Regulation

Elisha A. Pazner

1. INTRODUCTION

The scarcity of theoretical literature on what determines product quality testifies that the problem is analytically very difficult.[1] Yet it is of great practical importance in both regulated and unregulated industries. The aim of the present paper is to develop a simple model and use it to analyze the effects of market structure and various kinds of regulation on quality levels. While all such exercises must be applied with care, the analysis does lead to some quite interesting policy implications.

The plan of the paper is as follows. In section 2 we formulate the quality model and compare the outcome under perfect monopoly with that which would prevail under perfect competition. In section 3 we use the model of section 2 to explore the implications of various regulatory schemes as being best suited to cope with the regulatory problem. Section 4 contains a summary of our conclusions.

2. THE MODEL

Goods with different quality attributes command different market prices for two mutually reinforcing reasons. Both buyers' willingness to pay (demand) and production costs (supply) are increasing functions of quality levels. In this section we formulate a simple analytical model which tries to capture some of the features of the quality problem by introducing a quality variable on both the demand and cost sides. We will consider a composite good, consisting of a basic quantity component common to all items, and a quality component which varies across these articles. For example a Cadillac and a Chevrolet both represent one car, but the former is a car with more (i.e., higher) quality than the latter. In formulating both the demand and cost relationships we will thus include two separate arguments, the quantity of the basic commodity and its quality level. Throughout the paper the following notation is used:

Q quantity of the basic commodity $(Q > 0)$
T (continuous) quality index $(T > 0)$
p price of the (composite) commodity
$p(Q,T)$ inverse demand function with $\frac{\partial p}{\partial Q} < 0$ and $\frac{\partial p}{\partial T} > 0$
$c(T)$ average cost per unit of output with $c'(T) > 0$
ζ price elasticity of demand for Q (in absolute value)
Q^C, p^C, T^C equilibrium values of corresponding variables under competition
        perfect
Q^M, p^M, T^M equilibrium values of corresponding variables under perfect
        monopoly
$\pi(Q, T)$ profit function, $\pi(Q, T) = p(Q, T) Q - c(T)Q$

      As the functional form $c(T)$ suggests, in order to isolate the effects of market structure we assume that at any level of quality, the production function displays constant returns to scale.

      First, does market structure as such have any impact on quality? We start by examining the equilibrium configurations of quantity and quality in a given industry under the alternative assumptions of perfect competition and perfect monopoly. Assuming the objective of profit maximization in either case the first-order and the second-order conditions for maximizing profits are presented in table 1-1. The crucial assumption used in developing these results is that only one quality level will be offered at any one time.

      The conditions presented are for an interior maximum $(Q > 0$ and $T > 0)$ where some of the good is produced at greater than zero quality level. Note that condition (iii) implies that the output provided by a single firm is indeterminate, as is always the case in a competitive industry under constnat returns to scale. However, the output for the industry as a whole, as we will see, is fully determinate.

      The first-order conditions that determine product quality show that under both competition and monopoly (ii) and (ii)$'$ we get the same condition namely $\frac{\partial p}{\partial T} = c'$. This means that the quality level should be pushed up to the point where the marginal revenue from higher quality $\frac{\partial p}{\partial T} Q$ is equated to its marginal cost $c'Q$. This however is not enough to imply that quality choice is unaffected by market structure, i.e. that $T^M = T^C$. For, since the demand price, $p(Q,T)$, is a function of both quality and quantity so is $\frac{\partial p}{\partial T}$. Since in general Q will *not* be the same under both competition and monopoly, neither will be T.

Table 1-1. Conditions for Profit Maximization

		Perfect Competition		Perfect Monopoly
First Order Conditions	(1)	$\dfrac{\partial \pi}{\partial Q} = p - c = 0$ $\rightarrow p = c$	(1)'	$\dfrac{\partial \pi}{\partial Q} = p(1 - \dfrac{1}{\varsigma}) - c = 0$ $\rightarrow MR = c$
	(2)	$\dfrac{\partial \pi}{\partial T} = Q[\dfrac{\partial p}{\partial T} - c'] = 0$ $\rightarrow \dfrac{\partial p}{\partial T} = c'$	(2)'	$\dfrac{\partial \pi}{\partial T} = Q[\dfrac{\partial p}{\partial T} - c'] = 0$ $\rightarrow \dfrac{\partial p}{\partial T} = c'$
Second Order Conditions	(3)	$\dfrac{\partial^2 \pi}{\partial Q^2} = 0$	(3)'	$\dfrac{\partial^2 \pi}{\partial Q^2} = \dfrac{\partial MR}{\partial Q} < 0$
	(4)	$\dfrac{\partial^2 \pi}{\partial T^2} = Q[\dfrac{\partial^2 p}{\partial T^2} - c''] < 0$ $\rightarrow \dfrac{\partial^2 p}{\partial T^2} < c''$	(4)'	$\dfrac{\partial^2 \pi}{\partial T^2} = Q[\dfrac{\partial^2 p}{\partial T^2} - c''] < 0$ $\rightarrow \dfrac{\partial^2 p}{\partial T^2} < c''$
	(5)	$\dfrac{\partial^2 \pi}{\partial Q^2} \cdot \dfrac{\partial^2 \pi}{\partial T^2} - (\dfrac{\partial^2 \pi}{\partial Q \partial T})^2 =$ $- [\dfrac{\partial p}{\partial T} - c']^2 = 2$	(5)'	$\dfrac{\partial^2 \pi}{\partial Q^2} \cdot \dfrac{\partial^2 \pi}{\partial T^2} - (\dfrac{\partial^2 \pi}{\partial Q \partial T}) =$ $\dfrac{\partial MR}{\partial Q} Q (\dfrac{\partial^2 p}{\partial T^2} - c'') > 0$

Thus $T^C \neq T^M$ in an a priori unspecifiable way. Furthermore, other than generally knowing that $Q^C \neq Q^M$ we cannot specify a priori whether quantity will be greater or less under monopoly or competition. Indeed we do not even know whether or not the market assumption under which quality is higher also leads to greater quantity.[2]

In order to reach more determinate conclusions we shall make the additional assumption that: $\dfrac{\partial^2 p}{\partial T \partial Q} \equiv 0$. This assumption means that the change in the price customers are willing to pay for a given increase in quality is independent of the quantity they consume, and vice versa. That is to say, independent of whether one, two or three cars are bought, the consumer is willing to pay the same premium for a Cadillac over a Chevrolet. Thus when we compare two products with different quality levels, the difference in the price customers will pay is constant over units of quantity. This means that the demand curves (for different quality levels) are vertically parallel in price-quantity space, and so are the demand curves (at different quantity levels) in price quality space. Thus the rate of change in demand price as quality changes (the slope of the latter curves) depends only on quality levels, that is $\dfrac{\partial p}{\partial T} = \dfrac{\partial p}{\partial T}$ (T). This does not seem to be too strong an assumption, given the additional determinacy thus introduced. Whether or not substantial violence is done to reality is an empirically testable proposition.

This additional assumption now does imply that $T^M = T^C$. Under either competition or monopoly the quality of the product will be the same.

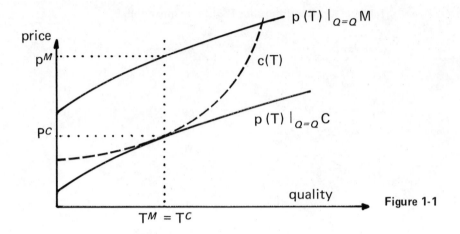

Figure 1-1

The reason for this result is easy enough to see in figure 1-1, where each demand curve for quality assumes a different quantity of output. Since our additional assumption assures that these are vertically parallel, the profit maximizing quality for *any* given quantity is the same. The competitive industry is driven to that quality to avoid non-negative profits, while the monopolistic firm chooses it. The latter makes profits per unit equal to the difference between the competitive and monopoly prices. Obviously, such margins rise as quantity declines; but past some point, so would the monopolist's total profits.[3]

The diagram also shows us that $Q^M < Q^C$ which can confirm formally by comparing equation (1) and (1)' in table 1-1. These imply $p^C = c = p^M(1 - \frac{1}{\zeta})$, since c takes the same value in both cases because c is a function only of T, and T is the same in both cases. Since ζ is positive by definition, we must have $p^C < p^M$. And, since $\frac{\partial p}{\partial Q} < 0$, this finally implies $Q^C > Q^M$.

In sum then, with the help of our additional assumption we are able to deduce $T^C = T^M$ and $Q^C > Q^M$. The evil of monopoly is thus entirely restricted to the usual contrived scarcity of quantity marketed. As far as quality is concerned, competitive and monopolistic regimes yield the same outcome. As will be seen in the next section this carries extremely important implications for regulatory policy.

3. EFFECTS OF REGULATION

We will ignore externalities, income distribution, second-best problems and other complications and assume that, given a monopoly, regulatory policy should be aimed at achieving the Pareto Optimal price-quantity-quality configuration reached under perfect competition. Since our assumptions insure that quality is the same under competition and monopoly, no direct regulation of quality is needed. The regulatory effort thus addresses itself to the smaller quantity and higher price prevailing under monopoly. Solving this problem, however, is not so easy as it might appear because the process of regulation itself can introduce distortions into the choice of quality by the regulated firm! In the three subsections that follow, we analyze three alternative forms of regulation: rate-of-return regulation, price regulation and markup regulation. Finally we will discuss alternative policy measures leading to an optimal outcome in terms of both quantity and quality.

(A) Rate-of-Return Regulation
Using the basic framework first presented in the well-known paper by Averch and Johnson[4] (cited here as A-J) we briefly show that their general conclusion on the choice of overcapitalized methods of production is unaffected by the explicit incorporation of quality choice into the regulatory problem. Furthermore, the expected impact of rate-of-return on quantity offered is also unaffected. More interesting, the expected change in quality turns out to depend on the same kind of considerations as those that determine the impact on quantity. Under equivalent assumptions on the production functions of the basic commodity and quality, the changes in quantity and quality caused by regulation will be in the same direction. Needless to say, rate-of-return regulation cannot lead to an optimal outcome, since both the choice of techniques is distorted *and* the quality level is affected.[5] To prove the various propositions we use the following notation:

K_1	capital employed in the production of Q
L_1	labor employed in the production of Q
$Q(K_1, L_1)$	production function of Q
K_2	capital employed in the production of T
L_2	labor employed in the production of T
$T(K_2, L_2)$	production function of T
$K = K_1 + K_2$	total amount of capital employed by the firm
$L = L_1 + L_2$	total amount of labor employed by the firm
r	rental price of capital
w	wage of labor
s	regulated "fair" rate of return, $s > r$.

Making all the assumptions used by A-J, and in particular $s > r$, the maximand of the regulated monopolist becomes:

$$\text{Max:} \quad F(K_1, L_1, K_2, L_2) = p\left[Q(K_1, L_2), T(K_2, L_2)\right] Q(K_1, L_1)$$
$$\phantom{\text{Max:}}_{K_1, L_1, K_2, L_2} \qquad -r(K_1 + K_2) - w(L_1 + L_2) -$$
$$-\lambda\left[p\left[Q(K_1, L_1), T(K_2, L_2)\right]Q(K_1, L_1) - s(K_1 + K_2) - w(L_1 + L_2)\right]$$

where λ is an unspecified Lagrangean multiplier. The first-order conditions for an interior maximum are:

$$\frac{\partial F}{\partial K_1} = \frac{\partial p}{\partial Q}\frac{\partial Q}{\partial K_1}Q + p\frac{\partial Q}{\partial K_1} - r - \lambda(\frac{\partial p}{\partial Q}\frac{\partial Q}{\partial K_1}Q + p\frac{\partial Q}{\partial K_1} - s) = 0, \qquad (6)$$

$$\frac{\partial F}{\partial L_1} = \frac{\partial p}{\partial Q}\frac{\partial Q}{\partial L_1}Q + p\frac{\partial Q}{\partial L_1} - w - \lambda(\frac{\partial p}{\partial Q}\frac{\partial Q}{\partial L_1}Q + p\frac{\partial Q}{\partial L_1} - w) = 0, \qquad (7)$$

$$\frac{\partial F}{\partial K_2} = \frac{\partial p}{\partial T}\frac{\partial T}{\partial K_2}Q - r - \lambda(\frac{\partial p}{\partial T}\frac{\partial T}{\partial K_2}Q - s) = 0, \qquad (8)$$

$$\frac{\partial F}{\partial L_2} = \frac{\partial p}{\partial T}\frac{\partial T}{\partial L_2}Q - w - \lambda(\frac{\partial p}{\partial T}\frac{\partial T}{\partial L_2}Q - w) = 0, \qquad (9)$$

$$\frac{\partial F}{\partial \lambda} = pQ - s(K_1 + K_2) - w(L_1 + L_2) = 0. \qquad (10)$$

It is easily seen now that from (6) and (7) we get in the usual manner:

$$\frac{\partial Q/\partial K_1}{\partial Q/\partial L_1} = \frac{r}{w} + \frac{\lambda(r-s)}{(1-\lambda)w} < \frac{r}{w} \text{ since } 0 < \lambda < 1 \text{ and } r < s, \qquad (11)$$

while from (8) and (9) we get:

$$\frac{\partial T/\partial K_2}{\partial T/\partial L_2} = \frac{r}{w} + \frac{\lambda(r-s)}{(1-\lambda)w} < \frac{r}{w} \text{ since } 0 < \lambda < 1 \text{ and } r < s. \qquad (12)$$

As shown by the inequalities in (11) and (12) overcapitalization will occur in the production of both Q and T. Furthermore, the discrepancy between the marginal rate of technical substitution between capital and labor and the ratio of factor prices is identical in the two cases. In this sense then, the "degree" of inefficient overcapitalization is the same for both Q and T. It can also be shown without any additional assumptions that both $\frac{dK_1}{ds} < 0$ and $\frac{dK_2}{ds} < 0$; and thus $\frac{dK}{ds} < 0$. That is to say, tighter rate-of-return regulation will induce the firm to employ more capital in both the production of Q and T and thus more capital in total.

With regard to the effects on Q and T themselves we need the additional assumption that capital and labor are complementary factors of production in the profit function.[6] Under this assumption we also obtain $\frac{dQ}{ds} < 0$ and $\frac{dT}{ds} < 0$. That is to say that as the allowed rate of return is lowered from its preregulated unconditional profit maximizing level, both quantity of output and quality of service will increase. While the increase in quantity is beneficial per se since the monopoly output was too low ($Q^M < Q^C$) the change in T is not desirable. Quality was at the right level prior to regulation. With scarce resources there can be too much of a good thing such as quality! The fact that the choice of inputs is distorted away from its efficient level is, of course, an additional reason for the suboptimality of rate-of-return regulation. In addition, it can also be shown that Sheshinski's proposition that "some rate-of-return regulation is better than none" in a (second-best) welfare sense does not apply when quality choice is explicitly introduced into the model.

However, without the assumption, $\dfrac{\partial^2 p}{\partial T \partial Q} \equiv 0$, we cannot say that the preregulatory quality level was correct, and hence it is not clear that the change in quality, caused by rate-of-return regulation, is necessarily undesirable. We have seen that under mild assumptions, lower allowed rates of return imply higher quality levels ($\dfrac{dT}{ds} < 0$). But since quality under an unregulated monopoly could either be too high or too low, it is quite unlikely that regulation under such circumstances would happen to bring quality to the correct (i.e., competitive) level.

(B) Price Regulation

While public utilities, airlines and other sectors are regulated with an eye on their rates of return, the variable which is often directly controlled in these industries is price. In this subsection we examine the implications of such direct price regulation with special attention to the effects on quality. Because in our model the price is for the "composite" commodity and there are no separate prices for each of its components, price regulation will be shown to affect quality and do so in a definite direction, provided that $\dfrac{\partial^2 p}{\partial T \partial Q} \equiv 0$. Furthermore, as in the previous case, that assumption implies that price regulation will move quality away from its optimal preregulated level. Thus, if the basic aim of regulation is to raise quantity from the monopolistic to the optimal competitive level, price regulation could lead quantity to either increase or decrease.

To prove these assertions and denoting the regulated price by $\bar{p}$ with $\bar{p} < p^M$ the monopolist's problem becomes:

Max: $L(Q,T) = p(Q, T)Q - c(T)Q - \lambda[p(Q, T)Q - mc(T)Q]$,
Q, T

where λ is an undetermined Lagrangean multiplier. The first-order conditions for an interior maximum are:

$$\frac{\partial L}{\partial Q} = \frac{\partial p}{\partial Q} Q + p - c - \lambda \frac{\partial p}{\partial Q} = 0 \tag{13}$$

$$\frac{\partial L}{\partial T} = \frac{\partial p}{\partial T} = Q - c'Q - \lambda \frac{\partial p}{\partial T} = 0 \tag{14}$$

$$\frac{\partial L}{\partial \lambda} = p - \bar{p} = 0 \tag{15}$$

With some manipulation we can rewrite (14) as

$$(1 - \frac{\lambda}{Q}) \frac{\partial p}{\partial T} = c' \tag{16}$$

It is readily seen by comparing (16) to (2)' that if regulation has teeth (i.e., $\lambda > 0$) T will change from its preregulation level. Using the second-order conditions presented in table 1-1 above, we find that T will go down when $\frac{\partial^2 p}{\partial T \partial Q} \equiv 0$ (i.e., that, as one would expect, quality will deteriorate under price regulation).[7] Furthermore, from (16) since $c' > 0$ and $\frac{\partial p}{\partial T} > 0$, equation (16) implies that $1 - \frac{\lambda}{Q} > 0$, which in turn implies $Q > \lambda$. But apart from this condition, nothing can be learned about Q. It will generally change under price regulation but in what direction is simply not known.

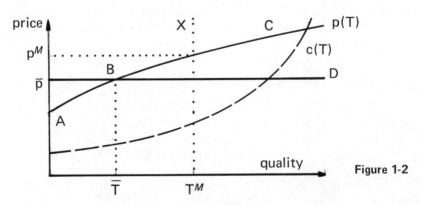

Figure 1-2

In intuitive terms, the conclusions are not surprising. As we can see in figure 1-2, if regulation is effective, no matter what quantity he sells, the monopolist in price quality space now faces as a demand function for quality, not ABC, but ABD. He thus chooses quality $T = \bar{T}$ since he cannot get a higher price for producing quality higher than $\bar{T}$, yet average costs increase as he goes beyond that point. (The assumption that $\frac{\partial^2 p}{\partial T \partial Q} \equiv 0$, furthermore assures us that no matter what quantity is chosen, it will never pay for the seller to increase quality above T^M, the monopoly level, since all the demand curves will be vertically parallel.)

Any change in quantity is due to two offsetting factors. On the one hand, the decrease in quality means that the demand curve in price-quantity space is shifted down. On the other hand, price has fallen. Thus the quantity demanded on the lower demand curve under regulation could be lower or higher than the quantity bought under monopoly. If quantity falls, then we would know that price regulation was undesirable since quality declines as well. If quantity goes up, however, the final outcome may be an improvement over the unregulated monopoly situation. What is clearcut, however, is the conclusion that price regulation cannot be optimal when quality variables are explicitly introduced into the regulatory model.

When $\dfrac{\partial^2 p}{\partial T \partial Q} \neq 0$ the change in quality is not necessarily undesirable, since monopoly quality was not in general optimal. But, in a probabilistic sense, the possibility that not only will T move in the right direction, but that it will actually be pushed to its optimal value, is an event of measure zero.

(C) Mark-up Regulation

Another interesting regulatory method is mark-up regulation, which has not been extensively practiced in the United States except as a temporary price control measure. Like price regulation, when no quality variations are possible this form of regulation could conceivably lead to an optimal outcome.[8] However, as we will see, when quality levels are not fixed, mark-up regulation will have an impact upon them. To characterize this policy, let m denote the allowed mark-up over costs. Assuming regulation to have teeth, this implies that in equilibrium we must have $p(Q,T) = mc(T)$ where $m > 1$.

One complexity is that this type of regulation can create an incentive for inefficiency. Ignoring quality for the moment, suppose that the mark-up constraint could only be satisfied at an output level such that marginal revenue was negative (i.e., total revenue was declining). Then the monopolist would have the incentive to incur unproductive, inefficient costs which would allow him in turn to raise prices, per-unit dollar margins and total profits. This follows because, by definition, demand is inelastic when the marginal revenue is negative. Thus, in what follows we will assume that no such incentive exists, and the regulated optimum occurs in the region where demand is elastic ($\varsigma > 1$) and marginal revenues are positive.

Assuming efficient behavior then, the regulated monopolist problem becomes:

Max: $L(Q,T) = p(Q,T)Q - c(T)Q - \lambda[p(Q,T) - \bar{p}]$,
Q,T

where λ is an undetermined Lagrangean multiplier.

The first-order conditions for an interior maximum are:

$$\frac{\partial L}{\partial Q} = \frac{\partial p}{\partial Q} Q + p - c - [\frac{\partial p}{\partial Q} Q + p - mc] = 0 \tag{18}$$

$$\frac{\partial L}{\partial T} = \frac{\partial p}{\partial T} Q - c'Q - \lambda[\frac{\partial p}{\partial T} Q - mc'Q] = 0 \tag{19}$$

$$\frac{\partial L}{\partial \lambda} = pQ - mcQ = 0 \tag{20}$$

Now, (19) can be rewritten as:

$$Q[\frac{\partial p}{\partial T} (1-\lambda) - c'(1-\lambda m)] = 0, \tag{21}$$

from which we derive

$$\frac{\partial p}{\partial T} = \frac{1-\lambda m}{1-\lambda} c' \tag{22}$$

Comparing this last result with equation (2)′ in table 1-1, it is clear that since $m \neq 1$ ($m > 1$) the solution for T cannot be the same in both equations. Thus under mark-up regulation quality will be different from the common monopolistic/competitive quality level which is optimal when $\frac{\partial^2 p}{\partial Q \partial T} \equiv 0$. Indeed, given that assumption, since $0 < \lambda < 1$ and $m > 1$, equation (22) shows that at the regulated equilibrium $\frac{\partial p}{\partial T} < c'$ (T). The second order conditions then tell us that as a result of regulation, quality (T) will increase, a result diametrically opposed to that under price regulation.

Intuitively, this result occurs because increasing quality above its previously optimal level can increase costs more rapidly than revenues, allowing the regulated firm to meet the mark-up constraint. From the second order conditions we know that at the unregulated optimum, T^M, the slope of the demand curve for quality has to be increasing more slowly than the slope of the marginal cost curve for quality. That is, $\frac{\partial^2 p}{\partial T^2} < \frac{\partial^2 C}{\partial T^2}$. Thus as quality increases from its previously optimal level, costs rise more quickly than revenues until the mark-up constraint is met.

The effect of mark-up regulation on the quantity is indeterminate. Again, the intuitive explanation is easy. On the one hand, $\zeta > 1$ implies that revenue can be decreased to meet the mark-up constraint by reducing Q. On the other hand, the more than proportional increase in costs relative to revenue caused by the increase in T means that Q may somewhat be increased in order to generate an increase in revenue so that the mark-up constraint may be met. Note that the indeterminate effect of regulation on quantity, both in this case and under price regulation, is at sharp variance with the unambiguous results from a model in which there are no quality variables. In that simple case, both price and mark-up regulation will always lead to an increase in Q beyond its preregulation level.

Again note that the analysis is essentially independent of the assumption that $\frac{\partial^2 p}{\partial T \partial Q} \equiv 0$. The only real role played by that assumption is to tell us that quality under mark-up regulation cannot be *optimal*. Yet, for exactly the same reasons that are given in previous subsections, virtually the same can be said even when the assumption does not hold.

(D) Optimal Regulation

None of the three regulatory schemes discussed so far can induce the monopolist to behave in an optimal way. Can we develop an alternative policy which is conducive to an optimal outcome?

Starting first with the case where $\frac{\partial^2 p}{\partial Q \partial T} \equiv 0$, we do not want the policy instrument to interfere with the monopolist's already optimal choice of quality. We simply want him to increase the quantity produced from Q^M to Q^C (and to lower the price from p^M to p^C). One way to accomplish this objective is to give the monopolist an appropriate excise subsidy per unit of output which is entirely independent of quality. It is easy to show that the right subsidy leads to the competitive/optimal quality and quantity.

Denoting the excise subsidy by e, the monopolist's maximization problem becomes:

Max: $\pi(Q,T) = [p(Q,T) + e]Q - c(T)Q$
Q,T

The first-order conditions for an interior maximum are:

$$\frac{\partial \pi}{\partial Q} = \frac{\partial p}{\partial Q}Q + p + e - c = 0 \tag{23}$$

$$\frac{\partial \pi}{\partial T} = [\frac{\partial p}{\partial T} - c]Q = 0 \tag{24}$$

Comparing equations (24) and (2)$'$, it is clear that if we assume $\dfrac{\partial^2 p}{\partial T \partial Q} \equiv 0$, quantity will be the same in both cases. Thus, even with the excise subsidy it will remain at its previous optimal level. So will c, which is only a function of quality. Now we want price, under optimal regulation, to be the same as the competitive price. We also know, from (1) that $p^C = c$. This allows us to substitute p^C for both p and c in (23) yielding

$$\frac{\partial p}{\partial Q} Q + p^C + e = p^C \qquad\qquad (25)$$

This in turn implies:

$$e = -\frac{\partial p}{\partial Q} Q = p - (p + \frac{\partial p}{\partial Q} Q). \qquad\qquad (26)$$

The optimal subsidy is therefore equal to the difference between price and marginal revenue at the desired optimal output Q^C. The demand and marginal revenue curves should be drawn for $T = T^C$, and where we evaluate $\dfrac{\partial p}{\partial Q}$ at Q^C. When this subsidy policy is followed, all variables indeed assume their optimal values! We have raised the monopolist's marginal revenue curve just enough so that it intersects his (assumed constant) marginal cost curve at the desired quantity.

The above discussion assumed $\dfrac{\partial^2 p}{\partial T \partial Q} \equiv 0$. This was critical because it meant that quality was not affected by monopoly, competition or our subsidy regulation. Hence, the single policy instrument of the subsidy was enough to lead us to the correct price-quality-quantity equilibrium. In the more general case, when this assumption is not valid, quality and quantity under monopoly could be higher or lower than under competition. Thus we would need two policy instruments (taxes or subsidies depending on whether Q^M and T^M were each too large or too small), one keyed to each target variable, to achieve the optimal result. All the regulatory policies discussed above fail in part because, in general, one cannot control two target variables with only one instrument.

Finally, note that in the subsidy case the profits of the monopolist will go up as compared to the profits prior to regulation. To those who object to this distributional change we recommend an excess profits tax at whatever rate (provided it is less than 100%) accommodates their social values. The allocational outcome will be unaffected by such a tax. In fact we now have three targets—and need three instruments. The two excise tax-subsidies take care of allocation (quality and quantity) and the profits tax alters income distribution.

4. CONCLUSIONS

While previous attempts at analyzing the quality problem led to highly indeterminate results, interesting conclusions emerge from the analysis presented in this paper:

(1) In general, without regulation one will expect different market structures to lead to different quality levels as well as to different quantities of the basic commodity. However, given an apparently reasonable assumption in this model, quality is the same under competition or monopoly while quantity produced and sold is smaller under competition.

(2) The regulatory problem thus becomes inducing the monopolist to provide a larger quantity while leaving his choice of quality unaffected. In our framework, the regulatory schemes prevalent in the United States (fair-rate-of-return regulation and price regulation) cannot lead the monopolist to behave in this optimal way. Since rate-of-return regulation cannot lead to an optimal outcome, even in the absence of a quality dimension, its failure in the presence of the quality problem does not come as a surprise. However, price regulation can lead to an optimal outcome when quality choice is absent. (In any case it induces the monopolist to change his output in the right direction.) Hence the logical impossibility of achieving an optimum under price regulation is an interesting result.

(3) Mark-up regulation too cannot bring the monopolist to optimality, even though the mark-up regulation may lead to an optimum when the quality dimension is absent. Interestingly enough, the quality level will go up under mark-up regulation while it will go down under price regulation.

(4) Finally there is a tax-subsidy which can lead to an optimal outcome. The failure of alternative regulatory schemes is because they cannot exert separate influences on quality and quantity. Hence, we propose policy measures able to do just that. Where market structure has no impact on quality in this formulation there is an excise subsidy per unit of output (independent of quality) that will induce the optimal quantity. When both quality and quantity are affected by market structure, two separate excise taxes and/or subsidies can always be chosen in such a manner as to lead to an optimal outcome.

In sum then, if the quality of service in some real-world regulated utilities is believed to be suboptimal, it would in general be a mistake to attribute this entirely to the structure of that industry. Instead regulation itself is as likely to lead one astray. Short of setting rigid quality standards (i.e., short of a rationing solution) the problem can best be solved by an appropriate excise tax-subsidy scheme.

Notes to Chapter One

1. G. C. Archibald despairs of finding any predictive content in models containing quality variables. G. C. Archibald, "Profit-Maximizing and Non-Price Competition," *Economica,* 31 (February, 1964). For an interesting discussion of the quality problem from the point of view of differentiated competition see R. Dorfman and P. O. Steiner, "Optimal Advertising and Optimal Quality," *American Economic Review,* 44 (1955). Our general formulation of the quality problem is actually quite close to theirs.

2. This type of indeterminancy is precisely what led Archibald in his above-mentioned article to an extremely pessimistic outlook on the use of economic theory in this kind of problem. As we show in the next section, however, even without additional assumptions, important conclusions can be drawn as far as the adequacy of various regulatory schemes is concerned.

3. This result is closely related to the conclusion reached by Peter L. Swan in a recent attempt to deal with the durability of consumption goods under competitive and monopolistic regimes. See Peter L. Swan, "Durability of Consumption Goods," *American Economic Review,* 60 (November, 1970).

4. H. Averch and L. L. Johnson, "Behavior of the Firm under Regulatory Constraint," *American Economic Review,* 52 (December, 1962).

5. We assume here that no taxes are imposed on the monopolist. For the importance of this assumption, see E. A. Pazner, "Effects of Taxes on a Regulated Monopoly," (mimeo, revised July 1971).

6. See E. Sheshinski, "Welfare Aspects of a Regulatory Constraint: Note," *American Economic Review,* 61 (March, 1971). The statement in the previous paragraph of the text regarding the sign of $\frac{dk}{ds}$ can also be checked there.

7. See White (chapter 2, of this volume) in which even though separate prices are used for what we call Q and T, a change in the price of Q only induces an indeterminate change in T. The fact that T changes is thus not due to this particular feature of our model. What is important, however, is that we can determine unambiguously the direction in which T changes, while White cannot.

8. This is at sharp variance with rate-of-return regulation, since the latter can never lead to an optimum configuration of inputs, outputs and prices. See Pazner 1971.

Chapter Two

Quality, Competition and Regulation: Evidence from the Airline Industry

Lawrence J. White

In studying the effects of regulation on product quality we must distinguish between two groups of cases. On the one hand there are the traditional public-utility sectors like electricity, gas, water and telephone where the cost structure of distribution systems makes geographic monopoly essential for technical efficiency. Such activities in the United States are typically carried out by licensed monopolies subject to rate-of-return regulation—where the regulators control the earned rate of return either directly or indirectly via their control over prices. In such sectors, concern with product quality has most often centered around whether the utility was providing good enough service, as opposed to skimping on maintenance or reliability in order to raise or maintain earnings.

There is however another whole class of regulated industries in which more than one producer is generally present: airlines, railroads, trucking, broadcasting, securities transactions, local taxicabs and most financial services. The avowed goals of regulation in such sectors are often the same as in the previous group: to keep prices down and quality up. Here also prices are often (but not always) subject to regulatory review. In general, however, in such cases, cost functions would not support a strong tendency toward local monopoly in the absence of regulation—as the presence of multiple producers indicates. Hence entry is often controlled and unconstrained price competition forbidden by regulators for the declared purpose of preserving profits which are seen as necessary for preserving quality. Yet, the resulting market structures are not

An earlier version of this paper was presented at the American Telephone and Telegraph Conference on Regulation at Dartmouth College, September 1971. I would like to thank Marc Roberts for his comments and suggestions and Marc Schwartz for his assistance in data checking and computations. Part of the research on this paper was supported by a postdoctoral research grant in public utility economics from the American Telephone and Telegraph Company.

always stable, and firms can resort to rivalrous interaction by raising quality while price remains unchanged. The hoped-for profits from the regulated price disappear into higher quality levels. It would be very useful from a policy viewpoint to understand this relationship more clearly. What is the effect of price regulation and the number of competitors (as determined by entry controls) on quality?

I have elsewhere developed a model of this second kind of regulated industry. After summarizing and clarifying that model, this paper will use it as a basis for exploring these relationships in the United States trunk airline industry. Some comments on the meaning and policy implications of the results will also be offered.

1. THE ASSUMPTIONS OF THE MODEL

(1) I prefer to think of a quality variable as a second output produced by a firm. It is tied to the first or primary output in both production and consumption. This second output has an identifiable cost, and there is an identifiable demand for it. In principle, a separate price could be charged for this second output, although in practice the primary output and the quality variables will usually be consumed jointly so that no separate price is observed. If there were separate prices, the two outputs would behave as complementary goods. Even if indivisibilities limit this apparent interaction, differences in quality levels would still influence the division of sales of the primary product among producers (e.g., my total consumption of airline flights may not be affected by the number of meals that airlines serve, yet, other things being equal, I will choose the airline which offers the most meals).

Some examples of this notion of quality can be given. If the primary output of a firm were airline transportation between city pairs, the secondary outputs might be meals, inflight comfort, ease of getting a seat at a convenient time, or luxurious downtown ticket offices. If the primary output were gasoline, the secondary output might be octanes. If the primary output were automobiles, the secondary output might be chrome, fancy showrooms, or advertising which conveys information and/or generates a sense of contentment with the product.

This notion of quality is somewhat akin to the notion of attributes that Lancaster developed in his reformulation of consumer theory.[1] The major difference is that the quality variables here have attributable costs and can thus be integrated into a theory of markets.

It is worth stating here that the results below do not depend crucially on the acceptance of this interpretation of quality variables. The calculus works equally well if one takes the more conventional view of a quality variable as something that is an input into the production process which somehow influences final demand for a product. It is just that I believe that my interpretation gives a better insight into what is going on behind the calculus.[2]

(2) The second assumption is that consumers see quality as varying along objectively definable dimensions that are the same for all firms in an industry. In essence, I have taken the uniformity assumption usually made for the primary product in a competitive industry, and extended it to the secondary product or quality variable. At least in all consumers' perceptions, the food provided by an airline can be described in homogeneous units of meal service, and equal octanes are seen to be identical among gasoline companies. I will measure quality so that consumers will be presumed to prefer more rather than less.

(3) The third assumption is that both the primary and secondary outputs can be produced under conditions of constant unit cost. The major purpose of this assumption is to allow straightforward comparisons between the behavior of a competitive industry and a monopolized industry. If, instead, one permits increasing or decreasing returns to scale, the simple act of consolidating a competitive industry of n firms into a monopoly will affect production costs and consequently other variables in the model. I prefer to focus on the direct effects of monopoly and competition on these variables and not on their indirect effects through cost changes.

(4) Quality variables can be thought of as falling into two major categories: variables which are normally expressed in terms of quality per unit of the basic output, and variables which are expressed in terms of the total quantity of the quality variable itself. Thus, meals per passenger, octanes per gallon, and chrome per car are examples of the first. While we may sometimes be interested in the total number of meals provided in the market, we are usually more interested in measuring this kind of quality in the number of meals per passenger. Advertising, spacious show rooms, and luxurious ticket offices would be examples of the second kind.

These two kinds of quality variables are analogous to Marshallian variable costs and fixed costs. In the short run we can vary the number of meals per passenger, but once that level is set, the total number of meals will vary directly with primary output (though advertising per passenger will, of course, vary inversely with primary output). But in the long run all costs are variable, and all quality variables become adjustable to primary output, and thus in the long run all quality variables collapse to the first variety.

The model below will use the first type of quality variable. Quality is expressed in terms of quality units per unit of primary output. One can thus think of it as a short-run model for the meals-octanes-chrome kinds of variables and as a long-run model for the other kinds.[3]

2. THE MODEL IN THE ABSENCE OF REGULATION

Suppose we have an industry of N firms producing a primary output Q_1 at a price P_1 per unit for that primary output at zero quality and a secondary quality output Q_2, which is expressed in terms of quality units per unit of primary output. Q_2 has an explicit or implicit price at P_2 per unit. Thus, overall price per unit purchased, P is given by $P = P_1 + P_2 Q_2$. The unit costs of the two outputs are C_1 and C_2 respectively, both of which include a normal return on capital. The market demand functions facing the industry are

$$Q_1 = f(P_1, P_2) \tag{1}$$

and

$$Q_2 = g(P_1, P_2). \tag{2}$$

The profit function facing each firm in the industry is

$$\pi_1 = P_1 q_{i1} + P_2 q_{i2} q_{i1} - C_1 q_{i1} - C_2 q_{i2} q_{i1} , \tag{3}$$

where π_i is the profit of the ith firm, q_{i1} is the output of the primary product by the ith firm and q_{i2} is the average amount of the secondary output that the firm appends to each unit of primary output. We know that total primary output

$$\sum_{i=1}^{n} q_{i1} = Q_1 , \tag{4}$$

and average quality output

$$\frac{\sum_{i=1}^{n} q_{i2} q_{i1}}{Q_1} = Q_2 . \tag{5}$$

If the industry behaves competitively, the prices of both outputs will be driven down to the level of costs, so that no excess profits are made. Thus, the competitive outcome will be $P_1 = C_1$ and $P_2 = C_2$. Because the quality variable may be tied to the primary output, P_2 may not be directly observable, but in principle it can always be derived. The appropriate quantities of Q_1 and Q_2 can be solved for in equations (1) and (2). Note that the exact output of each *firm* is not determined—as is generally the case with constant returns to scale in the competitive model. If a firm had a monopoly in the industry (and was not fearful of entry), it would set the price of one or both outputs above their marginal costs and reap its monopoly profits, Again, the appropriate quantities of Q_1 and Q_2 can be found from equations (1) and (2).[4]

Note that equation (2) tells us only about the average level of quality Q_2 that will be demanded. There is no reason why every unit of Q_1 should have only the average level of Q_2 appended to it. As long as consumers are willing explicitly or implicitly to pay the price charged for their quality units, the industry will be happy to provide them with as many or as few quality units per unit of primary output as the consumers want. Thus, with constant returns and a perfect market, an unregulated industry will provide a wide variety of quality levels. Indeed, each consumer will get his goods custom made with exactly as much quality as he is willing to pay for. Brief introspection leads me to conclude that this is not so unrealistic as it sounds. In actual industries in which significant economics of scale are absent—retail services, clothing, household goods, for example—there is indeed an extremely wide variety of quality levels available.

This is an important result from the unregulated market. As is indicated below, one of the important losses from price regulation is the loss of quality variety. The conclusion that unregulated markets will provide a variety of quality levels has been reached before both by Abbott and by Dorfman and Steiner.[5] But it did not figure prominently in their analyses, and it has been ignored in subsequent models involving quality variables.[6]

3. THE MODEL UNDER PRICE REGULATION

Suppose the industry comes under price regulation. The regulator tells the firms that they can charge only one price, P^*, for their output. This immediately changes the behavior of the market in a very critical way: *all goods will be of the same quality level*. Since no one can charge higher prices for higher qualities, higher qualities are not offered. At the same time, no lower quality goods will be sold, since no consumer would purchase anything less than the highest available quality level—which will not be limited in supply by the constant cost assumption. Thus Q_2, the average quality discussed above, is now the *actual* quality of all units sold, and we can write a well defined industry demand function of the form

$$Q_1 = h(P^*, Q_2).$$
(6)

To actually find that quality level, note that the profit function of a firm will be

$$\pi_i = P^* q_{i1} - C_1 q_{i1} - C_2 q_{i1} - C_2 q_{i2} q_{i1}.$$
(7)

With the price of the primary output fixed and the charging of a price for the secondary output (quality) ruled out, quality becomes the competitive variable.

Firms will compete among themselves by offering customers increasing amounts of the secondary output. Formally, the profit-maximizing firm will follow the rule

$$\frac{d\pi_i}{dq_{i2}} = P^* \frac{\partial q_{i1}}{\partial q_{i2}} - C_1 \frac{\partial q_{i1}}{\partial q_{i2}} - C_2 q_{i2} \frac{\partial q_{i1}}{\partial q_{i2}} - C_2 q_{i1} = 0. \tag{8}$$

Rearranging, we get

$$q_{i2} = (P^* - C_1)/C_2 - q_{i1}/(\partial q_{i1}/\partial q_{i2}). \tag{9}$$

Now we have not specified what the *firms'* demand functions are like. But we can argue that in a competitive industry, in which each firm ignores the effects of its actions on its fellow firms, each firm will see $\partial q_{i1}/\partial q_{i2}$ as being very large or infinite. It will believe that an added unit of quality will steal all of the customers away from the other firms. This is analogous to the assumption of infinite elasticity of demand facing a competitor in the usual price-quality analysis. As a consequence, the last term in equation (9) would approach zero, and we would be left with

$$q_{i2} = (P^* - C_1)/C_2. \tag{10}$$

Since all firms face the same price and costs, equation (10) tells us the single level of quality that all firms in a regulated competitive industry will produce. The consequent level of primary output for the industry could be found from equation (6). In words, equation (10) says that the quality offering of the regulated competitive industry will be equal to the "potential" net revenue per unit of primary output, divided by the cost of a unit of quality. Under conditions of constant costs, the competitive industry will compete away all potential excess profits by offering higher quality to customers.

Now suppose we have a monopolist facing similar regulation. He is constrained to charge P^*, and to provide adequate service in a nondiscriminating manner; that is, he must sell as many units at the given price and quality as people demand. Such a monopolist operates directly with the industry demand function (6), since he is a price taker just like the competitive firm (because of regulation). His profit function looks like (7), except that he can write it using Q_1 and Q_2, the industry magnitudes, which, after manipulation, gives us

$$Q_2 = (P^* - C_1)/C_2 - Q_1/(\partial Q_1/\partial Q_2). \tag{9'}$$

The monopolist of course knows that $\partial Q_1/\partial Q_2$ is less than infinite. When he offers an extra unit of quality to the marginal customer, he must offer it as well to all of the inframarginal customers. Again, this is analogous to the marginal revenue of a monopolist being below the demand curve in the usual price-quantity case. Since the denominator of the last term of $(9')$ is always positive, a monopolist regulated in this way will always offer a lower level of quality than will the regulated competitive industry.[7]

The differences are even more marked in the special case where quality has no effect on industry sales ($\partial Q_1/\partial Q_2 = 0$) but still influences the distribution of sales among competing firms. The competitive industry still approaches the result given by (10), while $(9')$ shows us that the monopolist provides "zero" quality since there is no gain to him from doing anything else.

Archibald (1964) has despaired of being able to generate general and meaningful predictions and conclusions from microeconomic models containing quality variables. The model summarized above, however, does yield a number of important conclusions:

(1) At a given price level, a price-regulated competitive industry will offer a *higher* level of quality per unit of primary output to customers than will a regulated monopolist. Consumers are thus always better off under competition than under monopoly.

(2) The competitive industry will produce a larger primary output than will the monopolist, if the same regualated price is imposed on both.

(3) The quality level provided by a competitive industry will be directly dependent on costs and the regulated price. As costs fall and/or the regulated price rises, there will be more potential net revenue to compete away, and a higher quality level will be forthcoming.[8] This relationship may not be true for the monopolist. A change in the regulated price may also change the size of the $\partial Q_1/\partial Q_2$ term. If, say, at a higher price, demand for the primary product becomes less responsive to quality, this magnitude could decrease by enough to offset the higher P^* in equation (9), and the resulting quality (Q_2) might actually fall.[9]

(4) The regulator cannot provide the competitive industry with supernormal profits. Any attempt by the regulator to grant supernormal profits by setting a higher P^* relative to C_1 will simply lead to a higher level of quality offered.[10]

(5) When a competitive industry with constant costs comes under this type of price regulation, consumers in general must suffer, because they lose their ability to choose the quality they prefer. Those who want to consume just the quality level indicated by equation (10) will be unaffected; everyone else is worse off. The regulator's choice of a price can only affect the determination of which consumers are hurt. The welfare loss or gain from regulating a previously unregulated monopolist is indeterminate. The monopolist presumably offered more than one quality level, so that consumers lose by being deprived of such variety, but they gain a lower price.

(6) If the regulator sets a high price relative to the costs of producing the primary output, a competitive industry will produce a high quality output. If consumers do not value the quality very highly, they (or

outside observers) may complain that competition is wasteful, although they nevertheless value it enough always to choose the firm that offers the highest quality, other things being equal. The fault here, of course, is not the competition but the high regulated price. At that same price a monopoly would offer a lower level of quality, and some observers may suggest this as an alternative. To the extent that consumers value the quality at all, they will be worse off under the monopoly.[11] A more efficient alternative is to keep the industry competitive and lower the regulated price. A yet more efficient alternative would be to eliminate the price regulation completely.

4. AIRLINE FLIGHT FREQUENCIES:
AN APPLICATION OF THE MODEL

The domestic American trunk airline industry, and the particular quality variable important to the industry, seat availability, provide an interesting case for testing the preceding formal analysis. The industry is regulated by the Civil Aeronautics Board (CAB) which controls both prices and entry into all interstate scheduled airline service. No new airline has been allowed to enter the industry since it came under regulation in 1936, and even existing airlines must obtain the CAB's permission to enter any new city-pair market.[12] CAB regulation is not exactly like that assumed in the model, since some quality differences (e.g., those between first and tourist class) can be reflected in differential prices. Airlines cannot, however, adjust prices for scheduling frequency and consequent seat availability, the variable we will investigate.[13] Do note that this quality parameter is not exactly like the ones we have just explored in the model. It is *in principle* not variable for each customer. Furthermore, in our studies we will use statistics characteristic of city-pair markets (i.e., multifirm averages) and not the quality levels offered by distinct producers. Thus we will not be able to explore differences in *variety*, but rather *the influence of various structural factors on quality levels.*

Why scheduling/seat availability as an object of study? From the consumer's viewpoint, several aspects of the airline service bundle in this area are partially relevant to his satisfactions. The likelihood of a convenient departure and of an available seat depends on the total number of flights (from all carriers), their distribution over the day and the total seats available relative to typical demand. In addition, the airlines have shown that they believe that consumers make choices about what airline to call for a ticket partly on the basis of these criteria. Many carriers have advertised heavily to depict in detail the convenience of their schedules for selected city-pair markets.

One variable that is easy to collect and compute and reflects many of these conditions is the ratio of available seats to passengers. It also fits an important condition of the quality variable of the model in Section 3: It is expressed in terms of quality per unit of primary output. The inverse of this measure is a familiar concept, the load factor, and it is this latter concept that will be used below.[14] In what follows, we hypothesize that the lower the load factor, the greater the quality on a given route.[15] Of course this measure does not perfectly reflect passenger convenience, since carriers' departure times could be distributed in various ways over the day.

On the other hand, load factors have another virtue in that they are likely to be correlated with other dimensions of service quality. In particular, newer aircraft are often larger aircraft. Such equipment, which presumably offers better service in various ways, is likely to produce some decline in load factors when first introduced, as we discuss below.

Another problem in relating the model to real data is that the formal analysis is limited to the purely competitive and monopoly cases. In what follows, however, we will be interested in the effects of varied degrees of oligopolistic interdependence on quality. Since economics generally lacks a well-developed formal model of oligopolistic interaction, we are forced to make the usual inference that markets which are structurally closer to monopoly will behave in ways closer to the monopoly pattern, and vice versa. The measure of "concentration" we will employ for this purpose is simply the number of carriers in a given city-pair.

The model predicts that the greater the tendency of firms to act competitively, the higher quality they will offer, or, in this case, the greater will be the availability of seats and the lower their load factors.[16] Furthermore, the present structure of airline costs and fares is such that fares per passenger mile fall less rapidly with distance than do standardized costs per passenger mile.[17] Thus, there is generally a larger potential net revenue margin in long-haul markets than in short-haul markets—note equation (10)—and we would expect firms that behave competitively to offer lower load factors on long hauls than on short hauls. We can make no a priori prediction about distance and load factor for monopoly markets however. Monopolists could be influenced by the fact that in markets of different lengths the cross relationship between primary demand and quality could be different, implying different optimal behavior.

The data for the test come from the CAB's general passenger fare investigation. For 1967, 1968 and 1969 data are available on roughly 250 city-pairs having nonstop service by the trunk carriers. However, the information for some of the city-pairs is incomplete, and the samples were weeded down to 151, 172, and 186 city-pairs for the three years, respectively.[18]

Table 2-1 presents the mean values of the variables used, and table 2-2 presents the regressions that relate load factors on routes to the distance and number of carriers on the route. (The numbers in parentheses are the t-ratios of the coefficients.) The regressions indicate that, for example, in 1967 the load factor on a monopoly route of (hypothetically) zero mileage would have been 65.64%, that a route of 1000 miles on the average had a lower load factor, which meant 3.5 fewer passengers per 100 available seats, that adding a second carrier

Table 2–1.   Mean Values of Variables, Analysis of Determinants of
Load Factors.

Variable[a]	All Markets	One-carrier Markets	Two-carrier Markets	Three-or-more Carrier Markets
		1967		
LF	58.66	62.52	57.67	54.13
D	934.36	882.65	962.10	964.28
N2	0.44			
N3	0.17			
N4	0.04			
S	103.52	101.20	104.85	104.69
no.	155	55	68	32
		1968		
LF	55.82	59.87	54.36	51.95
D	941.81	937.33	939.04	955.66
N2	0.44			
N3	0.18			
N4	0.02			
S	107.34	106.27	106.02	112.05
no.	172	61	76	35
		1969		
LF	51.43	53.44	51.31	49.47
D	900.41	1159.85	813.63	818.88
N2	0.53			
N3	0.18			
N4	0.04			
S	110.05	116.92	106.67	110.52
no.	186	46	99	41

[a] Notation:

LF = load factor = (passengers ÷ available seats) × 100
 D = distance in miles
N2 = 1 if two carriers serve a route, 0 otherwise
N3 = 1 if three carriers serve a route, 0 otherwise
N4 = 1 if four carriers serve a route, 0 otherwise
 S = average size of plane on a route = available seats ÷ flights
no. = number of city-pairs

reduced the load factor by 4.56 passengers per 100 seats below the monopoly level, that adding a third carrier reduced the load factor by 6.65 passengers per 100 seats below the monopoly level, etc.

The results of the regressions are those that the model predicts. In all cases the coefficients take the expected signs and are significantly different from zero at a 95% confidence level. Further, the presence of two or more carriers on a route yields significantly lower load factors than are found on comparable monopoly routes.

To test whether the additional carriers beyond two make a significant difference, it is necessary to run a regression constraining all of the coefficients on the two-, three-, and four-carrier dummy variables to be equal to each other and compare the sum of squared residuals from this constrained regression to that from the corresponding equation in table 2-2 by means of an

Table 2-2. **Regressions of Load Factors on Distance and Number of Carriers, All Markets.**

Year	Constant	D	N2	N3	N4	R^2
1967	65.64 (43.77)	0.0035 (3.25)	4.5647 (2.94)	6.6500 (3.25)	14.3784 (3.89)	0.1852
1968	63.6585 (52.12)	0.0040 (4.75)	5.5034 (4.43)	7.5333 (4.73)	10.2748 (2.75)	0.2489
1969	57.18 (36.98)	0.0032 (3.57)	3.2495 (2.30)	4.4854 (2.52)	7.4864 (2.48)	0.0954

appropriate F test. For 1967, the resulting F ratio had the value of 3.62, whereas the 95% confidence point for 2 and 150 degrees of freedom is 3.06. Thus, for 1967 we can reject the null hypotheses that the presence of two, three or four carriers in a market had identically the same effect on quality. More carriers did mean greater quality. For 1968 and 1969, however, this ratio had the values 1.49 and 1.27, respectively; and we cannot reject the null hypothesis.

It is worth noting that our conclusion about the influence of the number of carriers is fairly strong, because there are at least two factors that might tend to bias monopoly markets toward low load factors. First, some monopoly carriers might be in small markets where they are under local or CAB pressure to provide a minimum of daily service that is not otherwise justified on a profit maximization basis. This would generate lower load factors than the monopoly carrier would otherwise wish to provide. Such service (and low load factors) also helps ward off new entry since the CAB has frequently considered the "adequacy" of service being provided by the existing carrier or carriers in determining whether an additional carrier should be placed on a route. (This kind of entry-deterring behavior in two-carrier markets in 1968 and 1969—years in which the CAB was considering new route awards—may partly explain the similar performance in two-carrier and more-than-two-carrier markets in these years.) Despite these possible effects, the results do indicate that monopoly routes have significantly higher load factors (poorer quality) than non-monopoly routes.

As another test on the nature of competition or rivalry in city-pair markets, I included an additional 0,1 dummy variable for those monopoly markets in which a second carrier was offering a significant amount of one-stop service. For the three years, the coefficient on the additional variable was negative once and positive twice, and in all three cases was insignificantly different from zero. The existence of a second carrier offering one-stop service does not seem to improve the performance of a carrier having a monopoly on the non-stop service in a market.

As a further test of these relationships, the samples for each year were separated into one-carrier, two-carrier, and three-or-more-carrier markets and separate regressions of load factor (there were not enough four carrier markets to provide a large enough sample for a separate test) on distance were run. These results are reported in table 2-3. In monopoly markets, distance has a negative coefficient which is only significant in one of three cases. The R^2s are also quite low. Since our formal model does not give any specific predictions about the impact of distance on quality in monopoly markets, these results are not disheartening. In the two-carrier and three-or-more carrier regressions, however, distance is clearly significant in five or six cases. Again, the appropriate F tests indicate that the significant distinction is between the monopoly markets and all other markets.

Table 2-3.   Regressions of Load Factor on Distance, by Year and Number of Carriers per Market.

Number of Carriers per Market	Year	Constant	Regression Coefficient	R^2
1	1967	63.69 (25.17)	0.0013 (0.55)	0.0056
1	1968	63.43 (32.48)	0.0038 (2.19)	0.0752
1	1969	57.99 (17.02)	0.0039 (1.51)	0.0492
2	1967	62.05 (36.22)	0.0045 (3.06)	0.1245
2	1968	57.07 (40.33)	0.0029 (2.30)	0.0664
2	1969	53.39 (45.11)	0.0026 (2.21)	0.0483
3 or more	1967	57.08 (27.88)	0.0031 (1.81)	0.0982
3 or more	1968	57.73 (39.30)	0.0061 (4.95)	0.4262
3 or more	1969	52.33 (48.12)	0.0035 (3.44)	0.2323

A possible objection to the form of these regressions needs to be discussed. The National Economic Research Associates have argued that costs really do not fall faster than fares with distance, so that distance is not a good proxy for potential profitability.[19] The negative relationship between load factors and distance is spurious, they say, because the technology of the industry requires larger aircraft for longer distances and, hence, more available seats and lower load factors. The carriers are not able to compensate for the larger aircraft with fewer flights. Thus, the apparent negative relationship between load factors and distance, they contend, is really a negative relationship between load factor and aircraft size. When they added aircraft size on a route to regressions similar to those in table 2-2, the coefficient on distance became positive.

I do not find these arguments fully convincing. First, as is indicated below, aircraft size appears to be a competitive variable on various routes. Hence, the positive relationship that can be observed between size and distance may not be purely technological but rather may be a response to the lure of potential profitability. Accordingly, the lower load factors that accompany larger size may be catching the potential profitability effect of longer routes.

Second, even if size and distance were strictly linked technologically and this initially resulted in unprofitably low load factors, over time we would expect to see scheduling adjustments on long routes to raise load factors back to profitable levels. Yet, over the three years covered by these regressions, distance continued to have a significantly negative effect on load factors. This indicates either extremely slow adjustment to unprofitable situations—or evidence of the continuing lure of potential profits on longer routes.

Third, if distance and size are strongly related, multicollinearity problems will make the estimation of the effect of distance more difficult when both variables are introduced as explanatory variables. Nevertheless, I have also included size as a variable in the regressions reported above. These results, reported in tables 2-4 and 2-5, do not change the earlier results appreciably. The distance effect remains negative in the all-markets regressions (table 2-4) and the two-carrier and three-or-more-carrier regressions (table 2-5), though significance levels decline, as we would expect from the collinearity with size. An interesting story, however, is told by the comparisons of the monopoly markets with the two-carrier and three-or-more-carrier markets. In the former, the size variable is significant in two of the three years and the R^2s improve notably while aircraft size is insignificant in the more competitive markets. This is not implausible, since a number of monopoly markets already had minimum schedules. Thus, we could expect aircraft size to have the most impact on load factors in these cases because carriers cannot so completely engage in compensatory readjustments of flight frequency. This suggests that the significant role for size in the all-markets regressions is largely the result of the particular role of that variable in the monopoly case only.

Table 2-4.   Regressions of Load Factors on Distance, Number of Carriers, and Aircraft Size, All Markets.

Year	Constant	D	N2	N3	N4	S	R^2
1967	70.75 (16.58)	0.0026 (1.97)	4.4253 (2.85)	6.6241 (3.25)	13.8093 (3.72)	0.0587 (1.28)	0.1941
1968	71.42 (21.86)	0.0026 (2.54)	5.5268 (4.52)	7,1149 (4.51)	9.4011 (2.54)	0.0860 (2.55)	0.2773
1969	67.1056 (18.10)	0.0011 (0.98)	3.6041 (2.59)	4.5145 (2.59)	7.1543 (2.41)	0.1058 (2.93)	0.1367

Table 2-5.   Regressions of Load Factor on Distance and Aircraft
Size, by Year and Number of Carriers per Market

Number of Carriers per Market	Year	Constant	D	S	R^2
1	1967	70.89 (11.44)	0.0009 (0.29)	0.0901 (1.27)	0.0356
1	1968	75.32 (17.02)	0.0005 (0.24)	0.1411 (2.95)	0.1961
1	1969	75.99 (10.16)	0.0006 (0.23)	0.1867 (2.66)	0.1836
2	1967	68.48 (9.01)	0.0036 (1.97)	0.0699 (0.87)	0.1346
2	1968	55.00 (8.92)	0.0032 (2.02)	0.0224 (0.34)	0.0680
2	1969	57.23 (11.59)	0.0016 (1.00)	0.0430 (0.80)	0.0546
3 or more	1967	63.90 (4.80)	0.0023 (1.02)	0.0721 (0.52)	0.1065
3 or more	1968	66.38 (7.86)	0.0050 (3.19)	0.0860 (1.04)	0.4450
3 or more	1969	55.07 (9.23)	0.0030 (1.92)	0.0288 (0.47)	0.2367

Overall, then, the relationship between distance as a proxy for profitability and load factors does hold up, despite the possible objection raised above.

The low R^2 statistics for all the equations indicate that a good deal of the variance in load factors is unexplained. Some of this may be due to the interrelated multi-market structure of all airlines which necessitates equipment and scheduling decisions for individual city-pairs that differ from those that would occur if each market were being served independently. Unfortunately, there seems to be no way that this effect can be included in the regressions. Nevertheless, the distance and number-of-carrier coefficients are significant and sizable. The potential profitability of a route and the amount of competition (or rivalry) on a route really do influence the quality of service offered.

The changes in the coefficients over the years are also quite interesting. The period for which we have data, 1967-69, saw the introduction of the second generation jets, the DC-9, Boeing 727 and BAC 111, which were generally larger than the propeller and turboprop equipment they replaced. The airlines apparently introduced these newer, larger aircraft first on their more competitive routes, and only employed them in less competitive markets as they took additional deliveries in later years. This pattern is reflected in a number of ways. In table 2-2, the intercept (which reflects the zero-miles monopoly-route load factor) declines over time, while the negative coefficients on the number-of-carriers dummy variables become smaller. A Chow test on a regression pooling the observations for all years compared to the regressions for the individual years indicates that the differences in coefficients are significant; the same is true when Chow tests are applied to the individual market regressions of table 2-3. The behavior in both monopoly and more competitive markets does not appear to have changed significantly. Further, the effect of aircraft size in the equation for all markets (table 2-2) and for monopoly markets (table 2-3) becomes larger and more significant over time. Direct confirmation of this view is also provided by the averages of table 2-1, which show just this pattern of changes in load factors and aircraft size for three different sets of markets in each of these years.

5. EXPLAINING THE RESULTS

The regressions indicate that as few as two carriers are enough to generate a significantly higher quality performance in a market. This is something of a puzzle. Most economists expect that when two to four firms control 100% of a market with restricted entry, the monopoly outcome will generally develop via tacit collusion and recognized oligopolistic interdependence. True, the airlines are competing on "quality" and not "price," but why should that make such a difference?

A number of explanations can be offered. I am not sure that any of them is really adequate. The first is the influence of CAB. But it is not clear how this influence might have been exerted. Explicit agreements to curtail service have been ruled out until very recently, but what is at issue here are implicit agreements. If the carriers fear that the CAB would frown on the reduced service in the affected markets, why has this fear not prevented the higher load factors characteristic of monopoly markets?

Perhaps the airline corporation executives are really sales maximizers rather than profit maximizers. But, if so, why do we not see higher quality levels in the monopoly markets that might induce more sales in those markets?

Alternatively, oligopolists may collude on quality with greater difficulty than on price. Moves might be more difficult to notice and imitate. Each firm could believe that its product is superior and not easily imitated so that tacit collusion is not in its interest. Yet, the quality variable examined in this paper is easily observed and duplicated. One would have thought that collusion on load factors would not be that difficult to arrange.

Yet another possible explanation is that the perceived gains from achieving a scheduling advantage over a rival are so great that the risks of aggressive scheduling behavior seem worthwhile. Fruhan has argued that market shares show a strong S-curve relationship to shares of seats available.[20] The dominant carrier in a market (as measured by seat availability) will get more than its share of passengers and hence will be able to operate at higher, more profitable load factors. If each rival seeks to be the dominant carrier, a "prisoner's dilemma" results, with lower profits for all. Yet such relationships are present in other industries, as Fruhan recognizes. It is not clear that the advantages to the dominant firm are much greater in the airline industry than in other stable oligopolies.

Three factors may help to account for this pattern in the airlines case. First, airlines are a relatively young industry, so that more mature patterns of oligopolistic interdependence might have not yet been learned. If so, the recent CAB approval for meetings and joint agreements among the carriers to reduce flight frequencies may have ominous implications for the future. Once having experienced the gains from coordinated flight reductions, the carriers may be able to continue their coordination tacitly (in classic oligopolistic fashion) even if the CAB reverses policy and forbids these agreements at some future date. Second, insofar as the CAB will rescue carriers in financial trouble (through higher fares or route awards) the risks of aggressive rivalry are lessened. Finally, the airlines might believe that scheduling dominance in one city-pair helps in other markets, since customers will be more likely to fly a carrier they have flown on other routes. Such brand loyalty makes the rewards of achieving dominance in any one market correspondingly greater.

If this last explanation has some validity, there is an important implication for possible deregulation of the industry. Suppose deregulation did produce a number of specialty carriers, each serving only one or a few high-volume routes, as some have suggested it might.[21] Without the multiple city-pair structure of the current trunks, these specialty carriers might find it easier to collude tacitly. Thus it would be important to allow continued entry (or that possibility) as a constraint on oligopolistic behavior.

6. CONCLUSIONS

The airline industry is a regulated industry which seems to fit the model of section 3. Markets with more firms tend to have higher levels of quality than markets with fewer firms. Long-haul markets with higher potential net revenues have higher levels of quality than short-haul markets. If consumers' benefits from lower load factors are worth the costs, greater competition would appear to be one way to help achieve that result. I suspect that this is also true for other quality variables as well.

If, on the other hand, the extra quality is wasteful, if consumers do not value the quality in a way commensurate with the costs of providing it, adjusting prices to reduce the price-cost margins of carriers would be one possible response. The response might be delayed and a bit painful for the carriers, but with reasonably good rental and second-hand markets for aircraft we could expect that schedule reductions would take place. Reducing the number of carriers on a route will also tend to reduce the quality level—but without compensating price reductions, it would also tend to generate excess profits for the airline involved.

Given the current regulatory system, we have no chance to observe much price-quality variety among the markets for airline services. Of course, the quality measure we have actually used is characteristic of each market as a whole. But it is easy enough to imagine different prices and seat availability as characteristic of different carriers in the same market at any one time. The same can be said of price variations for different types of equipment, departure times, numbers of intermediate stops, seating configurations, packages of on-board services and so on. By limiting price variations, the CAB puts itself in the position of having to select the one "worthwhile" level of quality from the set of price and quality combinations that the behavior of the industry will generate. Under such circumstances the market gets no chance to tell us what quality levels consumers prefer by the levels they are willing to pay for.

Only a drastic relaxation of price regulation and of entry restrictions would produce the variety of prices and qualities that would maximize consumer welfare. Unfortunately, the prospects for such a change in policy are not bright. It would virtually eliminate the powers of the CAB and call into question the justification for its existence. No large organization is likely to look kindly on suggestions for its own demise. The established carriers would certainly not favor such a proposal, and they appear to be a much stronger lobbying group than any potential entrants or scattered passengers. The parallel vested interests of the regulator and regulated on this point are powerful blocks to any fundamental change.

Notes to Chapter Two

1. Kelvin Lancaster, "A New Approach to Consumer Theory," *Journal of Political Economy*, v. 74 (April 1966), pp. 132–157.

2. I also believe that this "two output" view of the quality problem is useful for interpreting other problems, such as the two-part tariff problem that has been discussed by Walter Oi, "A Disneyland Dilemma: Two-Part Tariffs for a Mickey Mouse Monopoly," *Quarterly Journal of Economics*, v. 85 (February 1971), pp. 76–96.

3. For a discussion of the advertising model, see L.J. White, "Quality Variation when Prices are Regulated," *Bell Journal of Economics and Management Science*, v. 3 (Autumn 1972), pp. 431–432.

4. A complete statement of the problem of a monopoly selling two goods, including the possibility of a .loss leader, is found in R.G.D. Allen, *Mathematical Analysis for Economists* (New York: Macmillan, 1938), pp. 359–362.

5. Lawrence Abbott, *Quality and Competition* (New York: Columbia University Press, 1955), pp. 71-72; Robert Dorfman and Peter O. Steiner, "Optimal Advertising and Optimal Quality," *American Economic Review,* v. 44 (December 1954), p. 833.

6. G. C. Archibald, "Profit-Maximizing and Non-Price Competition," *Economica,* v. 31 (February 1964), pp. 13-22; George J. Stigler, "Price and Non-Price Competition," *Journal of Political Economy,* v. 76 (January/February 1968), pp. 149-154; Elisha A. Pazner, "Quality Choice and Monopoly Regulation," chapter 1 of the present volume.

7. For a geometrical presentation of this model, see White, "Quality Variation," p. 428.

8. In Equation (10),

$$dq_{i2}/dp^* = -\, dq_{i2}/dC_1 = 1/C_2 > 0.$$

9. This can be seen by taking total differentials in equation (9') and solving for $\dfrac{dQ_2}{dP^*}$:

$$\frac{dQ_2}{dP^*} = \frac{\dfrac{1}{C_2} \cdot \dfrac{\partial Q_1}{\partial Q_2}^{2} - \dfrac{\partial Q_1}{\partial Q_2} \cdot \dfrac{\partial Q_1}{\partial P^*} + Q_1 \cdot \dfrac{\partial^2 Q_1}{Q_2 P^*}}{2 \cdot \dfrac{\partial Q_1}{\partial Q_2}^{2} - Q_1 \dfrac{\partial^2 Q_1}{\partial Q_2}}$$

The denominator is positive, since the second order condition for maximum is that

$$Q_1 \cdot \frac{\partial^2 Q_1}{\partial Q_2^{\,2}} - 2 \cdot \frac{\partial Q_1}{\partial Q_2}^{2} < 0.$$

The sum of the first two terms of the numerator is positive, since $\dfrac{\partial Q_1}{\partial Q_2} > 0$ and $\dfrac{\partial Q_1}{\partial P^*} < 0$. But the third term is unsigned. If it is negative and large enough, the entire fraction could become negative.

10. If the marginal costs of primary or secondary output rise with volume rather than remain constant, the industry will be able to earn excess profits in equilibrium as long as entry is prevented. See Stigler, "Price and Non-Price Competition," pp. 149-154.

11. One can still ask if monopolizing the industry leads to a gain in a social sense. Is society better off by devoting the resources elsewhere rather than to quality in this industry? This is clearly a Kaldor-Hicks compensation question: Could the monopolist fully compensate the customers for the lower level of quality and still come out ahead? It will depend on how customers value the quality variable. This point is also discussed by Richard E. Caves, *Air Transport and Its Regulators,* (Cambridge: Harvard University Press, 1962), pp. 423-424.

12. For a more complete description of the industry and its regulatory environment see Caves, *Air Transport,* and William E. Fruhan Jr., *The Fight for Competitive Advantage* (Boston: Division of Research, Graduate School of Business Administration, Harvard University, 1972).

13. The one major exception here is Eastern Airlines' Boston-New York City-Washington shuttle, for which a premium price is charged.

14. The highest load factor in a city-pair recorded in the three-year sample described below was 86.3%. We could thus think of the primary output as passenger service with that load factor.

15. Airlines may try to offer more quality by taking seats out of existing flights and giving passengers more room. This would *raise* observed load factors. Ideally, one would like to correct observed load factors for the seating configurations offered by the airlines. However, this should not be a serious problem for the test proposed here. The 1967-1969 period was one for which seating configurations were relatively standardized among airlines and relatively stable over time. There was no behavior comparable to the large scale ripping out of seats that characterized the airlines' response to very low load factors in late 1970 and early 1971.

16. Similar predictions are yielded by a model developed by James C. Miller III, testimony contained in U.S. Department of Transportation, *Load Factor and Seating Configurations: Before the Civil Aeronautics Board Domestic Passenger Fare Investigation,* Docket no. 21866-6 (1970), appendix C, pp. 1-6. Miller's model, though, is specific to airline load factors.

17. Caves, *Air Transport* p. 409; U.S. Civil Aeronautics Board, Bureau of Economics, Rates Division, *A Study of the Domestic Passenger Air Fare Structure: Staff Report* (1968), p. 142; Theodore E. Keeler, "Airline Regulation and Market Performance," *Bell Journal of Economics and Management Science,* v. 3 (Autumn 1972), p. 416.

18. In all cases, the rejected city-pairs were those for which the number of carriers reported on a route in the sample differed from the number which was listed in the Official Airline Guide for the year in question.

19. National Economic Research Associates, Testimony contained in Exhibit TW 9-t-B, U.S. Civil Aeronautics Board, Docket no. 21866-9 (1971).

20. Fruhan, *The Fight for Competitive Advantage,* pp. 126-129.

21. Caves, *Air Transport,* p. 431.

Part Two

Self-Regulation of Product Characteristics

Chapter Three

Trade Associations and Self-Regulation: Major Home Appliances

Michael S. Hunt

Though economists generally equate regulation of an industry with government regulation, other agencies besides the government regulate industrial behavior. Of these, the most common is the trade association. Virtually every industry has at least one association if not several. Even though their activities vary considerably, these associations often set policies that apparently constrain the behavior of their members and, hence, provide self-regulation for their respective industries. Yet, little research has been done on the impact of such self-regulation on industry performance.

Conventional wisdom among economists holds that trade associations are mere filters through which underlying structural forces are mediated. If an industry is unconcentrated, they will be powerless and ineffective. If it is concentrated, they will be redundant, even as agents for price-fixing and other forms of collusion. To help test the conventional wisdom, this paper examines the impact of self-regulatory activities of one trade association—the Association of Home Appliance Manufacturers (AHAM). Since I will argue that the conventional wisdom does not fully pass this test, I will also suggest some tentative alternative hypotheses as to the uses and desirability of self-regulation. It is to be hoped that these hypotheses will stimulate interest in, as well as provide starting points for, further research.

To provide a context, it is helpful to look first at the major home appliance industry and the history and organization of AHAM. The various

The author is indebted to the Association of Home Appliance Manufacturers and its president, Guenther Baumgart, for their cooperation in providing the information for this paper. A complete reporting of the interviews and data supplied by AHAM can be found in the "Association of Home Appliance Manufacturers," International Case Clearing House (4-372-344), Boston. The analysis and evaluation of AHAM's activities are entirely this author's and are neither supported nor denied by AHAM and its staff. The assistance of Joseph Bower and Marc Roberts in the project from which this essay derives, and of the latter in commenting on earlier drafts of this essay, is also gratefully acknowledged.

forms of self-regulation are then described; possible motives for firms adopting self-regulation are considered; and the impact of self-regulation on industry performance is discussed. The paper concludes by putting forward five hypotheses as to the causes and desirability of self-regulation.

1. THE MAJOR HOME-APPLIANCE INDUSTRY

In 1970 the major home-appliance industry, as considered here, included the producers of what the trade calls "white goods,"—refrigerators, freezers, ranges, disposals, dishwashers, clothes washers and dryers, and room air conditioners. The industry shipped 28.2 million units with a retail value slightly in excess of $6 billion. Over the period 1960-70, this industry had apparently quite desirable economic performance. First, prices declined. Unit sales in 1970 went up 82% over 1961 while dollar sales were only 65% higher.[1] This reflects the fact that average retail appliance prices fell by 10% between 1960 and 1970, while the consumer price index rose by 30%.[2] Nor can this decrease by explained by any decline in average product quality. Actually the industry saw continuing technical change. During the 1960s the number of features on an average appliance (e.g., automatic icemakers or self-cleaning ovens) steadily rose. At the same time, new features were introduced, the capacity of units increased (e.g., the number of cubic feet in a refrigerator) as did their reliability.

This apparently desirable performance was accompanied by only moderate profits. Return on assets for the industry as a whole was estimated to be 6% to 8%. Yet over the same decade concentration was high and rising. In 1970, only seven firms shared 75% of the market.[3] Furthermore, concentration in any one product line was generally even higher. Barriers to entry as traditionally defined—particularly economies of scale and product differentiation—appeared to be moderate to high.[4]

Traditional economic theory would *not* predict that a highly concentrated industry with such moderate to high barriers to entry would have this performance. I have argued elsewhere that these results can be explained by the fact that many of the major firms in the industry differed with respect to their economic position and their internal organization. The primary economic differences between firms were in their degree of vertical integration, in the breadth of their product line and in the amount of brand loyalty they commanded. Internally, there were differences in terms of formal organization, in control systems and in management reward systems. For example, some participants in the industry were a group or division of a diversified firm while others operated solely in this industry. Some firms rewarded managers for maximizing short run accounting profits, while other firms gave managers more autonomy. These organizational differences led managers to have different attitudes toward risk and different time horizons. Together these economic and organizational differences meant that managers of various firms differed in their views as to what price levels, R&D spending and so on should prevail in the industry. These differences were sufficient to prevent the firms from agreeing on how to behave so as to exploit the potential monopoly profits available.[5]

Though this is a brief sketch of a complex situation, it is a necessary basis for examining the trade association (AHAM). AHAM existed in a very concentrated industry that exhibited highly rivalous behavior among diverse participants. The differences in circumstances and opinions among managers made interfirm communication (not to say direct cooperation) difficult indeed. As the following discussion suggests, such circumstances increased the perceived need for self-regulation in the eyes of the managers with respect to certain aspects of firm behavior. Yet it also limited their ability to use self-regulation to coordinate their behavior and reduce competition in other areas.

2. AHAM: HISTORY AND ORGANIZATION

AHAM's history reflects these larger forces. The first mechanical home appliance, the clothes washer, was developed at the turn of the century. By 1915, a number of manufacturers formed the Washing Machine Manufacturers Association (WMMA) in order to educate consumers as to the need for and use of the new product. By mid 1920s other major appliances, particularly refrigerators, found expanding markets. The manufacturers of these products formed the consumer product section of the National Electrical Manufacturers Association (NEMA), again with similar functions.

Initially, both the consumer products section of NEMA and the WMMA had an executive secretary and a small staff in order to carry out the policy directives of the members. As the home laundry industry grew to include clothes dryers and ironers, the latter was renamed the American Home Laundry Manufacturers Association (AHLMA). The organizational structure of the two groups began to diverge in 1954, when AHLMA was reorganized. The position of executive secretary was upgraded and retitled "president," and he and the association's staff were allowed more initiative in making policy recommendations to the board of directors.

This reorganization was quite successful. Throughout the 1950s and 1960s AHLMA, with Guenther Baumgart as President, experienced increasing member satisfaction. Most of the self-regulatory programs in which the industry now engages were developed over this period at AHLMA. In sharp contrast, the members of NEMA's consumer product division, many of whom also belonged to AHLMA, became less enchanted with the former group. This was partly because NEMA's increasing budget was spent almost entirely on industry promotional activities and partly because NEMA—with a broad spectrum of concerns—was predominantly controlled by firms whose major interests lay outside the appliance industry. The solution to this growing discontent was for the consumer products section of NEMA to merge with AHLMA and form new umbrella group, the current Association of Home Appliance Manufacturers. This happened in 1967, when AHAM was formed with its membership open to any producer of major or portable home appliances.[6]

An executive of one of the member companies succinctly sum-marized the source of the trade association's success:

> The move to the professional management concept in the mid 1950s was crucial in developing an effective trade association. The change in itself, however, didn't guarantee an effective association. The association became effective by gradually developing the confidence of its members. This confidence allowed the staff a larger policy role.
>
> Even now if AHAM fails to serve its members it could lose this confidence and its effectiveness. A trade association at best is very fragile. Guenther's ability as a manager has undoubtedly been responsible for AHAM's growth and effectiveness. He knows and understands the members and is a diplomat of the highest order.

In 1971, AHAM was headed by a board of directors, elected by the members, which had to approve all association actions. Various program committees (made up of industry members) and the president and professional staff both reported to this board. More than 500 individuals from member firms served on the program committees, while the staff consisted of a dozen professionals and about 20 support personnel. The professional staff was organized in parallel with the various program committees.

The AHAM staff was a major source of initiative in developing new self-regulatory programs. It had both a significant ability to further such efforts and some reason to do so. The staff had several sources of power: (1) information regarding policies the government and organized consumer groups were considering, (2) the trust of its members built up over the years, (3) control over meetings agendas and other such administrative details, as well as (4) the formal power to recommend policy to the board. In addition, AHAM's staff had an obvious interest in developing self-regulatory activities since these expanded the role, importance and prestige of the organization and its members. The staff also had a different perspective on industry problems from that of some members. They not only associated with industry executives, but also spent a considerable amount of time with officials from government and organized consumer groups. This made them more keenly aware of the threat of government regulation. This position as an intermediary also meant that the staff was the direct recipient of most of the outside criticism of the industry. Reducing this criticism via self-regulation made life more "livable" for them.

Given that AHAM's staff had a substantially different set of preferences from the member companies, why did the members delegate as much power as they did to the professional staff? The answer to this question lies in the very nature of voluntary organizations. As Buchanan and Tullock have pointed out, collective voluntary action implies unanimity.[7] In a voluntary program none have to comply. But, where there are many decisions to be made and many participants, the effort needed in order to reach the necessarily complex bargains may be very expensive. In fact, it is quite possible that the decision-making costs are so sufficiently high as to negate the benefits of voluntary action. When many similar decisions must be made, the costs of reaching agreements can be reduced by creating a permanent bargaining mechanism--e.g., a trade association or a government. Under such circumstances it is not necessary that each member benefit from every decision. It is only necessary that each individual receive a net benefit from all the decisions. A strong trade association staff may be a way of reducing decision making costs. This arrangement may be in every member's interest even if all would have preferred a slightly different outcome.

This view would explain why the NEMA section failed and AHLMA succeeded. In NEMA the staff had little or no power, and NEMA's members came from a wide range of industries. Here, the high costs of reaching agreements prevented any major attempt at self-regulation or other complex activities. However, AHLMA, with a more homogeneous membership and a more powerful staff, could pursue self-regulation because the lower decision making costs were less than the benefits to the individual firms. This analysis likewise explains why a staff's power is fragile. As the members learn more about how the staff will behave, they will have an incentive to further reduce decision-making costs by delegating more authority. However, if at any point the outcomes on average become unfavorable to any member, he can "blow up" the whole process and demand a return to direct bargaining.

As noted, the staff can use some of the gains from consolidation to pursue its own interests by choosing the policies it desires from among the set of alternative acceptable policies. How much influence the staff has depends on the breadth of alternative acceptable programs, which in turn is determined over time by the distribution of views of the members and the aggregate benefits to the members from trade association self-regulatory programs. Indeed a strong staff may be a necessary—but not sufficient—condition for self-regulation, since the members still must perceive that they benefit from the self-regulatory programs. It is to an analysis of these self-regulatory programs that we now turn.

3. SELF REGULATION

By 1971, AHAM was pursuing a wide range of activities including such standard association functions as collecting and distributing industry data and serving as the industry's spokesman before the government. Here we are concerned only with those activities which were self-regulatory in nature—particularly (1) safety standards, (2) product standards, (3) certification and (4) the Major Appliance

Consumer Action Panel. For each of these I would like to discuss the program and the possible motives of the member firms for pursuing each form of self-regulation. The analysis of each program is concluded by an examination of its welfare implications.

Safety Standards

Safety standards specified the minimum level of characteristics or performance for a number of aspects of a product (e.g., wiring), as well as a method for testing to determine if this level was achieved. In the area of safety, AHAM did not develop its own standards, but rather made recommendations to the Underwriters Laboratory (UL) and occasionally to the American Gas Association (AGA). Still, AHAM was one of UL's prime sources of standards information, and the two groups worked closely together. Recommendations to UL came from the engineering committee. According to Herbert Phillips, technical director of AHAM, new recommendations were made "almost continuously."

This description of AHAM's safety standards program raises three questions. First, why do manufacturers want safety standards of any kind? Second, why do manufacturers prefer self-imposed standards to government-imposed standards? Finally, what is the impact of AHAM's safety standards on industry performance?

From the manufacturer's point of view there are several reasons for desiring standards. Standards, if AHAM's arguments are correct, reduce the threat of legal action against manufacturers by reducing the chance a consumer will be injured. Standards may also increase demand, since some consumers, who would not buy an unsafe product, given standards will buy the product. This, of course, assumes that the group of consumers who require safety is larger than the group of consumers who would be unwilling to buy the product at the higher price safety standards require.

Safety standards seem to be especially beneficial to full-line producers, because a consumer may associate an unsafe product with an unsafe brand. Hence, a bad experience with one product might lead them not to buy other products of that brand—even outside of home appliances. Thus, the more products a firm produces, the greater the potential cost in lost reputation of competition through less safe products.

Safety standards, in theory, might also affect the economic barriers to entry. They could increase economies of scale, or raise the capital required for entry by making necessary additional investments in plant and equipment. In this case, in fact, according to industry experts, the change in production technology due to standards is small, and the additional investment required is low. Safety standards can also make entry more difficult for foreign competitors. If a foreign country does not have such standards, then a foreign competitor must either sell a safer and more expensive product in his home country or switch his production facilities back and forth, probably raising his average cost per unit.

These various types of direct benefits to the members stemming from safety standards however, are independent of the agency which sets the safety standards. What then are the benefits to the industry member arising from safety standards developed by the members, when the alternative is not an unregulated environment but government regulation? Clearly, there would be little reason for members to pursue self-regulation if the government would choose regulatory policies identical to those the members choose or if the government's policies would lead to more profitable outcomes than would the self-regulatory process.[8] This is possible, even with similar regulatory outcomes, since government regulation is usually financed from general revenue, while private firms must support their own self-regulatory efforts. (At the same time, the total cost of regulation could well be lower for self-regulation because the industry may have data and expertise that it would be costly for the government to acquire.)

In a world of perfect information and no decision-making costs, self-regulation could not prevent the government from choosing more stringent regulation. But the world is not perfect. Both legislatures, which create government regulatory agencies, and those agencies themselves, have limited resources and limited information. If an agency has jurisdiction over several industries and a limited budget, then to deter the government from becoming involved, self-regulation needs not be perfect from the agency point of view. It has only to elevate the performance of the industry to the point where it does not represent a relatively attractive target to the resource-constrained regulatory agency. A similar argument applies to attracting the attention of the legislature. Of course, if all or most industries pursued self-regulation, then there would be less advantage to any one of them from doing so. To escape outside attention they would have to move closer and closer to the government-desired performance levels. However, since self-regulation is not now universal, this concern is not in fact relevant.

Deterrence of government regulation was explicit as a primary motive for self-regulation of AHAM. To quote Mr. Phillips, the technical director, again:

> In today's society any industry as conspicuous as the major home appliance industry is continually faced with the threat of government regulation. In my opinion, the only way to avoid government regulation is to move faster than the government. The alternative to government regulation is judicious self-regulation.

From a welfare point of view, it is even possible that the deterrence objective could lead AHAM to set standards just as stringent as the government would set. Clearly it would have no incentive to do this if it knew exactly what standards the government would set and what level of standards (presumably less than this) would be necessary to deter government regulation. In fact, AHAM does not know this. If AHAM is sufficiently risk averse, then depending on the costs of government action, it might choose safety standards more stringent than the expected level necessary for deterrence.

In summary, there may well be some direct profit benefits to the industry, or to some members stemming from safety standards. On the other hand, safety standards, above some critical level, could lower industry profits. Self-imposed safety standards are one means of deterring government imposition of still more stringent safety standards. Self-regulation, however, does not necessarily lead to safety standards less stringent than those the government would choose. The question still remains as to whether safety standards improve the welfare of consumers, and it is to this we now turn.

It is clear that in a perfectly competitive economy with constant returns to scale, no externalities, and where customers have perfect knowledge, safety standards would be harmful. In such a world (somewhat similar to the one analyzed by White in chapter 2) each consumer should be allowed to buy as little or as much safety as he wanted with his product. Forcing anyone to buy more safety than he wants by limiting product variety will lead to a decline in his welfare.

However, as AHAM's staff points out, consumers have little knowledge about safety and have only a limited ability to absorb this knowledge. Providing information to the consumer at the point of sale is also expensive—not only in terms of salesmen's time but also in terms of the cost of training the salesmen.[9] The implication of this viewpoint is that in a market without standards, a safer product with a higher price would be at a competitive disadvantage, and might not be offered. Without standards, any individual firm contemplating the introduction of a safer product would have to bear all the initial costs of providing general safety information to consumers and of salesman training. Such a firm would also be unable to prevent other firms from taking advantage of this expenditure, should the safer product prove successful. Thus the potential profit from introducing a safer product in a market without standards could be limited. Therefore, the association argues, standards are needed if safer products are available at all.

If one believes this argument, the social choice is between lower costs and lower safety, without safety standards, and higher costs and higher safety with them. Given imperfect consumer choice, it is not hard to opt for the latter alternative.

Product Standards

In contrast to safety standards, product standards specify certain performance dimensions of the appliance related to its main purpose (such as how much dirt a washer removes from clothes) and a method for testing that parameter. Product standards, however, unlike safety standards, have not contained a minimum acceptable level of performance. Instead they have been defined as a continuum. Such standards both allow manufacturers to compare their products with those of their competitors and provide consumers standardized data to help them compare brands.

Product standards for each appliance were developed by AHAM, but were submitted to the American National Standards Institute (ANSI) for certification as national standards. It was generally agreed by AHAM's management that ANSI's status helped create the impression (and the reality) of standards that covered aspects of performance relevant to consumer satisfaction. Six to twelve product standards might apply to a given product. Standards of all types were worked out by the engineering committee.

The manufacturer's motivation for developing and using product standards derives in part from the problem he faces in evaluating the performance of his appliance. An appliance has a surprisingly vast number of performance characteristics. For example, a washing machine could be measured in terms of how clean it gets clothes, how much water, soap and electricity it uses, how reliable it is, etc. In addition, the color and type of fabric as well as soil nature and content, might well differentially affect the cleanliness obtained by different machines. The washer also affects the life of the clothes in a manner which in turn depends partly on the fabric of the clothes. The number of possible performance measures is large indeed.

A manager needs to be able to monitor the performance of his own products both for intenal control purposes and because he can expect that changes in performance will affect his sales and profits over time. Yet such testing of his own products would be very expensive if many dimensions were included. Further, the manager can effectively use only a limited amount of information. This suggests that each firm, on its own, would be led to adopt a testing program with respect to a simplified, standardized set of performance measures rather like the current product standards.

But why has AHAM set common standards? In this oligopolistic industry firms compete not just via price, advertising, R&D, etc., but also over product performance. If no common industry definitions existed for performance parameters, it would be harder to compare one's own performance with competitors'. Defining and noticing "competitive moves," not to mention implicit coordination of behavior, all would become very difficult. However, if all firms use the same standards, the risks associated with changing a product can more accurately be assessed. A firm contemplating a change at least knows how the other firms will view his actions, so the relationship between industry behavior and such standards operates in both directions. Firms will seek standards that reflect the dimensions of competitive interest to them. At the same time, it is not unlikely that what is measurable—and measured—will become an object of interfirm rivalry and/or coordination.

An alternative, though compatible, explanation of product standards is that voluntary product standards, like safety standards, lessen the threat of government regulation. In this context AHAM, with its contacts outside the industry, can be seen as an effective device for generating standards that respond to the concerns of organized consumer groups and government. As with safety standards, these product standards are designed to prevent the government from adopting more stringent standards by elevating industry performance to an acceptable level.

The American automobile industry, in contrast, is an example of a case where the implicit standards the industry focused on during the last several decades did not serve this latter function of "self-regulation," even though they did provide a basis for interfirm coordination. These implicit standards appear to have been defined in terms of horsepower, size, newness of style, etc. Safety, pollution, and. to an extent, gas mileage were neither officially measured nor of crucial importance in the competitive moves of the companies. Whether or not consumers evaluated the product along the same dimensions as the industry, and whose views played a causal role in this relationship, is far from clear. However, it is clear that organized consumer groups and eventually the government came to evaluate the performance of the automobile in terms of different parameters. The result has been an ever-expanding program of government testing and regulation of exactly the sort that ASAM is no doubt trying to help avoid.

The welfare implication of standards is a special case of the problem of optimal product variety. At the moment, there seems no general theoretical framework to handle these matters so that any given case can be evaluated only on the basis of a specific and detailed normative judgement. Standards focus managerial attention on some areas of performance and lead managers to ignore others. Some aspects of performance will probably improve, while others may remain constant or even decline. Some consumers will prefer the set of products produced by any given standards to all other sets generated by alternative standards, but others will not.

If standards of some kind will exist in any case, does the fact that they are explicitly chosen by AHAM have adverse implications? In my view it is difficult to argue that explicitly set standards have influenced industry performance in a systematically adverse way that standards set less formally would not. If, in fact, performance standards are set to avoid government regulation by raising industry performance to some minimum acceptable level, and they are successful, then they would shift industry performance toward that which the government desires. Whether performance would be better still if government regulation occurred seems too problematic a question to try to resolve here, especially since such a process could generate many different final outcomes.

Product Certification

The third AHAM program, product certification, actually began with NEMA and arose from the competitive situation in the room air conditioner (RAC) market. Guenther Baumgart put it this way:

> In the early 1950s the RAC was advertised in terms of horsepower, BTUs/hr., watts, room-size cooled, tons, and other characteristics. It was impossible for consumers to compare most products. Also where products were comparable, manufacturers were forced into a position where claims were of doubtful validity and confusingly stated.

One industry executive explained the reason for this phenomenon as follows, "If one manufacturer lied, what could the rest of us do? For example, if one manufacturer sold a 5000 BTU/hr. RAC for $140 and his competitors found out that it was only a 4000 BTU/hr. RAC, they had little recourse other than to lower the capacity of their product." In describing the situation, Baumgart stated, "Consumers were dissatisfied; the FTC was investigating, and the whole industry was being hurt because a lot of people just wouldn't buy any RAC."

Through the trade association, NEMA in this case, it was agreed after lengthy discussion that the crucial measures of performance were watts, amps, and BTUs. A program was set up whereby an independent laboratory tested a sample of all the room air conditioners produced by firms in the program to see if the claims made were correct. The association published a quarterly directory listing the results of the tests. A sticker was put on each machine produced by a participating member, certifying that the statements made as to these three characteristics were correct as stated in the directory.

Participation in the program was voluntary but universal. Part of the reason for this was the pressure from retailers. AHAM's management believed that by 1971 no room air conditioners—including imports—were being sold in the United States that were not AHAM certified.

Other certification programs were the cubic space of refrigerators and pints of water per day removed by dehumidifiers. In all cases the costs of certification were covered by selling the certification stickers to the manufacturers. Seals for air conditioners cost 5¢, for dehumidifiers 4¢, refrigerators 1.6¢, and so on. The total cost of the certification program was $400,000 per year. In comparison the budget for the rest of AHAM's functions raised by dues was a little less than $1.2 million.

The manufacturers' incentive for certification of room air conditioners is clear. The confusing advertising that took place before the program began made systematic comparisons among units by the consumer quite difficult. Further, competitive pressures had caused the reliability of the information the consumer received continually to deteriorate, Hence, consumers who had little or no experience with such units, since the RAC was a relatively new product, were becoming increasingly reluctant to buy. This at least was the manufacturers' expressed view.

By limiting the aspects of performance to BTUs, watts, and amps, consumer choice was simplified, since products could be directly compared. By guaranteeing the accuracy of the information, the risk facing the consumer was reduced and the government was placated. Hence, the manufacturers felt that certification could increase the growth of the market and minimize the threat of government intervention.

The welfare implications of certification are fairly straightforward. Certification improves the information available to consumers—both in terms of allowing comparability and in guaranteeing its accuracy. It is hard to imagine that this information was not worth 5¢ to each potential buyer. Even if it was not for some, the welfare loss is surely small. Thus it seems reasonable to conclude that the direct effect of certification was to improve the performance of the industry. It made comparisons among units easier, discouraged artificial product differentiation and enhanced competition.

Whether the certification program indirectly produced some adverse effects on industry performance is difficult to say. One might argue that certification of some aspects of performance could lead to a reduction in quality along other dimensions—for example product reliability. But, in fact, the reliability of RACs improved over the 1960s.[10] One might also argue that certifying air conditioners facilitated the creation of focal points which would aid manufacturers, who in fact began to submit models at 1000 BTU intervals. Yet, the average price of RACs fell from $251 to $205 between 1961 and 1970 while the average BTU rating increased.[11] The decline in price of 18% was greater than the average price decline of 10% for the appliance industry as a whole. Of course, in both cases it is impossible to tell what would have happened to prices or durability without the certification program. But the case for adverse indirect effects is certainly weak on empirical grounds without the certification program.

MACAP

In the area of consumer affairs one of AHAM's most visible efforts was participation, along with Gas Appliance Manufacturers Association and the American Retail Federation, in establishing and funding the Major Appliance Consumer Action Panel (MACAP) in 1970. MACAP, however, was an autonomous panel whose members came from universities, consumer agencies and civic groups and had no industry ties. With the exception of the chairman, Dr. Virginia Cutler, panel members were compensated only for the expenses they incurred.

MACAP was chartered to resolve consumer complaints that had not been solved by the retailer or the manufacturer. The participating manufacturers agreed generally to abide by the decision of MACAP as to the way complaints should be resolved, but they were not legally or otherwise bound to do so. MACAP was also empowered to undertake broad studies of industry practices and make public recommendations where they felt changes were necessary.

In its first year and a half, the organization reviewed more than 3800 complaints. Of these, 3164 were resolved, with the consumer satisfied with the resolution in 3022 cases and unsatisfied in 142. In only 267 cases did MACAP actually consider the complaint, however. The other 2837 cases were resolved directly by the manufacturer when notified—at the top management level—that MACAP had received a complaint. Where MACAP considered the complaint itself, it found the complaint justified in over 60% of the cases and recommended that the company involved take specific action. According to AHAM's president, compliance with the recommendations was virtually 100%.[12] It was generally felt by AHAM's staff that MACAP's role in the industry would increase over time as consumers became increasingly aware of its existence.

At its second meeting MACAP decided to pursue its other functions as well and undertake studies of warranties, point of purchase information and service availability, cost and quality. The results of the warranty study and MACAP's recommendations were presented to the manufacturers and the Interstate and Foreign Commerce Committee of the House of Representatives. MACAP recommended legislation as to the minimum standards for warranties, clear disclosure of warranty terms and remedies for non-performance of contractual agreements. The other studies were in progress.

A major reason for AHAM's participation in MACAP was, according to AHAM's staff, a response to public critics like Bess Meyerson who felt that consumers had no one to turn to if they were dissatisfied with an appliance and the manufacturer refused to take action in response to their complaint. MACAP provided an appeal procedure for these consumers once other alternatives were exhausted. Hence, MACAP, like all of AHAM's other self-regulatory activities, was in some sense a PR move which also produced real results and helped to reduce potential public pressure for government regulation.

Several other benefits, however, may have accrued from the formation of MACAP. Albert Hirschman has argued that management discovers the decline in product quality or service only when customers either stop purchasing the product (exit) or when they complain (voice).[13] Further, he suggests that voice is often more effective—especially for communicating the nature of one's dissatisfaction. All the major appliance manufacturers had formal procedure for handling complaints. Top management, however, was seldom involved in, or aware of them unless these complaints pointed to a major mistake in product design or production process. MACAP—because it sent all complaints to the corporate president—provided information to top management both about their products and about the performance of their own complaint processing procedure. Thus, it served as an outside adjunct to internal corporate control structures. Further, since MACAP offered another outlet for voice it might deter exit. In other words, by producing a satisfactory resolution from the consumer's viewpoint—as well as making him feel he had some channel for complaint—MACAP might prevent consumers not buying the appliance again or not buying that brand of appliance again. This is an especially valuable service to multiple-product firms which face a potential loss in sales of other products.

From a welfare viewpoint, MACAP seems noncontroversially desirable. It offered the consumer another channel for seeking a favorable ruling on a complaint. The total cost was extremely low (less than $100,000 per year) and insignificant on a per appliance basis. Hence, some consumers (i.e., those who received favorable rulings) were made better off while, given the extremely low cost, none were made significantly worse off.

CONCLUSIONS

Drawing general conclusions from one case study is obviously unwarranted. However, especially in a relatively unexplored area, such a study can usefully be used to suggest hypotheses designed to guide and stimulate further research. Of particular interest are the factors that lead an industry to adopt self-regulation, the role the trade association professional staff plays in the formulation of self-regulation policies, and the usefulness of self-regulatory policy as an alternative to government regulation.

In each of the four examples in this industry there were two potential benefits to industry members stemming from self-regulation, (1) the possibility of increasing industry sales and/or margins and (2) the reduction in the likelihood of government regulation. Both of these presumably would help firm profitability. It was argued that government regulation could be avoided by the adoption of less stringent, less costly self-regulatory policy because the government has only limited decision-making and administrative resources. Hence, it is only necessary to improve industry performance sufficiently so that the industry no longer represents an attractive target for regulation. These observations suggest our first interindustry hypothesis. *Self-regulation is more likely to occur where it can help to improve industry sales and margins and/or where profit-reducing government regulation is believed to be probable if self-regulation is not undertaken.*

As was also noted, voluntary agreements require unanimity, which raises the cost of reaching self-regulatory decisions. If this is the case, decision making power may be given to an independent staff in order to reduce decision making costs. Indeed it may be that the whole enterprise is profitable for members only on this basis. In these circumstances if such a strong group exists already, particularly in a trade association, self-regulation becomes that much more likely. These arguments lead to a second hypothesis. *The existence and power of an independent organization which can carry out the self-regulation programs is positively related to the likelihood that such a program will develop.*

Further, the importance of such a staff increases as the number of participating firms and the number of policies under consideration increase, since these two factors affect decision making costs.

Suppose the trade association is uncertain both about what action is necessary to forestall government regulation and is also uncertain as to the regulatory actions the government will take. Then, if the firms are risk averse, the self-regulatory policies chosen will tend to be more strict, especially if the cost of government regulation is expected to be quite high. On the other hand, if the trade association believes that the government would take regulatory actions that would be impossible to implement, then the association may choose to let the government act and (in its view) fail. Hence, we have a third hypothesis. *Increased uncertainty as to the potential severity of government regulation, providing the government's alternatives are believed to be plausible, is positively related to the stringency of the self-regulation firms adapt.*

As was also noted, the degree of self-regulation necessary to forestall government regulation is partly determined by the resources available to the government and partly determined by the other opportunities available to the government for regulation. This view indicates a fourth hypothesis. *The stringency of self-regulation an industry adopts is positively related to the resources available to the government for regulation, public attention devoted to the industry and the extent of self-regulatory activities in other, similarly situated industries*

The preceding analysis also allows us to begin to answer the critical normative question—when can we view self-regulation as an acceptable alternative to government regulation? Where trade associations have the information and the expertise necessary to formulate regulatory policy, and the government does not, the cost to the trade association of formulating policy may be much lower. Indeed, if the industry is the only source of the data and expertise, it may be that the industry will have significant control regardless of where formal authority lies. However, the government can expect to gain by delegating regulatory responsibility only when it is able to measure and evaluate the performance of the industry. Otherwise the threat of government action if performance becomes unsatisfactory is not creditable. This suggests a fifth hypothesis. *The benefits of self-regulation to society will be positively related to the policy making efficiency of private groups relative to the government and positively related to the government's ability to measure and evaluate industry performance.*

There may be ancillary benefit to self-regulation. Much of government regulation is focused on inputs, not results, largely because compliance with respect to inputs is easier to monitor. It may not be true, however, that the specified inputs are necessarily the most efficient means for obtaining the desired results or that in fact they will even lead to those results. Forcing the *threat* of such regulation, based on an overall evaluation of industry performance may, therefore, have desirable results. It may allow more flexible techniques to be employed than the government could utilize. Further, self-regulation removes the excuse from industry that it followed the rules and that it is not the industry's fault that the rules didn't lead to the desired performance.

These last mentioned benefits, as well as the rest of the argument advanced in this paper, suggest the potential desirability of self-regulation in certain situations. Clearly the balance between good and bad effects will not always be positive, nor will industries always develop such programs on their own (see chapter 5 of this volume). In all, however, such efforts afford an interesting option for public policy. I should imagine that there will turn out to be a reasonable number of cases in which it is worth considering how to foster and shape self regulation where market performance is unsatisfactory and public intervention is being considered.

Notes to Chapter Three

1. *Merchandising Week* (February 11, 1971), pp. 22-23.

2. Hunt, *Competition in the Major Home Appliance Industry, 1960-1970*, p. 1

3. Ibid., pp. 48-50. This information was drawn from corporate annual reports as well as interviews and data provided by major producers.

4. Engineering estimates placed minimum efficient scale relative to market size as 25% for dishwashers, 18% for clothes washers, 11% for ranges, 10% for refrigerators, 5% for disposal and 2% for air conditioners. But there were also significant economies of scale in sales and distribution from selling and shipping all the major appliances. These economies stemmed from the fact that most retailers and construction firms bought several, if not all, types of appliances. Hence, one salesman could more efficiently use his time by selling the full line of appliances, and the order where several types of appliances were sold was more likely to be a full carload, reducing shipping costs. With regard to brand loyalty, the *Look National Appliance Survey, 1963* found that on average 70.1% of all consumers owning an appliance believed that if they were to replace their existing appliance they would replace it with the same brand they then owned.

5. See Hunt, "Competition in the Appliance Industry," chapters 2 and 9 for a complete explanation.

6. This paper focuses on AHAM's activities in the major home appliance industry. Portable appliances were organized as a separate division and received much less attention than major home appliances.

7. James M. Buchanan and Gordon Tulloch, *The Calculus of Consent* (Ann Arbor: University of Michigan Press, 1962), p. 90.

8. If the cost of formulating and administering regulatory policies is passed on to the members when the government provides regulation, then the members would prefer self-regulation to identical government regulation if the members' cost of formulating and administering regulatory policies was lower

than the government's. Though it is quite possible that the members do face lower policy making costs because they possess much of the relevant data and technical expertise which the government would have to acquire, it is not generally true that the government's regulatory costs are passed on to members. To the contrary, regulatory agencies are usually financed from general tax revenue.

9. A large manufacturer might sell to 30,000 retailers. Assuming six salesmen per store the company would have to train 180,000 salesmen. If personal contact is required for training, the cost could easily be several million dollars.

10. This conclusion is based upon confidential data on frequency of repair experience supplied to the author by major manufacturers.

11. *Merchandising Week,* February 22, 1971.

12. Data supplied to the author by AHAM.

13. Hirschman, *Exit, Voice, and Loyalty,* p. 4.

Chapter Four

Regulation and Self-Regulation in the Farm Machinery Industry

Robert T. Kudrle

The farm machinery industry provides an apt case-study of the causes and effects of public regulation and self-regulation of product characteristics. Both forms have long histories in this sector. Furthermore, the industry's market structure and product mix have changed so sharply over that period that we have some chance of associating differences in them with differences in regulatory practice and market performance. We will survey the following forms of product regulation:

1. Just after World War I, the varying quality of tractors marketed led to serious consideration of federal legislation. What emerged from the furor was a requirement by the state of Nebraska that all machines sold therein be certified for basic product characteristics at the state's testing station. Because of Nebraska's pivotal place in the farm equipment market and the wide circulation of the test results, this became in effect a national tractor test.

2. Self-regulation through trade associations and other intraindustry organizations has dealt with several dimensions of the product. Manufacturers have sought to standardize the types and dimensions of individual farm machines. In recent decades there have been serious attempts to make the implements and tractors of different manufacturers compatible (i.e., usable) with one another and to promote the use of parts that are interchangeable between the machines of different manufacturers.

3. The concern with product safety kindled during the 1960s has stirred both the industry and the federal government to ponder a new line of public or self-regulation.

These regulatory efforts have taken place in a diverse industry whose market structure has changed greatly over the last half-century. Farm machinery is not a homogeneous industry but rather a subsector of the economy, encompassing an easily identifiable group of sellers and buyers of complementary capital goods. In the nineteenth century farm implements were manufactured by hundreds of companies, often local or regional and usually specialized in particular machines or implements. Around the turn of the century the industry's structure began to change as some large firms broadened their lines of equipment. This practice gained enormous momentum in the interwar period. By 1972, seven "full-line" firms—offering a tractor, a combine, and an entire range of implements—accounted for about 65% of all farm machinery sold in the United States. Much of the remaining output is highly specialized and does not compete directly with the products of the top seven firms.

Michael Hunt points out that the theory surrounding self-regulation through trade associations is exiguous and develops a number of hypotheses that appear to hold for the major home appliance industry.[1] His most general hypothesis is two-fold: an industry will undertake self-regulation (1) when its profitability is likely to be improved or (2) when stringent regulation is threatened from outside but can potentially be averted by self-regulation entailing a smaller expected loss of profit. The farm machinery industry faced outside pressure just after World War I and again in the 1960s, but at other times self-regulation was internally generated, and thus this industry is presumed subject to the former hypothesis. We can expand the hypothesis that self-regulation may be undertaken to raise joint profits by using the theory of markets and industrial organization to identify the channels of influence.[2] We might observe voluntary adherence to regulation where (1) costs are reduced, (2) total demand for the industry's product is increased with participating firms sharing in that increase, (3) barriers to entry into the industry are raised or (4) sellers can enhance the level of collusion and policy coordination that they achieve. Because self-regulating schemes may operate on more than one of these variables, and not necessarily with a favorable impact on each, what matters is the net effect of any self-regulatory policy. The farm machinery industry offers several examples of self-regulation as a complex contributor to joint profits. Recognition of the multiple links between regulation and profit is also useful in helping to predict situations in which an industry may actually promote government regulation.

1. PRODUCT CERTIFICATION:
THE NEBRASKA TRACTOR TESTS

Prior to World War I, farm tractors were of only minor importance in North American agriculture. Annual United States production, only a few thousand in 1910, rose to 15,000 in 1914, 63,000 in 1917 and 130,000 in 1918, while the number of tractor manufacturers went from 15 to 142. During the postwar boom, a seemingly endless variety of machines was sold to poorly informed farmers by imaginative salesmen, and there are many stories of customers buying several successive machines before finding one that even approached its advertised performance. As early as 1915 discussion took place between some leading manufacturers and officials from the United States Department of Agriculture concerning a possible national testing station for tractors. Plans were drawn up, but Congress failed to appropriate the money. Complaints from the farm community continued to grow, and in 1919, the Nebraska legislature passed a law which made a special permit necessary for a tractor to be sold in that state.[3] The permits were to be issued only after the machine had been tested at an official state testing station for performance characteristics, including various measures of horsepower and fuel consumption. Despite the large number of local and regional manufacturers, the bulk of tractors even then were produced by only a few firms, and the disadvantage of exclusion from one of the largest tractor markets to any firm having pretensions to national importance led all to submit their equipment for testing. The performance results became universally recognized, and farmers everywhere came to resist machines not tested. The tests began in 1920, and of the 68 tractors tested "manufacturers of six tractors increased their engine speed, manufacturers of eleven lowered their horsepower rating, eleven made changes in their equipment, and three withdrew from the tests."[4] Within a few years, a large number of departures from the industry were recorded many of which were linked directly to inadequate performance rated by the official criteria.

There is no indication in contemporary accounts that the major tractor makers resisted the implementation of the Nebraska tractor tests in any way nor that they earlier resisted the proposed federal ratings. Several explanations may be offered for their quiescence, although the historical record is not complete enough to allow relative weight to be given to them.

First, the International Harvester Company, having agreed in 1918 to limit its activities in any one town to a single dealer, was being reinvestigated by the Federal Trade Commission as part of a general industry investigation (the 1920 report recommended that Harvester be dismembered into competing units). Harvester, which accounted for about one-third of all tractors produced in the United States between 1911 and 1917, may well have felt that opposition to what was clearly a popular outcry from the farm community would not sit well with the investigating agency.

Second, Nebraska's careful testing and widely publicized results could provide a rationale for the refusal of the large firms to engage in the endless string of tractor demonstrations that they were constantly being pressured to hold by various state and county agencies. The industry had attempted to limit these costly and, in the eyes of the makers, often meaningless demonstrations but with little success. Either local makers or a major firm trying to make a special regional impact would relent, and other firms would follow.[5]

Two more reasons for the support of compulsory government regulation by the major firms could be predicted from structural characteristics of the industry. Third, the new standards undoubtedly contributed to the mutual understanding of the major firms by highlighting certain characteristics of their differentiated products. It became much easier to identify the relevant performance characteristics of one's own machine and compare them to those of other manufacturers. This information would otherwise have cost duplicative efforts by the firms or collaborative efforts by a trade association. Either one of these developments might have followed had the Nebraska tests not been instituted when they were. The outcome of the tests offered the potential for better cooperative pricing as well. Price per horsepower corrected for special equipment seems to have been very close among the major makes since World War II. Although information is not available, horsepower measurement undoubtedly facilitated such coordination in the earlier period as well. In 1967, one firm suggested that prices were usually held within two and one-half percent of competitors' machines, and there was industry agreement that no firm wanted its price to be more than five percent "either way" from one of its principal competitors.[6]

Fourth, makes that were better engineered and serviced probably suffered from the shortcomings of the many unimpressive small competitors. Not only were the less adequate machines taking up a share of the market (no estimate is available), but also farmers' difficulties with the products may well have been retarding the expansion of aggregate demand.

There can be little doubt that the Nebraska tests contributed significantly to improved market performance. Their role in allowing price coordination was an unavoidable concomitant of easing the evaluation of important differences among machines; at least they forced the manufacturers to relate their price policies to significant characteristics of machine design. In the period since their inception, the test procedures have been adopted with minor modifications and extensions by official and semiofficial agencies in nearly every tractor-using country in the world. The Nebraska tests themselves have continued with only slight modification over the years; noise emission testing was added in 1970.

2. SELF-REGULATION THROUGH TRADE ASSOCIATIONS

Before the end of World War II, farm machinery was one of the most investigated industries in the American economy. Nearly all of the investigatory activities revolved around possible violations of the antitrust laws, however. None of the reports, including the 1200 page Federal Trade Commission study of 1938, devoted any substantial attention to product characteristics.[7] Two early studies of the industry, the United States Commissioner of Corporations' *Farm*

Machinery Trade Associations of 1915 and the Federal Trade Commission's *Causes of the High Prices of Farm Implements* of 1920, outline classic trade-association activity patterns: among the separate groups of implement makers before 1911, and after that by various sections of the umbrella National Implement and Vehicle Association (later the National Association of Farm Equipment Manufacturers, and in 1933 the Farm Equipment Institute).[8] Before 1920, common cost-accounting practices and cost projection schemes and direct price comparisons were used to coordinate prices among the firms. The frequent exchange of price lists was the subject of FTC complaint as late as 1938.

Cooperative Suppression of Variety

Of interest here, however, is the concomitant practice of standardizing the implements sold by participating firms. Long before World War I various branches of the implement trade held periodic meetings to decide on the materials and dimensions of the industry's offerings and in particular to limit variety. Most successful was the group selling plows and tillage equipment, which reduced the number of types of implements offered from 2156 to 255 (nearly 90%) between 1914 and 1926. Not only were costs supposed to have been greatly reduced but "it is claimed that the quality of implements is improved for two reasons: the manufacturing department can give more attention to the details of manufacture of a few implements, and experimental effort for improvement concentrated on a few implements can be made more effective than the same amount of experimental effort devoted to many implements."[9]

The government agencies investigating this practice were not impressed by the beneficent claims of the firms and essentially ignored the possible impact of standardization on cost saving, quality control and innovation in order to concentrate on the extent to which such activity contributed to "the elimination of price competition." Although price competition was probably not eliminated (there is no way of knowing how much cheating took place), the scheme's impact on price coordination may have been considerable. In the decade after World War I, most farm implements were being produced by thirty or forty different manufacturers, although many may have operated in only a few states. For most implements, eight-firm concentration ratios were below 50%, and price competition could have been intense in the absence of collusion. In addition, products proliferated easily in response to slightly varying regional preferences, perhaps often accidental in origin, because of the low marginal cost of adding another implement to the product line. Joint control of such product proliferation would be almost impossible in the absence of agreement; as was not the case with prices, joint control by agreement on product lines would not be undermined by cheating.

It must be stressed that, despite low concentration, even in this early period substantial barriers to entry into the industry resulted from brand preferences and the exclusive control of the best dealers by established firms.

The FTC's judgment about the negative impact of trade association activity on the farmer's welfare was probably correct. One must certainly question the plausibility of the industry's claim that quality control and technical progress were enhanced by suppressing variety. The simplicity of design of most of the equipment involved renders the first claim implausible, and there is no reason to believe that suppressing variety either promoted or hindered technical progress. The design of the equipment involved had largely stabilized, and standardization simply retained some designs while dropping others. The industry's claim of cost saving, however, deserves more serious attention, and the total impact of standardization cannot be properly evaluated without more evidence than is available.

On the one hand are the loss of variety itself and the increased collusion among sellers that it makes possible; on the other is the realization of scale economies. It is not inconceivable that the latter consideration could outweigh the others and render the self-regulated situation superior in performance. Many of the apparent differences among the diverse sizes and shapes of implements may functionally have been largely irrelevant, and the actions of the companies may have eliminated spurious differences which, in turn, were concealing from buyers the real differences among machines. In this situation buyers might theoretically support the restriction of variety; but even with buyers' demands fully respected, the apparent trade-off between variety and unit cost must still be considered.[10] One wishes that official investigations had paid more attention to the exact nature of variety suppression and to the magnitude of cost savings achieved through standardization, as well as to any relevant evidence on the extent to which price-cost margins were increased. None of these issues received any real attention, because most of the documentation focused on the mechanics of trade-association activity.

Power Farming and the Growth of Full-Line Firm

The kind of standardization outlined above became increasingly unimportant over time. The machines that were standardized became a smaller part of total industry sales, and such standardization was never attempted in power machinery. These facts are in turn related to two structural interwar developments which permanently changed the character of the industry: the revolution in "power farming" and the growth of the "full-line" firm. The value of tractor sales relative to that of other equipment before 1919 is not known, but the figure of 12% for that year had risen to 24% by 1937; it climbed to 38% by 1967. The rise of the tractor, however, was only the most important change in the product mix of the industry. Combines, whether horse or tractor-drawn, comprised less than 5% of industry sales in the late thirties but became self-propelled during the war and by 1967 accounted for nearly 15% of total sales. The new machines not only changed the product mix of the industry and rendered many important pieces of equipment obsolete but also displaced the sometimes standardized complementary implements. The thresher was displaced by the combine, and plows and tillage machinery for use with tractors required totally different design and stronger construction than those used previously. Indeed, almost none of the implements and machinery carefully standardized up to the mid-twenties survived the following twenty years.

The other major development was the growth of the "full-line" firm. After its inception from the merger of five harvesting machinery companies in 1902, International Harvester discovered that it could greatly improve year-round utilization of its factories by producing different kinds of equipment and that, in addition, considerable economies of scale in distribution resulted from selling a wide variety of machines through a single network of dealers. Deere and Company, founded and operated for decades exclusively in tillage machinery, followed Harvester's lead in 1910 and broadened its offerings. Case, the country's largest threshing machinery company, began expanding into other equipment in 1925. Massey-Harris, a Canadian harvesting machinery company, moved into tillage equipment in 1928, the same year Allis-Chalmers entered the industry with an instantly successful small tractor for which implements were soon offered. Minneapolis Moline and Oliver were 1929 amalgamations of several specialized machinery firms.

As late as 1938, none of these firms offered all 28 major types of implement, but powerful forces were drawing them all in this direction. The increased profitability that the broadened range of offerings brought to International Harvester not only provided an example for the other large firms but also gave Harvester a substantial advantage through the practice known as "full-line forcing" through exclusive dealers. The practice of exclusive dealing has a history in the industry going back well into the nineteenth century. It meant simply that a dealer could not sell two competing brands of plows, although he could sell the equipment of many different firms. International Harvester, particularly after the consent decree of 1918 limited it to one dealer per town, insisted that its dealers, usually the largest and the best, sell only its equipment. The other major firms were thus given powerful impetus to build their own networks of strong dealers handling as much of their lines as they offered. As they did so, they found themselves very successful in competing against the rather quiescent and conservatively managed Harvester. The giant held nearly 50% of the total equipment market right after World War I, and the next largest firm (Deere) probably less than 10%. By 1929, Harvester's share was less than 30%, Deere's 12%, and the other firms' a few percent apiece. Subsequently, overall concentration increased substantially as the result of further acquisitions and the great success of new tractor designs, particularly those of Allis-Chalmers. The seven major firms sold only 55% of all machinery in 1929 but 73% in 1937. Except for an innovative episode to be explored below, "closure of entry" into the farm machinery industry had been accomplished;

new equipment could certainly be brought to the market, but unless revolutionary or highly specialized, it was usually blocked from sales through the most trusted established channels.

The 1938 FTC report observed the inactivity of the power machinery department of the Farm Equipment Institute (FEI) in the standardization area but suggested that this resulted from the newness of the equipment involved. The report notes with alarm suggestions from some industry sources in the mid-1930s that certain tractor components be standardized and hints that this foreshadowed an attempt at collusive suppression of variety similar to that previously seen in tillage equipment and threshing machines.[11]

Any direct impact of the FTC report on industry behavior is not known. In any event, however, the changed structure of the industry rendered increasingly irrelevant such very detailed trade-association product regulation as had previously been attempted, despite the fact that the technical design of tractors and many other pieces of equipment stabilized after World War II. By the late thirties the full-line firms controlled over 70% of all equipment sold, and barriers to entry into the industry were enormous. In the early 1950s Bain determined that a combination of scale economies and capital requirements in the manufacture of tractors and combines and the formidable product differentiation advantages of established reputation and full-line dealers placed the industry in the highest category of barriers to entry.[12] The remaining important competitors could presumably follow price and product leadership exercised by International Harvester and Deere whenever it was profitable to do so, without the necessity of precise product specification. Further, the small number of firms, together with the high costs of proliferating models of complex machinery, would tend to keep variety in check.

Solely on the basis of the structural material just presented, one would predict higher profits for the industry after World War II than in the prewar period; in fact, the opposite is true. Although the data available do not permit a precise comparison, it appears that even counting the depression years, the major firms had a higher rate of return in the earlier period. Many explanations have been offered for the low postwar profitability of the industry, which saw the profit leader, Deere, earning only 11% on equity from 1946 to 1965 and the much smaller Case, similarly specialized in North American agricultural machinery sales, earning only 3.3%. The main explanation appears to lie in the false expectations the industry entertained about sales in the 1950s. Although all of the firms realized that the postwar boom could not last, they failed to foresee how much unit demand would drop after the early 1950s. Excess capacity, low profitability, low plant expenditure and productivity increase, and thus further low profits became the industry pattern.[13] It is also possible that doubts about the long-run future of North America as a production base for equipment as technically stable and easily imitated as most farm machinery may have retarded modernization while the threat of foreign competition may have somewhat limited price advances.

Interfunctional Compatibility

Despite structural changes, the industry continued to engage in some product self-regulation. Interestingly, the cooperative suppression of variety examined above does not appear as part of the official history of trade association activity. In the eyes of the Farm and Industrial Equipment Institute ("industrial" was added in 1964, principally in recognition of the role of slightly modified agricultural tractors in construction work), the first industry standard was that issued by its engineering committee in 1927, dealing with various parameters of the power take-off connection between tractors and implements.[14] The standard was promulgated directly by the trade association and subsequently ratified by the two related engineering societies, the Society of Automotive Engineers and the American Society of Agricultural Engineers. The SAE, which early in its history absorbed the tractor engineering society, considers all standards related to tractors. The ASAE, founded in 1907 as a broadly interested professional home for land-grant college agricultural engineers and later those in industry as well, deals with all standardization matters; it usually adopts the SAE tractor standards without modification. After World War II, the relations of industry committees to the professional groups change somewhat, perhaps in part because of the FTC attack on trade-association product activity. Now the industry issues no official standards but simply submits them to the societies for consideration.

The first major self-regulatory activity after the war came as a direct response to the most important innovation in the otherwise evolutionary development of the tractor: the "Ferguson system" of integrally mounted, hydraulically controlled implements. It extracted more effective implement capacity from a smaller tractor while at the same time greatly reducing the most dangerous element in previous tractor operation: the tendency of a tractor to tip over backward when a trailed implement met with unusual resistance. The innovation therefore contributed significantly to both economy and safety of operation.

Perhaps partly because it came wholly from outside the established industry—it was a British design, produced in the United States by Ford, with only a limited line of complementary equipment—the established firms at first paid little attention to the newcomer. By 1943, however, Ford-Ferguson had captured about a quarter of all tractor sales. Nevertheless, wartime government supervision of industry production restrained the output and model changes of the major firms, and they continued to believe that in the postwar period larger and more expensive tractors would regain strength. They hoped to assure this outcome by modernizing their offerings. Just as hydraulically controlled mounted implements were the basis of the Ferguson system, the old line firms believed that hydraulic control of trailed implements held the key to their success. A special committee of chief engineers of the major companies was formed with authority to make binding decisions on common dimensions of the hydraulic cylinders and implements, so that the implements of one firm could be used with the tractor of any other. Although one manufacturer had already marketed machinery with a design unacceptable to the others, a common standard was worked out in 1949, quickly ratified by the SAE and the ASAE and adhered to by all of the makers.[15] Ford and the now independent Ferguson, of course, did not take part.[16] One indication that the engineering societies at this time were completely dominated by the old firms is that the principle of the new system was never even discussed at any professional meeting until 1954, the first year an old-line firm (Oliver) imitated the revolutionary hitch; the system was nevertheless completely accepted by the industry within a few years.

What needs to be explained is why the firms were willing and even anxious to relinquish their ability to tie their lines of implements to their tractor designs (and to some extent vice versa). Loss of the tying practice not only weakened each manufacturer's differentiation from his rivals, in addition, standardization invited more competition from outside implement makers than would otherwise have obtained, by allowing them to realize economies of scale in both production and distribution (despite major-firm control of the best distribution channels).

In the face of the Ferguson challenge, there was doubtless a special urgency to establishing purchasers' confidence in the long-run acceptability of a common range of conventional equipment. It would support the farmers' expectations concerning the resale value of tractors and trailed implements even when they were resold separately. The story does not end there, however, in view of the industry's standardization ten years later (1959) of Ferguson-type implement mounting, after slightly differing variants had been adopted in the previous five years by all of the major firms. A more fundamental collective concern had, over the years, come to count in favor of standardization.

With a stable technology and a differentiated product, full-line tying and an absence of standardization would tend to stabilize and isolate firms' market shares. But these same conditions, in a time of major product innovation, would be destabilizing and disruptive of established oligopoly behavior patterns. This is because, without compatibility, a major innovation by one company would swing demand to its full line and not just to the innovative implement or device itself. The 1927 power take-off standard and its widespread adoption by the industry indicates that the new full-line firms were concerned with the magnified impact on market share of any sweeping innovation in tractors or implements so long as incompatibility prevailed. The fortunes of the firms making power equipment shifted radically in the 1920s as innovations came from a number of different sources, thus suggesting the value of compatibility to all. Market shares were more stable in the 1950s, after the first impact of the Ferguson system, but a similar concern probably motivated the 1959 standardization of Ferguson-type implement mounting.

This same preference for the stability of market shares, against chances for individual firms to increase the differentiation of their product lines, is suggested by the industry's practice of licensing patented innovations freely after only a year or two of exploitation by the originating firm. What is the overall impact of interfunctional compatibility of implements on market performance? It is possible that the increased potential for instability among the fortunes of going firms associated with absence of compatibility could have resulted in lowered price-cost margins, but it could also have driven some firms out of the market, thus creating the potential for even less favorable market performance. Compatibility gave buyers greater flexibility in choosing tractors and implements of somewhat varying design and greater ease of resale, together with the possibility of greater competition from outside implement firms. Furthermore, it is unlikely that interfunctional compatibility had any important negative impact on technical change. Any firm can move to off-standard equipment if it needs to, and most improvements in either tractors or implements, either realized or projected, have borne little relationship to compatibility.

Interchangeable Parts

Firms' adherence to SAE/ASAE standards for the design of parts appears to be largely confined to individual makers' interfunctional components, despite the rather large number of standards issued over the years that would have made parts interchangeable among machines of different makes (most of which were submitted to the professional societies by the engineering committees of the FEI). No hard data on adherence are available, but a 1967 Canadian study of parts of ten different machines used in the prairies is revealing.[17] The general conclusion was that, although differences among the parts examined were often very slight, there was little interchangeability, despite the frequent existence of ASAE standards.

The Canadian investigators surmised that the reasons why major firms would not standardize were inertia and a belief by the larger competitors that such standardization would help alleviate the disadvantage suffered by the smaller full-line firms in the expense of producing small-volume parts and keeping replacements in inventory. Although these factors are undoubtedly important, there are reasons why the industry as a whole might be loath to engage in parts standardization. The more parts within the industry are standardized, the greater its vulnerability to outside "to fit" competition—already an important factor in the provision of the best-selling replacement parts. Spare parts account for over 10% of total farm machinery sales and are regarded as a particularly profitable line. If standardization were more widespread, outside suppliers could gain additional production and distribution economies. Also, the availability of a really common bank of spare parts would lower barriers to entry for foreign manufacturers by allowing them to adapt their designs to common American standards and thereby alleviate the farmer's concern about the availability of spare parts.

The Canadians concluded that very little progress could be expected in parts standardization without governmental initiative; they suggested the establishment of an official agency to determine the practical limits to interchangeability, to advertise its importance and to publicize the extent to which machines of various makes meet interchangeability criteria.

The entire ASAE budget for voluntary standardization activities in 1970, just over $40,000, was still 70% higher than the 1969 figure[18] and both amounts are vastly in excess of what was available until the midsixties when the ASEA began soliciting funds from manufacturers for standardization activities rather than relying on membership fees. The increased resources raised sharply the number of standards promulgated, but there is no evidence of any substantial increase in adherence to standards that would increase interchangeability of parts among different brands. The firms also make a substantial direct contribution of manpower to FIEI, ASAE and SAE activities in setting standards. Although the total resources devoted to standardization are not large, it is still somewhat puzzling that the industry bothers to use part of those resources to formulate and adopt standards that are not subsequently used by the sponsoring firms.

To explain the facts, it may be useful to abandon the idea of the participating firms as unitary actors. The engineering committees of the FIEI are composed of distinguished engineers loyal to their profession as well as to their firm, and this is equally true of the relevant committees of the SAE and the ASAE. Professional explanations of the development of standards point to the desirability of reducing the "variety of components required to serve an industry, thus improving availability and economy for manufacturer and customer.[19] The engineering view is apparently that when there is no functional reason for parts of various manufacturers to differ, they should be standardized and attention directed to other problems. They do not condone the suppression of technical nuance, about which engineering teams at the various firms might well hold differing views, buth rather would dispose of such issues as the exact width of a drive belt or the distance between bolt holes on a wheel. Although engineers do not make the final decision about what to produce in an industry, their morale may be buoyed by allowing them to work for socially beneficial solutions. Once they have standardized a part, the problem is out of their hands.

The impact of lack of parts standardization on performance is not difficult to assess. Agriculture is an industry in which shutdowns at certain times of the year can be devastating, and provision of repair parts is perforce an elaborate and costly service. The simplification of this problem by standardization in the areas where the engineers are in agreement and possibly in many others not yet explored because of insufficient resources, would greatly benefit the farming community directly. Its indirect influence on entry barriers into parts and machinery production could make the industry more competitive. Yet this latter consideration suggests that standardization collides with the profit interests of the dominant firms and that no substantial progress of an entirely voluntary kind should be expected.

3. SAFETY, PUBLIC POLICY AND SELF-REGULATION

Government interest at the federal level in the industry began to reemerge in the 1960s as part of a general interest in product safety, despite the fact that the hundreds of pages written during the major federal investigations of the industry fail even to touch upon the subjects of health or safety. Earlier government attention to safety had been almost exclusively at the state level and was concerned with farm machinery as a road hazard. Examples of industry-government interaction in this area are the ASAE lighting standards developed in the 1950s and the triangular slow-moving vehicle emblem of 1964; generally, state governments have simply made ASAE standards mandatory. Most adaptation of equipment for this purpose has been cheap and simple and has engendered little controversy over the propriety of the government's role.

Farmer sentiment about the need for safer machinery has never been intense, and the generally conservative farm community has failed to produce even the vocal minority characteristic of users of other products. Experts, however, have pointed out many areas in which the machinery makers have failed to take even the most minimal initiative. Simple and inexpensive steps to reduce tractor noise emission, for example, were long delayed despite evidence that permanent hearing damage was being caused. The companies are believed to have thought that the farmer associated noise with power. Industry interest increased after the Nebraska tests were expanded in 1970 to include noise emission. An even simpler example concerns the heavy springing of the tractor clutch, which makes it sometimes difficult to depress in emergencies. The companies are alleged to think that heavy springing suggests quality of construction to the farmer.[20]

One of the principal difficulties in discussing machinery safety is that there is no accurate reporting of non-fatal accidents, and the most pertinent data surrounding fatalities are not always recorded with care. A report of the Department of Transportation to the Congress in 1970 proposed a comprehensive service for gathering safety statistics. Nonetheless, it has been known for a long time that the principal cause of work-related rural fatalities is the overturning of tractors, which accounts for as many as 600 deaths per year. This was a major factor which led to a much publicized (and statistically controvertible) 1969 Nader-report conclusion that farming was the "third most dangerous occupation" after mining and construction. It has also been established from Swedish data that nearly all such fatalities can be eliminated by some form of rollover protection. Such protection, however, adds between $200 and $1500 to the price of a tractor, depending on whether the method employed is a rollbar with seat belt or a safety cab.

What may be an example of industry action in an attempt to avoid government regulation was the adoption by the ASAE in 1969 of a crash program to reduce accidental rural deaths during the 1970s by 50%. The program was set up to study all aspects of farm safety outside the home and to convey its findings to all interested parties. Machinery deaths, most of them from tractor accidents, account for more than 40% of the fatalities, and the safety drive was suggested to the ASAE by a Ford executive while legislation was being prepared in the Congress to authorize an investigation of tractor safety by the Department of Transportation. During the course of the investigation, the industry pointed with pride to its ambitious efforts to cut down fatalities and injuries. Although the industry's sincerity about improving rural safety is not in question, some form of compulsory rollover protection was thought to be one of the most likely outcomes of the Department of Transportation's investigation, and this was probably regarded as a profit-reducing requirement by the industry.

When the manufacturers were questioned about their own view concerning mandatory safety equipment, the investigators concluded that "their reasoning, as near as could be determined, is that the farmer is certain to oppose such rule-making action, and manufacturers would not want to be on record as endorsing such specification."[21] While the committee is naive in assuming that this was the industry's prime motivation because "it stood to make a profit on the requirement," there can be little doubt that it adequately gauged rural opinion. In a national survey conducted by a farm magazine (and verified by testimony given before the Canadian Royal Commission on Farm Machinery at about the same time), it was discovered that less than half of the farm community thought its equipment less safe than it should be, and most dissidents held that a rollbar was the principal feature lacking.[22] Roll-bars were available as optional equipment, and those farmers interested would presumably buy one on their next tractor. There was no sentiment in favor of government regulation.

The industry's stand is scarcely surprising; government regulation was not popular with those most directly affected, and the industry might well have believed that the government's probable maximum proposal would be virtually the same as the industry's minimum substantive accommodation: nonoptional rollbar rollbar protection. Cabs are much more expensive, and their additional contribution to safety is not firmly established. This suggests a general proposition: the popularity of proposed government regulation among those directly affected may help determine the industry's strategy toward the regulatory agency; it will expect milder regulatory response when the provisions are not generally popular, particularly in the absence of intense minority lobbying. This is nothing more than the assumption that the regulatory agency is unlikely to seek trouble when there are no compensating payoffs.

When questioned about rollover protection during the transportation safety hearings, the manufacturers pointed out that although the industry had developed SAE/ASAE rollbar and cab standards in the late 1960s and all offered them as optional accessories, they believed they would be in violation of the antitrust laws if they jointly and voluntarily made such protection standard equipment. The transportation report continues: "Whether real or imagined, the fear appears to be that such agreement could be interpreted as price-fixing, or as constituting a move to force smaller, less well prepared manufacturers out of business."[23] It may well be true that this industry is particularly sensitive about antitrust issues, and International Harvester in particular has declared elsewhere that its policy is "to bend over backward in its interpretation of the law."[24] Nonetheless, in the light of virtually simultaneous moves in other industries to adopt nonoptional safety equipment and considering the fact that all of the tractor makers were already offering the equipment optionally (as the report itself acknowledges elsewhere), antitrust grounds for inaction are hard to take seriously.

If there is an antitrust issue involved in making such safety equipment nonoptional, it would appear to relate to the prohibition of tying in section 3 of the Clayton Act. Any piece of optional equipment available not solely from producers within an industry may become so popular that the industry's ability to appropriate the entire market outweighs what it loses by not offering some customers the product without the special equipment. Injury to independent manufacturers of the equipment might then provide a legal ground for complaint.

When safety equipment is involved, however, the manufacturers might seek an additional justification for their actions, and public or private support of mandatory factory installation could be their vehicle. Such a legal requirement might look attractive to regulatory agencies because it would obviate the expensive (for the regulators) and less effective methods of monitoring at the point of sale or inspecting equipment in use. It must be stressed that the hypothesis above relates to the *type* of safety equipment being considered in the farm machinery industry, but only in part to the structural conditions there. It does not explain any actions yet observed in the industry.

What are the welfare implications of industry and government provision of nonoptional safety features? The regulations related to highway travel of farm vehicles can be justified on the basis of externalities alone. The argument of ignorance of the risks faced can be applied to mandatory requirements that affect only the farmer himself or, perhaps, his family. The alternative of providing detailed information on risks and allowing for individual choice might not be superior, given the government's role as provider of last resort. These arguments also apply when the machinery is to be operated by employees and where additionally there is a longstanding tradition of not allowing variation in market wages to carry the entire burden of adjusting for danger to the employee.

Even if practically all circumstances argue for the legitimacy of government concern, however, weighing the costs and benefits of different devices with different degrees of effectiveness remains an enormous problem.

With respect to farm machinery neither the extent of the problem nor the effectiveness of various remedies has been established for any area except tractor turnovers, and even here the information is very rudimentary.

4. CONCLUSION

This discussion has attempted to demonstrate the usefulness of industrial organization theory in explaining self-regulatory activities and different postures towards government regulation in an industry that changed markedly in structure over the period of observation. Reducing cost, expanding demand, elevating entry barriers and improving industry coordination are all desiderata that appear to have motivated industry behavior directly, and they illuminate why self-regulation was sometimes adopted and sometimes avoided. Some measures of self-regulation by their very nature weakened the industry's position by one or more of the criteria while raising it overall.

The experience of the industry and possible future developments also confirm some hypotheses about the relation of an industry to compulsory regulation and suggest others: an industry may approve of government regulation when it limits fringe competition, particularly when the fringe may be reducing total industry demand. It will not voluntarily self-regulate when such self-regulation lowers profits and it sees its minimum accommodation as identical with that of the government's maximum demand. Its understanding of the government's maximum requirement may sometimes be confidently held on the basis of purchaser attitudes. It may under some circumstances support strong compulsory legislation, if such legislation sanctions an exclusive broadening of the industry's product line.

Notes to Chapter 4

1. Chapter 3 of this volume.

2. The structural and behavioral characteristics which lead to high profit rates are explored in Joe S. Bain, *Industrial Organization* (New York: John Wiley and Sons, 1959) and Richard E. Caves, *American Industry: Structure, Conduct, Performance* (Englewood Cliffs, New Jersey: Prentice-Hall Inc., 1964).

3. Information on the inception of the Nebraska tests can be found in R. B. Gray, *Development of the Agricultural Tractor in the United States.* (St. Joseph, Michigan: American Society of Agricultural Engineers, 1956), pp. 31-34; and Wayne H. Worthington, *50 Years of Agricultural Tractor Development.* (New York: Society of Automotive Engineers, 1966), p. 5.

4. Robert P. Crawford, *These Fifty Years* (Lincoln: University of Nebraska Press, 1925), p. 153.

5. U.S. Federal Trade Commission, *Report on the Causes of High Prices of Farm Implements* (Washington: Government Printing Office, 1920), pp. 503-4.

6. *Report of the Royal Commission on Farm Machinery* (Ottawa: Information Canada, 1971), p. 128.

7. U.S. Federal Trade Commission, *Report on the Agricultural Implement and Machinery Industry: Concentration and Competitive Methods* (Washington: Government Printing Office, 1938).

8. U.S. Department of Commerce, Bureau of Corporations, *Farm Machinery Trade Associations* (Washington: Government Printing Office, 1915).

9. FTC, *High Prices,* pp. 308–309.

10. These issues are discussed in the context of the Chamberlin large-group in R. L. Bishop, "Monopolistic Competition and Welfare Economics," *Monopolistic Competition Theory: Studies in Impact,* Robert E. Kuenne, editor (New York: John Wiley and Sons, 1967), pp. 255–260.

11. FTC, *Agricultural Machinery Industry,* pp. 249–250.

12. Joe S. Bain, *Barriers to New Competition* (Cambridge: Harvard University Press, 1956), pp. 167–81.

13. This explanation is developed in David Schwartzman, *Oligopoly in the Farm Machinery Industry* (Ottawa: Information Canada, 1971), pp. 149–74.

14. L. H. Hodges, "The Voluntary Standards Program for Agricultural Tractors," U.S. Department of Transportation, *Agricultural Tractor Safety on Public Roads and Farms* (Washington: Government Printing Office, 1971), p. A–125.

15. Worthington, *Fifty Years,* p. 12.

16. The seven full-line firms by the late sixties were not the same seven discussed in the prewar period. Ferguson merged with Massey-Harris in 1953, while Ford arguably attained full-line status only by the late sixties, after importing a combine and expanding its implement line. In the early sixties, White Motor Company took control of Oliver, Minneapolis Moline and the small postwar Canadian entrant, Cockshutt.

17. *Royal Commission on Farm Machinery,* pp. 533–37.

18. American Society of Agricultural Engineers, "The ASAE Co-operative Standards Program," in U.S. Department of Transportation, *Tractor Safety,* p. A–158.

19. Russell H. Hahn, "Voluntary Standardization and ASAE," *Agricultural Engineering,* April 1970, p. 231. Similar sentiments are expressed by engineers with great frequency: E. W. Tanquary, "Standardization: World-Wide," *Agricultural Engineering* (September 1963), p. 486; Arnold B. Skromme, "The Growth of ASAE and the Farm Equipment Industry," *Agricultural Engineering* (April 1970), p. 181.

20. Graham F. Donaldson, *Farm Machinery Safety* (Ottawa: Queen's Printer, 1968), pp. 50–51.

21. U.S. Department of Transportation, *Tractor Safety,* p. 41.

22. Ibid., pp. B–5–31.

23. Ibid., p. 41.

24. A. D. H. Kaplan, Joel B. Dirlam, and Robert F. Lanzillotti, *Pricing in Big Business* (Washington, D.C.: The Brookings Institution, 1958), p. 142.

Chapter Five

Competition, Standards and Self-Regulation in the Computer Industry

Gerald Brock

1. THE NEED FOR STANDARDS

Standards in the computer industry have a major impact on the level and pattern of competition. Effective standards greatly facilitate the interchange of data and programs among the machines of different manufacturers and allow the user to combine equipment from several suppliers. Although various attempts have been made by the industry to develop such standards, the most effective standards have been those organized by computer users—led by the federal government. This chapter reviews the development of two particular efforts, the COBOL and ASCII standards. It concludes that the divergence of manufacturers' interests— especially between IBM and other firms—has prevented voluntary self-regulation from accomplishing socially desirable ends. This situation is an instructive contrast to the home appliance industry discussed in chapter 3. The policy implications of the finding are discussed, and an increased role for government pressure based on the government's purchasing position, as well as for the National Bureau of Standards, is recommended.

To understand the role and value of standards more precisely we need to understand the structure of computer processing. This is a very capital-intensive activity, with capital distinguishable into four types. (1) The central processing unit or CPU is the actual computer, the unit which performs the calculations. (2) The peripheral equipment handles the data transfer into and out of the CPU. It includes tape and disc drives, card readers, printers and other devices. (3) The program is the set of instructions which controls the processing of the data. Such programs include both the general instructions which operate the machine (systems programs) and the particular instructions for a given procedure (applications programs). (4) The data which are being processed are

I want to thank Marc Roberts for helpful comments on an earlier draft.

also a capital item. They must be encoded on tapes, cards, etc. in the format required by the CPU, peripherals, and programs with which they will be used. In order for processing to take place, the various types of capital must be completely and precisely compatible. CPU design is obviously crucial because it determines what peripheral equipment, programs and data can be used.

No natural set of interfaces among CPUs, peripherals, data and programs exists. The interfaces chosen are dependent upon design considerations but are largely a matter of convention and convenience. Without an organized effort to produce compatibility among machine types, programs and data can be used only on the machines for which they were designed. Peripherals, programs, or data designed for use on the CPU of one manufacturer generally cannot be used on the CPU of a different supplier. As discussed below, such incompatibility has a major impact on the ability of users to switch suppliers and on the ability of new suppliers to enter the industry.

In the industry today, the mechanical capital (CPUs and peripherals) is either rented or bought by the user from one or more manufacturers. The systems programs for controlling the operation of the machines are generally supplied as part of the hardware. Applications programs are usually written by the user and are specific to his own data processing procedures. They must be written either in a language the CPU can read directly (machine language) or, as is much more commonly done, in one of the languages for which the manufacturer supplies a translation program (a compiler). User programs may also be purchased or rented from the manufacturer or independent companies. The user commonly spends as much on the development of programs for his application (software) as he spends for the rental of the CPU and input-output equipment (hardware).

The requirements on a user's data are both physical and logical. The data must be coded in a form that the CPU can understand and also be organized physically so that they can be read by the peripheral equipment. This involves a large number of parameters such as recording density, number of tracks used on a tape, disc-pack size, etc. The data must also be arranged so that the user's programs will find each increment in the expected location. The investment in collecting and organizing the data is so large that in many cases it is the most valuable part of the capital. Hardware which does not accept the user's data as recorded (or make some provision for their automatic conversion) is not usually considered at any price, since reproducing the data base by hand would be prohibitively expensive.

The compatibility problem was recognized early by users, but little was done about it. Soon after the first commercial computers were introduced, American Management Association Conference speaker Neil MacDonald complained:

> one of the biggest of all obstacles has been the lack of a common language among the information-handling machines of various types. . . .

> no machine, so far as I know, will take in recorded magnetic tape produced by one manufacturer and translate that information and record it in appropriate form on the magnetic tape of another manufacturer.[1]

As the industry prospered during the late 1950s, the number of products grew rapidly. No significant attempts were made to insure that data recorded on one machine could be read by another. A 1960 report on tape drives showed fifty models with physical tape widths ranging from one-half inch to two inches and the number of parallel data tracks ranging from seven to forty-eight.[2] Coding schemes for assigning binary digits to numbers, letters and symbols proliferated even more rapidly than tape characteristics. By the time the first official standard was adopted in 1963, sixty different internal codes were in use including eleven different ones used on IBM machines alone.[3]

Programming languages also multiplied with no provision for transferring programs written for one machine to another machine. Most early programs were written in machine language or symbolic machine language and were specialized to the characteristics of a particular machine. Input-output equipment was also specialized to the CPU for which it was designed. There was little transferability of peripheral equipment or programs even among different CPUs produced by a single manufacturer.

In 1960, the International Standards Organization (ISO) assigned responsibility for standardizing "terminology, problem description, programming languages and communications characteristics" to the American Standards Association (ASA), renamed the American National Standards Institute (ANSI) in 1966.[4] The organization which has become ANSI was originally founded in 1918 to coordinate the development of technical and safety standards. Both ANSI and the ISO are voluntary organizations whose goal is to promote standardization in industry without government force, based on the belief that the best standards are those developed by people who will be affected the most. ANSI neither writes nor enforces standards, but provides a framework for cooperative voluntary development of standards by industry groups. As is ordinarily done, the ASA recognized the Business Equipment Manufacturers' Association as the sponsor of computer standards efforts. However, in this case, the diversity of opinion among the manufacturers made it very difficult to obtain the consensus required by the ASA if it was to accept an industry's proposals.

The lack of transferability of peripheral equipment, programs and data among different CPUs forced users to purchase all their equipment for a complete computer system from a single supplier. A user would typically rent a CPU and peripheral equipment from a supplier and then design his programs and data base to fit the specifications of the chosen equipment. If the user wished to switch to a competitive CPU supplier, the original CPU and peripheral equipment could be returned and rented out to another customer with little loss to either the customer or supplier. However, the user's investment in programs and data was specialized both to his own particular business and to the CPU, causing the user's investment to be largely lost in the switch to the manufacturer of a noncompatible CPU.

The user's investment in specialized programs and data insulated him from the competitive efforts of alternative CPU suppliers unless the alternative supplier arranged to protect the user's investment either by using the same specifications or by providing a translation service to convert the data and programs into the new format. The potential entrant generally adopted the standards of the established company from which he hoped to lure his customers. The company copied most often was IBM (which controlled 70% of the market).

From the manufacturer's viewpoint, the value of standards depends upon his competitive position. If he is satisfied with his current market share, he will want to differentiate his product as much as possible from competing products and will thus be opposed to required standards. The supplier who wants to increase his market share will desire increased standardization in order to ease the task of drawing customers away from other manufacturers. In practice this means that IBM generally opposes required standards and the very small manufacturers support them. The major non-IBM companies (with two to seven percent of the market each) may or may not support standardization efforts, depending upon their particular competitive strategy at a given time.

The most successful example of standards copying was Honeywell's 1964 introduction of the H-200 to compete with IBM's 1401, then the most popular computer. Because Honeywell planned to replace both the CPU and the peripheral equipment of the 1401 system, it was unconcerned about the CPU-peripheral interface specifications. Honeywell aimed its H-200 program at protecting users' investment in both data and programs. The H-200 could read data originally prepared for the 1401. It could not accept 1401 programs directly, but with the H-200 Honeywell supplied a program called the Liberator which translated programs written for the 1401 into a form usable by the H-200.

Honeywell's price advantage over the 1401, combined with protection for the user's investment, brought immediate success; within six weeks of its announcement, Honeywell received 400 orders, many of them for 1401 replacements.[5] Standards for a machine such as the 1401, which had been on the market for several years, were well-known and relatively easy to copy. But the practice left the copying company vulnerable to competitive response. Four months after the H-200 announcement, IBM announced the System 360 with substantially changed programming and data coding standards. Because of IBM's power in the industry, the new 360 standards became de facto industry standards, and reduced the value of the 1401-oriented H-200 system.

The practice of copying dominant standards was extended to the CPU-peripheral interface in the late 1960s. A number of small companies began offering peripheral equipment equivalent in performance to IBM's units which used the same interface standards as the IBM equipment did. This allowed the competitive units to be attached directly to the IBM CPU, and eliminated the need to purchase the CPU and peripheral units from the same manufacturer. It was much easier to enter the market for peripheral equipment than the market for CPUs, primarily because customers could try out the independent equipment and then revert to IBM if it was unsatisfactory with very little lost effort or conversion expense. Consequently, the ability to copy the interface standards brought a rush of new entrants into the peripheral equipment segment of the market, transforming it from a tight oligopoly into a relatively competitive market.

Because the interface standards were set by IBM and not by an independent standards body, they could be manipulated for competitive advantage. A competitor could determine the standards only by making an examination of the physical equipment after it had been delivered. This caused a lag of from several months to a year between the time IBM could deliver a product with new standards and the time that the other firms could compete, regardless of the technological competence of the competitors.

The problems of standards secrecy can be illustrated by IBM's introduction of the System 370 series and the 3330 disc drive. The 370 and 3330 were announced in June 1970 for delivery in 1971. The independent peripheral makers knew that the interface specifications between the 370 CPUs and the 3330 would be different from those between the 360 CPUs and the 2314 disc drives. Although they had the technological capability to make a product equivalent to the 3330, they were forced either to wait for the 3330 delivery or to discover IBM's secret specifications, before developing a competitive product. Because a substantial delay in producing 3330-type products was considered a threat to the viability of some of the peripheral companies, many efforts were made to obtain IBM specifications by hiring IBM employees and by other means. IBM's increased security measures after 1970 to protect peripheral equipment information (primarily on the 3330 drive) from competitive peripheral companies were estimated at $3 million in a trade-secret suit won by IBM.[6] Although the trade secrets involved included many technological elements other than interface specifications, the interface specifications were one of the primary pieces of information ardently sought by the peripheral companies and just as intently protected by IBM.

As the above examples indicate, control of standards by one company can be a significant barrier to entry. Control by one company allows that company to change standards any time that so doing is in its interest, constrained only by the need to provide a measure of continuity and compatibility with earlier systems to its own customers. Control of interface standards among various parts of a computer system allows a company to tie the systems components together into one package and close the market to potential competitors which have the ability to compete effectively in segments of the market but not in the entire systems market. The tying aspect is significant because of the estimated $1 billion capital and shakedown cost for an effective integrated systems supplier, compared with the very minor cost for a peripherals maker.[7]

The intensity of the user's desire for standardization varies with the size of the installation. Very small-scale users are generally tied closely to a particular manufacturer and have only a minor stake in the standardization which would make it easier to switch suppliers. In principle, they would prefer standards which increase the opportunities for choice; but, particularly if they are satisfied IBM customers, they are unlikely to see standardization as an important goal. Large-scale users often have complete systems from more than one manufacturer and see a recurring need to switch programs and data among their computer systems. Besides seeing the immediate advantages in computing resource flexibility provided by standards, large scale users tend to be very aware of machine improvements among various manufacturers and of the costs of taking advantage of improvements which are not compatible with their current systems.

The largest computer user is the federal government. According to IBM Industry Marketing, the government occupied 17% of the entire computer market in 1968.[8] The government's selection procedures insure it a selection of equipment from many different manufacturers, causing it to be very aware of the problem of incompatibility among various systems. The government is the user with the most to gain from standardization and the only one large enough to force standardization through buying power. No major manufacturer is willing to be shut out of the government market entirely. Thus the government can establish a standard simply by announcing that it will only order equipment conforming to that standard.

The government has been aware of its losses due to computer incompatibility but has been reluctant to use its market power to foster standardization. The longstanding government position was expressed by Myron Tribus, Assistant Secretary of Commerce for Science and Technology in a speech to the American National Standards Institute: "We participate to the best of our ability in the voluntary program without overriding or restraining private initiative; we embark on mandatory standards . . . only when Congress has determined that there is no real alternative. . . ."[9] Congress determined there was "no real alternative" in the computer case following a congressional report which indicated that the government had 500,000 hours of unused computer time in 1965, much of it because data and programs could not be shifted from an overloaded machine to an underutilized one.[10] As the following two examples indicate, most of the progress that has taken place in computer standards has been as a result of government pressure.

2. THE DEVELOPMENT OF COBOL

So long as programming was done in machine language or symbolic machine language, there was little hope of standardization, because the language was necessarily so closely tied to the physical characteristics of each machine. The possibility of machine-independent programming was demonstrated by the development of Fortran by IBM in 1956. Fortran allowed the user to write in notation resembling mathematical symbols rather than in the actual machine language. A special Fortran compiler program was produced which translated programs written in the Fortran language into programs in machine language. With Fortran (or similar languages) it was necessary to have a separate compiler program for each machine language. However, the same user program written in Fortran could be translated automatically by the various compilers for use on different machines. IBM assigned the task of standardizing Fortran for use on IBM machines to its users group, but no effort was made to create a standard Fortran for use on machines produced by different manufacturers until much later. Many dialects of Fortran came into common use, as variations were made in the language specifications to fit them to various machine characteristics. Although the job of converting scientific programs from one machine to another was eased by the existence of Fortran, the language did not completely solve the program of running programs on different machine types without expensive manual conversion efforts.

Fortran was oriented to scientific applications and did not contain the instructions necessary to easily code common business problems. Typical business applications involve relatively simple calculations with large quantitites of data and fairly complex reports. This requires a different set of program instructions from those used for scientific work, which primarily involves extensive calculations with relatively small amounts of data and simple reports. By 1959, Fortran had achieved wide acceptance and had proved the value of compiler-translated languages over direct machine language programming. Both Honeywell and IBM began programs to develop a business oriented language which would extend the benefits of a high-level language to the rapidly growing group of business computer users. Recognizing the compatibility problems that would exist if each manufacturer produced its own business oriented language, a group of users, led by the Department of Defense, decided to push for a single standardized commercial language that would simplify both the programming of commercial problems and the translation of programs from one machine to another.

The Department of Defense called a meeting of interested users and manufacturers in May 1959, and organized the Conference on Data Systems Languages (CODASYL) to begin work on a common business oriented language. CODASYL's authority was derived from the voluntary cooperation of users and manufacturers, and its recommendations were not binding. CODASYL did not intend actually to produce compilers for the business language but to standardize the specifications as the user would see them in order to improve compatibility. However, the Department of Defense sponsorship of the effort caused the manufacturers to cooperate with CODASYL, because of the implied threat of mandatory cooperation if voluntary efforts were unsatisfactory.

The short range committee of CODASYL, originally assigned only the task of examining previously proposed language specifications for relevance to the new effort, had extremely active representatives and immediately began drawing up new language specifications.[11] Not all CODASYL committees were in agreement with the activities of the short range committee. For example, the intermediate range committee recommended that the existing Honeywell business compiler specifications be accepted as the standard rather than designing a completely new language. However, the CODASYL executive committee authorized the short range committee to continue its development of a new language (named COBOL for common business oriented language). The initial specifications were accepted by the CODASYL executive committee and published by the government printing office in June 1960.

The reactions of the various manufacturers to the January 1960 CODASYL vote making the COBOL-60 specifications official revealed their views of their own interests. IBM announced dissatisfaction with COBOL and said it would not implement the language on IBM machines. IBM said it would continue development of its own version of a business oriented language and would announce the specifications in April 1960. The company explained that it would continue participation in COBOL development and possibly alter its own language specifications to make them similar but not identical to the COBOL specifications. The probable reason for IBM's dissatisfaction with COBOL was given by the trade journal *Datamation* which expressed the belief that "COBOL appears to be the first real outside impetus to a more competitive industry."[2] The *Datamation* writer further explained that he expected the COBOL effort to fail because it was dependent upon manufacturer support and IBM could be expected to oppose the increased competition that would result from a common business language.

In contrast to the IBM position, both RCA and Univac saw COBOL as an opportunity to improve their standing in the business oriented computer market. Both companies began efforts to implement the COBOL-60 specifications by developing a compiler program to translate programs written in COBOL into their respective machine languages. On August 17, 1960, RCA achieved the first correct, complete COBOL translation, using the RCA 501 COBOL Narrator. Because Univac was also close to success in building a COBOL compiler, plans were begun for a public demonstration of program compatibility across machine types through the use of COBOL.

A government-written program in COBOL for the RCA 501 was given to Univac and an industrial profit-loss program written in COBOL for the Univac II was given to RCA, along with information on file layouts and other specifications needed to check out the programs. Several changes were required to convert the programs from one machine to the other, requiring about two man days of work. On December 6, 1960 both programs were compiled for the CODASYL executive committee on the Univac II, and on December 7 the same two programs were compiled and run on the RCA 501. The test was considered a success and demonstrated 90% compatibility by the use of COBOL on very different machines. The RCA-Univac demonstration proved that although complete program interchangeability had not yet been achieved, the use of COBOL could reduce the programming cost of changing machine types to a fraction of its previous cost.

RCA and Univac were the only manufacturers to implement COBOL–60, leading to doubts about COBOL becoming a truly common language. The lack of enthusiasm for the language among other manufacturers was due both to concern over its competitive effect and questions about the value of some of the specifications. Many changes in the language were proposed. Recognizing the need to allow the language to be improved and to be adapted to changing technologies and computer requirements while maintaining compatibility with earlier versions, the CODASYL executive committee set up a procedure to make necessary changes to the language without destroying compatibility. The COBOL features were divided into required features, which had to be implemented in any language version calling itself COBOL, and elective features, which could be implemented at the manufacturer's discretion. This procedure provided a common base language across machine types, and yet manufacturers could add elements to improve the language's use of their own machine's capabilities. The two-level language represented a compromise between the desire to have a completely common language, which would be transferable, and the realization that full use of every machine's design capabilities required specialization of the language to machine types. The specifications for COBOL–61 were completed in early 1961 and a manual was published in June 1961. All of the major computer manufacturers and some of the minor ones announced plans to develop a COBOL compiler for their machines and were given voting rights on the specifications.[13]

This change of heart by the manufacturers and the consequent increased development of COBOL compilers were due in part to a GSA question about COBOL capability in negotiations for new equipment contracts. More explicitly, the Air Force declared that COBOL capability would be "an important factor" in the future selection of equipment. The implied requirement for manufacturers to develop COBOL was made explicit with a regulation from the Department of Defense that manufacturers must either provide COBOL with computers purchased or leased to the government or prove that their performance would not be enhanced by the existence of COBOL.[14] With government pressure both from Department of Defense sponsorship of CODASYL and from threats to stop purchase from those who did not provide compilers, all companies with an interest in the business data processing market developed COBOL compilers. The alternative languages, IBM's Commercial Translator and Honeywell's Fact, were dropped in favor of COBOL.

Although COBOL was forced upon manufacturers in the early 1960s, it did not receive widespread use at first. The language changed rapidly as attempts were made to improve it. Accurate, effective compiler programs for a large number of machines were not initially available. In addition, the second generation machines of the time were severely limited in internal memory capacity, a resource which COBOL used less efficiently than machine-oriented assembly languages.

The use of COBOL increased greatly with the introduction of the third generation of computers around 1965. The tremendous program conversion effort required to move from IBM's second generation machines to the System 360 expanded the group of users concerned with compatibility problems and machine independent programming from a relatively small number of large-scale users to a large fraction of all computer users. The effectiveness and availability of COBOL compilers were improved. In addition, the new machines shifted the economic calculations of cost-minimizing users. Computer power, and memory in particular, was less expensive in the third generation, while programmer costs continued to increase. Because COBOL was less efficient with machine power and more efficient with programming time than assembly languages, the use of COBOL was more cost-effective. Among medium-scale ($5 to $10 thousand per month rental) second-generation computers, over 90% used assembly language as their major programming language, and fewer than 5% used COBOL extensively. Among third-generation machines of the same price class, over half used COBOL as the major programming language. Of the larger third generation machines in the $15 to $30 thousand rental range, two-thirds used COBOL as the major language, according to International Data Corporation.[15]

The development of COBOL under the auspices of CODASYL greatly facilitated the exchange of programs among machines but, as with Fortran, did not completely solve the problem. Many variants of COBOL were developed by various manufacturers in order to take advantage of specific machine characteristics. The compatibility of COBOL programs across machines remained around the 90% level of the original RCA-Univac demonstration in 1960. Although the variations in the language detracted from the original goal of compatibility, they were accepted willingly by most users because they increased the efficiency of the language. Consequently no urgency was felt by the ASA committee set up to formulate a single standard form of COBOL. With decreasing machine costs in the third generation and renewed concern for compatibility, some users began to feel the gain in efficiency from the COBOL variants was not worth the cost in compatibility. Finally, in 1968 an American national standard COBOL was officially approved by ANSI. Continuing its earlier COBOL activism, the Department of Defense quickly adopted the ANSI form of COBOL as a federal data processing standard, guaranteeing that major manufacturers would produce a compiler for the ANSI form of COBOL.[16] ANSI COBOL has been achieving increasingly widespread use but has not yet displaced the variant forms of COBOL. For example, IBM continues to offer COBOL D for small scale users and COBOL F for large scale users as well as introducing ANSI COBOL. Customers who regularly switch programs among machines have found it worthwhile to convert to ANSI COBOL to achieve complete compatibility, while those with less need for program interchangeability continue to use the variant versions to avoid the cost of converting to ANSI COBOL. In spite of incomplete compatibility, the efforts of the CODASYL committee and user pressure to produce a common business oriented language has made program conversion a less formidable barrier to competition than it would have been without COBOL.

3. THE DEVELOPMENT OF ASCII

The user's investment consists of programs and data. The COBOL development facilitated the interchange of programs but did not affect the exchange of data among different CPU models. The data exchange problem is primarily related to the coding scheme used. All computers operate only upon binary numbers. Letters, decimal numbers and symbols can only be processed after being coded into binary numbers. Codes may vary both in the number of bits used to define a character and in the actual binary number assigned to character. For example, the IBM BCD code for the 1400 series used a six-bit binary number to identify each number and character. This allowed a maximum of sixty-four characters to be defined. The IBM EBCDIC code for the 360 series used an eight-bit binary number for each character, providing for 256 symbols, characters, and numbers to be defined. The arbitrary nature of the assignment of characters and numbers to a binary representation, combined with the lack of standardization efforts, led to the use of sixty different coding schemes on various machines by 1963. Data prepared in machine readable form on one machine cannot be read by a machine with a different coding scheme without explicit provision for translation of the codes.

Although users recognized the disadvantages of multiple coding schemes, there was less user pressure for the development of a standard coding scheme than for the development of COBOL. The COBOL project was popular, even among users who were unconcerned with compatibility, because of the need for a convenient language oriented to business problems. Only users concerned about compatibility of data were interested in the standardization of a coding scheme. Users in general were less familiar with advantages and disadvantages of various coding schemes than they were with programming languages. The binary representations used were closely tied to the design of the machine and were considered the responsibility of the manufacturer. Early coding standards efforts were left to the American Standards Association with little user input.

The American Standards Association formed a subcommittee (X 3.2) in 1959 to begin standardization of a coding scheme. The subcommittee was led at various times by representatives of IBM, Burroughs and the Navy Management Office. Several existing codes were examined, and all were found to be inadequate. After much discussion the committee devised a seven bit code (with provision for expanding it to eight bits) eventually known as ASCII (American Standard Code for Information Interchange). ASCII was based most heavily on the army Fieldata code. The code contained an implied collating sequence consistent with the binary numbers assigned to the various symbols. (IBM's BCD binary number representations did not represent the collating sequence, requiring special hardware or software for sorting). A six-bit subset of the code was assigned to sixty-four information characters while the other sixty-four codes were reserved for control characters.[17]

When the final proposed code was ready in 1962, IBM voted against accepting it. W. W. Andrews, IBM's group director of standards, said that the rejection was to protect the heavy user investment in IBM's six-bit BCD (binary coded decimal) code. Andrews said that implementation of ASCII would add between twenty and thirty percent to the cost of equipment and asked that BCD be recognized as the standard.[18] With the support of the Department of Defense and the Bell System, the ASCII code continued toward final approval in spite of IBM objections. The Business Equipment Manufacturers Organization objected to the new code becoming an official standard but did not push opposition through the available appeal channels. The code was accepted as an official standard on June 17, 1963.

The code, as originally adopted, only assigned binary numbers to characters and symbols; it did not specify the representation of the binary numbers for punched cards, tape or other media. For data to be interchangeable, the tape, discs and cards written by one machine must be readable by another model. Even with a standard binary representation, the data are not interchangeable if varying assignments of a given binary number to tape tracks or punched-card holes are chosen by different manufacturers. Standards for the assignment of the code to various media were more difficult to develop than the basic code standard. In 1966 IBM opposition caused the proposed tape standards to be dropped. The punch card standard was killed on a split vote, with IBM opposing it.[19] In late 1967 a tape standard was agreed upon, and IBM informally withdrew opposition while remaining officially against the standard.

The federal government finally became disenchanted with the speed of implementation of ASCII. In March 1965, the Bureau of the Budget sent out circular A-71 which was labeled "administration policy" by President Johnson. The circular stated that policy would be to arrange for "voluntary commercial standards when it is in the best interests of the Government to do so, and to arrange for the development, approval and promulgation of Federal standards for ADP equipment and techniques on an interim basis, or permanent basis, when voluntary commercial standards are not available or usable."[20] An official of the bureau clarified the threat as meaning that the government preferred ASA to set standards but would not stand for lack of action because of the consensus requirements of ASA.[21]

In October 1965, Public Law 89-306 (the Brooks Bill, originally introduced in March 1963) was passed. It assigned responsibility to the National Bureau of Standards to develop computer standards for use within the government and to coordinate government efforts for joint standardization programs with industry. Following the precedent of its earlier report, the Bureau of the Budget issued policy directives to the Bureau of Standards for desirable levels of computer standardization. Explaining the implications of the law, Congressman Brooks stated, "The Federal government will continue to take a decisive role in standards development. We will cooperate and fully participate in the development of voluntary standards."[22] Joseph Cunningham, head of the ADP management staff at the Bureau of the Budget (the ADP management staff was responsible for carrying out provisions of PL 89-306) stated: "The agencies of the government have given strong technical support through the years to the various committees working on the development of USASI standards. While some standards have been developed, implementation to provide the user with a reasonable degree of compatibility has not been achieved."[23]

In spite of strong government suggestions for voluntary action, implementation of ASCII failed. Finally on March 11, 1968 (9 years after work was begun on ASCII, 5 years after ASCII was officially adopted by ASA, 2½ years after PL 89-306 was passed) President Johnson issued a memorandum establishing ASCII as a federal standard. It was the first important standard officially established under the authority of PL 89-306. All computers brought into the government inventory after July 1, 1969 were required to have the capability to use ASCII and its associated magnetic and paper tape representations. The day following the adoption of the standard, Congressman Brooks commented: "The adoption of this standard is a most important beginning to a broad frontal attack on the entire standardization problem affecting computer usage."[24]

In actuality, the Johnson order was much less significant than Brooks expected it to be. Implementation of the order was left to the National Bureau of Standards and the Bureau of the Budget. Because the actual form of the implementation letter was crucial to its effects on the manufacturers, the Johnson order set off a flurry of lobbying activity directed toward the officials responsible for implementation. The resulting disagreements within the government over the proper form of implementation led to a decision to delay the implementation letter until after the 1968 presidential election.

The opposition to ASCII implementation was led by IBM, with Control Data and Honeywell also strongly opposed. In spite of IBM's 1962 proposal that its six-bit BCD code be accepted as a standard, IBM had changed to an eight-bit code known as EBCDIC (extended binary coded decimal interchange code) with the introduction of the System 360 in 1965. IBM's management committee was given three reasons for choosing EBCDIC rather than ASCII for the System 360: (1) IBM's marketing group wanted a code compatible with BCD, (2) ASCII was not completely defined at the 360 decision time and (3) IBM didn't want ASCII to become a de facto code standard.[25] Because of IBM's move to EBCDIC, EBCDIC was adopted by other manufacturers as well and had become the most popular code in use at the time of Johnson's directive establishing ASCII as a federal standard.

By 1968, IBM had recognized that at least partial implementation of ASCII would be required but was determined to prevent ASCII from becoming an internal standard. IBM's eventual goal was to get EBCDIC recognized as the standard code. The standards strategy was presented to IBM's Management Committee as follows:

Objectives—

A. Have EBCDIC recognized as an 8–bit D.P. Standard code
B. Contain USASCII to a 7–bit information interchange code (communications)

Strategy—

A. Demonstrate a willingness to release control of EBCDIC
B. Keep USASCII from evolving into the 8–bit D.P. Standard
C. Encourage formal industry standardization of EBCDIC
D. *Then,* if others wish, work with them on an USASCII–8 standard
E. Eventually "back" EBDIC into an interchange standard[26]

IBM's opposition to ASCII implementation was based upon two principles discussed by the management committee: (1) "Implementation of standards are business decisions based on market consideration," and (2) "IBM participation in the adoption of a standard does not commit us to that standard." A key problem was listed as "the timing of release of information to gain maximum value to IBM without the loss of competitive advantage."[27] As a long-run consideration, the implementation of ASCII would have been bad for

IBM because it would have proved that a major standard could be imposed on the industry in spite of IBM's opposition, signaling IBM's loss of control over standards and possibly encouraging other standards efforts. At the immediate time of the Johnson order requiring ASCII, IBM was concerned about the fact that ASCII use would require translation equipment or possible redesign of its machines in use and planned future announcements. IBM took a risk in adopting a new but non-ASCII code in 1965 and could have suffered severe losses if total internal communications use of ASCII had actually been imposed in 1968. IBM's attempt to get EBCDIC accepted as an official standard represented a compromise between IBM's goal of control of standards and protection from complete compatibility and the government's goal of jointly-set standards together with compatibility. A formally standardized EBCDIC would improve compatibility but would reassert IBM's leadership of the industry because the entire industry would be adopting an IBM code rather than one worked out jointly.

IBM directed its efforts to contain ASCII to a communications standard primarily toward government officials and the Business Equipment Manufacturers Association (BEMA). A secondary effort was an educational program on the implications of ASCII directed toward computer users. The two officials most directly concerned with ASCII implementation were Joseph Cunningham of the Bureau of the Budget and Herbert Grosch of the National Bureau of Standards. Besides a number of meetings with Cunningham and Grosch, IBM planned a seminar for both men and their staffs on code technology "of an educational nature and presented in the spirit of cooperating with the government."[28] The seminar was "well received" by the officials involved.[29] Because of the technical nature of the ASCII implementation problems and IBM's advantage in technical sophistication over the government agencies, such seminars and discussions were considered necessary in order to make approrpriate decisions. Not all of IBM's public relations efforts were successful; one spokesman "pointed out the large number of people involved and the difficulties that we have in getting our point of view to prevail."[30]

IBM also lobbied among BEMA members for a delay or elimination of ASCII implementation. Consistent with the IBM strategy of containing ASCII to a communications standard, BEMA passed a resolution in July 1968 requesting that the government not adopt ASCII as a file standard without further development. The resolution further asked that BEMA be allowed to review the ASCII implementation plans before they were formally issued.[31] However, in spite of an IBM campaign, BEMA refused to endorse EBCDIC as code standard.[32] IBM felt that its difficulties in securing BEMA approval was due in part to the fact that "some of their committees are made up of furniture manufacturers and the like who are neither interested or qualified to rule on items regarding internal computer standards."[33] Consequently, the management committee concluded that "some reorganization of BEMA and X-3, the ASA committee charged with computer standards, is necessary to insure the right quality and quantity on key committees."[34]

The failure of BEMA to endorse EBCDIC as a standard caused IBM to drop that program from its strategy. There was little chance of getting favorable action from either ANSI or the government without BEMA support. However, IBM was successful in confining ASCII to an interchange code. When the implementation letter was finally issued in 1969 by the new secretary of commerce, Maurice Stans, it was less strict than had been anticipated, even by IBM.[35] ASCII was required only for communications and not as an internal code. Furthermore, the ASCII requirement could be waived by the head of any agency who felt that efficiency would be improved by not using ASCII.[36] The requirement could be met by building a translator which would convert from whatever internal code the machine used to ASCII. IBM chose the translator approach: "The SDD work in the immediate time period is predicated on accommodation of ASC rather than a full embracement. Although this will allow the government to use ASC, it will also clearly cause some degradation of the systems."[37] The translator approach caused degradation in performance because of the computer time spent translating codes from ASCII to EBCDIC and back again. If all communications were required to be in ASCII without exception, IBM's translator approach would have put it at a competitive disadvantage. However, because agency heads could waive ASCII use for efficiency, and IBM computers were clearly more efficient when not using ASCII, the implementation as written actually allowed extreme freedom to individual agency heads to decide whether or not to use ASCII, reducing its effect as a general standard.

In 1969, IBM announced the System 3 for very small scale users with a code that was neither ASCII nor EBCDIC; a test case for stringency of compatibility requirements on new equipment before the main System 370 announcements in 1970. Herbert Grosch of NBS reacted angrily to the S/3 incompatibility and called on the General Services Administration to boycott the new machines.[38] However, other officials in the government were less concerned. IBM management summed up the reaction as follows:

> The specific criticisms came from the National Bureau of Standards. which naturally has a vested interest in compliance with the ASC code.
> ... this concern is restricted to the Bureau and not spread throughout the federal government agencies.
> ... The MC has requested Commercial Development, Corporate Marketing, and SDD to get together to make sure our NS strategy as regards ASC is sound prior to announcement of the new system.[39]

IBM was able to continue marketing non-ASCII systems because NBS was the only agency strongly concerned with compliance, and the ASCII implementation letter left the decision to agency heads. The ASCII effort did produce an increase in compatibility even though it lacked total success. The computer manufacturers were forced either to use ASCII as the basic code or to offer a translator from their code to ASCII. Consequently, data could be exchanged between computers with noncompatible basic codes, but at a cost in computer time for the translation process. Tapes used within an installation that had only IBM hardware were generally written in EBCDIC to avoid converting and reconverting codes at each step. Those to be transferred to another machine could be written in ASCII if required.

4. CONCLUSIONS AND RECOMMENDATIONS

In summary we see that IBM has generally opposed the development of standards in the computer industry that would result in an increase in computer compatibility. This is to be expected from IBM's market position and is in the company's interest, given its strategy of differentiating its product. In the absence of outside pressures, IBM can control the effective standards of the industry simply by virtue of its market position. Smaller companies are forced to follow IBM's lead in order to compete for IBM customers. IBM can modify the standards at will when so doing will improve its competitive position or allow IBM to improve the technology of its products.

Because of IBM opposition, very little progress has come from (or can be expected from) the American National Standards Institute. This is because ANSI requires a consensus among those affected by the standard for it to become official. Given the voluntary nature of all of ANSI's activities, no change can be expected in this requirement. Only when users became involved in the standardization process, has progress been made. With the exception of the federal government, individual users are so small relative to the market that organizational difficulties and self-interest prevent them from exercising a strong voice in standardization efforts. The federal government has enough market power either to force standards on its own or to organize other users into an effective pressure group. Thus future progress in standards efforts is largely dependent upon how active a role the federal government takes in demanding compatibility.

From a public policy point of view, the advantages of government imposed standards must be weighed against the disadvantages. The primary advantages are freer competition, increased flexibility for the user in choosing equipment and a reduction in the real resources spent converting from one company's standards to another's when an equipment change is made. Control of standards by one company either protects that company's market from competition (if other companies choose separate standards) or imposes extra costs on competitive companies in order to discover and abide by the changing standards of the dominant company. Consequently, imposed standards could remove part of the product differentiation barriers to entry in the industry, as well as reducing the capital-cost barriers to entry through an increase in the ease of constructing an integrated computer system from components produced by diverse manufacturers.

The basic disadvantage of imposed standards is that restrictive standards could lead to a reduction in technical progress or to an inefficient machine configuration designed to abide by the standards. Progress has been extremely rapid in the computer industry, increasing the difficulty of standardization. The arguments made elsewhere in this volume about the difficulty of having the government set good standards in the appliance industry apply with even more force to the computer industry. The product is complex and most of the technical knowledge about it is possessed by the companies, not the government agencies. Standards do affect the design of machines, and it may require intimate knowledge of the design process to calculate the potential of proposed standards for holding back technical progress.

The government's position as a large user gives it the opportunity to increase useful standardization without putting unwieldy legal constraints on the industry. The Brooks Act has established the legal framework for the National Bureau of Standards to set standards for the federal inventory of computers. This power should be used to require standards rather than waiting for manufacturers to set voluntary standards. The fact that the standards are only required for government computers prevents them from slowing progress. If a major innovation is developed which does not fit the established standards framework, the manufacturer could petition the National Bureau of Standards for an exception or a change in standards. Even if a misinformed or unresponsive NBS refused a legitimate request, the computers containing the nonstandard specifications could still be sold to all but the government market. If the innovation was useful, the standards would most likely be changed to allow it either at its introduction or after it had been successfully tested on non-government users. Although the standards would be required only on federal computers, the government buys such a quantity of computers that the federal standards would probably become generally accepted throughout the industry. The government's buying power and the Brooks Act allow the government to set semirequired standards without the inflexible legal restraints that would be required to establish standards by law.

An an example of what could be done, the most pressing current need is standards for the interface of peripheral units with CPUs. Much of the recent competition in the industry has been the result of multiple sources of supply for peripherals compatible with IBM CPUs. Both the user and the independent peripheral manufacturer suffer loss through IBM's control of the interface standards and practice of keeping them secret until the equipment is delivered. The National Bureau of Standards has investigated the feasibility of requiring a single interface standard for all peripherals and CPUs. At the end of

1972, the NBS reported that a single standard was not technologically feasible but recommended a set of specific standards, one for the interface of each type of peripheral unit to CPUs.[40] If these standards were developed and made mandatory for federal government equipment, many users could expect lower prices and increased choice among peripheral units.

Compared with other industries in which self-regulation has operated, the computer industry shows the limits of the approach. Two distinctions can be drawn between the examples discussed in this chapter and the successful examples of self-regulation in farm machinery and home appliances discussed above. The first is a difference in the effect of the standards examined on the industry. Both safety regulations and product certification programs primarily affect the relationship between the industry as a whole and the consumers rather than the relationships among companies. As Hunt argues, appliance makers recognize that consumers have difficulty evaluating the safety of appliances. Consequently it is unprofitable for a single manufacturer to improve the safety of its product. However, if all follow the same safety standards, total industry sales may improve, as the industry obtains a better image in the eyes of consumers. Even if some companies believe that safety standards will reduce total industry profits, they are unlikely to oppose them vigorously because the costs of the standards fall equally on all companies and thus are unlikely to put any company at a competitive disadvantage.

The standards discussed for the computer industry relate to the ability of consumers to switch suppliers, and thus have a significant effect on the competitive strategies among the firms. Consequently, they can be expected to be endorsed by those firms which expect to gain and opposed by those firms which expect to lose from the standards. For example, COBOL was enthusiastically accepted by RCA and Univac and opposed by IBM. ASCII was favored by NCR and opposed by IBM and Honeywell. It is this difference in the way proposed standards affect the various firms that makes voluntary standards through a consensus agreement unworkable. A similar problem was found in the farm machinery industry. Although the industry formulated standards to make parts interchangeable, the standards were not followed by the companies, presumably because interchangeability affected the competitive relationships and therefore would not be accepted voluntarily by the companies that expected to lose from the increased competition.

The second reason why voluntary standards have been less successful in the computer industry than in other examples relates to the structure of the industry. Because IBM is such a dominant company in the industry, IBM's standards become de facto industry standards in the absence of cooperative effort. It is hard to imagine a case where it would be in a company's self-interest to submit to cooperative standards-making if the alternative were to set all standards itself. Public relations considerations require IBM at least to participate in cooperative standards efforts, but not necessarily to abide by the results of the cooperative endeavor unless the results are consistent with IBM's own plans. As IBM's management committee reported about its change of heart on the CODASYL data base proposed standards:

> Our previous concern was that the proposal under study was inconsistent with our product plan, particularly AM-1. Since our December report, AM-1 has been stopped because of poor performance and our probable new direction is much more consistent with the CODASYL work.[41]

Thus, IBM is willing to abide by voluntary standards if they are consistent with its product plan but has no incentive to do so if they are detrimental to IBM's interests. In industries with no dominant firm, there is much more incentive for all firms to cooperate in setting standards than in the computer industry.

Although self-regulation in the computer industry has been much less successful than in the appliance industry, there is nothing in the computer industry examples to contradict Hunt's hypotheses about when self-regulation will be effective.[42] However, two more hypotheses could profitably be added to Hunt's list. First, *self-regulation is more likely to occur in situations where the regulations do not upset the competitive relationships among firms.* Second, *self-regulation is more likely to occur if firms are somewhat balanced in size causing the regulations to affect each firm equally.* The key point is that self regulation is a voluntary process requiring unanimity among the companies affected and therefore will occur primarily in cases where firms view the regulations equally. Any industry which could experience relatively easy price coordination could also achieve self-regulation with relative ease. Industries with a dominant firm, or firms with extremely different outlooks and goals, will have difficulty achieving self-regulation. In those cases, effective standards are unlikely to be achieved without the intervention of consumers or the government.

Notes to Chapter Five

1. Neil MacDonald, "Processing Information Using a Common Machine Language: The American Management Association Conference, February 1954." *Computers and Automation* III (April 1954), 6.

2. "Digital Magnetic Tape Recorders," *Datamation* VI (March-April 1960), 20-21.

3. R. W. Bemer, "The American Standard Code for Information Interchange, Part 2," *Datamation* IX (September 1963), 29-44.

4. Richard F. Clippinger, "The Standards Outlook: Objectives Set," *Datamation* VIII (January 1962), 35.

5. "Happiness is a Thing Called Honeywell," *Datamation* X (March 1964), 17.

6. "Findings of Fact, Telex vs. IBM," Northern District of Oklahoma, no. 72-C-18 and 72-C-89 (September 14, 1973), 147.

7. Gerald Brock, "The United States Computer Industry 1954-1973," (Unpublished Ph.D. dissertation, Harvard University, 1973), 144.

8. Reported in Elmer G. Schuster, *Selective Demand Determinants in the Computer Acquisition Process,* Ph.D. dissertation, The American University, 1969, (Ann Arbor: University Microfilms, Inc.), 30.

9. Speech of Myron Tribus to American National Standards Institute, quoted in *The Magazine of Standards* XLI (January 1970), 25–26.

10. Joseph F. Cunningham, "The Need for ADP Standards in the Federal Community," *Datamation* XV (February 1969), 27.

11. The short range committee consisted of representatives from Burroughs, IBM, Honeywell, RCA, Univac, Sylvania, the Air Material Command of the Air Force and the Bureau of Ships of the Navy.

12. "Some More Facts about COBOL," *Datamation* VI (March-April 1969), 29, 70–71.

13. Joseph F. Cunningham, "Need for ADP Standards," 28; Howard Bromberg, "The COBOL Conclusion," *Datamation* XIII (March 1967), 45–50; "COBOL is the Language!" *Datamation* VI (January-February 1960), 54–55; Charles Phillips, "CODASYL Emphasis Shifting to Development Committee," *Datamation* VI (July-August 1960), 70–71; "RCA Supports Common Business Oriented Language," *Datamation* VI (July-August 1960), 35; "RCA Stirs Simmering COBOL Pot," *Datamation* VI (September-October 1960), 3; Jean E. Sammett, "More Comments on COBOL," *Datamation* VII (March 1961), 33–34; "Codasyl O.K.'s Publication of COBOL-61," *Datamation* VII (July 1961), 40–41; Howard Bromberg, "COBOL and Compatibility," Datamation VII (February 1961), 30–34.

14. Saul Rosen, "Programming Systems and Lanugages, A Historical View," in Saul Rosen, ed. *Programming Systems and Languages* (New York: McGraw-Hill, 1967), 13.

15. Joseph F. Cunningham, "Need for ADP Standards," 27.

16. "Computer Language Standardized," *The Magazine of Standards* XL (October 1969), 25.

17. R. W. Bemer, "The American Standard Code for Information Interchange, Part 1," *Datamation* IX (August 1963), 32–36.

18. "IBM Votes 'No' on Seven Bit Code," *Datamation* VIII, (August 1962), 17, 19.

19. "Onwards Towards ASCII," *Datamation* XII (August 1966), 17.

20. James McCrohan, "Government Sets DP Guidelines," *Datamation* XI (April 1965), 70–71.

21. Ibid.

22. Jack Brooks, "The Federal Government and Computer Compatibility," *Datamation* XV (February 1969), 24–25.

23. Joseph F. Cunningham, "Need for ADP Standards," 26–28.

24. "Feds Adopt ASCII Standard," *Datamation* XIV (April 1968), 153, 155.

25. IBM Management Committee Minutes, May 7, 1968.

26. IBM Management Committee Minutes and Charts of Presentations, Feb. 6, 1968.

27. Ibid.

28. IBM Management Committee Minutes, March 21, 1968.

29. IBM Management Committee Minutes, July 12, 1968.

30. IBM Management Committee Minutes, April 14, 1969.

31. IBM Management Committee Report to the Management Review Committee, "ASCII Review," July 19, 1968.

32. IBM Management Committee Minutes, Nov. 1, 1968.

33. IBM Management Committee Minutes, Feb. 17, 1969.

34. Ibid.

35. IBM Management Committee Minutes, March 17, 1969.

36. Ibid.

37. IBM Management Committee Report to the Management Review Committee, "Standards," October 21, 1969.

38. "Grosch Bucks the System 3," *Datamation* XV (February 1970), 167.

39. IBM Management Committee Report to the Managemen Review Committee, "Standards," October 21, 196⊆

40. E. Drake Lundell Jr., "Common Interface Vetoed, NBS Asks Some Standards," *Computer World* VII (January 17, 1973), 1-2.

41. IBM Management Committee Report to the Management Review Committee, "Standards," July 26, 1971.

42. See Chapter 3 above.

Chapter Six

How Should the Content of Entertainment Television Be Determined? Self-Regulation and the Alternatives

Marc J. Roberts

1. INTRODUCTION

Given that entertainment television might have a significant impact on those who watch it, what institutions and policies should we adopt for producing and regulating this product? Motivated in part by such concerns, other countries have chosen to provide television via government corporations or through organizations controlled by various religious groups. Instead the United States relies on licensed commercial owners to exhibit "leadership" and "responsibility" when it comes to broadcast content, that is to engage in self-regulation.[1] Simultaneously, regulatory authorities, politicians and critics produce a continuous stream of suggestions, pronouncements and demands to provide guidance for the industry. Can this hodgepodge of informal and implicit arrangements be improved upon, and if so, how?

In raising this issue we are forced beyond the usual assumption of welfare economics that tastes are not affected by policy choices. The first step in our analysis, then, will be to explore what criteria we might use to recognize a "good" outcome when tastes are in fact endogenous. Then I will describe and evaluate the performance of current arrangements in light of those criteria. Finally, I will examine various alternative arrangements and explore whether they offer any improvement over what we have now.

The argument leads to the view that less rather than more regulation of program content is desirable, and that to secure variety and effective decentralization, we need significantly to expand the number of television signals available to each viewer, e.g., through cable transmission or home

The author is indebted to Bruce Owen, Jim Rosse and Charles Meyers for stimulating comments and suggestions as this work was being prepared and to Richard Caves for his help at every stage, but especially for his criticisms of earlier versions. Some very helpful research assistance was provided by Suzanna Kayson.

playback devices. Furthermore, until (if ever) such new technology becomes widespread, expanded formal regulation would not necessarily bring very great changes in program content. Such changes as seem likely might or might not be desirable, depending on one's perspective. In sum, since political mechanisms too are often "imperfect," a finding of "market failure" may imply that less rather than more government intervention is the desirable response.

2. WELFARE JUDGMENTS WHEN TASTES ARE ENDOGENOUS

Despite the fashionability of the contrary assumption in theoretical exercises, in controlling television program content we are not simply seeking the one "optimum" outcome. In the real world we do not confront a well-defined opportunity set. It is not clear what is "feasible" or "possible" in technical or institutional terms. Instead, in formulating public policy we are simply seeking a set of social and economic arrangements which we can identify as better than either the current situation or any other alternatives we can identify.[2] In making such judgments, we must have due regard for uncertainty, our limited knowledge and the imperfect reversibility of all arrangements once physical capital and patterns of self-interest become attached to them.

As a way of defining "better" outcomes, let us begin from the economist's usual perspective of individuals' evaluations of their own circumstances. The literature offers two main suggestions for making welfare statements when tastes are affected by experiences. Rothenberg and von Weizsacker suggest that there is a "correct" or "equilibrium" set of preferences.[3] Alternative outcomes are evaluated by asking about the distribution of individual utility levels, as derived when using that "correct" basis for evaluation. Alternatively, Harsanyi considers tastes simply as a means.[4] Welfare judgments are made by considering the distribution of utility levels for different price-income-tastes combinations assuming, of course, that we can make such comparisons among situations in which tastes differ.

Neither of these suggestions is fully satisfactory, for several reasons. First, which tastes are "correct"? Using "later" valuations is surely not sufficient. People can develop bad habits, and this approach would lead to approval of all successful programs of propaganda and indoctrination. On the other hand, considering all tastes ethically equivalent ignores that individuals (and policy makers) may have preferences about their own (and others') tastes and preferences. In that sense tastes are themselves a "good," and a public good at that. Furthermore, more is at issue than just preferences for economic goods. Questions about morality, violence and the image of minority groups are central to the debate about the impact of television broadcasting. And using either the von Weizsacker or Harsanyi formulations would involve measuring each person's "utility," a task whose scientific and psychological reasonableness is much in dispute. Yet we would have to do just that because, as Arrow has pointed out, if all one knew about other people's utilities were arbitrary ordinal index numbers, there would be no way to decide if any given gain to man A was sufficient to justify imposing a given loss on man B.[5]

In order to develop a satisfactory account of what is at stake in regulating television content, we need a model of individual choice behavior psychologically more sophisticated than the economist's usual construct. We need to take account of individuals' attitudes toward their own and others' tastes and toward noneconomic as well as economic goods. The formulation I propose derives from the observation that many divergent psychological theories share the view that individuals are motivated by a moderate number of distinct needs, drives or satisfactions.[6] Every psychological theorist has his own distinct terminology and his own account of the underlying psychological mechanisms. Sidestepping all these disputes, however, I will simply try to capture the insight that subjective experience has a number of dimensions, and that both economic and noneconomic "goods" provide a variety of distinct types of satisfactions or fulfill a variety of needs. For example, houses can both provide shelter and enhance one's status.

Thus I suggest that we describe an individual's experiences in terms of a need/drive/satisfaction space—the dimensions of which will be labeled D^i. These are not arbitrary constructs, but rather are meant to correspond to psychological reality as accurately as we are able to make them, given our limited knowledge. (One illustrative list would be material pleasures, love/ friendship, power/status, duty/morality, etc.) At this point the reader can be left to specify and label these dimensions as he sees fit. Choices over that space will be represented by $Q(D)$—where Q in principle is not observable and has no experiential counterpart. Unlike the D^i's, it is just an index, embodying individuals' values about how to choose among various bundles of experiences.[7] More specifically, let us say that each individual picks some vector x out of the set of all possible choices X. Also, unlike conventional consumer theory where control and target variables are the same, we recognize that each specific x also results in certain values for a distinct vector, r of target variables, according to the relationship $r = r(x)$.[8] Since an individual might well care both about the x's and the r's we can write his overall multidimensional choice function as

$$max \; Q = Q[D^1(x,r(x)), D^2(x,r(x)), \ldots, D^N(x,r(x))]. \tag{1}$$

This formulation reintroduces the old distinction in economics between values and tastes. While $Q(\cdot)$ represents values, tastes can be taken to refer to the structure of the $D(\cdot)$ relationships that generate material satisfactions.[9] The traditional formulation of the "economic problem" can be seen as the maximization of some subset of the D's with respect to some subset of the x's. Whether or not this suboptimization will in fact lead to a maximization of Q depends on the separability of the various relationships; that is, on the effect of economic choices on noneconomic choices and satisfactions.

To introduce yet another complexity, let us call $Q(\cdot)$ the *perfected*, or *idealized* choice function, representing the consistent choices that an individual *would* make if he had perfect information and unlimited time and analytical resources. In practice data are costly; time is limited, both in the long run and the short run, and so is each person's decision-making capability. Men do not perfectly understand the world (i.e., the relationship between target and control variables $r = r(x)$) nor their own psychology (the $D(\cdot)$'s), nor do they have fully consistent and perfected values ($Q(\cdot)$). Thus the globally optimal approach to choice, indeed the only possible one, involves making and then sequentially adjusting imperfect decisions arrived at by using various strategies and rules of thumb to economize on scarce problem-solving capability.[10]

If we try to consider outcomes from the perspective of each individual's experience, there is no way to look at the levels of $Q(\cdot)$ because those are arbitrary and not interpersonally comparable. In contrast, the multiple and presumably psychologically real dimensions of actual experience denoted by the D^i's, can be subject to empirical investigation. Thus, our social welfare function would be of the form:

$$w = w[D_1^1, \ldots, D_1^k, \ldots, D_N^1, \ldots, D_N^k]. \tag{2}$$

Where D_N^k is the kth satisfaction enjoyed by the Nth individual.

Furthermore, our conceptual framework allows us to distinguish among three different ways that broadcast content could affect viewers' behavior.

(i) There might be a change in an individual's psychology, in the experiences he enjoys in various "states of the world." This implies some change in the $D(\cdot)$ functions.

(ii) The change could involve an individual's values, that is, his choices among various bundles of experience. This would involve a change in $Q(\cdot)$.

(iii) The broadcast might simply affect the individual's information about himself, ($D(\cdot)$ and $Q(\cdot)$), or his information about the world and the consequences of his actions—i.e., his beliefs about the $r(\cdot)$ functions that link control and target variables.

Using (1) and (2) as a framework for making policy choices (especially when the above changes take place) does help to overcome two of the limitations of the traditional approach noted previously. First, the assumed multidimensionality of experience lends itself naturally to our considering not only a viewer's direct reaction to TV programming but also his responses to both his own and others' psychology and values and to the larger world. In addition, insofar as this model is psychologically more accurate, it offers greater possibilities for the development of valid, reliable and operational data-gathering procedures. But the problem of which tastes to use, when tastes change, remains unresolved. Do we want to use current tastes, equilibrium tastes, correct tastes or what? And the possibility of consumer error, which we have also introduced, raises still additional difficulties. Do we want to use each viewer's actual (and perhaps misinformed) reactions or his "idealized" response with unlimited knowledge and calculating ability?

In practice, regardless of how we answer these normative questions, individual reactions on the basis of *current* tastes are all we can reasonably hope to collect. If these are not the correct, informed or equilibrium responses we would like to know about, we have little alternative but to use them nevertheless, with whatever cautious interpretation seems in order. Given these limits, data good enough to resolve crucial problems could well be so costly as to make the process of looking at individual responses not very attractive as a choice strategy. In particular, Harsanyi's suggestion that we run large-scale social experiments to bring about and evaluate various alternative taste-price-income options seems quite impractical in the context of television programming.

In what follows I will use whatever can be easily found out about current individual responses to broadcast content. But the difficulties just noted suggest that we need to look beyond the "consumer sovereignty" framework we have been discussing thus far. One option would be to consider the psychology, values and behavior of individuals as themselves being an object of public choice, analogous to merit goods.[11] While to some extent such considerations are ethically unavoidable, there are both practical and philosophical objections to making such matters the explicit focus of administrative or legislative decisions.

Insofar as we care about the impact of broadcasting (and not just what is *shown*) we face very great inference problems in making decisions about content. Many aspects of the society play a role in transmitting culture and information and shaping psychology and values. Determining the differential impact of entertainment television content on such variables is difficult indeed. Presumably this is a long, slow, cumulative process. As a result, the existing experiments, which focus on an individual's immediate reactions to sex or violence on a given show, are largely beside the point.[12] It is even difficult to conceive of realistic circumstances under which more relevant data could be generated.

More fundamentally, there are also objections from political theory to making formal public choices on those matters. Such decisions are sure to be quite divisive. There is little agreement in the society as to what would be a "correct" portrayal of many aspects of the world. There is still less agreement about whether entertainment television should even try to be "accurate" in any sense. A prominent TV producer recently asserted that as a patriotic act he intentionally portrayed the police as more effective and upright than they were, as an antidote to the social confusion of the times.[13] Others have explicitly defended fantasy and escapism (i.e., inaccuracy) as a legitimate aspect of art and entertainment.[14] The debate over values is even more explicit. For example, what attitude should television convey toward various types of sexual conduct? Trying to resolve those issues through formal political or administrative mechanisms would implicitly legitimate the debatable notion that the society has the right to manipulate the media consciously for the purpose of shaping citizens' beliefs and values. Creating such institutions would thus involve a significant and undesirable centralization of social power.

The problem is that achieving specific short-run goals can conflict with our values about the long-run procedural and institutional structure of the society. Institutions and practices are analogous to problem-solving strategies; they direct our attention in specific ways and make alternative policies and outcomes more or less likely. Procedural and structural values, as rules for choosing institutions, are in turn like rules for choosing strategies. They save us from the costly task of reanalyzing in each case the implications of proceeding in various ways.[15]

In trying to achieve good by controlling television programming, we could all too easily create arrangements which violate our procedural values, which do not conform to our rules of thumb about institutional structures. Especially in this area, I contend, there is a very strong case for increasing the diffusion of power among independent centers of decision making. Simple considerations of personal freedom—which is both a means and an end—surely imply such a view. The artistic, personal and social consequences of the imposition of an official approach to the content of entertainment, as in the case of "socialist realism" in the USSR, are obviously unattractive to many.[16] Furthermore insofar as anyone believes that tastes are not all "relative," and that it is possible to discover or develop "better" tastes or values, there is much to be said for decentralization as a "research strategy." Do recognize, however, that by restricting anyone's capacity to do "harm" we also limit anyone's ability to do "good" by manipulating broadcast content. Decentralization would imply that the president could not try to use the content of entertainment TV to discourage drug abuse, as he in fact tried to do recently, any more than he could use it to discourage political dissent.[17]

Our options are actually too complex to simply be described along the centralized-decentralized continuum. Any institutions for providing programming will inevitably be constrained to some extent by cultural traditions and laws on obscenity if by nothing else. Expanding those constraints means allowing the internal, bureaucratic choice processes of the producing organizations to control output "quality," as opposed to using formal, external political mechanisms. Yet both those internal bureaucratic arrangements and the processes that impose external constraints could be organized in many different ways. In particular, the extent of variety in the institutional system that provides programming is of substantial significance. Recent work suggests that the behavior of various private and public organizations depends not only upon their factor and product market circumstances but also upon their internal organization and the kinds of individuals in key positions—especially when external constraints are lax enough to allow for alternative strategy choices.[18] This means that expanded programming opportunities will lead to the multiplication of distinguishable viewpoints only if producing entities with differing motives, structures and opportunities are at work.

Do note, however, that variety in this sense has little to do with the measures of variety that several economists have used in studying television programming.[19] They analysed the extent to which programs of different types (action, drama, comedy, etc.) were available at any one time in a given area. This does not speak to the issue of whether those broadcasts exhibited the more basic differences of perspective and belief that are relevant to this argument. Nor does variety in the sense used here mean catering to special tastes like opera, or to those minorities who prefer program types not currently available.[20] Rather the focus is on the views and values, images and attitudes communicated within the set of "light entertainment" programming which predominates today on broadcast television.

In practice, the point where any one person chooses to strike the balance between doing good on the one hand and decentralization and variety on the other will often depend on how he expects to like the outcome of alternative arrangements. Those concerned with the possible moral corruption of others are more likely to prefer a mutual veto approach, where no show can offend any significant segment of opinion. In contrast, minorities with tastes that might be objectionable to others will tend to argue for fostering maximum variety and providing something for everyone.

Rather than trying to work out a more detailed normative position in the abstract, it is more useful to get a better idea of what the situation we are concerned with is actually like. For the moment I will assume that, in varying ways and degrees, we all care about how viewers evaluate the current pattern of program content, what impact that content has on viewers and how that content is determined. What, then, are our current arrangements like, what results do they produce, and how can we evaluate that situation?

3. THE CURRENT SITUATION

The entertainment programming currently available on American television reflects the objectives and the opportunities of the three television networks which produce the bulk of these broadcasts. Program content is a problem for network management exactly because the pursuit of profit has consistently provoked the threat of, or demand for, increased external regulation. The result has been a continuing effort at self-regulation, undertaken both informally and via explicit agreements, including the National Association of Broadcasters code.[21] The networks must balance current profitability against the risks of endangering their own long-run autonomy, and do so within constraints generated by the absence of full vertical integration within the industry.

The programs that result are typically polished and well produced. They often follow traditional formulas or imitate other recently successful shows. They generally take a sanguine view of contemporary American society and institutions, although normal life-situations are seldom depicted. Action, adventure, suspense and violence are found in abundance, as is broad comedy. The treatment of potentially controversial material, such as sexual conduct or the role of minorities, reflects a cautious attempt to follow current trends. What we see, I contend, is the result of an ongoing attempt by management to compromise among evolving political and social pressures both manifest and latent.

The competitive forces on television broadcasting are complicated because, like other advertising-supported media, it operates simultaneously in two markets: those for entertainment and for the transmission of advertising messages. Success in the first is crucial to success in the second. One can only "sell" the viewers one has. Even giving programs away at zero price is not sufficient to guarantee audiences, since viewers pay a substantial opportunity cost in watching any one show—including the cost of not watching other broadcasts.

The market for television advertising time is elaborately organized. While networks have posted rate cards, negotiated agreements are the rule on major sales. An advertiser can get a better deal if he risks waiting to buy until a week or two before show time.[22] The networks compete for advertising not only with each other and with other media, but also with individual stations. Stations can sell certain amounts of advertising time around network programs or when showing non-network fare. Most stations, in fact, are independently owned and are only tied to the network by an affiliation contract (FCC rules prevent networks from owning and operating more than five VHF stations).[23] Typically stations are represented by professional time brokers, while advertisers retain advertising agencies whose media specialists do the purchasing. Given expert buyers and sellers, any price differences are generally due to real, as opposed to image or reputational, differences in services provided. (Newspapers are not in fact a perfect substitute for network TV for some purposes.) This is a responsive, competitive market where changing supply and demand balances are signaled rapidly.

The rates individual stations and networks charge for various shows depend critically on audiences—since competition tends to equalize those on a "cost per thousand" viewers basis. This is why ratings are, and will remain, so important to all decision making, no matter how much the various types of ratings data can be criticized on a statistical basis.[24]

Intra- and inter-media competition have clear effects on program content. First, production costs in dramatic series shows have steadily increased—reflective of improved "production values" like more location filming.[25] While this movement was provoked in part by the success of movies on television (which are generally expensively produced), it is far from clear that the elasticity of total viewing with such expenditures is high enough to make current spending levels jointly profit maximizing. Instead, it appears that even a three-member oligopoly cannot tacitly agree to limit such competitively tempting and difficult-to-monitor product competition. At the same time, the networks have succeeded in shortening the season and expanding reruns, which does serve to keep costs down. Such coordination, however, focuses on a parameter which can be noticed at essentially zero cost.[26]

Similarly, for competitive reasons the networks tend to employ as much violent action as they feel will be accepted without overly risking public intervention. Industry executives believe that viewers want to see more happening on the screen than just "talking heads." The dramatic tension created by fights, shootings, car chases and so on, it is said, serve to attract and involve viewers and discourage them from switching channels.[27] One of the more subtle aspects of such programming is the implied moral code, the need to present private (or public) violence as legitimate, provided only the person involved is really the "good guy." You cannot build a show around someone doing the "wrong" thing week after week, if only because self-regulation requires that evil not be rewarded. For similar reasons, shows tend not to portray normal family groups, but rather to concentrate on loners or single-parent situations.[28] This allows the star more flexibility for adventuring, provides the basis for various love interests and gives (at least part of) the audience something to fantasize about.

The same market pressures, paradoxically enough, caused the cancellation of several apparently highly successful shows, including Red Skelton, Lawrence Welk and Jackie Gleason. Partly in response to magazine advertiser pressures, ABC television began to emphasize the fact that its nominally smaller audiences were younger, more urban, had more purchasing power and hence were more attractive to advertisers. The increased interest in "demographics" that resulted helped to bring about a refinement and expansion of the information provided by the rating services. By provoking a significant advertiser response, such claims in turn forced all the networks to reevaluate their schedules. At CBS in particular, which had a significantly older audience, this issue became central to an internal power struggle between Robert Wood, the new network president and Michael Dann, long-time programming vice-president. Wood won; Gleason and Skelton were canceled with much fanfare, and Dann left the network.[29]

The same arguments led to brief experimentation with shows with younger protagonists who would deal with "relevant" social problems. By and large, those shows did not attract viewers and did not survive. Perhaps this was because, as one executive suggested, the youth they were directed at were not attracted by the "compromises" television had to make in dealing with such themes.[30]

Finally, intermedia competition is also evidence in television's treatment of sexuality. In 1973 the NAB code was revised to allow the treatment of sexual subjects previously unacceptable.[31] Extramarital and premarital sex, homosexuality, abortion and so on all rapidly became subjects of television treatment. Indeed, one of the highest rated shows of the 1973-74 season, "A Case of Rape," sported a title—not to mention a subject—taboo only a few years previously. Such changes occurred for several reasons. The increasing frankness of motion pictures both demonstrated the gains to be made in this direction and provided a competitive incentive for broadcasting to move along those lines. Those changes also reflected and helped to create a changing climate of public opinion which diminished the risks and protests such themes would once have entailed.[32] But it was profitability that led the networks to alter their behavior when they thought that the frontiers of acceptability had sufficiently shifted.

The networks must make such programming decisions in the midst of much uncertainty. It is difficult indeed to know what the public will choose to watch. Since new shows are often scheduled opposite successful shows, the success rate of new ventures is quite low—one-half to two-thirds, or even more, lasting only one season. In part the success rate is so low because success is stringently defined—an audience share of 28 to 30 percent.[33] But why retain a show doing less well than this when its replacement just might do better?

Such uncertainty, in turn, leads to a tendency toward programming cycles and imitation. A proven idea will be used again and again to minimize the risks of new shows.[34] However, most such cycles occur with at least a one-season lag because of the eighteen-month period required for program development. The program which eventually does get on the air usually begins as a brief "treatment" of a story idea. It then must pass through successive stages as it is developed, scripted and shot as a pilot episode.[35] At each stage costs increase rapidly and the number of projects a network pursues correspondingly decreases. Throughout, the risks involved create a bias for using program sources with "a proven track record." By using such suppliers, network executives not only lower risks but are also in a position to defend their own actions as plausible in the all-too-likely event of the show's failure.

The nature of the relationship between networks and suppliers also has implications for program content. Most suppliers are independent producers or companies (of quite varying size) whose financial arrangements with the networks are not at all standardized. A network generally contributes some share of the capital for producing the show in return for some rerun rights or foreign rights or a percentage take or whatever.[36] Because success breeds success, producers have more to gain and less to lose than the network by producing shows which attract viewers, even if they run greater risk of public outcry or government intervention than the networks might prefer. Thus, with respect to both sex and violence, the networks find themselves engaged in a continuing effort to "communicate the realities of Washington" to the "creative" community.[37] In these circumstances, a normal, arms-length market relationship would not serve to transmit a sufficiently complex set of signals. Instead, a form of quasi-vertical integration arises, with the networks' production and program practices departments often maintaining intimate day-to-day working relationships with suppliers. When a disagreement arises as to content, a bargaining process often takes place;[38] and on a successful show, those associated with the program possess significant bargaining power since they cannot be replaced without risking loss of the show or at least seriously diminishing its effectiveness.

Different risks and benefits from programming results also account for the now almost universal trend toward having the network oversee program development. In the 1950s, advertising agencies often took the entrepreneurial role of finding a show for a client and then delivering the whole package to the network.[39] Today advertisers typically buy only announcement time in and around the programs the network has scheduled and can thus reduce their risks by spreading their investments over a number of projects. The networks—which stand to lose more if there were expanded regulation—gain greater control over the details of program content. The networks' concern with content is especially great because they believe that a significant segment of the audience will continue to watch whatever channel it turns to first. Hence the "costs" of a low rating are even higher to the network (whose schedule for the rest of the evening suffers) than to the sponsors associated with the show. A show which a sponsor might be willing to keep going for prestige reasons may, therefore, be a bad bargain for the network concerned.

A sponsor with a substantial commitment to a regular show (or his advertising agency) will usually review scripts before episodes are produced.[40] In general, sponsors are most concerned about images related directly to their own products—although they have on occasion become more extensively involved.[41] After much adverse publicity about their role in early years, their current influence is apparently more limited, in part by the predominence of the network as packager. The low frequency of sponsor interference, however, also no doubt reflects the effectiveness of network self-censorhip, which makes greater activity on their part unnecessary. But when the sponsors do get very concerned, as they did in the case of the cancellation of the Smothers Brothers (a comedy/variety show notable for its off-color humor and antiwar editorializing) they do appear to have some influence.[42]

Given the risks of program development, there has been a steady attrition in the number of organizations supplying shows to the networks. Indeed the typical financial arrangements are such that outside producers do not make money unless the show is successful enough to go into reruns or a second year of production—something that happens only to 5% to 15% of all shows shot as pilots.[43] This seems to imply that suppliers are at best risk-neutral or even "risk lovers" of the sort analyzed by Friedman and Savage—accepting unfair gambles in the hope of major gains.[44] Alternatively, many may believe that their own superior talent confers on them an above average chance of success. The large rewards reaped by those associated with successful shows has to be seen in this context.

In addition to problems with suppliers, networks' programming choices are also constrained by the behavior of affiliated stations. Those stations do not always "clear" network shows, in part for financial reasons. The payment by the network to the affiliate (to compensate the latter for "clearing" a network broadcast) generally is less than the value of the advertising time the affiliate loses in the process.[45] Affiliates cannot afford not to "clear" too many shows, however, for fear of losing audiences. Given this basic financial context, affiliates can and have refused to clear shows whose content, in their view, might be objectionable in their particular community. Widespread non-clearance is very dangerous to the network because of its impact on audiences and hence advertising rates (including those for succeeding shows).

Because programming is aimed at national "average" tastes, affiliates in regions with more extreme attitudes are those that tend to be subject to local pressures; whether they come from newspaper editorials, protest meetings or informal social contacts. In practice, this has occurred most often in conservative areas, especially in the South and Midwest. For example, pressure from affiliates in those areas is acknowledged to have contributed to CBS's decision to cancel the Smothers Brothers.[46] Similarly, fear of widespread non-clearance in the South also appears to have delayed the development of programming with black leads.[47] Indeed, the efforts of the FCC to encourage and preserve local ownership of stations to some extent only serves to increase exactly this sort of responsiveness.

However, no one aspect of the situation necessarily dominates forever—especially with other aspects of the environment changing significantly. In the case of minority representation, changing social attitudes, the threat of outside regulation and the discovery by advertisers (and the movies) of the black audience has produced notable changes in recent years.[48] The networks now keep close track of minority representation in their programming in order to implement the self-regulatory process.

Overall, the threat of increased public regulation apparently provides the greatest incentive to pursue policies opposed to short-run profit maximization. For example, recent concern over children's television has led to formal industry agreements on limiting commercial time and commercial content on such shows, as well as to announced intentions to lower the violence depicted.[49] Similarly, some years ago, at the height of agitation over evening TV violence, at least one network had special meetings with its producers to outline revised guidelines on content. As one network executive depicted the change:

"It used to be that at the end of the show, the hero shot the villain and the second lead said, "Well, that saves the taxpayers some money." Now the bad guy is injured just enough to take him prisoner, and as he is rushed off in an ambulance someone says, "He will have his day in court."[50]

Over the years, the Congress, and especially the Senate, have generally been the focal point of concern over broadcast content. The FTC only becomes involved in television where advertising is concerned. The FCC, fearful of raising the spectre of censorship, has limited its own inquiries in license renewals to the amount of programming of various types (e.g., educational, news, religious, etc.) and to the issue of "balance" and "community service" in programming; and that renewal process has been largely automatic. Furthermore, any expanded outside interference in content would appear to require new legislation, which also implies that congressional opinion is critical. The fact that all television stations operate on federal licenses, their terms subject to legislative specification, certainly helps to increase industry sensitivity.

Television violence has appeared as the subject of congressional hearings again and again in the last fifteen years.[51] Yet the various subcommittee chairmen who have initiated those hearings have not, in general, been faced with traditional interest groups pressing for such action. The political gains to be achieved were primarily in terms of national media exposure and reputation. Thus, like other areas of "public interest" politics (auto safety, environmental protection), the political system has proved capable of inflicting concentrated, individually acute costs to secure diffuse, individually small benefits—the reverse of what traditional "pressure group" analysis would suggest.[52] The lure of possible national office and the expanded role of the Senate as the starting place for such candidates appears capable of generating such "exceptional" results on a regular basis. Violence on television is an ideal issue for such a crusade because it is a cause that demonstrates a man's moral vision and his concern with the average voter while making few, if any, enemies. Since the airwaves are nominally public property, and broadcasters do have "responsibilities" as licensees, such concerns seem all the more legitimate.

Under current arrangements then, government influence over content is most likely to occur around issues where the virtuous position is evident and apparently noncontroversial (note the anti-drug abuse campaign mentioned earlier). National loyalty also has generated such pressures under certain circumstances. In addition to several notable experiences of the 1950s, a prime example is the delay in the broadcast of a controversial show about returning Vietnam prisoners, "Sticks and Bones" (with substantial affiliate pressure in the latter case).[53] In contrast, sexual morality has generally not played the same role, in part because some groups have always vigorously favored less restrictive standards.

Many of the subtle effects of external pressures on programming have never appeared as explicit controversies or disputes. Violence has been an overt issue because commercial pressures continue to push programming in that direction. Where there is no incentive to risk controversy, the constraints are seldom visible because effective self-regulation keeps content well within "safe" limits. Most notably, the generally positive portrayal of American life and institutions reflects the same forces and processes. Recently several critics and commentators have discussed the generally favorable, even unrealistic, view of doctors, policemen and so on given in television broadcasting.[54] The extent and causes of doctors' very high incomes and the systematic corruption of the police in many cities seldom if ever appear in entertainment programming. But why produce such programming? It would lead only to much controversy and criticism from the relevant interest groups while offering no significant commercial advantages.

Not all pressures come through congressional channels. Sometimes groups simply ask for changes while their recourse to governmental or political mechanisms remains in the background as an implicit (or explicit) possibility. Nor are all claims equally successful. CBS refused to cancel the controversial rerunning of two episodes of "Maude" about abortion, despite intense pressure from the Catholic Church.[55] Yet the network did cancel a whole series, "Briget Loves Bernie," which had been objected to by Orthodox Jews for showing interfaith marriage in a favorable light.[56] In the first case, the network ran several risks if it had agreed: countercomplaints from the women's movement, trouble with a notoriously difficult but successful producer, the loss of revenue from a successful show and the encouragement of further attempts at "censorship" from special interest groups. This last possibility was especially serious since more-explicit sexual subjects are clearly the direction in which profitablity is now propelling programming. Finally, only two episodes were involved, and the storm would soon pass. In the second case, continuing the series meant risking a continuing debate. Also, there were no organized pro-intermarriage forces on the other side to be offended. Perhaps most significantly, although it got high ratings, "Briget Loves Bernie" was to some extent being carried by the shows before and after it, both of which attracted even larger audiences. Thus, a switch might even be profitable since a still stronger show might be found.

In all, programming is the crucial strategic decision affecting the profitability both of the network and of the owned-and-operated stations associated with them. The risks and uncertainties are great, the information poor, and many unquantifiable consequences must be weighed. Not surprisingly, therefore, these decisions are centralized in the hands of top management. While various parts of the organization all have their input (sales, affiliate relations, programming, etc.), crucial problems routinely go to the network president—or higher, since all the networks are parts of larger corporate structures.[57] Even at a preliminary stage, in developing ideas, scripts and so forth, the vice-president for programming will be involved in most even moderately significant choices. Thus, at least as far as show selection is concerned, top management can directly implement strategic and policy choices. (Altering the more subtle aspects of continuing shows is more difficult, as noted previously.)

To keep matters in perspective, the major networks are not the only source of television shows. About 80% of the population can receive either or both a noncommercial and a non-network commercial station.[58] Furthermore, not all the broadcasts on network affiliates come from the network. Yet the non-network entertainment programming on commercial stations is essentially indistinguishable from network fare. Old movies, reruns, and game shows constitute the bulk of such efforts. Only public television offers any significant variety as to institutional structure, incentive patterns and the type of output that results. Yet while BBC imports and foundation-supported children's programming have been major "successes," non-commercial television hardly offers an alternative to the bulk of network prime-time programming.

The reactions of viewers to all this programming appears to be complex. Two parallel national samples in 1960 and 1970 reveal that general attitudes toward television became discernably less favorable over the decade. For example, in 1970, 27% thought TV provided "too much" escape from everyday life whereas 15% held that view in 1960.[59] Other polls, including a Roper study done in 1972, show similar results.[60] On the other hand, at least one poll suggested that viewers seemed to enjoy shows slightly more in 1970 than in 1960. Furthermore, over the decade viewing increased in all age groups, but especially among the 25-50-year-old bracket. In 1960, these people watched less than those older or younger—but not so in 1970. (However, much of this increase occurred in early evening hours, and reflected expanded news audiences.)[61] It is also notable that in both years, better educated individuals found broadcasts less enjoyable and were more likely to say that they themselves spent too much time watching television (roughly one in four so responded).[62] A clear majority of viewers say that they prefer some recent programming changes, including the increases in evening movies, expanded sports on weekends and having more shows with blacks in prominent roles, although they were nearly evenly divided on the desirability of the decline of the Western.[63]

The picture that emerges is of a medium whose programming has managed to capture the attention (but not the devotion or respect) of its audiences—except in the news area. The extent to which viewers' negative evaluation of television is a "general" belief, as opposed to one produced to impress an interviewer, is difficult to say. No survey has really tried to elicit from viewers their opinions about the impact of television upon them. Yet the available data suggest that while people are indeed "buying" more of the "good" of television broadcasting than ever before, a substantial proportion of them are not happy with either the programming or their own use of it. Perhaps such doubts are just a routinized cultural gesture—a secularization of Puritan suspicions of dancing, the theater and having a good time. And no doubt much of the concern with television and violence amounts to a rather naive "devil theory" that seeks a simple and superficial cause for a complex and deeply rooted aspect of the society and its functioning. But the fact that much of the recent discussion centers around children's programming does imply that the "educational" (i.e., taste- and value-forming) aspects of programming are clearly at issue in the public mind. Indeed, a recent network "corporate image" advertisement explicitly stressed the "pro-social" motivational message of its new and nifty children's television show.[64] The multidimensional choice model reviewed earlier implies that we have to take these self-conscious concerns into account, along with any expressed or exhibited satisfactions, in evaluating the impact of broadcasting on viewers.

For me, at least, several aspects of the structure and content of current broadcasting do raise serious normative problems; notably, the uncritical viewpoint of American society and the legitimization of righteous violence. Scientific difficulties really do prevent us from knowing how important broadcasting is as a source of such ideas and attitudes. Still, considering the ideas themselves as a "merit good," they are, nevertheless, not obviously highly desirable—at least not to me. When one observes that this result comes from a system which is structurally concentrated, homogeneous and much subject to organized social and political pressures, the evaluative conclusion that emerges is not entirely positive. On the other hand, our problem is not whether the current system is perfect but whether we can identify ways of improving it.

4. ALTERNATIVES

One response to violence, the limited role of minorities and so on would be to develop more formal and confining constraints on program content; for example, through an administrative agency or by means of more explicit legislation enforced in the courts or via an expanded industry effort at cooperative self-regulation. Perhaps because direct government action has implications of censorship and raises possible first-amendment problems, expanded self-regulation has been the option most seriously considered. In 1969, Senator Pastore proposed the creation of a joint industry prescreening board, focused especially on violence; a proposal which was at first accepted by both NBC and ABC, and only failed because of CBS objections.[65]

Yet it is far from clear that such a step would be desirable. Such measures would centralize social power and produce still greater homogenization of perspective in broadcasting. Furthermore, while such regulation might control obvious aspects of programming, like the depiction of violence, it is not at all clear that it could or would get to more subtle issues like the attitudes expressed toward the legitimacy of violence in various circumstances. Similarly, insofar as more formalized controls have any impact relative to sexual morality and the portrayal of American life, they seem likely to move content in a more conservative or traditional direction. Special-interest groups like the Catholic Church would undoubtedly prove more effective in influencing administrative proceedings than in having an impact on overt political decisions. At the same time, more regulation does not seem likely to produce massive changes in program content. The extant process of self-regulation does a good job of avoiding major arguments with powerful interests groups. Indeed, it is possible (as Hunt notes in his essay elsewhere in this volume) that because of risk-aversion and poor information, self-regulation could go even further than external regulation would in fact require.

What is it about television that makes the notion of controls over content seem peculiarly legitimate? Movies, books and newspapers also influence individuals, and all operate with few if any limits on what they portray. The relative ease of access to TV programs appears to create a sense that the viewer does not really choose what he sees. Together with the small number of channels, this view leads to the notion that somehow programs are *imposed* on people and that they therefore must be defended from them. Perhaps we should rely more on the principle of consumer sovereignty—with all its obvious limitations—given the political and social risks of doing otherwise.

An alternative to more regulation would be reforming the current structure to increase both decentralization and variety. The FCC has, to an extent, been concerned with such matters. It has tried to promote UHF broadcasting to expand the number of signals available in each area and has imposed the so-called prime-time access rule which both limits the role of the networks in non-network program supply and restricts the amount of pro-gramming a station can use from network sources.[66] These measures have been justified in part as devices for expanding the number of independent sources of programming and program decision making. Unfortunately, such policies are not an effective response to the structural problems we have identified. Non-network program suppliers face many of the same constraints and incentives as do the networks, nor is their output readily distinguishable from network broadcasts except, perhaps, by its less expensive mode of production.

A different approach to expanding output, urged by Noll, Peck and McGowen, would involve changing the allocation of stations among cities and increasing the power and range of some in order to permit the creation of additional networks. They do not even claim, however, that such changes would necessarily increase variety in programming in the sense being discussed here. Instead, the justification for the proposal is that viewers have exhibited a willingness to pay significant sums for access to an expanded number of essentially similar programming services.[67]

All these schemes are confined by the limited capacity of the electromagnetic spectrum. Television signals use a great deal of that capacity— and the more of the spectrum devoted to TV, the less there is for other competing and also valuable uses.[68] Furthermore, in order to prevent inter-ference, the location and power of transmission facilities does have to be made consistent by some process. Thus, so long as current technology provides the basis for transmitting television signals, we can expect that those signals will be both limited in number and provided by organizations sensitive to the political system that controls their most basic operating resource. Furthermore, so long as each program uses a significant share of that apparently scarce public resource, issues of propriety and public responsibility (i.e., calls for the self-regulation of content) are sure to arise.

Fortunately, several technologies offer the possibility of shifting television signals from a relatively scarce public medium to a relatively abundant private one—notably cable television and various home playback recording systems.[69] While some controls are likely to be present under any scheme, alternative systems could legitimate a withdrawal of political and social intervention from the programming process. Especially if the new structure allows viewers to pay on a per show basis (via pay TV over the cable, or by buying recordings), the image of "unchoosing" or "unwilling" consumers may become less salient in our social decision-making on this issue. Of course, new technology does not have to produce such results. The FCC, for example, has chosen to try to treat cable TV operators as "broadcasters," as opposed to common carriers, precisely in order to deploy all the social, political and legal pressures that now constrain the over-the-air system. Given our analysis, this seems to be exactly the wrong way to proceed on these matters.

By limiting centralized control over content, each person's favorite socialization/informational goal for entertainment television may be made less attainable. With more variety, it would tend to become less easy to impose one sort of signal or another on viewers. People will be better able to avoid "good" shows if they want to, although from many perspectives there ought to be more "good" shows available. The possibility arises that the audience will become fractionalized in the way that the radio audience is today, with devotees of various types of music (including various minority groups) paying special attention to "their" stations. Such self-segregation would diminish the "melting pot" role of the medium—for good or ill, depending on one's perspective. At the same time, a real multiplication of perspectives for the "middle brow" mass audience would also require the existence of program sources organized and financed in a variety of ways (e.g., permanent funding for the public television sector, as Levin discusses elsewhere in this volume). The somewhat outlandish offerings that have appeared on the public access channels on the New York cable system do suggest the breadth of perspectives, now largely unavailable, that could become accessible with a new institutional arrangements.[70]

We should recognize, however, that not everyone would perceive himself as better off under the reforms being discussed. Individuals who enjoy current broadcast fare, now pay for it in the form of higher goods prices to support advertising expenditures. Any shift to direct payment would benefit non-viewers over viewers, low viewers over high viewers, and people who purchase more of those commodities heavily advertised on television over those who purchase less. It would also benefit those who would prefer to view "something else" but cannot find it on the limited number of channels now available. With a pay scheme they might be able to support programming they found more desirable. In contrast, fans of current fare, who also paid directly for programming, would find the direct cost per viewer higher than the indirect cost they now pay. The remaining (smaller number) of viewers no longer would be able to see shows that were, in effect, supported by both non-viewers and those with other tastes.

Notice that the expansion of channels will also allow television to cater to minorities with respect to program type, as well as potentially making possible the multiplication of perspectives within the "light entertainment" category. At the same time, the value and meaning of such a change needs to be examined carefully. Nowhere is it written on stone tablets that television "has to" or "should" provide a mixture of all media functions. The (effectively) zero short-run marginal costs of an additional viewer imply that decreasing average costs exist in very strong form in this industry. Such technological and economic imperatives inevitably do and will move either broadcast or wire television in the direction of being a "mass" medium. Television seldom offers either highly specialized information or superior "serious" music; but this is neither surprising nor necessarily very unfortunate when there are widely available and inexpensive printed and recorded materials to provide those services. Thus, even after relaxing the channel constraint and instituting a pay system, we may not be able to see and hear good Bach played regularly on Thursday nights at a "reasonable" price. Given the quality of TV sound systems and the costs of production, such programming efforts just may not be able to attract enough viewers in competition with tape, record and radio alternatives. The same can be said about the potential market for economics lectures. Thus, the actual distribution of viewers over options, even in a system with no effective channel constraint, is likely to be significantly more highly concentrated than in radio. In the latter case, production costs are so low that those with minority tastes can support programming of sufficiently good quality that they are not driven to choose high-budget–high-quality majority programming instead. Yet the reverse could easily occur in many-channel television.

The overall conclusion of this analysis is, I am afraid, quite negative. A lengthy discussion of morality and economics leads to the suggestion that the way we should regulate the product in this instance is to de-regulate it; even relaxing the implicit controls and self-regulation which now characterize the industry. The argument ultimately turns on the dangers of anyone having well-developed control over the "educational" functions of entertainment television. This analysis, therefore, would not necessarily persuade someone who believed strongly in the desirability of certain values and who felt that some explicit controls would lead to programming that would significantly foster the norms he favored. Given the limits of our discriptive, and especially our normative models, the analysis here represents but a first, and very rough, cut at public policy with respect to a particularly complex and illusive dimension of product quality.

Notes to Chapter Six

1. For a survey of the regulatory situation in the industry see W. B. Emery, *Broadcasting and Government.* (East Lansing: Michigan State University Press, 1971). The best treatment of the economics of the industry is R. G. Noll, M. J. Peck, and J. J. McGowen, *Economic Aspects of Television Regulation.* (Washington, D.C.: The Brookings Institution, 1973). Two more informal, but useful, works are L. Brown, *Television, The Business Behind the Box.* (New York: Harcourt, Brace, Javonovich, 1971); and E. Barnouw, *The Image Empire.* (New York: Oxford University Press, 1970).

2. This implies rejecting Samuelson's formulation in "The Evaluation of Real National Income," *Oxford Economic Papers,* 2, no. 1 (January 1950), p. 129. On the ambiguity of technical possibilities see Z. Griliches, "Comment," in *The Rate and Direction of Inventive Activity,* published for the National Bureau of Economic Research (Princeton, N.J.: Princeton University Press, 1962), p. 346. For a full exposition of this point see M. J. Roberts, "Social Choice Criteria: A Normative Approach," Harvard Institute of Economic Research Discussion Paper no. 223, (December 1971).

3. J. Rothenberg, "Welfare Comparisons and Changes in Tastes," *American Economic Review,* 43 (December 1953), pp. 885-889 and C. C. von Weizsacker, "Notes on Endogenous Changes of Tastes," *Journal of Economic Theory,* 3 (1971), pp. 345-72.

4. J. Harsanyi, "Welfare Economics of Variable Tastes," *Review of Economic Studies,* 21 (1953-54), pp. 204-13.

5. K. Arrow, "Notes on the Theory of Social Choice, 1963," in *Social Choice and Individual Value,* second edition. (New York: John Wiley and Sons, 1963).

6. See for example, A. Angyal, *Foundations for a Science of Personality.* (Cambridge: Harvard University Press, 1958); A. H. Maslow, *Toward A Psychology of Being* (Princeton, N.J.: D. VanNostrand and Co., 1962); E. Erickson, *Childhood and Society,* second edition. (New York: W. W. Norton, 1963); and, for a general review from a psychoanalytic viewpoint, see D. Rapaport, "The Theory of Attention Cathexis: An Economic and Structural Attempt at the Explanation of Cognitive Processes," and "On the Psychoanalytic Theory of Motivation," M. Gill, ed., *The Collected Papers of David Rapaport.* (New York: Basic Books, 1967), chapters 61 and 65.

7. If the individual is to make transitive choices among options defined as joint probability distributions over the D^is, then the index must satisfy the von Neumann-Morgenstern consistency properties. But that does not imply that there is a measurable, unidimensional psychic quantity which Q reflects. On the theory of such multidimensional choice functions see, R. L.

Keeney, "Multidimensional Utility Functions," Technical Report no. 43, Operations Research Center, MIT, (October 1969).

8. Such functions are a useful generalized representation of such phenomena as the "technology of consumption." See K. Lancaster, "A New Approach to Consumer Theory," *Journal of Political Economy*, 74 (April 1966), pp. 132–57.

9. See for example F. Knight, *Risk, Uncertainty and Profit*, (Chicago: University of Chicago Press, 1936).

10. H. Simon, "A Behavioral Theory of Rational Choice," *Quarterly Journal of Economics*, 69 (February 1955), pp. 99–118, W. J. Baumol and R. Quandt, "Rules of Thumb and Optimally Imperfect Decisions," *American Economic Review*, 54 (March 1964), pp. 23–46; M. J. Roberts, "On Time," *Quarterly Journal of Economics*, 87 (November 1973), pp. 646–50.

11. R. A. Musgrave, *The Theory of Public Finance*, (New York: McGraw-Hill, 1959), pp. 13–15.

12. Two recent examples of the research done on the effects of television violence are R. K. Baker and S. J. Ball, *Violence and the Media*, Staff Report to the National Commission on the Causes and Prevention of Violence (U.S. Government Printing Office, 1971) and U.S. Public Health Service, *Television and Growing Up: The Impact of Television Violence*, Report to the Surgeon-General of the United States (U.S. Government Printing Office, 1972).

13. Quinn Martin, producer of "The FBI," quoted in *TV Guide*, April 27, 1974.

14. See the comments by Herb Schlosser, NBC network president, about the "human need for escape programs," *Broadcasting*, May 1, 1973.

15. J. March and H. A. Simon, *Organizations*. (New York: John Wiley and Sons, 1958), chapters 6 and 7.

16. See for example, H. Swayze, *The Political Control of Literature in the USSR, 1946–59*. (Cambridge: Harvard University Press, 1962).

17. See, *Broadcasting*, August 24, 1970. See also W. F. Baker, "Power and Decision Making in American Television," Ph.D. Thesis, Department of Speech Communication, Case-Western Reserve University, January 1972, p. 210 for an interview with Edwin Vane, vice-president of night-time programming at ABC who described reactions to an April 10, 1970 meeting at the White House, "When the White House makes a suggestion like that, this industry is very responsive . . . The result was, I think, we all went overboard . . . By October 15, I think the nation was right up to its eyeballs in drug stories."

18. For a general statement of this approach to explaining organizational behavior, see M. J. Roberts, "A Framework for Analyzing the Behavior of Resource Allocating Organizations," Harvard Institute of Economic Research Discussion Paper no. 264 (December 1972).

19. E. Greenberg and H. J. Barnett, "Program Diversity—New Evidence and Old Theories," and H. J. Levin, "Program Duplication, Diversity and Effective Viewer Choice," both in *American Economic Review*, 61 (May 1971).

20. Thus we are not using variety in the same sense as those who have analyzed models of program choice based on audiences composed of distinct viewer groups with different tastes for show "types." See P. O. Steiner,

"Program Preferences and the Workability of Competition in Radio Broadcasting," *Quarterly Journal of Economics,* 66 (May 1952); J. Rothenberg, "Consumer Sovereignty and the Economics of TV Programming," *Studies in Public Communication,* 4 (Fall 1962); and P. Wiles, "Pilkington and the Theory of Value," *Economic Journal,* 73 (June 1963).

21. This code is reprinted annually in *Broadcasting Yearbook,* published by *Broadcasting,* the main trade journal in the industry.

22. See Baker, "Power and Decision Making," pp. 230–239 for an interview with Carl Tillmanns, vice-president and general sales manager at CBS.

23. Actually, a group can operate up to seven television stations in all, provided two are on UHF, and seven each of AM and FM radio stations—although for new applications and transfers no two stations of any type can be in the same market. See FCC rules §73:35 §73:240 and §73:636, reprinted in *Broadcasting Yearbook* 1974, pp. C27–27. All three networks have owned and operated stations in New York, Chicago and Los Angeles. In addition, NBC has Washington D.C. and Cleveland, CBS has St. Louis and Philadelphia, and ABC has San Francisco and Detroit; *Broadcasting Yearbook,* pp. E-10 to E-16.

24. For a review of the ratings see U.S. Congress, House of Representatives Committee on Interstate and Foreign Commerce, *Broadcast Ratings,* Hearings 88th Congress 1st and 2nd Session (1963–64), Brown, *Television, the Business Behind the Box,* pp. 32–35.

25. Noll, Peck and McGowen, *Economic Aspects of Television Regulation,* pp. 65–67: Barnouw, *The Image Empire* p. 306. See also B. Owen and W. Manning, "The Television Rivalry Game," Stanford University Program on Information Technology and Telecommunication, Report #5 (July 1973).

26. I am indebted to Professor Bruce Owen for this point. Note that in fact the networks have similar behavior with respect to many product parameters. Cultural shows are traditionally on Sunday, children's shows on Saturday morning and soap operas on daytime. All have half-hour news shows, etc. Yet at least some of these parallelisms are the result of competitive, not collusive, behavior. See the discussion by Robert Wood, president of the CBS network, on how a decision was reached on when to begin the evening schedule in light of new FCC rules, in Baker, "Power and Decision Making," pp. 447–49.

27. Brown, *Television, the Business Behind the Box,* p. 31.

28. R. H. Bell, "A Study of the Image of the American Character as Presented in Selected Network Television Dramas," Ph.D. Thesis in Education, Ohio State University, 1961, p. 82. See also Barnouw, *The Image Empire,* pp. 308-9.

29. Brown, *Television, the Business Behind the Box,* pp. 238–41; Baker, "Power and Decision Making," pp. 45–61.

30. NBC executive vice-president, David Adams, interview given in Baker, "Power and Decision Making," p. 460. "...the audience for which those shows are aimed are much too hip for the sort of compromises television does in doing 'relevant' or contemporary shows." See also Brown, *Television, the Business Behind the Box,* pp. 305–310.

31. For example, until the latest revision, the Code included the following language. "Profanity, obscenity, smut and vulgarity are forbidden, even when likely to be understood by only part of the audience . . . Respect is maintained for the sanctity of marriage and the value of the home . . . Illicit sex relations are not treated as commendable. Sex crimes and abnormalities are generally unacceptable as program material." Now the comparable sections read "Obscene, indecent or profane matter, as proscribed by law, is unacceptable. The presentation of marriage, the family and similarly important human relationships, and material with sexual connotations, shall not be treated exploitatively or irresponsibly, but with sensitivity." See, for example, *Broadcasting Yearbook,* 1969, pp. D-3, D-4 and *Broadcasting Yearbook,* 1974, pp. D-27, D-28.

32. CBS president Robert Wood told the Better Business Bureau of Nashville in October 1973, " . . . our society's standards and tastes are undergoing enormous changes and . . . TV must reflect the growing maturity of the audience." *Broadcasting,* October 22, 1973. He went on to defend the network's broadcast of shows about abortion on "Maude," which caused a controversy discussed further below.

33. Brown, *Television,* pp. 51-2.

34. Barnouw mentions a spy cycle, a war cycle and a supernatural cycle in *The Image Empire,* pp. 261, 266, 308. Brown, *Television,* p. 100 discusses the five imitations of "Mod Squad." A television agent quoted by him says, "You bring something to them and they start with the plastic surgery, and what you wind up with is something very reminiscent of one or two shows that have been seen before. Everything on television becomes a composition of stale ideas that once worked." p. 126.

35. See the description by James Aubrey, the president of the CBS network in Federal Communications Commission, *Television Network Program Procurement, Part II* (U.S. Government Printing Office, 1965), pp. 217–18; also, Brown, *Television,* pp. 131-3. Occasionally a well-known star will return without a pilot ever being produced: Baker, "Power and Decision Making," p. 310.

36. On financial arrangements, see the testimony of James Stabile, then general attorney of NBC in FCC, *Television Network Program Procurement,* p. 270. A review of all the networks' schedules and the varying origins of the programs on them is given in Baker, "Power and Decision Making," pp. 480-96.

37. Robert Wood, in Baker, "Power and Decision-Making," ". . .we try to be as sympathetic to the creators as we can be. . . . We'd like to go as far as we can go on the things they want to do, but we're privy to other considerations that they are not. So we bring the government to them in a way. We bring the Washington environment that they otherwise might not know about," p. 300.

38. See the account of a producer of a children's show of a disagreement over whether he could show the hero carrying gunpowder to blow up a bridge and being limited to two killings per episode, in M. G. Cantor,

"Producing Television for Children," in G. Tuchman (ed)., *The TV Establishment* (Englewood Cliffs, N.J.: Prentice-Hall, 1974), pp. 108–9.

39. Baker, "Power and Decision-Making," pp. 224, 240–41, shows that this older practice still holds true for daytime television. For some data on the declining role of sponsors see *Television Network Program Procurement*, pp. 792–95.

40. Baker, "Power and Decision-Making," pp. 220–29.

41. CBS vice-president of sales, Frank Smith, says, "We used to have, it seems to me, a fair amount of [involvement in program content by sponsors]. . .you know the old joke about the Ford Motor Company saying they didn't want the Chrysler Building in their picture. But I've got to tell you that's a very, very rare thing today," in Baker, "Power and Decision-Making," p. 226.

42. Baker, "Power and Decision-Making," p. 431.

43. A network typically will shoot 20 to 25 pilots, put five to ten new shows on the air, and of those, on average, one-half to two-thirds will not be renewed. See Aubrey in *Television Network Program Procurement*, p. 218. Of the 25 new series the networks introduced in 1973–74, only 3 were renewed for 1974–75. See *TV Guide*, July 13–19, 1974, p. A–2. To be successful, a show must achieve an audience share of 28 to 30 per cent. See Brown, *Television*, p. 51–52.

44. M. Friedman and L. Savage, "The Expected Utility Hypothesis and the Measurability of Utility," *Journal of Political Economy*, Vol. 60, (December 1952), pp. 463–74.

45. Brown, *Television*, pp. 244–79.

46. William Lodge, vice-president of affiliate relations of CBS, ". . .but boy we had plenty of complaints from stations, which added to our desire to get rid of it"; Baker, "Power and Decision-Making," p. 256. Similarly, Kenneth Bagwell, manager of the CBS affiliate in Cleveland noted affiliate unhappiness about the show and said his station edited some of the broadcasts (p. 277).

47. Barnouw, *The Image Empire*, pp. 223–4, Brown suggests that network executives also feared that whites would not watch blacks, pp. 218–19.

48. Each network, in recent years, has tried to keep at least one show with a prominent black lead.

49. Under substantial pressure from the FTC, the networks have proposed to cut commercial minutes on children's broadcasting from twelve to ten per hour over a three-year period. See *New York Times*, July xx, 1974. On the lowering of violence, see *Broadcasting*, April xx, 1974. This issue has been alive for some time. See the comments of Dean Burch, then FCC chairman in *Broadcasting*, Sept. 20, 1971.

50. Jack Schneider, executive vice-president of CBS, Inc., interview with the author, July 1973.

51. See Barnouw, *The Image Empire*, pp. 83, 200–204, 317–318, 325; Brown, *Television*, p. 40; *Broadcasting*, June 17, July 29, August 18, 26, 1968 and March 27, April 24, 1972. The networks' announcements in April 1973 for the 1974 season again heavily emphasized their voluntary efforts at controlling violence. Apparently network response over the years has varied

quite a bit as a function of this attention. See Baker's interview with William Tankersley, CBS vice-president for program practices in "Power and Decision-Making," pp. 334-5.

52. J. Q. Wilson, "The Politics of Regulation," unpublished manuscript, February 1973.

53. See *The New York Times,* March 7, March 20, July 14, 1973; also *Broadcasting,* March 19, 1973 and July 16, 1973.

54. See the comments of former NYC deputy police commissioner, R. Daily, *The New York Times Magazine,* Nov. 19, 1972, pp. 39ff; also Joseph Wambaugh, policeman and novelist, interviewed in *Variety,* July 4, 1973, "Jack Webb and company are nothing but propagandists grinding out a phoney party line." See also Dr. Michael Halberstam's analysis of medical shows, *The New York Times Magazine,* January 16, 1972, pp. 12ff. The Chairman of the censorship committee of the American Writers Guild has also charged in congressional testimony that shows in both categories are reviewed by police groups or the AMA, *The New York Times,* March 5, and March 12, 1972.

55. *New York Times,* August 10, 14, 1973. See also *Broadcasting,* August 13, 20, 1973. About 35 affiliates refused to carry the reruns and *none* of the advertising time was sold, as all series sponsors backed out.

56. The criticisms are reported in the *New York Times,* Feb. 7, 1973. On March 30, 1973, the cancellation is reported along with network president Robert Wood's claim that the cancellation is "independent" of and "disassociated" from the criticism.

57. See Baker, "Power and Decision-Making", pp. 426–65, for a discussion of various specific decisions. Also Brown, *Television,* pp. 56–8 for William S. Paley's role as the final arbiter of the CBS schedule for 1971–72. As chairman of the board of CBS Inc., between him and Robert Wood, president of the CBS Television Network, there were three layers of management; Frank Stanton, CBS president; Jack Schneider, executive vice-president, and Richard W. Jencks, president, CBS Broadcast Group.

58. Information supplied by A. C. Nielson and Company.

59. G. A. Steiner, *The People Look at Television.* (New York: Alfred A. Knopf, 1963) and R. T. Bower, *Television and the Public.* (New York: Holt, Rinehart and Winston, 1973). See the latter, p. 76. Similarly, in 1960, when offered a choice of five media, 44% said television was the one getting better all the time while 24% said it was the one getting worse all the time. In 1970 only 38% picked it as the one getting better while 41% picked it as the medium getting worse, Bower, p. 14.

60. Reported in *Life,* Sept. 10, 1971, pp. 40–44.

61. Bower, *Television,* pp. 29–31, 43–44, 72–73, 91.

62. Bower, *Television,* pp. 36–37. Among white viewers, college educated ones have a smaller proportion both of heavy viewers and of those who say they are watching more television now than ten years ago than do lower education groups: 40% for grade school vs. 29% for college in the first case and 48% vs. 31% in the second (p. 49). Also, 76% of college educated viewers say they sometimes watch noncommercial television vs. 55% for grade school graduates (p. 53).

63. Bower, *Television,* p. 93.

64. See the CBS advertisement for "Fat Albert and his Friends," on the back page of *The New York Times,* April 1, 1974.

65. "Stanton vs. Pastore." *Variety,* March 19, 1969, p. 1; Baker, "Power and Decision-Making," pp. 461-2, 465.

66. Noll, Peck and McGowen, *Television Regulation,* pp. 83-89; The rule was adopted after vigorous lobbying by the non-network groups that owned multiple stations who stood to gain most by expanded access to an enlarged market for non-network fare. See Baker's long interview with Donald Mc-Gannon, head of Westinghouse Broadcasting and chief proponent of the rule, "Power and Decision-Making," pp. 535-540.

67. See Noll, Peck and McGowen, *Television Regulation,* pp. 118-120 and 269-70, where they discuss the concentration of control in the networks, the lack of program diversity and the scarcity of conventional options. The first two of these issues are explored without considering the self-regulation process, while by diversity they mean catering to minority tastes. They argue that the last problem is "the one of greatest economic significance," a conclusion which, like the rest of the analysis, rests on the assumed exogeneity of consumer tastes.

68. This is discussed at length in H. Levin, *The Invisible Resource,* published for Resources for the Future (Baltimore: The Johns Hopkins Press, 1972).

69. A review of various technologies is given by Noll, Peck and McGowen, *Television Regulation,* Chapter 9.

70. One group showed "a five-minute clip from a film about a female masturbation class consisting of several nude females performing yoga exercises," *The New York Times,* June 18, 1974.

Part Three

Product Mix, Technological Change and Market Structure under Regulation

Chapter Seven

Market Structure and Embodied Technological Change

Richard E. Caves

Innovation and technological progress are important dimensions of economic performance. Our judgment about the effects of direct regulation should certainly take account of its effects on progressiveness. Regulation can affect progressiveness directly. It can block innovation by setting constraints on prices or further it by inducing the substitution of capital for labor. Such direct effects of public control on progress have been found for most regulated sectors.[1] Less attention has been paid to a more complex form of "wiring" that connects the regulatory control to the normative outcome: Progressivenes depends on a regulated sector's economic elements of market structure and behavior, and the regulators constrain and mold these elements of structure and behavior.

One could imagine several wiring diagrams taking this form: "Monopoly and market *Lebensraum* are favorable to progressiveness. Regulation blockades entry and removes immediate competitive threats. Therefore regulation furthers innovation;" or, instead: "Progressiveness is encouraged by the carrot of innovative quasi rents and the stick of market rivalry. Regulation excises the innovative rents and guarantees an acceptable minimum profit and a quiet life. Thus regulation deters innovation."

In this essay I shall be concerned, not with these familiar linkages, but with a different and more complex schema. It is built on an assumption observed empirically for several regulated industries: that their progressiveness is largely due to technological change embodied in capital goods that they buy at arm's length from another industry. Progress in electric power and in air transport closely matches this description, and the pattern holds in other regulated industries to a large if lesser extent. The connections between market structure (and behavior) and progressiveness then run through the structures of both the capital goods-using ("user") industry and the capital goods-producing ("producer") industry. This bilateral market link may color the information it transmits from the user to the producer industry about the social productivity of different innovations. The transmission may not only be affected by the bilateral structure of the intervening market; the industries' structures may in turn be altered over time by the character of innovation and the process of its diffusion.

This assumption and the hypotheses it yields contrast sharply to those plied by both the Schumpeterian and neoclassical investigators of structure-progressiveness relations. Broadly speaking, both groups leave the producer industry out of account, either as the vantage point from which innovative rents must be foretold or the site at which research and development outlays are committed. I suggest in this chapter that, whatever the influence of regulation on the user industry's structure, this vertical market may be very important.[2] The first section sets forth the general analytical argument. The second uses the electric power industry and the turbine-generator manufacturers to test some features of the model.

1. BILATERAL MARKET STRUCTURE AND PROGRESSIVENESS

In this section I list assumptions under which the market structures of the user and producer industries and the rate and character of technological change are all jointly determined in the long run. The resulting model will not be the last word in generality, but it does match the observed structures of several regulated industries and illustrate the potential importance of an arm's-length market link in the innovatory process.

Here is the argument in preliminary sketch: The producer industry consists of oligopolists, each making his own line of capital goods and pricing them to maximize profits. Any machine yields different quasi rents to differently situated user firms, or subsectors. The producer oligopolists design machines they think the user industry will buy; when incurring the fixed costs of designing a "new model," they aim (*ceteris paribus*) at the user-industry subsector with the largest potential demand. If capital rationing affects the user industry, this subsector may well be the one currently most profitable and thus be able to finance the replacement or expansion of its plant. Any effect of the regulatory process on the structure of the user industry or the relative profitability of differently situated user firms can thus slant the qualitative character of capital-goods innovations. This slant, in turn, alters the relative profitability of user firms and—assuming that the novelty succeeds—portends further changes in the user industry's market structure. The slant may make the rate or character of social progress either better or worse than what the interaction of other market structures and regulatory constraints would generate.

Assumptions
This sketch indicates the relations we have in mind between market

structure and technological change. Here are the assumptions underlying the sequence:

1. Technological change in the user industry must be mostly embodied in capital goods made by firms located in the independent producer industry. This assumption (this pair, really) is necessary to get the model off the ground. If new capital goods account for an insignificant portion of productivity growth, no amount of bias in their design in favor of particular user firms will affect that group's cost or net-revenue position relative to its market rivals. If user firms construct their own capital goods or assemble them from standard components bought at marginal cost, asymmetries between user firms either disappear or boil down to a simple matter of fixed costs spread over differing output.

2. Some relation must exist between parameters of the user firms and of the capital goods they buy. Suppose that the parameter is scale (output or capacity per unit of time), although one can imagine others. The producer firm developing an improved capital good can attack existing equipment of small, medium or large scale. It chooses some one scale, and succeeds. Its successful innovation lowers the unit cost curve for user firms operating at the corresponding scale in the user industry. If the productivity of the chosen-scale capital goods increases enough, of course, some user firms will substitute that scale for others; large firms can always employ multiple units of smaller equipment, and small firms can potentially operate large units at less than capacity. These substitution opportunities are a matter of degree, however, and an innovation can change the relative profitabilities of user firms substantially without the losers being able to take evasive action and adopt the innovation.

3. Product differentiation in the user industry is not necessary to this argument, but it supplies another link between the traits of the user firm and of the capital goods it buys. This link is most evident in a service industry where the firm's capital goods can affect the buyer's view of the qualitative traits of its output. Air passenger transportation provides numerous examples, because the physical properties of the capital goods intimately affect the quality and character of the "product" that the airline offers to the prospective traveler (speed, comfort, noise level, etc.). In the United States the larger carriers fortuitously have the longer hauls, especially transcontinental. Large airlines would thus be favored by a faster rate of advance in the productivity of long-distance aircraft, even if no other association with size existed. Airlines need not all offer the same mixture of product attributes, and submarkets could be based on difference in equipment. For example, one can imagine an airline industry consisting of small firms that provide (on a given route) expensive but fast service and large ones that give cheap but slow service.

4. The producer industry incurs fixed costs of research, development, and tooling for manufacture of each variety of capital good, and more fixed costs are involved in translating the innovations into new capital goods designed for other segments of the user industry. For instance, we assume that

research underlying the construction of a new electricity generating unit, larger than any previously built, does not proportionally lower the unit cost curve for electricity production in new smaller generating units, and does not necessarily lower it at all. Once a breakthrough occurs in the producer industry's research, a new generation of capital goods may appear that ultimately offers a new type to each segment of the user industry. But even if, in the extreme, all user-industry sectors ultimately enjoy the same cost reduction (or revenue-per-unit increase), most will be disadvantaged in the transition before "stretched" or "shrunken" versions of the basic innovative machine are developed. For instance, the jet airliner must be designed first for airlines with *some* average route density and length of haul, and those carriers enjoy an advantage until modified versions appear that are as well suited to their rivals' route structures.

5. Various assumptions can be made about the producer industry's market structure, and at this stage I merely indicate the range of possibilities. The producer industry cannot be a perfectly discriminating monopolist, because he would by definition leave no surpluses for the user firms and hence have no differential effects on their competitive positions. The producer industry's seller concentration must also be kept above a floor level. Perfect competition would be inconsistent with proprietary product innovations and raise awkward questions of how firms recoup their outlays on developing new equipment. We need to suppose that a producer investing in development of a new capital good can contemplate the potential demand of a specific group of user firms. Other producers may offer partial substitutes for his innovation. Thus, in effect, we are talking about producer industries that are differentiated oligopolies.

Market Behavior

The features of behavior that matter in this bilateral market situation are the producer's method of deciding the most profitable product innovation to develop and the bargaining process in bilateral oligopoly between the producer and user firms.

Suppose that some advance in basic science makes possible the development of a superior capital good, such as the jet aircraft. Heavy fixed development and testing costs assure that no producer can initially bring more than one design to market. The firm considers the most profitable form in which to market the innovation. For the decision to be socially optimal, the timing and qualitative characteristics should be chosen to maximize the present value of increments to consumers' (and producers') surpluses imputable to the innovation itself. Various factors might cause the market bargain struck between producer and user firms to miss the optimum choice, even if the users are gifted with perfect foresight. Alternatively, the quasi rents from different forms of the innovation may simply be foreseen differently by the user firms and the producers—making no assumption about their respective forecasting abilities. Differences in attitudes toward risk or other features of firms' utility functions could lead to divergent judgments. In bilateral oligopoly it is not clear that Pareto-optimal risk-sharing contracts will always be drawn.[3]

A single producer-innovator would certainly aim at the largest subsector of the user market that is potentially homogeneous in its interest in the innovation at hand.[4] If oligopolistic rivalry marks the producer industry, rivals may aim innovations at the same largest subsector of the user market rather than spreading them around. The Hotelling model of spatial duopoly may have some analogy value in suggesting the reasons why rival innovative designs can cluster together.[5]

This largest subgroup of users may carry out operations at the most efficient scale, both before and after the installation of any possible variant of an innovation. (Recall that "scale" stands for any parameter along which user firms might vary.) If Darwinian processes have thus generated an efficient organization for the user industry, we can expect that users and producers together are picking the most socially valuable locus for innovation. In regulated industries, however, firms are often constrained in scale and other dimensions by franchise limitations that cannot be traded away when they prove economically inefficient. The dominant subgroup of user firms is likely to reflect some mixture of economic and regulatory influences.

When the producer firms pick a submarket as target for an innovation, they are likely to take account of different user groups' relative profitability. If capital rationing constrains the users' rate of investment outlays, current and past profits come to affect the rate at which new equipment will be ingested. This constraint may be particularly important when capital goods innovations promise cost savings to firms that are running losses using present technology. It may be hard for lenders to secure a prior claim on substantial quasi rents that the users can gain from new equipment, and so funds may not be forthcoming. The railroads provide an obvious example: innovations with high internal rates of return are allegedly difficult or impossible to finance. In such an industry, evidence that the more profitable firms are the quickest to adopt an innovation can hardly serve without further inquiry to confirm the Schumpeterian hypothesis about the way freedom from competition encourages innovation.[6]

The likelihood that innovations will be slanted toward those who can pay creates an important channel for the influence of regulation. Regulatory control of price can affect the relative profitability of different user groups, in ways unrelated either to the social return to increments of output or the social productivity of an innovation. Coupled with the typical regulatory constraints on entry *de novo* or the migration of enterprises among segments of an industry, profit constraints due to regulation could slant innovation away from or toward a particular sector (or industry).

Market structures of both the producer and user industries can influence the course of innovation, and regulation can bend this influence through the control of either market structures or rates of return. But the innovation also releases forces that can change market structures. Once the innovation has been acquired by some of the user firms, it affects their relative profitability. If they are not a collection of natural monopolies or rigidly limited in their markets and market shares by regulatory constraints, the user industry's market structure becomes subject to change as a result of the innovation, in turn shifting the relative payout expected from the next innovation. Market structure and progressiveness thus are mutually dependent.

Suppose once more that the user industry subgroups are distinguished by size of firm.

1. Even if a differential advantage due to innovation afflicts only one generation of capital goods, it can become cumulative through its effects on the profitability and liquidity of different segments of the user industry and their relative ability to pay for subsequent generations of equipment. That is, imperfect capital markets (in particular, the imperfection of lenders' risk) tend to cumulate positions of advantage resulting from this process.

2. The variance of firm size in the user industry will fall, and concentration will increase if the large firms have been favored. If the user industry's product is differentiated the range of product varieties offered to final customers will tend to contract.[7]

3. Seller concentration in the producer industry may also be affected, if the user industry is its principal set of customers. Serving an increasingly homogeneous group of customers and facing high developmental risks, producer firms have fewer chances to prosper by catering to minor segments of the user industry. They compete in product strategy for the main user group and thus play an increasingly all-or-nothing game. This should raise the mortality rate of producer firms and increase concentration if entry is impeded.

4. If embodied technological change favors large firms *and* increases firms' capital-output ratios (which it has not always done) large firms would be more capital intensive than small ones. The model can thus explain an empirical result that is commonly observed, although usually in studies not confined to individual well-defined industries. The correlation of innovation with increasing capital intensity would of course be consistent with the predictions of the Averch-Johnson-Wellisz model of the regulated firm.

Regulatory objectives can be affected in various ways by these forces operating on the user industry. For instance, many regulatory bodies try to encourage or enforce cross-subsidy in order to satisfy social objectives of providing service to intrinsically less profitable segments of a market (or simply to favor politically powerful groups of customers). The process of innovation described above increases productivity in the more profitable sector and, hence, the size of the potential profits available for cross-subsidy. However, it also lowers the relative attractiveness of servicing the less profitable segments and taxes the regulators' ability to keep the internal subsidy flowing. By raising seller concentration, the process may also complicate the regulators' lives if their politicoeconomic leverage declines as their subjects grow larger and less numerous.

2. THE ELECTRIC UTILITIES AND
THE TURBINE-GENERATOR INDUSTRY:
A CASE STUDY

This model rests on a lengthy list of assumptions that will obviously apply—if anywhere—only to a select group of industrial sectors. It was concocted largely out of reflections on the airlines and airframe manufacturers; its explanatory power in that sector is weighed in chapter 8. Here we test it on another regulated service sector—the electric utilities, and the turbine-generator industry. Because capital spending by this sector has exceeded 10 percent of annual investment by all United States industries, the efficiency of the process and its attained rate of productivity gain is of no small importance. The fit turns out less than perfect, and the model's predictive worth is limited both by the evidence available and by its own low analytical horsepower.[8] Nonetheless, it raises substantial questions about the sector's performance and organization that might otherwise escape notice. We first consider the fit of the model's assumptions, then check its predictions against the record of behavior and the course of structural change in electrical sector.

Assumptions of the Model
Technological change in the electric utilities has been rapid and seems mostly to have been embodied in generation and transmission equipment bought from supplier industries. Kendrick found that productivity grew in the electric power industry by 5.5 percent from 1900 to 1955, more than three times the rate of increase for the economy as a whole.[9] It is not easy to allocate this impressive growth rate respectively to improvement in its capital goods and to disembodied and organizational changes in the electric power industry itself. Nonetheless, several kinds of evidence suggest that the supplier industries should get most of the credit. First, in the predominant steam-generation technology, user costs of major pieces of equipment account for a large slice of total unit costs. Electricity generation accounts for 51 percent of the total delivered cost of power; the turbine generator accounts for 32 percent of the total investment cost (excluding land) of a modern coal-burning plant, and the boiler plant (including coal and ash handling, feedwater system, etc.) another 43 percent.[10] Apparently this cost pattern will not differ greatly in plants employing a nuclear steam supply;[11] if anything, capital costs will be proportionally higher. Second, research outlays by the turbine-generator manufacturers have been heavy—about 10 percent of sales of this equipment for General Electric and Westinghouse, the

dominant firms in the United States market. Third, research and development outlays by the utilities themselves have been extremely modest—$5 million annually according to the Federal Power Commission, around $50 million according to the Edison Electrical Institute. Utilities have contributed importantly to productivity through system-design work, including plant design and siting and efficient transmission—but mostly through the accumulation of experience and know-how rather than formal research.[12] Thus the electric-power sector fulfills the first assumption reasonably well: productivity gains depend heavily on innovations embodied in capital goods purchased from another industry.

The second assumption requires that some parametric link, such as size or capacity, exist between the capital goods employed by the user industry and the structure of the user firms. It can be shown that the total size of utility systems has been correlated with the scale of their capacity additions and that the substitute strategems for small systems seeking to make large efficient-scale additions are all inferior. This connection between system size and generating-unit scale is important because of the major scale economics in generation; typical figures suggest a reduction in unit capital costs of 25 percent as scale is increased from 200 to 1000 megawatts, with an additional 16 percent saving in fuel costs.[13] The maximum size of a generating unit that a utility system buys is constrained by its prospective peak-load requirements—not literally, but via the operating rule of thumb that no single unit should comprise more than 7 to 10 percent of a system's capacity when it is installed. A single unit's failure then can be covered by the utility's normal 15 to 25 percent reserve capacity, and the chances of disrupted service due to forced outage of a single unit are kept acceptably low.[14] William Hughes studied the relation over the years 1954 to 1964 between the nameplate capacity of turbine generators purchased and various characteristics of the buyers' systems, including forecast peak load. The elasticity of unit size to peak load showed no trend, and both were growing then at about the same rate. For systems outside the largest 14, the elasticity was about 0.4; even for the largest 14, the relation of unit size to system peak persisted, though in weakened form.[15]

Utilities have found various techniques for relaxing this constraint on the maximum safe size of generating units. These range from interties between systems for the short-term exchange of power through staggered construction of new units (*cum* long-term sales contracts) and the joint ownership of large generating plants. Although desirable, these arrangements have been found to be incomplete substitutes for outright consolidation of utility systems as ways to exploit the available economies of scale. A statistical test by Leonard Weiss indicates that generating pools seldom install units as large as do comparable systems under single ownership although the member firms do employ larger units than independent utilities of similar size.[16] The implications of Hughes's calculations are similar. Thus we conclude that a relation exists between (peak load) size of utility system and size of generating unit.

The model's third assumption is clearly violated by the electric-power sector. Electricity is an undifferentiated product to the consumer, and the electric utility's equipment decisions affect its market position only through their influence on unit cost and reliability of service. Although this assumption is not fundamental to the model, its fulfillment can strongly amplify the model's behavioral underpinnings; compare the air-transport sector.

The next assumption bears on the relation between innovation in the capital-goods sector and the range of equipment offered on the market. An important frontier of innovation since World War II has been simply that of larger scale. If gains in turbine-generator productivity resulted solely from the construction of larger units, the differential effect on the position of large and small utility systems would be manifest. On the other hand, innovations such as supercritical steam pressures might conceivably affect all scales of equipment in the same proportion. The rather complex evidence developed by Hughes, Sultan and others suggests that pure extensions of scale have proved the major source of productivity improvement. Econometric studies suggest that improvements to units of a given scale have effected some saving of fuel and labor inputs but that these gains are small compared to those stemming from the shift to units of larger scale.[17] Furthermore, other innovations such as supercritical pressures and cross-compound design have not been neutral with regard to scale; rather they have tended, as one would expect for technical reasons, to lower unit capital costs more for large-scale units.

The turbine-generator industry's product line is not restricted to a few standardized types or sizes. On the contrary, units are nearly custom designed for individual utility customers, and product units thus are in effect completely variable in their major design parameters. In this they differ from, say, the types of passenger aircraft offered at any one time by the airframe manufacturers. This variability of units of the product thus dampens the bias of advantage that innovations could otherwise create among utility customers, but the net bias toward larger scales remains a quantitatively potent effect. Furthermore, the turbine makers appear sometimes to concentrate their research efforts on particular technological frontiers—each manufacturer making a different choice; hence the significance of alternative R&D strategies persists even though research results are not embodied in homogeneous product units.

This observation leads us to the final assumption concerning the structure of the turbine-generator industry. The model requires that it be neither atomistic nor a perfectly discrimating monopolist. The turbine makers have been highly concentrated for many years, with the two dominant firms holding relatively stable market shares. Over the period from 1948 to 1962 General Electric accounted for 57.3 percent of all turbine units ordered, Westinghouse for 33.8 percent, and Allis-Chalmers for 8.9 percent. Concentration would be greater if measured on a value-of-shipments basis, because GE's sales were concentrated in the largest and medium-sized units, Westinghouse's in medium-sized units, and Allis-Chalmers's in small turbines. During the past decade the appearance of import competition and the fluctuating fortunes of Allis-Chalmers have complicated this pattern somewhat while leaving the industry a highly concentrated one.[18]

Seller Concentration and Behavior in the Turbine-Generator Market

The thermal-based electric utilities and the turbine-generator manufacturers fit reasonably, if not perfectly, the structural assumptions of the model. We now trace certain behavior patterns in the bilateral relations between these sectors—behavior that responds to these structural predictions and implies certain consequences for market performance and the further modification of structure. We shall see that the market structures of the utilities and the turbine-generator industry have in fact interacted to influence their market performance in both profitability and progressiveness. The structure of the utility sector, furthermore, has changed in the fashion predicted by the model. This change is due in large part, however, to forces not endogenous to our bilateral market model.

The story begins with the behavior of the major turbine-generator manufacturers, which has been analyzed in detail by Sultan. General Electric has long been the dominant firm, its technological lead and close ties with its utilities customers going back to 1910. GE can be counted the price leader in the industry in regard to changes in list or book prices. According to Sultan's diagnosis, the firm has employed a strategy to maintain its leadership without coercion of its rivals. A keystone of this strategy has been technological leadership—since World War II principally in the extension to larger and larger scales, but also through increases in steam temperatures and pressures as mentioned above. GE, like Westinghouse, has spent about 10 percent of its sales revenue on research and development; but, with a sales base double that of Westinghouse, it has enjoyed much the greater *masse de maneuvre.*[19] As a result, GE's share has been the greatest in large-scale turbine generators, including many pilot units that opened up new technical frontiers. But it has also held a large share in the bread-and-butter medium sizes. Sultan provides the following tabulation of the percentage share of orders received by the three domestic producers over the years 1948-1962, by maximum rated output of turbine generators.

	Up to 100 MW	*100 to 199 MW*	*200 to 299 MW*	*300 to 399 MW*	*400 MW and over*
General Electric	54.9%	61.3%	63.6%	54.7%	76.2%
Westinghouse	34.6	32.4	31.4	35.8	23.8
Allis-Chalmers	10.5	6.3	5.1	9.4	0
Total	100.0%	100.0%	100.0%	100.0%	100.0%
Number of units	1129	413	188	53	21

The differing comparative advantage of the three sellers would probably show up even more sharply if a shorter period of time were observed.

In the late 1940s and early 1950s, Westinghouse sought to combat GE's research advantage by promoting standardized turbine-generator designs. Its hope was to effect cost savings large enough to combat utilities' preferences for custom specifications. Drawing on experience acquired during World War II, Westinghouse enjoyed a fair success with this approach, and 33 of 92 new power plants surveyed in 1952 were of preferred standard design.[20] This approach failed, however, as the pace of innovation speeded up, and the delays and compromises involved in standardized designs came to offset their cost advantages.

GE's dominant position, once attained, has been perpetuated through its innovative success. The average unit purchased has been steadily pulled toward the technical frontier at which GE had already obtained production experience. But other forces also sustained this market position. GE's pricing policy, at least through the early 1960s, was designed to maintain reasonably generous profits on the bread-and-butter medium sizes, relatively thinner margins on the small, relatively obsolete ones, and profit on innovative units not so large as to tempt rivals to leapfrog into the lead. The definitions of "small," "medium," and "large," of course, changed with the growth of average turbine size, and the periodic adjustments of GE's prices were designed to boost margins on those sizes (or designs) passing into average status and establish promotional margins on units now at the frontiers. This strategy maintained satisfactory profits for GE and its oligopolistic rivals. At the same time it preserved a certain segmentation of the market and made rivalry less pervasive than it might otherwise have been.[21]

Other aspects of behavior also influenced the turbine-generator market. Delivery time is an important parameter of the seller's offer, because a new order goes into the queue and may wait several years for fulfillment. Thus the manufacturing capacity of the generator producers is crucial for their market shares, and any bid for a substantially increased share must be prefaced by an expansion of manufacturing capacity to allow fulfilling an enlarged flow of orders. Any sustained clashes over market shares would register themselves in advance in the manipulation of capacity—a variable subject only to slow change. This buffering of rivalry would, of course, work better for the firms during times of active business and be subject to breakdown when business was slack and queues short. GE, however, also has performed a short-run buffering function, allowing its rivals to undercut GE's bids when order queues were shortening but pricing more aggressively as they lengthened during a recovery. GE's orders thus show a greater intertemporal variance than those of Westinghouse or Allis-Chalmers.

GE's profit rate may have been higher on large and pioneering units than on the middle-of-the-line group. What does become clear, though, is that the turbine manufacturers failed to capture any large portion of the quasi rents due units of larger size and more advanced design. Most, if not all, of the differential capital-cost advantage of larger units was passed along to the utility customers in the form of lower prices per KW of generating capacity. The result seems fully consistent with GE's long view of its position in this highly concentrated industry. This is especially so considering that favorable prices on large-scale turbines probably influenced the consolidation process among utilities, thus changing the size distribution of customers in GE's long-run favor.

The outcome of behavior in the turbine market has depended not only on relations among the turbine makers but also on the bargains they strike with the utilities. Turbines were, of course, one of the products subject to the famous price-fixing conspiracies of the 1950s, with collusion covering the rotation of bids and the determination of bid prices. Like the other collusive arrangements, it was neither continuous nor perfectly adhered to; Sultan's statistical analysis suggests that it was probably not effective in raising turbine prices during the slack period of the mid-1950s, but may have become effective later in the decade (Sultan himself is skeptical). For the analysis at hand, it is important only to establish that any collusion on transactions prices and bidding priorities was no better than imperfect, and the evidence seems clearly to support that proposition.

That effective collusion would be difficult for a product like turbine generators is no surprise. Orders are large and discontinuous, and the individual seller will often be willing to accept a thinner profit margin than normal (or take some risks) to secure business. Furthermore, the product is intrinsically complicated. Bids of rival sellers can differ in the efficiency ("heat rate") guarantee, schedule of progress payments and a host of other economic and technical factors. Evaluating rival bids is a complex job for the electric utility, and consulting engineers are often employed for this purpose. Whether or not particular utility customers are tied to individual turbine suppliers is not at all clear. There is a strong tendency for the larger utility systems to buy from the larger turbine manufacturers, but that merely reflects GE's predominance in larger generating units. Sultan argues that the statistical evidence for the period up to 1962 signifies some brand loyalty,[22] but an appropriately defined nul hypothesis probably cannot be rejected. Indeed, on some occasions major utility systems passed their orders around among the turbine makers with the conscious goal of keeping up the number of healthy sellers in the market. Sultan cites evidence that several major utilities rotated their orders among the three domestic producers, and American Electric Power explained its decision to switch purchases to Brown Boveri (Switzerland) as a conscious effort to bring another seller into the United States market.[23] The Tennessee Valley Authority may have behaved in similar fashion.

The pricing of innovative units is a special case and one important to this analysis. One might expect them to yield the manufacturer a higher profit than would more seasoned units, because of the lack of competition and potential real economies to be shared between buyer and seller. For at least one major reason, however, pioneering units have yielded relatively low margins. Their performance cannot effectively be guaranteed, and the buyer can expect to experience substantial shake-down costs in operating a unit that breaches the frontiers of scale, steam conditions or other features. Forced outage rates during the 1960s were much higher for large and relatively new units than for seasoned equipment: less than 3 percent for units smaller than 200 MW, over 7 percent for units larger than 400 MW.[24] Thus the pioneering large-scale units, which in any case can appeal only to systems able to make correspondingly large additions to their generating capacity, are further restricted to those willing to struggle with the teething troubles of new equipment. GE and American Electric Power, before their rupture, had sustained a partnership in installing and shaking down new units. In other cases, such as early large-scale nuclear units, "come-on bids" have allegedly been made to get pioneering units into use, with prices elevated once the breakthrough is made.[25]

Turbine makers might offer low come-on bids for various reasons, including simple miscalculation. The point is that a pioneering unit involves a joint risk for both the maker and the user, and some bargain must be struck that will yield an expected outcome acceptable to both. This fact is of cardinal importance for showing how progress in turbine construction, and thus productivity gains in generation, have been constrained by the size and number of customers willing to try out the pioneering units. If generating capacity had been more concentrated, it is at least possible that a higher rate of innovation and productivity gain could have prevailed. Other evidence supports the force of this constraint. The argument implies, for instance, that the growth rate of generating units at the technical frontier would be constrained by the growth rate of the peak loads of the larger utility systems. Some relation apparently exists. Sultan notes that the growth of average turbine sizes was closely related to the growth of utility system peak loads. This relation is almost necessary, given the constraint on the portion of a system's capacity that a single unit can comprise. The relation between the size of the *largest* turbines and the largest utility systems' peak loads is less close, the turbine size having grown several percent per annum faster during the past two decades. The constraint on research frontiers may have been either the number of large customers willing to experiment with pioneering units or the number of utility systems willing to buy tested units at any given scale frontier.[26] Either way, the structure of the utility sector could have influenced the rate of technical advance in generator technology.

Buyer Concentration and Behavior in the Turbine-Generator Market

The analysis has identified links between the structure and behavior of the turbine-generator manufacturers and price effectiveness of equipment available to the utilities. Cost reductions on larger units and those closer to other technical frontiers were passed on to a degree reflecting GE's partial technical monopoly and the fluctuating extent of oligopolistic rivalry away from these frontiers. It is now time to inject the structure of the purchasing utilities as an endogenous variable. The utility sector has undergone substantial concentration since the early 1950s, at a rate doubtless influenced by the scale economies accruing in large turbine generators. The influence of the turbine-makers' structure and behavior on the utilities' cost curve, and thus the change in their market structure, should be established. The endogeneity of concentration in electricity generation, however, does not stop there. Had utility concentration been different (greater, say) at any one time, it would have changed the opportunity set open to the turbine makers. The distribution of turbine-generator demand would have been shifted toward larger-size units (and favored the generator makers better able to provide them). GE, as technical leader among the manufacturers, would have found more utilities large enough to serve as playmates in the experimental installation of generators breaking through existing technical frontiers. Thus concentration in the two sectors, the division of innovative rents between them, and the rate of technical progress all mutually determine each other.

One element of mutual dependence in this market follows directly upon our expectations. The more concentrated were the buyers of generators, the more bargaining power they should carry in the turbine market. Holding constant the degree of monopoly among the turbine makers, increased concentration of buyers should have lowered the sellers' profit margins overall, and especially on the larger units. Sultan found that transactions prices for turbine units depended not only on the size of the unit but also on the size of the purchasing utility, with large buyers driving better bargains. Another factor lowering the transactions price was the utility's use of a consultant firm to appraise the manufacturers' bids; apparently the turbine makers feared that these consultants were more likely to detect price discrimination than the utilities themselves. Thus the standard hypothesis about bilateral market power seems to hold.

The concentration of utilities' generating capacity has been increasing, especially since the mid-1960s. Concentration had been high forty years ago, before the Public Utility Holding Company Act directed the Federal Power Commission to undertake a two-decade job of disassembly. In 1935, 90 percent of all electricity generation was concentrated in 45 large holding companies, 11 independent operating companies, and the Tennessee Valley Authority. In 1964 the ten largest operating systems (including public, but excluding federal hydro-marketing agencies) accounted for 33 percent of all generating capacity, and the hundred largest systems for 90 percent. These figures had been relatively stable through the 1950s. Since the mid-1960s concentration has begun to increase again, and some industry spokesmen predict that it will continue over the coming decades.[27]

This rapid pace of concentration reflects many determining factors. One, of course, is the changing scale economies of generating costs described above.[28] This pace also reflected other influences, including the structure of state and Federal Power Commission regulation. Had these been different (or wielded a different influence on the rate of concentration), the market's solution of the other variables discussed above would have differed as well. We cannot allocate the rate of concentration of generating capacity among its various causes. It seems clear, though, that the regulatory institutions had *some* influence and thus presumptively made some difference for the overall outcome.

The Public Utility Holding Company Act, in pursuit of the dragon of financial manipulation, may paradoxically have imposed a significant cost in technical efficiency. The cost would presumably have come, not during the 1930s when gross additions to generating capacity were modest, but in the booming times after World War II. The act was thorough, requiring not only the horizontal dismantling of the holding companies but, indeed, banning ownership ties between the utilities and manufacturing or engineering firms, to avoid the milking of captives. Still, the costs of dissolution are easily oversold. The 1920s had brought their surge of enthusiasm for "superpower," a technocratic vision of coordinated large-scale generating units. But in 1935, only one-fifth of the large holding companies were confined to single interconnected (but not necessarily contiguous) areas, and most of them enjoyed little or no technical integration.

The commission's disassembly job, completed in the early 1950s, did not break up any interconnected systems. The commission probably did stall the expansion of interconnection and integration, however; and it failed to use its statutory power to undertake studies designed to promote integration. Its influence, in fact, may well have been hostile to technical efficiency because at the outset it created an incentive for utilities to sever their interstate interconnections in order to keep transactions from falling under federal rate-regulation. Some new transmission lines were built with a close eye to state boundaries. Hughes concludes that the commission's influence on power pooling was probably neutral up to the mid-1960s, positive only after that time.[29]

Regulation of utility rates by state commissions is another influence on the pace of integration. Assume that scale economies in generator units have, over important ranges of output, actually been capital saving per unit of output.[30] Assume the absence of a regulatory lag. If the regulatory commission holds a utility to the same rate of return after it has integrated its generating capacity into a larger system, it would wind up with a smaller total profit. On these assumptions, commission regulation is seriously hostile to integration and technical efficiency. Fortunately, other empirically defensible assumptions tend to undermine this conclusion. Regulatory lag, or a willingness by the state commission to let the utility keep part of the rent from real economies, would restore the incentive to seek them, although in a dampened form in comparison to an unregulated situation. Students of the industry also stress the utilities' strong desires to avoid having to seek increases in their rates from the regulatory commissions. The right conjunction of inflationary pressures and economies available from integration could translate this motive into a force for optimizing the capacities of newly installed generating units. Of course, technological change and cost inflation would only by accident take values conducing this result.

A final institutional drag on consolidation lies in the preference of small municipal and REA systems to retain their own generating capacity rather than buying from large-scale privately owned systems.

The evidence will support no quantitative judgment about the drag of regulatory institutions on the consolidation and coordination of the nation's thermal generating plant. It seems a fair judgment, though, that it imposed some drag at least to the mid–1960s, when the Federal Power Commission began taking a more active hand in encouraging interconnection and other forms of coordination. Hughes provides an estimate of the technical inefficiency of the system due to all causes. It inflated total bulk power cost by a fraction lying between 3.5 and 9.6 percent, with allowance made for savings in direct generating cost, reserve capacity, diversity capacity, and various miscellaneous sources, and with an offset included for the higher transmission costs that would result from concentrating generation in larger and more centralized units.[31]

Could we achieve these cost savings without suffering offsetting efficiency losses elsewhere? The answer to this question depends on the interdependent structure-performance relations in the model. The increase in concentration and reduction in the size variance of integrated generating systems was probably subject to a net deterrent effect of public policy for three decades, and it may still be deterred by the insulating effect of state commission regulation and the dog-cat relation between public- and investor-owned utilities. Had this integration of generating facilities proceeded faster, the turbine makers would have found themselves a more homogeneous market in terms of average nameplate ratings demanded. To predict the effect of this on the domestic turbine triopoly (and world oligopoly) would require some boldness. The general tendency would be to reduce the segmentation of the market and the insulating effect of the different strategies followed by the domestic sellers. This probably means higher concentration, or tighter interdependence in market conduct. But the turbine makers would also be bargaining with a more concentrated group of buyers, so the situation would simply be one of tighter and more homogeneous bilateral oligopoly. The rate of technological progress would probably have been speeded up, and the lag of average technology behind best practice reduced. What would happen to the allocative efficiency of the bilateral market relation between turbine makers and utilities is anybody's guess, but the share of innovative rents captured by the turbine makers would probably not rise. Thus the secondary effects on performance considered so far would be indeterminate or positive.

One performance dimension has so far gone unnoticed—allocative efficiency of the electricity generator-distributors in relation to their final customers. Does increased concentration in a regulated industry portend decreased effectiveness of regulation and increased effective monopoly power? This is not the place for the nth review of the evidence on the effect of regulation on profits: my view is that the state and federal regulatory networks impose some constraint on utility profit rates without entirely eliminating monopoly rents. Would the force of this constraint weaken significantly if the generating systems had achieved a higher level of integration and concentration? Possibly, but the offsetting social losses—the welfare triangles—are apt to be small relative to the efficiency-gain rectangles measured by Hughes. Consider a proposal that has intrigued Hughes, Weiss and others: untie the electricity distribution systems (which are natural monopolies) from the generating-wholesaling systems (which are not). Could the distribution networks in major markets bestir enough competition among bulk suppliers to avoid the highly undesirable "chain of monopolies" effect? Weiss calculates concentration ratios for generating facilities within 100 and 200 miles of ten major load centers. These ratios are high, but not out of line with those in many industrial markets where public policy seems to view the amount of monopolistic distortion as tolerable. An arm's-length market between electricity generation and distribution is not a sure bet for economic viability, given the long-lived and immobile capital and transactions costs and various political and economic risks, but the merits of an independent generating sector deserve consideration.

Notes to Chapter Seven

1. See William M. Capron, ed., *Technological Change in Regulated Industries* (Washington, D.C.: Brookings Institution, 1971).

2. This structure-performance link may, of course, be important outside of the regulated industries. An interesting question is why they provide so many examples of the phenomenon.

3. We will not pursue the influence of differences in producer firms' information sets and preference functions. Instead, we limit our attention to the effects of structures of the user and producer markets, because the former are subject to influence by regulatory authorities, and the latter are (at least) empirically observable.

4. This statement implies the absence of important differences among user subsectors in their elasticity of derived demand for the innovation. By permitting production functions to differ between subsectors, one could generate differences in elasticities. However, no fruitful hypotheses seem to lie along this road.

5. H. Hotelling, "Stability in Competition," *Economic Journal, 39* (March 1929), 41–57.

6. Compare Edwin Manfield, "Innovation and Technical Change in the Railroad Industry," *Transportation Economics,* National Bureau of Economic Research, Special Conference Series, 17 (New York: Columbia University Press, 1965), pp. 164–197.

7. Note the implications of this model for interpreting cross-section research on cost curves and scale economies, especially through the "survivor technique." Increasingly numerous and relatively profitable classes of firms are not necessarily operating at scales that minimize social cost. See William G. Shepherd, "What Does the Survivor Technique Show about Economies of Scale?" *Southern Economic Journal,* 34 (July 1967), 113–22.

8. The ritual complaint about the available evidence is not meant to impugn the imaginative studies recently made of the utilities and the turbine-generator industry. Apart from the published sources cited below, this paper has benefitted greatly from access to two unpublished studies: Ralph G. M. Sultan, "Competition in Oligopoly: An Econometric Analysis"; and William R. Hughes, "Coordination and Integration in the Electric Power Industry: A Study in Industry Structure and Performance."

9. John W. Kendrick, *Productivity Trends in the United States* (New York: National Bureau of Economic Research, 1961), pp. 136–137.

10. U.S. Federal Power Commission, *National Power Survey* (Washington: Government Printing Office, 1964), Part 1, pp. 26, 68. Although the boiler plant bulks larger in capital costs, Sultan argues that it consists of relatively simpler components, less subject to price management by suppliers.

11. U.S. Federal Power Commission, *The 1970 National Power Survey* (Washington: Government Printing Office, 1970), Part IV, p. IV–1–57. Nuclear power may account for one-quarter of installed generating capacity by 1980. The 1970 survey predicts that nuclear installations as large as 6000 MW may ultimately prove efficient.

12. Philip Sporn, *Technology, Engineering, and Economics* (Cambridge and London: MIT Press, 1969), Lecture III, esp. p. 97.

13. Sultan, chapter 12; *Electrical World,* March 31, 1969, p. 33.

14. William R. Hughes, "Scale Frontiers in Electric Power," *Technological Change in Regulated Industries,* ed. W. M. Capron (Washington, D.C.: Brookings Institution, 1971), p. 55. Utilities have, if anything, become more conservative in avoiding outage risks; see Sporn, pp. 94–95. The size of a planned unit is now optimized through a complex calculation, but the general result is the same.

15. Hughes, "Scale Frontiers," pp. 55–57; "Coordination and Integration," chapters 13 and 14.

16. Leonard W. Weiss, "An Evaluation of Antitrust in the Electric Power Industry," *Competition and the Regulation of Industry,* ed. Almarin Phillips (Washington: Brookings Institution, forthcoming), chapter 5. Hughes summarizes the coordination techniques that are in use.

17. R. Komiya, "Technological Progress and the Production Function in the United States Steam Power Industry," *Review of Economics and Statistics,* 44 (May 1962), 156–166; Y. Barzel, "The Production Function and Technical Change in the Steam-Power Industry," *Journal of Political Economy,*

72 (April 1964), 133-150. Cf. W. D. Seitz, "Production Efficiency in the Steam-Electric Generating Industry," *Journal of Political Economy, 79* (July/ August 1971), 878-886.

18. Sultan, chapter 13.

19. Prior to 1960, Allis-Chalmers had spent only 3 to 4 percent of its turbine sales revenue on turbine research. Attempting a leap into major innovation, it spent at a rate of 15 percent in 1961 and 1962. This did not produce sufficient prospects of profit, however, and the firm's 1962 annual report announced its decision to withdraw from the industry. It returned again in 1970 via a joint venture with *Kraftwerk Union AG* of West Germany, itself a consolidation of *Siemens AG* and *AEG Telefunken.* (See *Electrical World,* March 2, 1970, p. 108.) Equipment for sale in the United States was to be manufactured domestically, and the German partner's designs and process licenses were apparently viewed as a principal weapon against the research advantage of Allis-Chalmers's domestic rivals (see the company's 1971 annual report).

20. See *Electrical World,* May 12, 1945, pp. 96-98; February 12, 1949, pp. 81-83; April 7, 1952, pp. 119ff.

21. One might also ask why the "natural monopoly" tendencies inherent in GE's position did not cause its rivals to disappear from the market. One can always invoke the short-run costs of price warfare and the vengeful furies of the antitrust laws. Even without them, however, GE would have captured the balance of the market only with difficulty. Innovations have, apparently, not been subject to patent or proprietary secrecy. Furthermore, the application of new technical features or properties to units of different scale and design apparently does not readily become routine. Hence GE could not practicably exploit all applications of frontiers in turbine-generator design before its rivals had carved out niches for themselves.

22. Chapter 14.

23. Sultan, *loc. cit.; Electrical World,* January 1, 1968, pp. 15-16. AEP's switch was related to its massive corporate fight with GE in the damage suits following the electrical conspiracies, but AEP in 1968 also alluded to a specific element of price rivalry: the refusal of GE or Westinghouse to quote firm prices earlier than 36 months before delivery of equipment (orders may be placed 60 months prior to delivery).

24. Edison Electrical Institute, *Report on Equipment Availability, 1960-1970* (New York, 1971), p. 13. One recent simulation identified differences in expected outage rates as a critical constraint on the maximum efficient size of turbines for a large utility system. See *Electric World,* September 29, 1969, pp. 41-44.

25. Sporn, *Technology, Engineering, and Economics,* pp. 48-54. Sporn also emphasizes that the risk of extrapolating from 200 MW to 1000 MW nuclear units was "not inconsiderable based upon experience in other technological areas and in conventional power" (p. 60).

26. At a time when no unit larger than 500 MW was in service, GE reported it was "actively developing designs" for 1500 MW units and considering 2000 MW units "to assure availability of the facilities and production techniques

required to produce the larger units *as the demand for them arises.*" (Emphasis added.) See Edison Electrical Institute, *Report on Current Research and Development in the Electric Utility Industry* (New York, 1963), p. 5.

27. Hughes summarizes the relevant data in "Scale Frontiers," pp. 54–55.

28. William Iulo's study, while confirming the relation between turbine scale and generating costs, did not find a relation between utilities' total size and average total unit costs. See his *Electric Utilities – Cost and Performance* (Pullman: Washington State University Press, 1961).

29. Hughes, "Scale Frontiers," p. 59; "Coordination and Integration", chapter 2.

30. Sultan, chapter 16, suggests that this has been the case.

31. Hughes, "Coordination and Integration," chapter 15.

Chapter Eight

The Market for Commercial Airliners

Sidney L. Carroll

1. INTRODUCTION

Recent studies of the aircraft industry, particularly a book by Almarin Phillips,[1] give strong evidence that market structure in the airline industry may be strongly affected by technological developments in the products of the industry which supplies their chief capital goods. The thrust here will be to analyze the conduct of the firms which participate in the market for jet aircraft and to marshal behavioral evidence to explain the structural and technological data in the aircraft industry.

The commercial turbine airliner market is quantitatively quite significant, highly volatile in terms of sales variability and growing rapidly if unevenly. The period from 1958 forward can fairly be termed revolutionary in the sense that in ten years almost the entire capital stock of an important industry was replaced by a qualitatively new type of machine. The airlines' "diesel revolution" came much more quickly than did the railroads'! In what manner this revolution was achieved, as well as the role of government regulation and intervention, are matters of interest. The investigation will proceed as follows. Structure in the airline (user) industry and then in the airframe (producer) industry are briefly reviewed. Then comes the recent historical record of behavior and profits performance in the market. Next is a more general analysis of conduct in the market. Finally, the importance of all of this for economic performance is investigated.

2. AIRLINE STRUCTURE

The airline industry, as can be seen from table 8-1, is a fairly concentrated one, even at the national level. Since most carriers are fundamentally regional in character, national concentration understates true levels of market con-

Table 8-1.   United States Airline Scheduled Service,
First Six Months of 1972

Airlines	Revenue Passenger Miles (000)	Percent of Total
United	11,414,300	16.8
Trans World	9,831,920	14.5
American	9,275,627	13.7
Pan American	8,921,563	13.1
Eastern	8,239,537	12.2
Delta	5,500,760	8.1
Northwest	3,325,829	4.9
National	2,731,822	4.0
Others	8,530,179	12.6

Notes: Others includes Braniff, Caribair, Continental, Northeast and Western.

Source: *Avaiation Week and Space Technology,* December 18, 1972.

centration. However, for the purposes of this chapter, the national size distribution of firms is pertinent, for it is the derived demand for its chief capital good, aircraft, which is at issue. Without further elaboration at this point, it suffices that the five or six largest trunk lines are crucial to the introduction of a new generation of commercial aricraft.

Structure in the airline industry is far from the result of national market forces. Rather it has been closely shepherded and controlled by the Civil Aeronautics Board. The CAB carefully constrains the airlines' route structures so that they cannot be rearranged in response to changes in the costs and operating characteristics of new aircraft. Further, at least during the period of primary interest here, the CAB set fares and constrained price competition, channelling rivalry into product competition—new aircraft and frequency of scheduling being the chief tools.

Innate characteristics of air transportation dictate that, *ceteris paribus,* longer routes between densely populated areas are the more profitable ones. It has been the CAB's policy to insure that such routes are served by more than one trunk line and to control fare levels on these lines so that competition is forced into product differentiation. Since it has been amply demonstrated that newer, faster aircraft are a powerful tool of product differentiation, the pressure to get new craft into service on such routes is quite intense. Conversely, the need for newer equipment is much less severe on the shorter, less dense routes which are often monopolistic.

The upshot of this type of CAB regulation is that when a technological breakthrough occurs in aircraft technology, (e.g., a new engine development), the innovating energies of aircraft designers are directed to the most lucrative first market for a new generation of planes; the long-haul, dense traffic routes. On these routes the five or six largest trunk carriers will have significant first orders and so will be the prime targets as customers for aircraft producers.

While in the absence of regulation one can envision other scenarios, the facts of CAB regulation and airline economics combine to rather narrowly prescribe the main customers for new aircraft as well as the desirable characteristics for such planes: namely, larger long-haul versions.

3. STRUCTURE IN THE AIRLINER-PRODUCER INDUSTRY

There are at most four United States firms which could be considered either actual or potential producers of large modern airliners. These are Boeing, McDonnell-Douglas, Lockheed and General Dynamics. In addition, there are a few foreign firms on the fringes of the market, but their impact on the domestic market has been quite limited. Table 8-2 gives an indication of the early dominance of Boeing in this market.

Table 8-2.   Jet Aircraft in Service on United States Airlines

Year	Boeing	BAC	General Dynamics	McDonnell-Douglas	SUD	Lockheed	Other[a]	Total
1958	6							6
1959	66			18				84
1960	113		14	75				202
1961	170		39	93	17			319
1962	216		60	100	20			396
1963	237		65	104	20			426
1964	357		67	114	20			558
1965	476	17	65	134	20			712
1966	645	54	63	196	20			978
1967	661	54	63	205	20		3	1003
1968	883	57	59	321	20	1	3	1340
1969	1146	60	52	503	20			1781
1970	1331	60	47	610	20			2068
1971	1408	59	46	622			1	2136
1972	1395	62	49	619		1	6	2132
1973	1341	58	49	650		18	2	2118

Notes: The above figures are as of December 31 each year except 1973, when the effective date is August 31. Others includes Dassault and Hamburger Flugzeugbau.
Source: "Aircraft in Operation by Certificated Route Air Carriers," U.S. Department of Transportation, Federal Aviation Administration, *FAA Statistical Handbook of Civil Aviation,* various years.

Additionally, each of these firms has quite substantial defense and space contracts as table 8-3 indicates. The intimate interconnection with government is even understated by table 8-3. An examination of total backlogs of several airframe companies shows that only Douglas had large commercial backlogs at the beginning of the period.[2] Each of the four firms which entered commercial jet production had at least an $800 million cushion in unfilled government orders. The importance of such life insurance to one company was recognized by an industry observer:

Table 8-3.   Commercial Sales as a Percentage of Total Sales

Year	General Dynamics	McDonnell-Douglas	Boeing	Lockheed
1957		31.5	2.1	
1958		21.2	4.0	12.5
1959		11.9	25.4	
1960		46.7	31.1	
1961	10.8	37.5	22.7	
1962	13.3	22.8	23.8	3.0
1963	19.4	22.4	14.7	
1964	20.5	23.5	35.6	
1965	21.9	33.2	49.6	
1966	22.0	46.4	52.3	5.0
1967		32.2	57.1	
1968		46.5	69.2	
1969		46.0	64.3	6.0
1970	1.3	29.6	78.4	4.0
1971	1.7	28.5	76.7	3.0
1972	4.3	40.9		

Note: A blank indicates data were not available.

Source: Company Annual Reports, various years, *Moody's Industrials* and *Moody's Handbook of Common Stocks,* various years.

Having a family of jets and having them first has unquestionably played a large part in the Boeing success. But this alone could never have put the company where it is. Throughout its recent history, Boeing has specialized with one major customer, the United States government.[3]

That government money provides much of the technology and plant for commercial aircraft is beyond dispute. The Boeing 707 in its tanker version sold several hundred planes. The 707 itself was built in a plant leased from the government.[4] Lockheed sells commercial versions of its C-130, C-141, and C-5A. Airbuses and the Boeing 747 were spawned by technical advances on the engines used for the C-5A. Every generation of new civilian transport has relied heavily on technology developed for the military.[5]

Airframe firms are fully aware that the government probably will not allow a company with huge defense backlogs to fail because of commercial misfortunes. Hard evidence here is difficult to obtain. However, the feeling is demonstrated by the following:

> One New York financial source said that the government, airline, and banking officials had agreed that the Douglas situation would not be allowed to reach crisis proportions because of the economic and military consequences that might follow.[6]

Douglas was eventually wed to McDonnell.

The foregoing does not suggest that the government guarantees satisfactory performance results for any company in its commercial endeavors, but rather that large backlogs of "safe" government contracts—coupled with the government's reluctance to let a truly large contractor entirely disappear—embolden firms to undertake risky commercial ventures.[7]

Recognition of the high risks in commercial aircraft production has led to one rather significant development in the last few years. Airframe manufacturers have shown increasing interest in devices which shift some of the risk of the venture either forward or backward. For its 747, Boeing "devised an unprecedented risk-sharing scheme . . . in which subcontractors are putting up at least $100 million of the development capital."[8] At the same time larger airline progress-payments than customary were stipulated.[9] Similar risk-sharing provisions were obtained by each airbus manufacturer.[10] Despite these devices the market remains quite risky for the manufacturer.

The cost characteristics of aircraft production are singularly interesting and contribute vitally to the marketing process. First, developing a new aircraft version requires huge expenditures on research and development, tooling, etc. Second is the "learning curve" phenomenon which operates in all new aircraft production. Briefly, the learning curve reflects the idea that as each successive unit is produced, techniques become more familiar and refined, usage of materials becomes more efficient, and more and more kinks are ironed out of the operation. Studies of various airframe development projects have reached the conclusion that, for example, there tends to be about an 80 percent learning curve for unit labor costs in airframes; that is, for each doubling of output, about a 20 percent reduction in unit costs occurs. Further, there appears to be no practical limit to the applicability of the learning curve. The larger the number of units produced, the lower the unit cost on the last unit.

These cost aspects insure that economies of scale are very important as well as practically limitless in production of a specific aircraft. High initial costs insure rapidly falling average total cost, while the learning curve phenomenon insures that incremental and average variable costs will continue to decline. Thus, costs for a particular airframe type take on the aspects of a natural monopoly with continuing economies of scale.

Other institutional and technical factors which contribute to the marketing climate are the following: (1) lumpiness in orders with only a few large orders dominating the scene; this results from regulatory effects on airline structure as outlined earlier; (2) the multidimensional nature of the product. What is purchased is not merely an aircraft, but an aircraft for delivery on a specified date. Production costs depend not just on the total number produced, but also on the rate of production. Similarly, carriers typically prefer an early delivery date to a later one, for competitive reasons; (3) knowledge that there is at least one other competing producer; (4) asymmetric knowledge of price and other bargaining positions; the buyer is usually well informed of the facts while the seller remains at least partly in the dark; (5) the standard contract policy of making price cuts to additional customers apply to all earlier orders. Hence, though orders are placed over a period of months, price for a particular plane remains substantially uniform.

4. THE RECENT RECORD: BEHAVIOR

The hallmark of airliner marketing has been intense and persistent interfirm rivalry. Price cutting and price equivalent quality and financing concessions are repeatedly evident. If any collusion, market sharing or market splitting has occurred among the airframe companies, it has been well hidden indeed. There have been three cases where substantially identical competing aircraft were offered to the airlines. These cases are to be investigated with an eye toward knowledge of the market process. Quality competition, financing concessions and other competitive gambits will also be explored. Following this, interproduct and foreign competition is reviewed. Finally, some attention is given to possible reasons for the lack of oligopolistic accommodation in this market.

Exact pricing maneuvers during the introduction of the DC-8, Convair 880, and Boeing 707 are lost in the corporate negotiations of the latter half of the 1950s. It is clear, however, that both price concessions and quality adjustments were rife during this period of first-round large orders. Early in the negotiations, "with Boeing on a spot owing to United's order, American president C. R. Smith was in a position to dictate terms."[11] The result was a redesigned 707, four inches wider, to be one inch wider than the DC-8. Other implicit concessions were evident. General Dynamics redesigned the 880 into a larger 990 specifically for American Airlines and then accepted from American, as a "$25 million" down payment, twenty-five DC-7s, worth perhaps half that.[12] Boeing's president, William M. Allen, complained of competition in prices "so low as to make no economic sense."[13] As for Douglas: "To get into the market at all, Douglas had to shave prices to a point where nearly half of some 150 jets it has so far sold . . . will be delivered at prices below factory costs."[14] Only after the large airlines had been sold and Boeing had established its primacy did any upward price leadership occur.[15]

Competition in the two-engine short-haul market took a slightly different form. Douglas began production of its DC-9 considerably ahead of Boeing with its 737. Only the BAC 111 provided a deliverable aircraft in fairly direct competition, and this threat faded considerably with technical difficulties.[16] Despite its time advantage, production difficulties and underpricing teamed up to help make the DC-9 a financial failure. In addition, Boeing was not dormant, despite its lack of an aircraft. It had announced its own short-haul aircraft (the 737) and was offering several concessions to prospective buyers. One excellent example of this is afforded by the United Airlines order of the 737. As a part of that deal, Boeing agreed to lease United a fleet of its 727s at nominal cost until the 737s were delivered.[17] Boeing was also able to offer a wide variety of configuration options, as its design was not rigidly set.[18] Thus,

Douglas's position was not nearly so secure as it might have seemed, and it faced real competition from a substantially identical plane as well as from less similar aircraft.

Most recent of the waves of competition is that between Lockheed and McDonnell-Douglas over sales of the three engined "airbus." Some details of these negotiations are publicly available and demonstrate rather well the nature of the market. The conception of the airbus follows quite normal lines. A breakthrough in engine technology, spurred by government procurement activities (in this case the C-5A), made it feasible to construct a much higher capacity two- or three-engined airliner. American Airlines engineers recognized this possibility and approached the four commercial aircraft makers. All showed some interest, and eventually Lockheed and later McDonnell-Douglas seriously began design work.[19] By this time the three-jet airbus configuration was set. The two aircraft designs were nearly identical. This was no accident as "similarity of the DC-10 and the L-1011 designs is close and resulted primarily from cross fertilization of design information by the airlines."[20]

American Airlines was the first carrier to go into negotiations with the companies. The record of these negotiations demonstrates that the cross fertilization of information by the airlines does not extend to price data. American picked the $16 million DC-10 over the $16.7 million Lockheed L-1011, ordering twenty-five options. One observer characterized the nego-tiations as follows:

> Probably the most valid speculation is that Lockheed miscalculated on price. It had pegged the airbus high, partly to be able to make last minute bargaining cuts, and partly because Douglas had taken such a bath on its DC-8's and 9's that Lockheed didn't believe the competition could engage in another price war. But Lockheed never got to the final hours when it could start cutting. And McDonnell-Douglas did cut its price under Lockheed's by approximately $1 million per airplane.[21]

At this point the American order, secured by underpricing Lockheed, seemed to give McDonnell-Douglas a leg up in the "race."

Next in line to order the jets were Eastern and TWA. In a complicated financial maneuver involving Rolls-Royce and an international holding company (Air Holdings, Limited) and fraught with political impli-cations, Lockheed garnered orders for over one hundred planes.[22] Lockheed in this instance seems to have grabbed off the order largely through slashing its price to $15 million. Although such things as favorable delivery time were of importance, price again held greatest sway:

> Negotiations twisted through scores of bargaining points ranging from delivery positions and progress payments to cabin con-

figurations and the effect on the U.S. balance of payments. But in all the intrigue and midnight telephone calls, the dominating issue was price. Says one airline officer with glee: "It was great. The longer negotiations lasted, the more we got."[23]

In the second round it is McDonnell-Douglas which appears to have taken price as a datum. Lockheed was not to be undersold, however, as this observation illustrates:

> Lockheed dropped its unit price in the closing phases of the intense competition by increasing its breakeven number of aircraft rather than through cost revisions or modifications. McDonnell-Douglas retained a more conservative breakeven number, possibly, in the view of one airline official, because of incomplete intelligence on what Lockheed was doing.[24]

At this point only United Airlines, of the largest carriers, had not placed an airbus order.[25] Further, McDonnell-Douglas did not contemplate production without this additional large order. The almost predictable order was not long in coming. McDonnell-Douglas cut its price to $15.5 million and obtained the United order for thirty planes and thirty options.[26] Of most interest in this development is the fact that McDonnell-Douglas was contractually obligated to adjust American Airlines' and other prior customers' contracts retroactively to United's more favorable terms.[27] Lockheed undoubtedly would have been similarly obligated had it won the United order.

The airbus machinations provide many insights into the dynamics of this type of noncollusive duopolistic bargaining. At a later point behavior under such conditions will be more systematically examined. To sum up the assessment of the marketing process by the airframe officials engaged in it, one following, plaintive citation is offered: "This is a competitive business, and it's understandable that someone is ready to scratch and bite to get his share. But all of this nonsense has been unfortunate."[28]

Competition between different types of aircraft (and from foreign planes) supplements the head-to-head rivalry between nearly technically identical aircraft. Each carrier's route structure makes its aircraft needs unique; technically dissimilar craft often may have quite comparable cost characteristics for certain route systems. Further, existing basic types of aircraft are usually reengineered into "stretched" or shrunken versions which can more easily compete with other types of craft.[29] Many versions of a basic type of craft were in use or on order by United States carriers in mid 1969.[30] The many models and passenger capacities of the DC-8 are a good example of the modifications that can be made to a basic aircraft type.

The capability to redesign airliners to different specifications is demonstrated by several instances. Convair's 880, a somewhat smaller craft than the Boeing 707 or the DC-8, seemed better suited for United Airlines' route structure. Boeing answered this challenge by redesigning the 707 into a smaller version, the 720, with lower operating costs than the 880 and was thereby able to get United's order.[31] Stretched versions of the DC–9 have provided some rivalry to the substantially unique Boeing 727. Larger versions of the DC–8 have been offered as substitutes for the airbuses, and the Boeing 747.[32] On the Eastern Airlines' route system, the stretched versions of the DC–8, and the 61 and 63 series, have been said to have operating costs on a par with the Boeing 747.[33] As one final instance of this interproduct competition phenomenon, a National Airlines official has noted that "the airbus could very well make the difference between exercising our options on the 747 and ordering airbuses instead."[34]

That United States airframe manufactuers have dominated sales to United States airlines is beyond dispute. In early 1969 the twelve large United States trunk airlines had total reported fleets of 1,504 turbine aircraft. Of these only 63—20 SUD Caravelles and 43 BAC 111s—were made by foreign companies. In the total world aircraft fleet, 2747 of the total of 3494 (or 78.6%) are United States made.[35]

This evidence of United States dominance only reflects the end result of the sales race. It does not imply that the foreign threat seemed insignificant at the time orders were being finalized. In the late fifties, for example, the threat of foreign competition seems to have been considered quite serious.[36] Another instance of serious foreign competition in the United States market was in the short to medium haul craft. American Airlines' order for thirty BAC 111s in lieu of Douglas DC–9s may very well have caused Douglas to underprice its plane in competitive reaction.[37]

There is ample evidence of highly competitive behavior among the commercial turbine-airliner builders. The competition is manifest in both price and product competition, and it is reflected in each successive new wave of aircraft. Not only is there just some competition, but rather the competition has been so intense and unbending as to make the market generally and perpetually unprofitable.

5. THE RECENT RECORD: PROFITS PERFORMANCE

Only four domestic airframe companies—Douglas, General Dynamics, Boeing, and Lockheed—have participated or seriously considered participating in the production of large airliners since 1955. The enormous research and development costs insure that only very large firms with access to abundant capital can weather the early period of great expenditure without immediate returns. By far the most striking feature of the market is the consistent and repeated aggregate financial loss suffered by the industry.

Examples of this phenomenon are abundant. Boeing in its attempt with several pre 707 planes suffered heavy losses;[38] Lockheed's losses on its

Electra totalled approximately $141 million before taxes;[39] General Dynamics in 1961 reported combined write-offs for development costs and inventory write-downs of $435 million;[40] Douglas reported staggering losses on both its DC-8 and DC-9;[41] and even most-successful Boeing's president reported "everybody making commercial jets has lost a piece of his shirt, although in some cases it has been only the tail."[42] It is sufficient to point out here that there is a pattern of poor profits and that the pattern is known to the industry. As James J. McDonnell said of the commercial jet market, "the risks as compared to the possibilities of gain are completely incommensurate."[43]

Further, it appears clear that conditions of cost and demand have been such that a monopolist of a species of airliner could have been successfully profitable. The nature of the market process, nevertheless, apparently decrees that, at most, one producer will be successful, and that the *a priori* expectation of a nonmonopolistic entrant into a race for sales should be one of great risk and (probably) a negative expected value of profits.

Under such conditions it is pertinent to investigate the reasons for past entry and losses. It seems improbable that a firm, even with knowledge of likely industry losses, would enter the market with the anticipation that it would sustain a substantial setback. In light of realized losses, then, there must have been serious errors in forecasting, and indeed there were from both demand and cost standpoints. Particularly interesting is the tendency to underestimate both development and production costs. Cost underestimation has not been an isolated phenomenon. Overoptimism is common on both development and production costs and has been characteristic of all companies. Some examples are these. In early February 1959, it was said that "by sometime in 1960 Dynamics expects it will have caught up its $200 million investment in commercial jets, and will begin to make some profits."[44] Less than a year and a half later General Dynamics had reported combined write-offs for development costs and inventory write-downs of almost $500 million, with more still to come. At Douglas "all of last year's (1959) commercial deliveries were at prices below actual factory costs."[45] Douglas seriously miscalculated costs on its DC-9, too As an illustration, it was anticipated that the DC-9 would have a twenty-plane breakeven point. But the first twenty averaged $1.25 million losses ($.5 million more than expected), and after production of fifty planes, Douglas was still losing $.2 million in manufacturing costs and $.2 million in overhead costs on each plane.[46] Similar but less disastrous miscalculation hit Boeing on its 707[47] and its 727.[48] Thus, almost as a rule, manufacturers underestimate both development costs and the height of the realized learning curve.

Other factors influence the decision to build airliners. One powerful impetus might be termed management ego or, more kindly, the desire to enhance the firm's image. Many executives seem to be quite interested in building the commercial portion of their sales. As one put it, "our great ambition is to produce the finest commercial transports in the world."[49]

Unreasonable optimism is not unknown. Frank Pace, president of General Dynamics in 1959, was quoted as saying "ours is a business that, with a little luck, is surely slated for greatness."[50] Much of this greatness was to be achieved in commercial aviation.

There are several other features of the industry which help lead to participation in commercial aircraft. Airframe companies often seem to be drawn to the commercial market by the lure of large sales and to be insufficiently mindful that adequate profits may not follow from these sales. This overwhelming concern with orders per se has led to management actions which are in retrospect dubious to say the least. Two instances serve to illustrate this type of management problem. In 1957, early in the Convair 880 program, an engineer in the purchasing division of General Dynamics is reported to have routinely calculated that the cost of vendor-supplied components alone would total more than the average price then being negotiated by the plane marketers. Management, presumably concerned with simply pushing ahead with the project, dismissed the engineer. Two years later, when the accuracy of his estimates was rather painfully clear, he was rehired.[51]

The DC–9 experience is another case illustrating difficulty in coordinating sales and production efforts. Learning curves represent the unit cost of the nth aircraft at the optimum *rate* of production. If production lags behind this rate, then fixed costs cannot be spread over enough units; if production must be done at a higher-than-optimum rate, bottlenecks, shortages and overtime rapidly increase unit cost. For the DC–9, as with most aircraft orders, a plane is sold to be delivered on a particular date, with penalties assessed for late delivery. A lack of coordination between marketing effort and production realities caused Douglas to obligate itself to unrealistically high rates of delivery. The ensuing attempts to meet these promised deliveries resulted in substantial losses.[52]

A final impetus to entry into commercial production stems from intense interfirm rivalry among the largest firms. Each firm sees a few other highly visible firms as its rivals as complete aerospace companies. The prospect of one of the other firms stealing a march as the sole producer of a lucrative commercial aircraft often seems to weigh heavily in the final decision to produce.

The preceding discussion enumerates some reasons for the entry of airframe companies into the commercial field. It further illustrates how their behavior may lead to large losses. What it does not do is demonstrate the necessity for such actions in a market with this type of structure. Indeed, most small-number oligopolies are able to reach some accommodation or understanding through tacit collusion, market leadership or attrition which prevents continuance of noncollusive negative-sum rivalry. Nevertheless, this industry so far seems to have demonstrated a nearly complete lack of either implicit or explicit price collusion or even market sharing.

6. A MORE GENERAL ANALYSIS OF BEHAVIOR
IN THE COMMERCIAL AIRCRAFT MARKET

Since demand for new aircraft is derived from the demand for air travel, carriers must make some estimates of the demand they can expect during the lifetime of their planes.[53] If aircraft could be purchased "off the shelf" as needed, such estimates would be rather routine. In practice, though, aircraft fleets are ordered well ahead of delivery and in rather large quantities.

Many complicating elements enter into the estimation of demand for future periods. First, a carrier's demand is intimately interrelated with the actions of competing carriers; the sizes and types of aircraft flown by other carriers greatly affect results. In addition to decisions by carriers, actions on routes by the Civil Aeronautics Board can greatly alter future aircraft needs. Another factor whose impact must be predicted is that the type of aircraft and its appeal to passengers may quite substantially alter the equation; for example, most travelers prefer jets, *ceteris paribus,* to piston planes. Added to these problems are the standard factors of growth in incomes, uncertainty and interdependence of costs, rates and quantity demanded.

In view of these problems it is little wonder that even estimates of aggregate demand have been erratic. Though carriers have not disclosed their methods in detail, it seems fair to conjecture that the process remains more art than science.

The most interesting period in the history of a particular generation of aircraft occurs during the first-round ordering process. Typically, the producers announce a new product, release tentative price and performance estimates, and attempt to line up "sufficient" orders to justify beginning production. At this point the major trunk airlines must make decisions about their own needs. The possibility that an airline could purchase new, older-generation craft or used craft either to replace substantial portions of existing fleets or to expand capacity greatly can be ignored. Such actions generally are competitively infeasible. Further, older aircraft models are not usually in quantity production, so that their aggregate fleet can be considered fixed.

The airline is then faced with two types of decisions. First, it must decide the quantity of new equipment to order for capacity expansion. Second, it must address the question of how rapidly existing capacity should be replaced with new equipment. The former decision, ignoring complications, would involve comparing the capital costs (including ground equipment, training costs and similar items) with the discounted value of future net revenues. Jets would be added to the total fleet until their cost exceeded incremental net revenues. In the latter case, the relevant comparison would be the fully allocated cost of the new aircraft with the operating cost (presumably rising over time) of existing craft on a route by route basis.

To this point nothing exceptional has been presented. Some peculiarities of the market, however, inject themselves to complicate this type of mechanical calculation. First is the sequential nature of production runs for new aircraft. An order for planes specifies not only the number of aircraft taken but also *position* in the delivery schedule of the producer. Thus, purchasers must queue up for new airplanes, so that for a considerable period purchases cannot be routinely made to augment the fleet or to replace spent aircraft. In such a situation neither the availability nor the price of the aircraft is certain in the future.[54]

Historically, each new generation of aircraft has exhibited substantially lower operating costs than the preceding group, at least for a large proportion of the routes. Thus, the large jets of the late 1950s were said to have 40 percent lower direct operating costs than the pistons they replaced.[55] Using a concept called the "theoretical fare," T. F. Cartaino finds that a two- or three-engined airbus would have a "fare reduction potential of about 15 percent compared to the 727–100—then the standard in the medium-haul range. He also finds a 12 to 14 percent cost advantage for new transcontinental craft.[56] In the case of the first jets (707 and DC–8), these realized cost advantages were even greater than had been anticipated.[57] Even with pessimistic expectations, substantial orders are usually indicated.

Cost advantages and delivery position strategies are only two factors working in favor of large initial equipment orders in the first round. Other equally strong factors are at work. Average aircraft costs are not independent of the number of planes in the fleet. That is, there are minimum efficient fleet sizes for maintenance purposes.[58] One further factor militates in favor of large orders. Airlines have needs for differing airplane configurations according to their route structures. Larger airlines have been successful in having planes tailored somewhat to their own specifications in return for the guarantee of a large order. Thus, the Convair 990 was "designed by American and sold to them at a fixed price while still on the drawing board,"[59] and Pan American got the 747 "virtually tailored to its system."[60]

In sum, major trunk airlines tend to order large numbers of new aircraft at one time, early in the life of a new generation of aircraft, for each of the following reasons: (1) there seems to be a minimum efficient-size fleet for maintenance purposes, (2) there are economies in training, break in and coordination if the number of different types of aircraft in an airline's fleet is kept small, (3) for several reasons the larger the potential order of an airline, the greater the concessions to be had on design, price, delivery time and financing, (4) delivery positions need to be guaranteed to prevent being locked out of the market for a considerable period of time, (5) there is typically a competitive struggle among trunks to place "modern" equipment in operation and (6) substantial productivity gains are usually available in new equipment.

So once the decision has been made to purchase, it becomes desirable to place orders for sizable fleets. Further, the fairly concentrated nature of the air carrier industry insures that the orders made by individual airlines are large relative to the total market. From this, and the situation of the sellers, a large airline derives considerable market power from its purchasing decision.

The market power conferred on trunk airlines is greatly enhanced if the manufacturers are offering competing designs; that is, where there exist competing products with quite similar operating characteristics and negotiable price and quality features. This has, in fact, been the usual situation in aircraft markets, particularly in the first-round ordering phases.

Usually, when a new genre of aircraft, representing a quite different technology, configuration or size appears, there are two or three potential producers seeking to secure firm orders for enough planes to get them close to what they consider to be their breakeven point.[61] Simultaneously, most of the large airlines are dickering with the companies using the possibility of a large order as a bargaining tool.

Given the learning curve phenomenon, a reasonable outcome for such a process might very well be the eventual production of the aircraft type by a single firm. Whichever firm garners the first order surely has a large cost advantage over competitors. That firm's position further out on a hypothetical learning curve would constitute a formidable barrier to entry to less fortunate firms. Further, price and quality concessions could be made on subsequent (and prior) orders taking advantage of lower unit costs and spreading out sunk costs to bar potential competitors. In view of the underlying cost conditions, then, one might expect the normal outcome of natural monopoly.

Regardless of how reasonable the natural-monopoly scenario may seem, it is not the one which has actually appeared for commercial aircraft. Indeed, almost invariably at least two quite similar competing aircraft have actually been produced. Examples are these: DC-6, Constellation, and Stratocruiser; the DC-8, 707, and 880; the DC-10 and L-1011; and the DC-9 and 737; and myriad intermediate and stretched aircraft. This multiple-source procurement phenomenon, which is of paramount import for performance of the industry, has several possible causes which will be explored next.

Several factors combine to enhance the tendency toward multiple source competing production. The first of these results from the fact that an airline's fleet of planes is an important product-differentiating tool. Airlines stress their more-advanced aircraft in competing with each other for passengers. This type of differentiation has two apsects, both of which work toward multiple sourcing. The first of these is delivery-time competition. If one producer has built a substantial order-backlog lead, the airlines which have not placed orders are able to secure earlier delivery from a competitor with a leaner list of orders. The second aspect involves "plane tailoring." An ordering airline, particularly if it is placing the initial large order (or the second, "breakeven" order) can elicit favorable specification changes in exchange for the crucial order. Examples of this were given earlier in the case of the Boeing 747 and Convair 990, and the interesting case in which the Boeing 707 design was widened as a condition for American Airlines ordering thirty of the planes.[62]

Competition among airlines is not the sole impetus behind the multiple-sourcing phenomenon. Trunk airlines are scarcely incapable of "cooperation," even in the purchase of airplanes. In one instance of this, two airlines alternated deliveries of the Lockheed Electra.[63] Further, carriers frequently lease craft from each other, as National did from Pan American to begin the first domestic jet service.[64] Finally, use of the same craft by more than one line on a joint flight is not uncommon.

Even so, although there are examples of attempts by carriers to *limit* the varieties of craft by colluding on purchase, these efforts have usually failed. The following account illustrates one such attempt.

> Apparently President Patterson of United led a substantial effort to get these four large trunk carriers to agree to order a single airplane. There were numerous reasons for United to make such a move. It was not clear that both the Boeing 707 and Douglas DC-8 would actually be produced in commercial quantities, and a scattering of orders for each would have produced an awkward situation. Pooled purchases would probably allow the chosen manufacturer to offer a lower price.[65]

Despite this attempt, the pool did not come off and Pan American ordered both planes.

It is possible that the carriers did not agree to Patterson's plan because of their inability to cooperate. What seems more likely is that at least President Juan Trippe of Pan American felt that the best interest of the carriers lay in having, if possible, more than one source of supply. Several crucial assumptions are implicit in the argument for a single source. The first is that if multiple development occurs, no producer will be able to obtain the economies of its learning curve, as each will have a "scattering of orders." The second is that developing two or more craft will entail expensive duplication of effort and that the carriers will have to *bear* these costs for each producer.

Historically, neither assumption has been justified. In each generation of competition there has been a distinct "winner" (or least loser) who produced a large number of planes while the other producer absorbed substantial losses. Thus, not only was one producer usually able to take advantage of its learning curve, but also the price of aircraft reflected those costs (both fixed and variable) and not some markup over the average of all producers' costs.

Finally, as was surely recognized, any price concessions available from single source collusion by the airlines would be most difficult to secure in any second wave of reprocurement. At that point the trunks would be faced with the unpleasant alternatives of dickering independently with a strong monopolist or once again attempting to collude in the uncertain world of bilateral monopoly.[66]

While representatives of the carriers are rather close-mouthed about such matters, it seems unlikely that such considerations were unknown to them. The best evidence, of course, is their actions. As one industry observer remarked of Trippe's move: "He guaranteed first delivery for his airline and incidentally assured that there would be two manufacturers of commercial jets."[67] Moreover, the desirability of there being competing aircraft is mentioned sporadically in trade journals.[68]

In sum, airlines reap substantial advantages from the existence of competing aircraft that are close substitutes. They gain substantial bargaining advantages in both initial orders and in reprocurement. Actions of the carriers contribute to the multiple-production phenomenon in their response to competitive pressures among themselves. Moreover, it seems most likely that there is a conscious (collusive or not) recognition of the advantages of multiple sources, and that actions are taken in an attempt to insure its occurrence.

Besides the pull of demanders there is considerable push from the engine makers (General Electric, Pratt and Whitney and Rolls-Royce). Recent actions by General Electric serve to illustrate this. After an early lead in airbus orders, McDonnell-Douglas had been passed by Lockheed's L-1011. The crucial airline order for the General Electric-powered DC-10 was that of United Air Lines, and United was reportedly leaning toward Lockheed. At this point General Electric stepped into the breach by offering "massive" financing aid to United. This swung the United order to the DC-10 and sealed the McDonnell-Douglas decision to go into production.[69]

That there is pressure working for multiple sources both from the carriers and the engine makers is clear. What is not so evident is why these forces have been so irresistible. Regardless of the pressures, the decision making process of the manufacturers will help to explain their actions.

The airframe manufactures are a small, highly visible group, undoubtedly acutely aware of each others' actions and of their own highly interdependent fates. In such a situation the common resolution, so often repeated in concentrated industries, is the evolution of some sort of mutual accommodation, especially with regard to "indiscriminate" price cutting. As yet, even after many years, no such accommodation seems to have been reached.

An examination of some of the particulars of the situation in which a potential supplier of new planes finds itself sheds some light. The simple learning curve phenomenon illustrates the great importance of large orders to the supplier. For example, suppose a manufacturer believes that his variable costs are such that he can produce the fiftieth plane at an incremental cost of $5 million. Assuming an 80 percent learning curve, then his average variable cost for the first fifty planes is $7.1 million. If the minimum price acceptable to the manufacturer is, say, $8.0 million, then the incremental profit received is $45 million minus the costs of tooling and initiating production. However, if the order available is for one hundred planes, then a price of $6.13 million yields the same profit results.[70]

As has been demonstrated, a firm, mostly because of falling costs, is able to offer a lower price, ceteris paribus, the larger the present order and the larger its backlog of past orders. This gets one very little along the way toward an explanation of the whole bargaining process. Returning to the first large order for a type of plane, the pricing process is yet to be explained. Indeed, the situation depends on relative bargaining strengths and tactics. All that can be said is that the airframe firms start with initial proposals on price and configuration and the potential customer continues to exact concessions until finally choosing what seems to be the best possible offer.

It is the second and subsequent round of orders that are, at first blush, puzzling. In the second large order, the competing plane makers are no longer coequal. The producer which has already garnered the first order seems to have distinct advantages. The first order guarantees that at least some progress along the learning curve will be achieved. Therefore, if the firms' cost conditions are at all similar, it is clear that the manufacturer with orders in hand could produce a new order at distinctly lower costs than could another firm. Despite these advantages, as is evident from the earlier review of sales rounds, the customary outcome is for a second manufacturer to win an early large order and for the second producer to gain enough orders to send it into production.

One reason for the multiple source phenomenon is the realization on the part of the airlines that there are many advantages in bargaining with noncollusive sellers of a type of product. This alone might or might not be enough to bring a second seller to production. There are, however, further substantive factors that mitigate the seeming inequality of bargaining position between the firm which makes the initial large sale and its less fortunate competitors. It is not suggested that Pan American sacrificed its own profits for the benefit of its industry as a whole, but rather that it felt that the benefits to itself of ordering both airplanes for its fleet outweighed the economies of restricting itself to a single plane. Standing at the head of each line served both as a boost to its prestige and as an insurance policy against the failure of either aircraft.

A second reason for multiple producers lies in the limitations on production rates most firms encounter. The learning curve, presented alone, is an oversimplification in many ways. It does not reflect the fact that there are separate learning curves for separate tasks; it abstracts from the aggregation of those curves. These simplifications are not of a serious nature because their inclusion would make little difference to the qualitative conclusions for the firms' actions.

One difficulty with the use of the simple learning curve cannot be dismissed so lightly. This is the fact that the cost of producing the nth airplane is not merely dependent upon the number, n, but also is affected by the rate at which production takes place. More specifically, given the total number to be produced, average and incremental costs increase with an increase in the rate of output.[71] This would not alone seriously upset the calculation if the production function were linearly homogeneous and factor supplies elastic. This, however, is not typically the case. Each firm usually has readily available a limited amount of floor space, specifically, an airplane plant to be devoted to commercial production. For these facilities, rates of production can be efficiently varied only within fairly narrow ranges. Drastic increases in the rate of output could be achieved only by construction of new facilities and injections of large amounts of resources into commercial production.

Effectively, then, the early leader in orders must offer potential customers more remote delivery times than a competitor with shorter backlogs. Here the strong competitive advantage to the airlines afforded by the early introduction of a new type of aircraft enters the picture. For the orderless firm can offer a qualitatively different product to its customer—one delivered at a much earlier date and offering a much more effective response to competition from trunks with guaranteed delivery date. Another significant advantage remains. The unsuccessful producer, not having committed itself to a definite production configuration, has much greater flexibility in "tailoring" its product to the wishes of the remaining large customers.

In sum, the advantages of an early lead in orders, while great, prove insufficient for establishing a monopoly. Once two producers are committed to production, though, fixed costs must be ignored in the scramble for orders, and the pressure on prices grows relentlessly.

Competitive practices resembling those of the airframe industry are hardly unknown elsewhere. Rather, industries with similar structures have often exhibited price wars, "ruinous competition," and the like. The unique element in the commercial airline industry is the persistence of an inherently unstable situation. "Destructive competition" is labeled such primarily because of its instability; if allowed to persist, the structure of the industry must eventually change through the disappearance of one or more firms. Often, of course, firms realizing their interdependence are able to reach understandings that create stability.

Some features of the airframe industry which make the need for collusion less pressing were discussed earlier. The last of these, large government defense and space involvement, provides the safety net that catches a plummeting airframe company. Large backlogs of government contracts furnish rather steady income during periods when commercial activities make sales and earnings volatile. Government-sponsored research provides the bulk of airframe technology. Finally, the government simply will not allow a huge defense contractor to fail completely, whatever its commercial sins.[72]

To summarize, several factors combine to bolster the noncollusive nature of the industry. Though relative weights are impossible to assess, each of the following apparently is of some importance: (1) Fully allocated average costs depend on projected total output (and rate of output). Consequently costs are indeterminate so that there is no a priori average cost curve for an individual plane, and therefore no guideline to a reasonable price. A profitable price can vary widely depending on admittedly vague "breakeven points." (2) Non-duplicable price-equivalent quality changes or other concessions are easily made. (3) In any large negotiation, price adjustments are kept secret from rival sellers by buyers and thus cannot be readily or exactly matched. Thus, price cutting can be, at least in the small, a worthwhile, nonduplicable tactic. (4) The lumpy and discrete nature of orders makes competitive concessions quite tempting; they may result in huge swings in orders. (5) If there are significant intertemporal relations in a firm's sales level, then the faster the growth of the market, the larger the present value of extra expected future profits to the firm associated with a unit of sales today. (6) There may be a "learning curve" operating for the development of successive models of subsonic jets, as well as in producing a larger number of the same model. (7) Perhaps most important is the infrequency with which manufacturers meet each other in commercial marketing. Only every few years does a truly new airplane competition come along. In the interim the producers are engaged in a milder, less disastrous form of product competition for the government airframe dollar, and so are not sufficiently inured to the rigors of true price competition. (8) These companies, to an unusual degree, retain individual "personalities." In most instances, if they are not controlled by pioneer figures in the aircraft industry, their management philosophy is not so far removed from that of their founder. (9) Finally, the ultimate solution to substantial large losses—forced exit by bankruptcy or takeover—is much mitigated by heavy overhangs of less risky government contracts.

Whatever the reasons and whether worth the candle, the game is played. Collusion is not a fact of life among these producers, and its absence leads to some quite interesting phenomena of the marketing process.

7. LONG-RUN STRUCTURE, TECHNOLOGICAL PROGRESS AND RESOURCE ALLOCATION

Pervasive and multifaceted government influences in conjunction with the natural structural features of the industries involved have yielded several important economic results for the commercial air-transport industry. Long-term structural changes in both the user and the producer industry have been shaped by these complex and interacting forces. Further, both the speed and character of technological change have been affected. Finally, the particularities of the market have significantly altered the amounts of resources devoted to development and production of new generations of aircraft.

CAB route decisions cause demand conditions which militate for large first-round orders of long-haul aircraft by a few large trunk lines. The nature of product differentiation in a newer, faster aircraft insures that those who receive first delivery have significant competitive advantages and thus greater profit potential than those standing farther back in the queue. But these first comers are precisely the large, strong trunks. Thus are the characteristics of structure in the airline industry reinforced and magnified by the introduction of new capital equipment. Further, the process rejuvenates itself each time a new technological leap occurs. As is so often the case, structure influences behavior, which affects performance, which alters structure completing the chain. The long-term structural characteristics of the airframe industry have been reviewed.

The inherent risk in airframe development and production raises further questions about the effect of government activity on structure. In similar situations in other industries, development of highly risky and expensive new types of capital equipment is done either by vertically integrated firms or through joint ventures. Here, though, explicit government policy has ruled out formal vertical arrangements.[73] Whether vertical ties would be the norm if not prohibited cannot of course be known, but their possibility should not be ignored. Structure would be manifestly quite different in a vertically integrated industry.

The interconnections between the type of aircraft developed and market characteristics have been duly noted. Still unexplained, however, is the timing of development of new types of aircraft as well as the rapidity with which they spread through the industry after introduction. As to timing, strong arguments have been advanced that this "depends on non-economic and essentially exogenous developments in science."[74] The speed of introduction is undoubtedly increased by the product differentiating character of a new aircraft, the profitability of purchasing firms, and the cost characteristics of new equipment.

Some major resource allocation questions are dealt with in the following:

> To the extent that firms excessively duplicated each other's efforts in these areas, resources were misallocated. Moreover, if multiple sourcing kept all firms high on their learning curves, then production costs were, on average, higher than necessary. This consideration, of course, is the central dilemma in all types of airframe procurement. A monopolist *could* lower cost and charge a lower price, but he would perforce be a monopolist and would thus have discretionary power with respect to both pricing and costs. As a second-best choice for commercial airframes, multiple procurement seems preferable if pricing and production are to be done solely by private enterprise. The strongest arguments for multiple sourcing are that pressure eliminates production slack and lowers cost and that competition has good long-run product development effects, in that several firms vie to make new kinds of airframes.
>
> Government procurement activities have provided most of the general technological base which enabled production of commercial

aircraft. Does the failure of commercial jet builders to explicitly purchase this technology (for example, engine improvements) represent a further subsidy and thus misallocation? It seems not. The vast majority of military and space expenditures would probably have been made without regard to possible commercial applications. If so, the use of that technology in commercial applications was costless and should not be charged for. Care must be exercised here, however. To the extent that possible commercial by-products and spin-offs are really an important argument in the government demand function, then increased resources should be allocated only if payments are made and justified by commercial returns on the investment.

Finally, the results given above support the hypothesis that airframe companies could overinvest in risky commercial ventures because of the good prospect that government contracts and assistance would be available in case commercial efforts failed. If this has indeed been the case, then the government contracting process has in effect continually encouraged overinvestment of resources in commercial airliner development and production. Simultaneously, economic profits in the government airframe work were masked by the accounting processes which combined both commercial and government results in aggregated figures.[75]

Finally, it is abundantly clear that government regulation, expenditure, research and legislation have deeply affected both long- and short-run structure, behavior and performance in the industries involved and, moreover, that non-trivial resource misallocations have occurred. The quantitative significance of these actions remains a matter of some conjecture.

Notes to Chapter Eight

1. Almarin Phillips *Technology and Market Structure: A Study of the Aircraft Industry* (Lexington, Mass.: D. C. Heath and Co., Lexington Books, 1971).

2. Sidney L. Carroll, "An Economic Analysis of the Airframe Industry in the United States," unpublished dissertation, Harvard University, 1970, p. 159.

3. "Boeing Soars Ahead of Douglas in Jet Race," *Business Week* (February 11, 1961), p. 65.

4. Carroll, "The Airframe Industry," p. 161.

5. This is not strictly true if one considers the DC-9 and Boeing 727 as distinct generations. Only the broad technology base for these aircraft is government sponsored.

6. "Douglas Reaching Key Stage in Fund Talks," *Aviation Week and Space Technology*, 85 (December 12, 1966), p. 36. See also "Lockheed Hits Heavy Headwinds," *Business Week* (February 14, 1970), pp. 46–48.

7. An obvious example is the recent Lockheed loan of $250 million.

8. John Mecklin, "Why Boeing Is Missing the Bus," *Fortune,* 77 (June 1968), p. 154.

9. Ibid., p. 154.

10, See C. M. Plattner, "Growth Capacity Emphasized for L-1011," *Aviation Week and Space Technology,* 88 (April 22, 1968), p. 71 and "Douglas Subcontractors Join in Novel Plan," *Steel,* 152 (May 20, 1963), p. 31 for some details of these plans.

11. "The Selling of the 707," *Fortune,* 56 (October 1957) p. 246.

12. R. A. Smith, *Corporations in Crisis* (Garden City, New York Doubleday, 1966), p. 94. Also see "General Dynamics Writes Off Jet Cost," *Aviation Week and Space Technology,* 73 (October 3, 1960), p. 47.

13. "Boeing's Allen Cites Trend to Mergers," *Aviation Week and Space Technology,* 71 (December 28, 1959), p. 81.

14. Charles J. V. Murphy, "The Plane Makers under Stress," *Fortune,* 61 (June 1960), p. 299.

15. Even this was not completely successful: "There have been two rounds of 'basic airplane' price increases, the latest revealed last week by Boeing (4-6%) and Douglas (5%). Convair raised 880 prices $200,000 a year ago, and now is quoting the 880 at $3.6 to $3.8 million. Boeing and Douglas run $5 to $6 million. Convair, which has been stressing its lower prices, plans no increase now." William H. Gregory, "Rising Costs Delay Jet Transport," *Aviation Week and Space Technology,* 72 (May 2, 1960), p. 177.

16. "BAC 111 Postponed," *Economist,* 214 (March 20, 1965), p. 1308.

17. *Commercial Aircraft Industry* (Coleman and Company, Institutional Department, 1960), p. 3.

18. Richard G. O'Lone, "Flexibility in Manufacturing Permits Wide 737 Options," *Aviation Week and Space Technology,* 74 (June 6, 1966), pp. 54-57.

19. Even recently ravaged General Dynamics cast a wistful look at the proposal. It, rather understandably, never got into serious development. William H. Gregory, "Lockheed Revises C-5A Market Approach," *Aviation Week and Space Technology,* 84 (June 13, 1966), p. 52. Boeing's already swollen capital and engineering commitments probably precluded its serious participation. "Airbus Hits Competitive Squall," *Business Week* (March 16, 1968), p. 40.

20. "L-1011 Sold as International Effort," *Aviation Week and Space Technology,* 88 (April 8, 1968), p. 32.

21. "Racing to Catch the Airbus," *Business Week* (June 15, 1968), p. 164. Even though the DC-10 and the L-1011 are extremely close in most important respects, American chose the DC-10 because it was substantially cheaper. "Airbus Hits Competitive Squall," p. 40.

22. The ability of the carriers to cooperate is demonstrated by TWA president, Charles Tillinghast: "Well, Lockheed coudn't go ahead with just a few planes. Floyd Hall (Eastern Airlines President) and I discussed this casually and agreed we wanted commonality of planes," The two lines have a joint maintenance agreement. *Newsweek,* 71 (April 8, 1968), p. 90.

23. Mecklin, "Why Boeing Is Missing the Bus," p. 84.

24. William H. Gregory, "Price, Schedule Keys in L-1011 De-

cisions," *Aviation Week and Space Technology,* 88 (April 8, 1968), p. 36.

25. Pan Am was committed to 747s.

26. "United Order for DC-10 Spurs McDonnell-Douglas Production," *Aviation Week and Space Technology,* 88 (April 29, 1968), p. 32.

27. Mecklin, "Why Boeing Is Missing the Bus," p. 85.

28. Lockheed's C. L. Johnson, vice-president for advanced development projects, "Racing to Catch the Airbus," p. 166.

29. Cartaino has calculated almost identical theoretical fare characteristics for stretched DC-8s and 747s in the entire range from one to four thousand miles, for example. See T. F. Cartaino, *Air Transport in the 1970's: Problems and Opportunities,* RM-5268-PR (Santa Monica: The Rand Corporation, 1968), pp. 16 and 19.

30. For instance, there were seven versions of the Boeing 707.

31. Smith, *Corporations in Crisis,* p. 93.

32. *Aviation Week and Space Technology,* 88 (February 26, 1968), p. 93.

33. Gregory, "Price, Schedule Keys in L-1011 Decisions," p. 36.

34. "Airline Observer," *Aviation Week and Space Technology,* 88 (May 20, 1968), p. 50.

35. *American Aviation,* 32 (May 12, 1969), p. 102 ff.

36. Richard E. Caves, *Air Transport and Its Regulators: An Industry Study* (Cambridge: Harvard University Press, 1962), p. 102.

37. "Plane Builders Feeling Foreign Competition," *Aviation Week and Space Technology,* 74 (July 29, 1963), p. 153.

38. "The Selling of the 707," p. 130.

39. Charles J. V. Murphy, "Lockheed Scrambles for the Battle of the Primes," *Fortune,* 71 (February 1965), p. 130.

40. R. A. Smith, *Corporations in Crisis,* p. 68.

41. Murphy, "The Plane Makers under Stress, II" *Fortune,* 62 (July 1960) p. 112.

42. Murphy, "The Plane Makers under Stress, II" p. 299. Also John Mecklin, "Douglas Aircraft's Stormy Flight Path," *Fortune,* 74 (December 1966), p. 167 ff.

43. Richard J. Whalen, "Banshee, Demon, Voodoo, Phantom—and Bingo!" *Fortune,* 70 (November 1964), p. 262.

44. Robert Sheehan, "General Dynamics versus the U.S.S.R.," *Fortune,* 59 (February, 1959), p. 168.

45. Murphy, "The Plane Makers under Stress, I," p. 137.

46. Mecklin, "Douglas Aircraft's Stormy Flight Path," p. 256.

47. See "Boeing's Allen Cites Trend to Mergers," and Murphy, "The Plane Makers under Stress, II," p. 112.

48. Mecklin, "Why Boeing Is Missing the Bus," p. 154.

49. "The Selling of the 707," p. 129. It is interesting to note that many of the aircraft pioneers are still active in major firms—James McDonnell, Leroy Grumman, and Donald Douglas are three.

50. Sheehan, "General Dynamics versus the U.S.S.R.," p. 88.

51. Smith, *Corporations in Crisis,* p. 90.

52. See Douglas Aircraft, *Annual Report,* 1966.

53. For an earlier and more extensive treatment for airliners, see

Caves, *Air Transport,* chapters 5 and 13.

54. Competitive strategy greatly reinforces this desire to get in early. Caves, *Air Transport,* p. 307.

55. *Commercial Aircraft Industry,* p. 12.

56. Cartaino, *Air Transport in the 1970's,* pp. 14-15.

57. Indeed, the airlines seem to have been unprepared for such a great increase in productivity. See *Commercial Aircraft Industry,* p. 45. TWA found that not only was its "breakeven point" as low as a 50 to 52 percent load factor versus 64 percent for piston planes, but that one jet could be utilized to replace nearly three piston planes (in passenger miles per year) as opposed to earlier estimates of two. See "A Deadline for Howard Hughes," *Fortune,* 60 (July 1959), pp. 112, 233.

58. Caves, *Air Transport,* p. 103.

59. Smith, *Corporations in Crisis,* p. 95.

60. William H. Gregory, "Pan American Order for 747 Opens New Era in Airline Jet Transportation Equipment," *Aviation Week and Space Technology,* 84 (April 18, 1966), p. 38.

61. Or perhaps beyond their breaking point. As one author has put it: "Typically an aircraft manufacturer goes ahead with plans to produce a plane only when he has enough firm orders to insure him no worse than a bearable loss." (Caves, *Air Transport,* p. 305.) Even this may be overly generous, unless anything short of bankruptcy is considered bearable. Allowing for this misjudgment and overoptimism, the *repeat* phenomenon of huge losses is hard to explain with a risk avoidance model. However, at this point it is sufficient simply to note that there is a threshold level of orders that usually must be reached before a production decision.

62. "The Selling of the 707," p. 246. Additional examples are contained in Smith, *Corporations in Crisis,* p. 95, and Gregory, "Pan American Order," p. 38.

63. Caves, *Air Transport,* pp. 131 ff.

64. "Jet Age Arrives in the U.S.," *Financial World,* 110 (October 8, 1958), p. 5.

65. Caves, *Air Transport,* pp. 311.

66. Subsequent reorders were quite large. Whether their magnitude was anticipated or not, their possibility probably was recognized. Boeing's production record for 707s is instructive. In 1959 and 1960 it produced 141 planes, but in 1961, only 11. By 1966 it was again producing 77 aircraft. There were ten new orders for 707s in 1971. (Boeing Company *Annual Reports,* 1966, 1971; Aerospace Industries Association of America, Inc., *Aerospace Facts and Figures,* (1967), p. 35.)

67. "Boeing Soars Ahead of Douglas in Jet Race," p. 65.

68. For example, the airlines expressed a desire for at least two complete prototype SST's in "Airlines Suggest Two SST Prototypes for Evaluation," *Aviation Week and Space Technology,* 75 (March 23, 1964), p. 27.

69. John Mecklin, "Rolls-Royce's $2 Billion Hard Sell," *Fortune,* 79 (March 1969), p. 140.

70. The fall in price is almost all a learning curve phenomenon. For instance, if the manufacturer insisted on a fixed markup of 10 percent on average cost, price would fall from $7.81 million to $6.248 million. There is nothing very remarkable in any of this. It simply demonstrates how falling costs confer market power on the large orderer.

71. For a discussion of total cost and its dependence on the program of output, see Armen Alchian, "Costs and Outputs," *The Allocation of Economic Resources,* Moses Abramovitz, editor (Palo Alto, California: Stanford University Press, 1959), pp. 23-40.

72. Lockheed's financial predicament with the commercial L-1011, L-500, and military C-5A illustrate this well. According to one analyst, "The magnitude of Lockheed's potential losses seems open-ended." Yet, "the government, of course, is not about to kill off its biggest contractor." ("Lockheed Hits Heavy Headwinds," pp. 46-48.) An intriguing further development is the offer by Howard Hughes to lend $100 million to Lockheed to finance a long-range version of the L-1011 jetliner. (*The Knoxville News Sentinel,* September 12, 1973.)

73. Caves, *Air Transport,* pp. 100-101.

74. Phillips, *Technology and Market Structure,* p. 22.

75. Sidney L. Carroll, "Profits in the Airframe Industry," *Quarterly Journal of Economics,* 86 (November 1972), p. 561.

Chapter Nine

Liquefied and Synthetic Natural Gas—Regulation Chooses the Expensive Solutions

Thomas R. Stauffer

1. INTRODUCTION

The purpose of this paper is to analyze the regulatory incentives which promoted the importation of liquefied natural gas (LNG) into the United States and fostered the creation of a new industry for manufacturing "synthetic" natural gas (SNG). Both involve innovative technologies and were justified on grounds of helping to close the "gas gap." Yet the several relevant regulatory bodies, federal and state, had explicitly recognized that SNG and LNG were several times more costly than the price the Federal Power Commission (FPC) allowed for domestic gas. However, those same regulatory commissions just as explicitly declined to pursue two other much less expensive (and technically less innovative) options which could have reduced the "gas gap" even more effectively—stimulation of domestic natural gas supply or implementation of an efficient rationing program. This policy thus warrants careful scrutiny because it seems so clearly ill-advised. As an illustration of "regulatory perversity," it provides some very useful insight into the pathological phases of the regulatory process.

The immediate impetus for LNG imports and the manufacture of SNG came from the regulators' recognition in the early 1970s that they did indeed face a "gas gap." In 1967/68 consumption of natural gas exceeded new discoveries by a large margin, and the gap thereafter widened in each succeeding year.[1] That decline in gas discoveries was not a transient phenomenon; by 1972 the annual consumption of gas was twice the replacement rate, and the U.S. inventory of proved reserves had been depleted dangerously. The number of gas wells drilled had peaked in 1960/61 and fell steadily thereafter to two-thirds the earlier level, in spite of a 50 percent increase in gas demand (see Figure 9-1). The more recent wells were deeper and notably more costly, and the yield ("productivity") per foot drilled had also diminished with time. Moreover, the

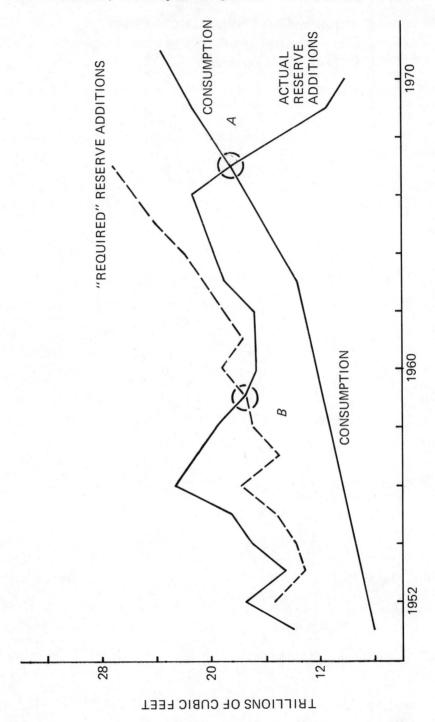

Figure 9-1.   Gas Consumption. Reserve Additions and "Required" Reserves

declining volumes of newly discovered gas were increasingly dedicated to the unregulated intrastate market, thereby exacerbating the shortage in the regulated, interstate market.[2]

The fact that the U.S. natural gas industry was no longer self-sustaining became obvious to all after 1968 when total reserves began to fall absolutely. The trend was discernible ten years earlier, but the FPC consistently failed to detect the signals or to respond to the warnings of the gas-producing industry.[3] Much of the extensive evidence which the industry introduced in numerous proceedings was clearly self-serving but it was nonetheless correct, and commissioners, hearing examiners, FPC staff, and judges all failed to read the signs.

In 1970/71 some of the major interstate gas pipelines acknowledged that they were unable to serve new or even existing customers with increasing volumes of gas. Indeed, several of the major pipelines by then were unable even to honor existing contractual commitments and were therefore forced to curtail deliveries to customers with "firm" contracts and a prior history of uninterrupted service. The shortfall in supply to *existing* customers for the period November 1972–March 1973 was forecast at some 500 billion cubic feet or approximately 7 percent of consumption in the interstate market. This understates the actual "gap" because it excludes a comparable level of curtailments to interruptible customers. The gas industry, which furnished about one-third of U.S. primary energy, was potentially some 15-20 percent in default.

This situation was the legacy passed on to FPC Chairman Nassikas in 1969 by his predecessors Chairmen Swidler and White. Moreover, future prospects were still worse. Both the FPC's own staff and the Future Requirements Committee, an adjunct of the American Gas Association, forecast that the unsatisfied excess demand for gas would grow rapidly. The "gap" would widen; conventional sources of domestic natural gas were believed to have reached a plateau, while demand would increase exponentially for the foreseeable future, since gas was priced well below alternate fuels in most markets.

The decisions to develop SNG and LNG as supplemental sources were taken in view of the cheerless prospect of an ever deepening shortage persisting through 1990, once most parties had come to recognize the gap as compellingly serious.

The price differences were dramatic. In 1971/72 the FPC limited the price of domestically produced natural gas purchased for resale in interstate commerce to 22.5-23.5¢ per thousand cubic feet (Mcf) in the Rocky Mountain region and 22.5-26¢ for the "Other Southwest" area. On the other hand, the FPC during the same period certified imports of LNG at 90¢-$1.10 per Mcf (subject to programmed—and unprogrammed—escalations imposed by the foreign seller). Similarly, SNG manufactured from imported feedstocks was approved by state regulatory bodies at target prices of $1.00-plus per Mcf, again subject to any rise in international hydrocarbon prices.

In the narrowest sense the regulators, state or federal, did indeed proceed rationally—given the constraints which they themselves had created or which were imposed exogenously. But regulatory history—the accumulation of precedent and practice—in effect foreclosed the efficient options and left the regulators no alternative but to promote inefficient solutions to a gas shortage that had resulted in large measure from their own prior actions. The regulatory process had acquired a momentum of its own, guided by the rules of evidence and unhindered by any economic criteria. The path from the Phillips decision of 1954 to the creation of the SNG industry and massive imports of LNG was unerringly straight—based upon its own purely internal logic—just as that path was unrelentingly inefficient.

Our interest here is to analyze the economic costs of supplemental gas sources (LNG and SNG) relative to the alternatives of domestic supplies of "natural" natural gas or fuel-substitution strategies, and to sketch the steps which led both the Federal Power Commission and the state utilities commissions to such economically aberrant policies.

Part 2 describes the innovative features of LNG imports, as used for base load supplies rather than peak-shaving, and the manufacture of SNG.

Part 3 focuses on the economic costs, excluding transfers, of "non-innovative" conventional alternatives—domestic *natural* gas production and fuel-substitution/natural gas rationing strategies. The analysis here involves only data or information available to the FPC in order to emphasize the internal inconsistency of its preference for innovative policies. We have undertaken rather detailed studies in part because the apparent misallocation appears to be so large that one wants to make quite sure of the result before making an argument based upon it.

The options are compared in Part 4. Stimulation of domestic gas is shown to be the cheapest scheme with fuel-substitution/rationing next, and SNG and LNG being notably more expensive. The analyses are based upon the hydrocarbon price structure that prevailed prior to October 1973—the period when the regulatory decisions were made. The currently much higher prices for imported hydrocarbons only reinforce the cost disadvantages of SNG and LNG.

Part 5 explores the perverse logic which led to the approval of SNG and LNG schemes. The regulators' inability to elect the efficient options is related to both the prior history and to conflicts between jurisdictions. The postures of the state regulators and the gas utilities, which acquiesced in, or even welcomed, these decisions is also considered. The analysis is brief and oversimplified, and most of the procedural history or legal details, so essential to the jurist but so distracting to the outside observer, have been omitted. Part 6 summarizes the results and suggests the more general implications for the regulation of energy industries.

2. THE INNOVATIVE OPTIONS

The importation of liquefied natural gas (LNG) involves the adaptation of a technology which has been reasonably well proven in providing supplies at periods of peak demand to the continuing supply of base-load gas, a totally different set of circumstances. This adaptation requires an increase in the scale of such facilities, which augments the technological risk. To make the manufacture of synthetic natural gas (methane) from heavier hydrocarbons commercially viable, a new technology is required to increase the energy content of the synthesized gas stream (methanation). It also entails a scale-up of about four-to-one in the size of the plants.

Chairman Nassikas of the FPC quite explicitly acknowledged that both options involved: "prices to consumers of two to three times the delivered price of natural gas from traditional domestic sources."[4] The commission also explicitly recognized the innovative character of the new sources of methane. The Columbia/El Paso LNG project was described as ". . . a pioneering enterprise" while the first SNG plant was characterized as "unprecedented as to size and scope."[5] The justification for such high costs and risks was expediency. In confirming the Columbia LNG project, the FPC reiterated that it approved ". . . the importation of foreign LNG because of shortage of gas in the United States." State authorities were similarly motivated, noting that SNG and LNG were the most readily "available" options within the jurisdictions of the regulatory bodies.

Before discussing the technical aspects and the financial implications of the two options we note that SNG manufacture, as approved thus far, entails the *transformation* of a premium light liquid hydrocarbon into gaseous methane and thus does not represent a new source of primary energy. LNG in contrast is such a new source since it constitutes a method of transporting natural methane to the U.S. from areas otherwise beyond the economic reach of pipelines. Thus SNG costs are related directly to market prices for petroleum products, plus SNG plant and fuel costs. The cost determinants for LNG are quite different, but its prices will ultimately be closely (if indirectly) linked to the prices for crude oils, reflecting the opportunity cost of the gas in other markets.

Synthetic Natural Gas (SNG)

The paradoxical term "synthetic natural gas" applies to a manufactured gaseous stream of which 95 percent or more is methane (CH_4), which in turn is the dominant chemical constituent of "natural gas" from oil or gas wells.[6] In principle, any hydrocarbon, down to coal or even lignite, can be processed to yield methane. The plant complexity, the processing costs, the thermodynamic losses of conversion, and the technical uncertainties all increase as one uses feedstocks of higher molecular weight or higher carbon-to-hydrogen ratios. Consequently, almost all of the SNG projects have used as an input either liquid petroleum gases (LPG), consisting of mixed streams of propane, butane and smaller volumes of heavier hydrocarbons, or low boiling-point naphthas. The latter are refined products of mixed molecular structure and weights inter-mediate between gasolines and kerosenes and commanding related price premia in the marketplace.

The manufacturing process involves three stages: desulphurization of the feedstock; producing a "synthesis gas" of carbon monoxide and hydrogen from the desulphurized feedstocks; and chemically transforming the synthesis gas stream into methane and carbon dioxide. The first two stages are technically well established at smaller scales, while methanation entailed considerable development effort.

To calculate the manufacturing cost of SNG we must take account of five components: 1) the feedstock; 2) process fuel and electricity; 3) capital charges; 4) variable operating costs—labor, catalysts, etc.; and 5) a thermo-dynamic degradation penalty. The capital investment per thousand cubic feet per day (Mcf/D) of synthetic methane ranges between \$300 for a light liquids plant,[7] to upwards of \$1500 for a coal-based plant. Other operating costs are similarly proportioned. The cost structures for the two cases are given by the following formulas:

$$\text{SNG Cost (liquid)} = 1.04 \, P^{Feed} + 0.08 \, P^{Fuel} + 25\cancel{c}$$
$$\text{SNG Cost (coal)} = 1.03 \, P^{Feed} + 0.42 \, P^{Fuel} + 70\cancel{c}$$

Here P^{Feed} and P^{Fuel} are respectively the price per BTU of the feedstocks and the fuel used to provide process heat. These estimates have been distilled from technical studies and cost-of-service fillings; they presume utility-type financing (including return on capital) and baseload operation at 330-350 days per year.[8]

These formulations say that SNG costs consist of a fixed processing charge (25¢ for liquid feedstocks, 70¢ for coal) plus a multiple of the cost of the heating value of the feedstocks and process fuel. Manufacturing SNG is thermodynamically inefficient, in that the output contains less usable heat than the fuels plus feedstocks employed (less any co-product credits). Energy is lost both in reforming the molecules of the feedstock and because lowering the carbon-to-hydrogen ratio of the fuel degrades its thermodynamic potential. An additional four to eight percent of the original fuel energy is sacrificed in order to achieve a synthetic fuel with a more convenient form. These losses in total amount to about 12 percent for a liquids-based plant and upwards of 50 percent or more for a coal-based plant. In 1972 and 1973, with naptha feedstocks, such thermodynamic losses added 11-13¢ per Mcf to the cost of SNG. At today's higher prices, these conversion losses imply a cost of 25¢ or more, over and above the plant costs of 25¢. Given feedstock prices, it is simple enough to use the above formulas and standard conversions to obtain a price per Mcf for SNG of \$1.37-\$1.48.

Liquefied Natural Gas

The novelty associated with LNG imports is incorporating storage facilities for the liquefied methane into tankers. Because liquefaction reduced the volume of natural gas by a factor of 600, it was explored quite early by the gas industry as a means for storing gas during off-peak periods in order to meet peak demands. Such facilities were stigmatized after a disastrous Cleveland fire in 1944, but since the early 1960's almost two score such central or satellite peak shaving LNG plants have been constructed throughout the United States.

LNG import facilities differ from those plants in three major respects. The plants involved are more than ten times as large as the peak-shaving facilities. Moreover they are destined for base-load service, with a load factor of ostensibly 90% or more.[11] Such trade also required the development of cryogenic tankships with hulls and fittings specially designed for a low-density cargo at an ambient temperature of *minus* 260°F.

Although transportation represented (1972) the largest individual component in the delivered cost of LNG delivered to the U.S. East Coast, the other components—the wellhead value of the natural gas itself, gathering and liquification charges, the import terminal with its storage and regasification, and delivery links to the customer utilities—are significant in the aggregate. The Federal Power Commission exercises no effective jurisdiction over taxes, costs, or prices abroad. But the certificates issued under Section 7 of the Natural Gas Act stipulate that conventional cost-of-service calculations for rate-making purposes apply to all stages of the project after it leaves the export terminal.

The market value of overseas natural gas is quite difficult to ascertain. It frequently depends upon a partly conjectural estimate of its value in other remote markets. Or it can depend upon the projected market for, and costs of, petrochemical, methanol, or fertilizer production where gas is a possible feedstock. There are reasons, however, that arise both from market forces and from institutional arrangement, which suggest that the price of natural gas in international trade should track the prices of liquid hydrocarbons. First there is enough substitutability among gas and other fuels to imply that rational buyers and sellers will not allow price differences among various fuels to long exceed their differential convenience values. In addition, since OPEC nations supply much LNG, they can be expected to revise the price of that product in keeping with any major oil price announcements. As a precedent we note that both domestic and export gas prices from the substantial Dutch fields are linked to domestic and international fuel oil prices.

The reported terms of the major schemes submitted before the FPC are summarized in Table 9-1. Even if the Algerian supplier does not unilaterally readjust the F.O.B. export prices, both the transportation and terminal costs are subject to escalation based upon the actual investments. Further, in some instances the not inconsiderable costs of supplementary storage tanks and the regasification plant have not been included. For the case of the Colombia (El

Table 9-1. Terms of Applications to Import Liquified Natural Gas, 1972.

Applicant	Volumes (10⁶ CF/Year)	Prices (c.i.f.ᵃ) (per MMBTU)	Escalation
Distrigas Corp.	15,400	68-85	0.6¢ p.a.
Distrigas Corp.	45,000	74	1.5% p.a.
Columbia LNG Corp. ("El Paso I")	390,000	77-83	(See text)
Easco LNG Inc.	238,000	91	1.5% p.a.

ᵃCosts of regasified LNG, delivered into the utilities' main distribution system are up to 30 cents/MCF higher than the quoted "ship rail" figures.

Source: Federal Power Commission, *Annual Report–1972,* Appendix E.

Paso, I) LNG project, the additional costs incurred up to the point where the regasified "LNG" is delivered into the Consolidated/Colombia and Southern Natural Gas systems were estimated at 17¢ and 20¢ per Mcf, respectively.[12] The resultant streams—at 90¢ to $1.10 per Mcf—were three or more times more costly than the maximum area rates for domestic gas, as decreed by the same regulatory authority, and about four times the economic cost of new domestic natural gas, again as derived from data used by the FPC in its own rate hearings (see below, Table 9-2).

Table 9-2. Estimates of Economic Costᵃ of Producing Domestic Natural Gas under Alternative Rates of Return and Reservoir Decline Rates.

Rate of Return on Capital	Reservoir Decline Rate	"Nationwide" (FPC)	South Louisiana Area (FPC)	(Companies)
		(1)	(2)	(3)
8%	zero	23.0¢	20.8¢	24.9¢
	5%	21.1	19.1	22.9
10%	zero	26.3	23.9	28.5
	5%	23.8	21.5	25.8
12%	zero	29.9	27.1	32.2
	5%	26.6	24.0	28.7

ᵃ"Cost" excludes royalties, severance taxes, lease bonuses, and any income taxes, but it does provide for a *d.c.f.* return to capital, as shown in the first column, of 8-12%.

Source: (1) Data base—Federal Power Commission Order R-389-B, April 1973, Appendix B, and Order R-659 (Appendix 8A)

(2) Analytical methods—T. R. Stauffer, "Economic Cost of U.S. Crude Oil Production," *Journal of Petroleum Technology, op, cit.*; also "Natural Gas Policy Issues and Options," *op. cit.*

3. THE CONVENTIONAL SOLUTION:
"NATURAL" METHANE

Expanding Domestic Production

In this section I propose to determine the economic *cost* of new domestic gas—as distinct from its administratively regulated *price*. Only if that cost indeed proves to be lower than the "innovative options" can one unequivocally challenge the economic rationality of FPC policies. In view of the regulatory constraints, tax subsidies, externalities, and transfer payments in this case—such as the tax write-offs for intangible drilling outlays or the percentage depletion allowance, as well as the fact that the corporate discount rate may be higher than the social opportunity cost of capital—there is specific reason to suspect that cost might possibly exceed price.

We shall estimate the two separate components of the economic or resource cost of developing incremental domestic natural gas supplies. The first is the cost of gas itself at the wellhead. The second is the incremental resource cost of moving additional volumes of such new gas from the Gulf States area, say, to either the upper Midwest or the East Coast (the two areas in which SNG or LNG projects have been proposed).

Present gas reserves cannot sustain current levels of production and consumption, so that a new supply involves the discovery of new reserves and investments for new production facilities.[13] The finding cost is the expenditure needed to discover one thousand cubic feet of producible gas reserves and is measured by dividing gross increases in reserves in an area, over a specified time period, by the exploration outlays in the same area. This necessitates an arbitrary allocation between oil and gas exploration, since both are joint products of total exploration effort.

The cost of developing gas reserves, once they have been discovered, consists of two basic items. The larger one is the expenditure per unit output for the producing wells themselves (development wells). It depends both upon the initial flow rates of the wells and also the rate at which the reservoir pressure and the production from the reservoir declines. The second cost item—"lease facilities"—covers the investments in dehydrating equipment, gas compressors, other gas field equipment, or producing platforms offshore. Since the development of a new gas pool or field spans several years before full production is achieved, there is a time lag associated with this stage as well.

The final constituents in the economic cost of production are the annual cash operating costs and the byproduct credits. Variable operating costs are a comparatively small item for natural gas and comprise the labor charges for gas field personnel, maintenance costs, and an allocation of corporate overhead charges. The byproduct credit, which is *deducted* from gross costs in order to determine a net cost figure, arises from the recovery and sale of petroleum liquids (LNG) or gases such as butane or propane (LPG) which are entrained in the methane stream flowing from the wells. This co-product credit amounts to as much as 15% of the net gas cost.

Estimates of the economic cost of *new* gas at the wellhead for Southern Louisiana, together with a nationwide "average" value computed on the same basis, are displayed in Table 9-2. The costs were calculated for three rates of return on capital—eight, ten and twelve percent—and for two values of the reservoir decline rate—zero and five percent.[14] These span the range of values of relevant practical interest. Two alternative estimates are given for the South Louisiana area; those in column (2) reflect the relative optimism of the FPC staff as to the rate at which gas reserves can be discovered per foot of exploratory drilling and their similar optimism as to the average number of wells needed to develop discovered reserves. On the other hand, gas producing company witnesses in various FPC proceedings claimed that higher outlays for drilling were required and also made less optimistic forecasts for the geological yields.

We will choose the average of the two extreme values for South Louisiana as the best proxy for our purposes, i.e., 25.7¢ per Mcf (rounded up to 26¢) which is all but indistinguishable from that for the average value in the nation-wide analysis (25.5¢). The mid-range figure based upon the FPC's own staff's data is somewhat lower at 23.2¢ per Mcf.

In order to compare "conventional" methane in the Southwest with SNG/LNG in the North Central states or on the East Coast; we must take account of transport costs. In the currently important case where interstate pipelines have excess capacity, the cost of transporting incremental gas up to their design capacity depends solely upon the additional compressor fuel needed. All other costs are fixed and thus are independent of the throughput of the pipeline. The precise specification of the incremental compressor fuel requirements involves detailed design data on each pipeline. However, broadly speaking, two dominant, countervailing considerations affect the compressor fuel required for transporting incremental volumes of gas through a partly empty pipeline. The horsepower required rises rapidly with the rate of flow of gas, but the joint efficiency of the prime movers and compressors increases.[15] These forces determine the incremental fuel requirements and thus the marginal transportation cost. The average accounting charge for compressor fuel on the major interstate pipelines which connect the Southwestern or Gulf states with the Chicago area or the East Coast ranges between 0.6¢ and 1.7¢ per Mcf, compared with the pipeline tariffs of some 20-25¢ Mcf. This item is thus small, but an important correction is needed.[16] The gas used for pipeline fuel is charged into the accounts at the weighted-average regulated field price. The social opportunity cost of incremental compressor fuel gas, however, depends upon the cost of the alternative fuel for which the delivered gas might substitute. This cost varies from case to case, and the detailed calculations could become quite complex.

Since even the shadow price for compressor fuel gas is relatively small compared with other magnitudes, it suffices to approximate the opportunity cost as one of two values: $1.25 per Mcf, reflecting the real cost of SNG or LNG, or 25¢ per Mcf, the economic cost of new domestic gas estimated above. The upper and lower bounds for the incremental pipeline transport cost are reported in Table 9-3 under the additional assumption that the pipeline is operating at 10% below prior capacity levels, so that the marginal fuel consumption equals 2.03 times the average values cited above.

Table 9-3.   Estimates of Incremental Transport Cost of Natural Gas.

Pipeline	Route	Estimate "Low"	"High"
Panhandle Eastern	Oklahoma-Michigan	1.8¢/Mcf	8.9¢/Mcf
Texas Eastern[a]	South Texas-N.Y./N.J.	3.1	8.9
Transco	South Texas-N.Y./N.J.	2.7	13.4
Trunkline	South Louisiana-Southern Illinois	1.2	6.0

[a]Cost/price correction applied only to compressor gas; cost of "other" compressor fuel assumed unchanged.
Source: See text.

If the FPC's own gas cost data is correct, then the "low" estimate for incremental transportation cost is appropriate. The "high" figure should be used *only* if an SNG/LNG plant were sited on the Gulf Coast and the surrogate gas were shipped to market via an otherwise partially empty pipeline.[17] Given our production cost estimates above, the data in Table 9.3 yields an estimated economic cost for new gas delivered to both the Chicago or New York/New Jersey areas of approximately 27¢. We note again for emphasis that this figure is less than a fourth of even the optimistic figures for the SNG and LNG plants which were approved by the FPC and the several state regulatory bodies, even before the precipitous rise in feedstock prices in the fall and winter of 1973. Even if one were to accept the evidence for a higher discovery and production cost for domestic natural gas that the FPC rejected, the cost of surrogate supplies is still at least triple that of domestic, conventionally produced natural methane.[18] The disparities based upon price differential do indeed reflect true differences in economic costs.[19]

Fuel Substitution

A second alternative to LNG or SNG would have been the systematic substitution of other fuels, such as fuel oil, light distillate fuels, coal, or LPG, for those applications of natural gas where such substitution is technically feasible. Instead of concentrating upon developing supplementary sources of supply, this involves correcting the imbalance in the market by curbing demand via an economically efficient set of rules and priorities for switching some users of gas to alternative fuels. We shall analyze only the economic implications of this option. Discussion of jurisdictional constraints and institutional factors is deferred until Section 5.

Three facts are crucial for the possibility of fuel substitution:

1. The gas supply deficiency has become real. Not merely is there no foreseeable increase in "natural" gas supply, but most major pipelines are already curtailing supply to existing attached customers.
2. The spectrum of fuel-switching/substitution costs is inordinately wide. The costs of converting equipment to other fuels can vary by a factor of fifty-to-one per unit of gas consumed, depending upon the type of equipment and its size.
3. Quite apart from the conversion costs themselves, all environmentally attractive fuels are significantly more expensive than natural gas delivered at the regulated prices to interstate markets.

These facts have certain immediate consequences. Given that regulation prevents the price of gas from rising to its "commodity value" relative to other fuels[20] no user will voluntarily substitute an alternative fuel for natural gas. Second, the wide diversity in conversion costs implies that the economic cost of fuel substitution will be quite sensitive to the details and priorities used in implementing the scheme.

The additional costs involved in substituting other fuels for natural gas break down into four components, over and above the price differential between gas and the replacement fuel:

- Transportation costs
- Conversion costs
- Costs due to differential sulphur content
- Different efficiencies of fuel utilization.

Our analysis deals exclusively with *existing* uses, and we exclude the more general case of alternate fuel choices in *new* plants or equipment. The former is indeed the relevant scenario, since supplementary gas supplies are destined in large measure to reduce the level of curtailments to existing users. The Commission was itself fully cognizant of this possibility. Indeed, pursuant to FPC order, the rationing procedures proposed by some two dozen interstate gas pipelines were being reviewed concurrently with the hearings on supplemental sources of gas.

LNG/SNG plants have been proposed both at the tail end of the interstate pipelines—in the upper Midwest and along the East Coast—and, more recently, in the Gulf Coast itself. There thus exist four possible configurations for replacing incremental high-cost gas by cheaper, more conventional fuels, as diagrammed in Figure 9-2. In case A.1, substitution could be made near the point of importation of the LNG or manufacture of the SNG, while in Case A.2 fuel substitution in the Gulf Coast area would release gas to be transported to the Northeast, where it could then replace incremental LNG. Conversely, in

Figure 9-2.   Alternative Locational Patterns for Substitution of Fuel Oil for Gas.

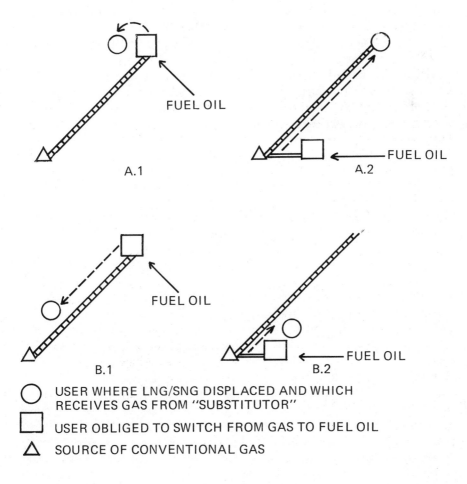

A.1

A.2

FUEL OIL

FUEL OIL

B.1

B.2

FUEL OIL

FUEL OIL

○ USER WHERE LNG/SNG DISPLACED AND WHICH RECEIVES GAS FROM "SUBSTITUTOR"

□ USER OBLIGED TO SWITCH FROM GAS TO FUEL OIL

△ SOURCE OF CONVENTIONAL GAS

Case B.1, fuel-switching in Chicago or New England would obviate the transport of some volumes of gas to those areas and eliminate the need for LNG/SNG in the Gulf Coast area. In Case B.2 increased fuel oil consumption and LNG/SNG displacement all take place in the Gulf Coast area.

In Cases A.2 and B.1 the gas for incremental compressor fuel must be valued at the cost of the cheapest alternative fuel, which we estimate below at an average of 80¢ per MMBTU. Thus the incremental cost of shipping extra gas to the Midwest or the East Coast becomes 4.5¢ and 7.0¢ per Mcf, respectively (Case A.1).[21] In Case B.1 the *saving* in transportation cost would be 4.5-7¢ per Mcf.[22] We focus hereafter upon Cases A.1 and A.2 and emphasize that substitution in this context necessitates the conversion of existing gas-burning facilities over to another fuel.

The economic costs of displacing natural gas from existing uses vary with the type of facility, its size, and the prices of the particular alternative fuels it can utilize. Most steam-raising boilers can be converted from gas to oil with relative ease. Other equipment is much less readily convertible, and at the extreme, many metallurgical applications of natural gas cannot be converted at all, so that a completely new facility designed expressly for some other fuel must be constructed. In such extreme cases the conversion penalty can exceed $4-5/Mcf of gas displaced. In general conversion costs (per unit of gas) depend strongly upon relative size, with very marked economies of scale. Most fundamentally, all alternative fuels, with the occasional exception of high-sulphur coal, are more expensive than gas. Moreover, some conversion processes (such as the modification of a gas-fueled turbine-drive in a pipeline compressor station to use a liquid fuel) require a higher-quality fuel—such as No. 2 oil. The resulting variation among fuel-switching costs is quite large. Economies of scale are often compounded by the fact that large boilers (e.g., in utilities) typically exhibit high load factors—60% or higher—whereas most smaller units operate at 25% or less. As a result, for the smaller unit, the higher conversion cost per unit of capacity is spread over fewer units of throughput. Excluding fuel price differentials, conversion costs range between zero (for units already equipped to burn fuel oil) to 10-12¢ per Mcf, for a new utility conversion, up to 75¢-$1.00 for small industrial boilers. The costs of more difficult conversions (non-boiler uses) can rise as high as $4.00 or more per Mcf displaced. An array of the costs of conversion, which duly allows for reductions in capacity of the converted units, differences in thermodynamic efficiency, or technologically imposed differences in fuel quality, is presented in Table 9-4.

Although little is known about the volumes of gas consumed in different applications,[23] large volumes are known to have been used in the low conversion cost category. In 1972/73 approximately 3.5 TCF, or almost 20% of marketed gas production in the United States, was burned under electric utility boilers for which conversion costs are the minimum—circa 10¢ or less per Mcf displaced. Indeed, approximately one-third of that volume was consumed in

Table 9-4.   Conversion Costs per Mcf of Gas Saved, Alternative Fuel-using Facilities[a]

End use	Additional Equip. Cost	Fuel-Quality Penalty	Total
Electrical utility boiler	5-10¢	-0-	5-10¢
Large industrial boiler	5-10¢	-0-	5-10¢
Large combustion gas turbine	5-12¢	20¢	25-32¢
Small industrial boiler			
80% Load factor	8-10¢	20¢	28-30¢
25% Load factor	25-35¢	20¢	45-55¢
Single-dwelling heating system	35¢-$1.30	60¢	$0.95-1.90
Industrial make-up air heaters	75¢-$1.70	25¢	$1.00-1.95
Metallurgical heat-treating furnaces	$3.00	50-90¢	$3.50-3.90

[a]Cost differentials for alternative fuels are not included. Low-sulfur No. 6 fuel oil is the alternative fuel assumed.

Sources: U.S. Senate, Committee on Interior and Insular Affairs, *Natural Gas Policy Issues,* Serial 92-22, Part 2 (Washington: Government Printing Office, 1972); FPC Docket No. RP73-115 *et al,* Exhibit 20-S. Cost data for 1970/71 were multiplied by 1.3 as an approximate inflation allowance.

boilers which already had dual-fuel capability, so that the conversion costs for displacing one trillion cubic feet of gas, or more, would have been zero exclusive of any increase in fuel costs.[24] That volume is comparable to the total output of the supplemental gas projects approved or pending through the end of 1973. Hence, an efficient gas curtailment or rationing program, might have preserved gas for "higher priority" end uses by selectively curtailing the natural gas burned by large dual-fuel electric utility boilers without requiring any capital outlays whatsoever.

The cost of shifting gas to the East Coast, for example, by displacing gas from utility boilers in the Gulf Coast area equals the cost of low-sulphur fuel oil plus the incremental transportation cost of moving the gas across one-half of the U.S. The nationwide average price for low-sulphur residual fuel oil delivered to electrical utilities in 1972-73 (prior to the global price increase) was about 80¢ per million BTU. Fuel oil substitution thus cost circa 87¢ per million BTU. The prices for imported LNG (see Table 9-5) were more expensive by 10 to 30¢ per MMBTU. SNG manufacture, since it consumes a light feedstock considerably more valuable than low sulphur No. 6 fuel oil, involved a much larger economic penalty of 55-60¢.

One further consideration qualifies the full comparability of the preceding cost estimates—the higher sulphur content of even low-sulphur residual oil as compared with natural gas. We have used fuel oil with 0.3% weight content of sulphur as the frame of reference. LNG and SNG thus warrant some sulphur premium value, since their sulphur content is effectively nil. We may approximate the "value" of this quality by relating it to the putative cost of removing 0.3% weight of sulphur from fuel oils consumed elsewhere in order

Table 9–5.   Economic Costs of Unconventional and Conventional Substitutes for Domestic Natural Gas.

Substitute	Unit Cost (¢/Mcf)	Annual Cost ($million/TCF)
Un-conventional		
Liquefied natural gas	90-115	900-1,150
Synthetic natural gas	137-148	1,400
Conventional		
"New" domestic gas	27-29	280
Fuel substitution		
Efficient	90	900
Inefficient	200-280	2,000-2,800

Source: See text.

that aggregate emissions not increase. Desulphurization costs range from 25¢-$1.00 per percent of sulphur removed per barrel of oil. This implies a "sulphur premium" for LNG vis-a-vis low sulphur residual fuel oil of 1.5-5¢ per MMBTU.[25]

4. ECONOMIC COMPARISONS: THE FOUR OPTIONS

The results of the two preceding sections may now be combined to permit a comparative assessment of the four potential solutions to the "gas gap." In order to be specific we concentrate upon the case where fuel substitution involves the replacement of fuel oil for gas in the Southwest and the transport of the displaced gas to customers in the Middlewest or on the East Coast (Case A.2 of Figure 9-2). This choice ignores all questions of equity or regulatory jurisdiction. The results are displayed in Table 9-5 under the assumption of a price of 80¢ per MMBTU for low-sulphur residual fuel oil. The latter is reasonable for the time period in question, i.e., 1971-73. The costs are shown per Mcf of gas and also for the case where each option supplies or makes up for one trillion cubic feet per year (TCF).

It has been necessary to differentiate between two extreme subcases for the fuel substitution option. It was demonstrated earlier that large volumes of natural gas could be saved by curtailing use in electric utility boilers at a conversion cost of zero or at most a surcharge of ten cents, i.e., a full cost of substitution of 80-90¢ per MMBTU. This was the minimum cost case. However, the FPC enunciated its own set of curtailment priorities for dealing with gas supply deficiencies on the interstate pipelines.[26] The FPC rules for fuel substitution are so weakly selective in terms of their potential economic impact as to be almost random. Their priority rankings are based upon contractual history and/or the size of total volumes of gas used by a customer at a single location. Boilers are identified as "low priority" but without reference to size.

Since the economics of conversion are governed by *type* of use and by the *size* of each piece of equipment which must be converted, there is only a fortuitous correlation between the FPC's categories and the economically significant classifications.

Consequently, we must introduce the second sub-option allowing for extremely inefficient substitution priorities. The economic rankings of these alternatives, in order of decreasing desirability are:

Rank	Options	Excess cost over new domestic gas per Mcf	Yearly/per TCF
1	New domestic gas	—	—
2	Efficient substitution	61-63¢	$620 million
3	LNG imports	61-88¢	$600-900 million
4	SNG manufacture	$1.08-1.21	$1.1-1.2 billion
5	Inefficient substitution	$1.70-2.50	$1.7-2.5 billion

The economic costs of the various strategies depend in part upon prevailing oil prices. The cost of new domestic natural gas is actually negatively correlated with the prices of liquid hydrocarbons, because of the offsetting effect of the co-products credit. On the other hand, the absolute levels of cost for SNG or fuel substitution depend directly upon oil prices, but the difference between the costs of these two options is essentially independent of liquids prices. The relative ranking of (1), (2), (4), and (5) thus remain invariant even though the absolute differences increase if oil prices rise. However, the cost advantage of LNG imports relative to SNG manufacture or inefficient fuel-switching will obviously be affected if LNG contract prices do go up (as we argued they might) when other hydrocarbon prices increase.

Subject to these limitations, we may conclude that SNG is always economically more expensive than efficient fuel substitution. A program of developing one trillion cubic feet of SNG manufacture per year implies an unnecessary annual cost of $500-600 million or a present value cost of $5-6 billion,[27] compared with fuel switching. Similarly, at current prices LNG imports in the same volume involve a lesser economic waste of $100 to 300 million per year, but this extra burden could rise dramatically if LNG prices move towards parity with liquids.

The economic costs attendant upon both of the nonconventional supplemental sources of gas, LNG or SNG, are even greater when compared with the option of developing more conventional domestic gas supplies. The annualized extra costs of LNG and SNG, versus new domestic natural gas, are approximately $800 and $1,200 million respectively. The present values of the extra costs of the two nonconventional sources become $7 and $10 billion, respectively, and the magnitude of the inefficiency cost would be reduced by only some $100 million per year if one accepted the higher estimates for the costs of finding and producing new gas supply in the U.S. which were argued by the producers but rejected by the FPC.

On the other hand, if for institutional reasons, the regulatory authorities are in fact unable to provide even modest incentives for developing new gas and simultaneously fail to design efficient fuel substitution priorities, then under such conditions of "regulatory perversity" LNG imports are clearly less wasteful than SNG manufacture. A program of one TCF per year of LNG costs at least $300-500 million per year less than the same volume of SNG, *provided* that the LNG contract prices do not escalate commensurate with liquid hydrocarbon prices. Similarly, *in extremis,* SNG itself becomes a "third-best" solution if the only option proves to be inefficient curtailment.

5. "THE REASON WHY"

Our final task is to illuminate why the Federal Power Commission and state utility commissions chose the more costly and technologically more risky options for reducing the natural gas "gap." This result can be understood only in the historical context of the positions of the various parties and in light of the forces acting upon them. This interpretation has unabashedly been stripped of all the complexities and collateral issues which have enriched a generation of lawyers, consultants, and stenographic and duplicating services.

The central role in this drama was played by the FPC—particularly during the 1960's when the crucial relationship between measured, historical costs and allowed prices evolved and crystalized. This pricing policy, only broadly mandated by the Supreme Court, was the genesis of the gas gap of ten years later. The other actors had to choose from a small set of options which had already been circumscribed by the FPC.

It is therefore necessary to scrutinize the FPC's method for establishing the regulated price of natural gas, since this is what inhibited development of domestic gas supplies. Then we will also be able to see why the FPC resorted to high-cost supplements rather than increase the domestic price and elicit additional supplies. Fundamental to the answer is the FPC's obligation under the Natural Gas Act to establish a "just and reasonable" price based upon objective costs and an appropriate profit margin. To do this, the FPC patched together a price formula borrowed partly from the electric utilities and pipelines and partly derived as a compromise with expediency.

Following established procedures of utility regulation the FPC tried to determine a rate base for the regulated gas producer and to specify an allowable rate of return on that rate base. The "just and reasonable" price for the gas is the sum of all items of current cost plus a profit margin equivalent to the allowed rate of return on the rate base. Between 1954 and 1960 the FPC struggled with defining rate bases for the producing assets of some 6,000 or more gas producers. Catapulted into an extractive industry with which it was quite unfamiliar, the Commission faced new rate-making problems—the treatment of exploration costs, the allocation of dry hole outlays to successful ventures, the dissection of joint costs such as certain exploration expenditures, and the assignment of co-product credits. This first effort to extend conventional rate-making techniques to the gas industry foundered, because of the administrative burden on the FPC and the long delays.

In 1960 the concept of regionally-defined gas prices (area rates) was introduced, reducing the number of cases from 6,000 or so to seven. Instead of adjudicating a rate base for each individual producer, representative *average* costs and investments were determined for each of several nominally homogeneous regions. Questionnaires and surveys were used to establish basic cost parameters for each area—the discovery and development outlays per Mcf of reserves, operating costs, state taxes, etc. The procedures that were employed in analyzing this data embodied several errors, omissions or unsupportable assumptions, all but one of which worked to underestimate the appropriate price, even if the input data were otherwise unobjectionable:

1. Reservoir depletion rate.

It can be shown that the FPC methods and the formula they used were correct only if the rate of production from the gas reservoir declines linearly with time. Because actual gas reservoirs' outputs hold at a roughly constant level for the first 6-10 years, and thereafter decline with reduced reservoir pressure, this error introduces a downward bias in the price of 10-20 percent.[28]

2. Quasi-capital outlays.

Expenditures for exploration or dry holes are treated as current-period expenses. The FPC's adherence to this accounting convention assumes that gas reserves are produced in the same year in which they are found, which contradicts engineering experience. This is tantamount to excluding any rate of return on approximately one-half of the pre-production outlays, and it further biases the regulated price downwards.

3. Retrospective "cost" basis.

Case law precedent has required that historical test periods be used to measure discovery and development costs. Inflation aside, costs necessarily rise in any area because the cheapest reserves are discovered first. Depletion means recourse to ever more marginal geological prospects as new reserves lie deeper or require offshore drilling. This physical phenomenon has been exacerbated by inflation and only partially offset by the technological progress in drilling through the late 1960's.

4. Income taxes.

Income taxes on production income and the deductions from tax liabilities arising from dry hole costs or the expensing of intangible drilling costs for tax purposes were both omitted.

5. Lease bonuses.

Payments for the acquisition of mineral rights were included as an item of "cost," even though such payments reflected the expected difference between price and cost. The logic is thus circular, but the impact was partially to offset the downward bias due to the preceding elements. This error cannot be quantified, but it must be noted that bonuses will always be offered on the most promising prospects (intramarginal potential reserves) even when prices are too low to permit discovery and development of all potential reserves. Thus not all of the "costs" due to bonuses can be eliminated without introducing still another error.

Biases in the price calculation also arose from systematic rejection of evidence by the Commission. Particularly significant was the decision on the time lag between the spending of exploration or development funds and the onset of gas production. The actual lag ranges between two and three years. Yet the maximum figure allowed by the FPC, in spite of an extensive evidentiary record, was six months. This omission was all the more remarkable—given the penchant of the FPC and the courts for analogies—because interest charges during construction, which reflect the time lag in constructing power plants, are routinely allowed in setting rates for electric utilities.

The errors perpetuated by the FPC's price formula are central both to the development of the gas shortage and to the FPC's inability to remedy the shortage by raising the price. The prices defined by the FPC formula are compared with the results of the more accurate calculations in Table 9-6; all input data and assumptions are otherwise the same. The error in the "just and reasonable" price is as low as 20¢ per Mcf—if one believes the FPC's notional 6-month time lag for the exploration/development cycle—but as great as 40¢ per Mcf, assuming the more plausible two-year lag. Hence the FPC's formula alone results in a two-to-one underestimation of the "price" derived from their own cost and productivity data.[29]

As noted above, the disincentive effect on exploration of the FPC's underestimation of the regulated price was in fact discernible by the early 1960's, even though the impact had become obvious to the regulators only in the early 1970's. By 1960 new gas discoveries had ceased to keep pace with the level of reserves needed to sustain the growth rates in production, ten years before gas curtailments were apparent. We have plotted this relationship on Figure 9-1 presented previously. "Required reserves" are defined to equal the annual production volume *plus* the additional reserves needed to sustain the increase in production in each year.[30] Actual additions were less than "required" new reserves in every year after 1959, and the gap had narrowed, beginning in 1957, only three years after the Phillips decision had clouded the producers' price expectations.

Thus, by 1971/72 the FPC was trapped in a Greek tragedy. The growing "gas gap" demanded immediate action. Yet in responding the Commission was fettered both by its own erroneous definition of the "just and

Table 9-6. Federal Power Commission Formula Cost and Corrected Cost of Natural Gas per Mcf

Cost estimate[a]	"Belco Case"	"R-389-B"
	(1)	(2)
1. FPC Formula	35.7¢	38.5¢
2. Corrected calculations		
a. 6-month lag	55.7	64.0
b. 2-year lag	68.7	78.9
3. "Bonus" component		
a. 6-month lag	(8.3)	(10.1)
b. 2-year lag	(10.3)	(12.4)

[a]Assumed: reservoir decline rate equals zero; rate of return equals 15%; lifetime is 20 years; depletion is 22% of gross income.

Source: col. (1), FPC Opinion 659, Docket C173-293 *et al.,* 30 May 1973; col. (2), staff studies issued 11 April 1973 and 21 March 1974 in connection with Notice of Proposed Rulemaking, Docket R-389-B.

reasonable" price and by the legal constraints of the Natural Gas Act. The Commission and its staff could not raise prices without raising questions about their own previous analyses and decisions and without doing violence to their judicial and legislative mandates. In addition there was the political storm that such a move might well have generated. Thus, absent new legislation, SNG and LNG appeared to be the only available options for new supply over which the FPC had control.

The postures of the various state regulatory agencies paralleled that of the FPC. The states certificated SNG facilities quite simply because there was no alternative. They could only speculate on what, if anything, the FPC might do to increase gas availability, whereas SNG plants did promise additional supplies. Conventional gas was clearly preferable—especially at historically low prices—but its availability could not be guaranteed. SNG became the chosen option because it was more certain, without any illusions as to its higher costs.

At first blush the enthusiastic interest of the gas distribution companies in constructing SNG plants can similarly be interpreted as a response by default to a gas shortage exogenously imposed by the FPC. Indeed, SNG plants did constitute the only form of "self-help" open to the distribution companies. But their motivation was more complex. High-cost SNG supplies did not burden the gas distribution companies financially since they could treat the capital costs as part of the asset base on which they could earn the regulated rate of return and pass the extra variable cost (for feedstocks) directly on to their customers via the purchased fuel adjustment clause.[31] Moreover, the impact on price of using sources 6-8 times more costly than conventional methane was blunted by the practice of "rolling-in" these costs. That is, in setting prices, the high cost of the incremental SNG/LNG is averaged with the low cost of much larger volumes of vintage gas. This lowered the risk of political and consumer complaints as a result of the strategy.

Moreover, SNG actually can prove profitable to gas distribution companies under certain conditions. Prospects for expansion are scarce in the gas industry today, and SNG plants comprise additions to the rate base, which otherwise might be declining. In some cases, SNG is needed to forestall actual reductions in total sales volumes, due to supply limitations. Such reductions and their accompanying revenue losses could jeopardize the financial condition of the company and its ability to maintain the necessary surplus of revenues over fixed (interest) charges. It is difficult to recover such losses through rate increases, so that avoiding such developments provided a very strong impetus to add supplemental supply like SNG, almost irrespective of cost.

The inability of the many parties to adopt an efficient system for allocating gas and inducing fuel substitution has a comparably, if different, intricate history. The FPC had failed to grasp the economic implications of fuel switching and thus emphasized purely legal, contractually-conditioned fuel-switching priorities. The states were caught in a conflict between equity considerations and the unknown or unknowable policies of the FPC beyond the regulatory boundary. The interstate gas pipelines and the intrastate gas distribution companies focused on the revenue effects of different rationing plans and felt understandably little concern for overall efficiency.

The existence of the regulatory boundary between state and federal jurisdictions considerably compromised the FPC's ability to implement any scheme for efficient substitution of other fuels for natural gas, even if the Commission had developed the appropriate criteria. The FPC could order or authorize the interstate pipelines to curtail gas deliveries to their few direct industrial customers or to the gas distribution companies. It was not unequivocally empowered however to compel intrastate distribution companies to curtail supplies to final users on the basis of the same system of priorities. The Commission thus ran the risk that an enlightened, efficient curtailment program at the pipeline level could be completely vitiated if the state-regulated distribution companies chose to allocate the shortage differently among the ultimate consumers. Conversely, the state utilities commissions could not provide curtailment priorities until they knew what rules the FPC might invoke. This uncertainty as to the direction and timeliness of FPC action with regard to rationing priorities was the recurrent theme in the state-level hearings that began to proliferate after 1971/72, once the spectre of the national gas shortage became real.

Superimposed upon this uncertainty was the greater exposure of the state authorities to the political repercussions of curtailment. Since alternative fuels are very much more expensive than gas, the financial impact upon the curtailed parties is very great. Any decision was bound to be bitterly contested. The state utilities commissions therefore had a clear incentive to avoid such unwelcome and financially discriminatory decisions, hoping that the FPC would assume the burden. For them SNG was the more promising recourse.

The need for end use priorities as part of a fuel-switching program posed a confusing set of conceptual and legal problems for the FPC (and for state regulators) because it seemed to resemble a well-known, yet different, policy question. The FPC was familiar with the well-established distinction between firm and interruptible classes of service, where "interruptible" customers' requirements were subordinate to those of "firm" customers in times of peak, (usually weather-responsive) demand. Accordingly, when chronic *supply* shortages—in contrast to the normal, short-term cold-weather *delivery* shortages—emerged as a new phenomenon, the FPC proceeded to apply the familiar priorities appropriate for temporary, peak situations. It interpreted the issue as the narrow legal one of contractual priorities. This approach could only give the correct economic answer if the uses of gas served under interruptible contracts coincided with those for which the fuel-switching costs were minimal, which proved not to be the case.

With only one exception, no pipeline or distribution company evidenced any interest in end use priorities, and most opposed economic rationing criteria with rare vehemence.[32] Each firm wanted a rationing plan custom-tailored to its own system. The consumption patterns on each line, or within each distribution company, were markedly different. Thus the impact of any rationing plan upon the distributor's revenues depended on the specifics of the situation. It would have been an extraordinary coincidence if the curtailment plan that minimized the revenue losses to company "X" had happened to approximate the economically efficient plan.

6. SUMMARY AND EPILOGUE

The FPC potentially had in its arsenal four different weapons to combat the "gas gap" which had become obvious by 1971/72:

- Increased prices or full deregulation of gas prices.
- Elimination of the excess demand via end use priorities for curtailment (economically efficient rationing).
- Promoting a new SNG industry based on liquid hydrocarbon feedstocks.
- Development of imports of LNG for base-load service.

The economic cost of domestic gas production, as based upon the FPC's cost data, was a fraction of projected costs of SNG/LNG. The costs of an efficient fuel-switching scheme lie between those domestic gas production and supplementary supplies, whereas an inefficient gas rationing system could have been even more expensive than SNG or LNG.

The absolute measure of the resulting misallocation of resources depends upon the costs of imported hydrocarbons and the pricing of imported

LNG. Based on prices prevailing in 1971/72, SNG/LNG involves an annual extra resource cost of $1,000 million for each trillion cubic feet per year, compared with the same volume from incremental domestic production. Based upon 1974 prices for oil—and assuming that LNG does not trade at a price less than its parity with oil—the cost penalty for supplemental sources would rise to some $3,000 million per year.

These cost differentials notwithstanding, the regulatory authorities opted to promote the higher-cost supplemental supplies of gas in order to cope with burgeoning excess demand in the 1970's. Regulatory policies came to subordinate allocative efficiency to other goals through an historical process that evolved through a number of crucial steps.

1. The Supreme Court created the predicate by extending the Natural Gas Act of 1938 to encompass the regulation of gas prices in the field. The courts thereafter abdicated any constructive role and deferred to the expertise of the Federal Power Commission.
2. After 1960 the FPC, under Chairmen Swidler and White, implemented a method for determining the "just and reasonable" price which intrinsically understated the full cost of producing most of the potential gas reserves. This downward bias in the regulated price was thereafter perpetuated by virtue of legal precedent and bureaucratic commitment.
3. With price set below marginal *and* average cost, reserve additions ceased to keep pace with production. The "gas gap" thus emerged in the early 1960's.
4. Ten years later, when the "gap" became apparent even to the uninitiated, the FPC—trapped in a *cul-de-sac* largely of its own construction—undertook to certify supplemental gas supplies. The high costs of those supplies, unlike those of domestic alternatives, were objectively measurable. Thus they were "just and reasonable" within the terms of the Natural Gas Act, while domestic price increases were not, given the record and precedents the FPC had amassed.
5. The state commissions, lacking any authority whatsoever to affect price, and thus powerless to encourage or elicit conventional supply, similarly endorsed LNG and SNG plants as the only "self-help" measures within their jurisdictions.
6. The interstate pipelines and the gas distribution companies, who could average the high cost of new supplemental gas against the much lower costs of vintage gas supplies, were not financially disadvantaged by SNG/LNG supplies. Some benefited from expansion of their rate bases or from greater protection for their fixed charges.
7. Efficient fuel-switching was unwelcome to all protagonists because the non-uniform financial impact on certain firms, industries, or states evoked virulent opposition.
8. The Congress, which alone was empowered to legislate either deregulation or some more enlightened pricing concept, remained inactive. Its members

had few incentives to enter an arena in which rationality implied the unpopular step of higher consumer prices.

This interpretation of the internal logic of regulatory perversity still fails to fully explain why the FPC persisted in its erroneous calculation of the "just and reasonable" price and why it failed to react to the "reserves gap" of the 1960's which was the bellwether of the "gas gap" itself.[33] In the mid-1960's, for example, the FPC might have altered its definitions of "cost," before those concepts were fossilized by an accumulation of case law. The sympisons of the gas shortage—a declining reserve-to-production ratio and a downward trend in new exploration drilling—were then clearly perceptible. Even then the gas producers were stridently proclaiming the deficiencies, real and otherwise, of the FPC's pricing policy.

Why, then, was there no response? Any definitive answer is impossible without access to confidential staff memoranda and the full minutes of the commissioners' deliberations. However, one may posit two central factors. The first is the failure of the adversary process to provide for evaluation of economic evidence. Repeatedly, both FPC examiners and review courts adopted compromise formulae which were tantamount to independent, unsupported renditions of economic or technical facts. Often the results unwittingly involved incorrect, implicit assumptions about parameters whose magnitudes had in fact been explicitly discussed in evidence. A prominent example is the rate of return formula itself. While the courts and commission explicitly rejected the concept of discounted cash flow rates of return, they failed to recognize that the specification of any formula did indeed implicitly determine some *dcf* equivalent rate of return, so that the issue was decided by default. The legal authorities appear to have been unable to assimilate economic evidence or to discern whether the economic consequences of their legal decisions were consistent with the economic or financial evidence. Indeed, it may be questioned whether the FPC had legal authority to consider questions of economic efficiency.

The second factor is more subtle and elusive. One may speculate that the FPC was desensitized to any auguries of the pending gas shortage because of their political commitment to the goals of low prices and the elimination of unwarranted producers' rents. The thrust of the Phillips decision was the protection of consumer interests against the monopolistic power of the gas producers. That preoccupation persisted into the 1960's even though the predicate was unfounded—monopsony, rather than monopoly, characterized the natural gas industry.[34] These misapprehensions, plus the political advantage of offering short-term gains to consumers in the form of low gas prices, may have blunted the ability of commissioners, examiners, and staff to assess evidence, quite aside from the technical errors discussed earlier.

The trade-off between short-term consumer savings and longer-term misallocations of resources is difficult to assess. The costs of the shortage today are expensive retrofits to switch fuel, high-cost supplemental sources, and the multiplicative effects of forced plant closures for want of fuel. Given the political advantages of immediate kudos from offering low prices, given the long lags before supply and demand respond to price signals, and given an obsession with possible producers' windfalls, it is all too understandable why the regulators may have been reluctant to recognize the initial indications that their policy had failed.

This case study of gas price regulation by the FPC offers important insight into the problems of controlling prices for an industry characterized by long gestation periods and based upon a depletable resource. Historical costs are an intrinsically biased metric for prospective costs, and the long lead/lag times ensure that the signals needed for corrective responses are delayed. Five to eight years must lapse before the consequences of misregulation become apparent and another full cycle of five to eight years is necessary before those errors can be rectified. Like any servomechanism with a long time constant and system dead time, such an industry can be destabilized by a badly-designed control loop. This potential instability is exacerbated by the virtually irresistible political temptation to incur future costs—perceived only after several electoral terms—in order to offer palpable, short-term benefits. The exigencies of the political process and the procedural inadequacies of the legal/judicial process thus pose special problems in the regulation of such an industry, and both are illustrated in the evolution of gas regulation since 1954.

Notes to Chapter Nine

1. In 1954 reserve additions dropped below consumption, but the year was an isolated exception. This discussion excludes the large reserves found in Alaska, since these were not readily accessible to market.

2. Federal Power Commission, *Annual Report, 1973,* And PFC, Bureau of Natural Gas, *National Gas Supply and Demand: 1971-1990* (Washington, 1972).

3. See Part Five for illustrative documentation.

4. J. N. Nissikas, Statement before the Interstate Commerce Committee, U.S. Senate, February 19, 1974.

5. Federal Power Commission, Opinion No. 622 (CP 71-68 *et al.*), June 28, 1972 and Opinion No. 637 (CP 72-35 *et al.*), December 7, 1972.

6. The manufacture of lower energy-content "town gas" involves a known, almost hoary technology; the large-scale manufacture of "high-BTU" gas, however, is an entirely new development.

7. Derived as representative from diverse sources: *Oil and Gas Journal,* June 25, 1973, pp. 119-31; *ibid,* April 16, 1973, pp. 99-102; July 17, 1972, pp. 83-88; April 9, 1973, p. 32; costs based upon reforming crude oil are some 20-30 cents higher per million BTU, but the feedstock cost is less by roughly the same amount.

8. See Babcock and Wilcox, *Steam* (New York: Babcock and Wilcox, 1972), chapters 6 and 7, or C. G. Segeler (ed.), *Gas Engineers Handbook* (New York: Industrial Press, 1965), section 2, chapters 3-5.

11. Several such facilities have already been built: in Brunei and Alaska for shipment to Japan, in Libya for Italy and Spain, and in Algeria for the U.K.

12. Concurring opinion of Commissioner Rush Moody, FPC, Opinion 622, *op. cit.*

13. See T. R. Stauffer, "Economic Cost of U.S. Crude Oil Production," *Journal of Petroleum Technology,* 25 (July 1973), pp. 643–53, for one exposition of the methodology; also U.S. Senate, Committee on Interior and Insular Affairs, *Natural Gas Policy Issues and Options,* Committee Print, Serial 93–55 (Washington, 1973), pp. 200–214.

14. As a gas field is depleted, the reservoir pressure declines and deliveries from the field are reduced. The effective decline rate over the lifetime of the field is 2-5%, while that observed in later years is much higher—10% or more. The FPC cost of service studies presume this rate is zero.

15. For detailed formulas embodying these relations see H. H. Ratchford, *Oil and Gas Journal,* 71 (July 16, 1973), pp. 93–96; American Gas Association, *Gas Engineers Handbook* (New York: Industrial Press, 1965), pp. 8/73 ff.

16. Additionally, the reported charge ignores the fact that compressor fuel must also be transported along the pipeline, and some 4% of the system capability can be devoted to carrying fuel for ultimate pipeline use. The FPC format ignores that effect, too, but it is part of sunk costs and does not enter into our enquiry.

The derivation of the relationship between average and marginal compressor fuel consumption has been deleted. Both the non-linear dependences of compressor horsepower upon flow rate and compressor efficiency upon capacity factor were included.

17. A figure of 3¢/Mcf is reported in the initial opinion of Examiner Levy in Docket No. CP 72–100 (30 Aug. 1973), but without substantiation.

18. The FPC procedure also assumed unrealistically short discovery and development lead times (six months). More representative figures of two to three years add some 6-9 cents to the cost, but this effect would now be more than offset by the much higher co-product credit for natural gas liquids.

19. Balance of payments effects are ignored; if included, these would increase the real cost of imports of LNG or feedstocks to SNG plants. See Stauffer, *Journal of Petroleum Technology, op. cit.,* or Cabinet Task Force on Oil Import Control, *The Oil Import Question* (1971), App. H. (pp. 265–98).

20. The commodity value varies among markets. It is no less than the cost per unit of energy of an alternative fuel *plus* a "form value" premium which reflects the technical advantages of gas. An approximate lower bound is 10¢ per million BTU above the cost of low-sulphur heavy fuel oil.

21. These intermediate values were obtained as the arithmetical averages of the high and low cases from Table 9.3; the average of the gas prices in the two cases is very close to 75¢, so greater accuracy—compared with an 80¢ alternative fuel cost—is not warranted.

22. The incremental transport cost in these cases is larger than that cited above because alternate fuels are very much more costly than "new" gas.

23. An approximate distribution was presented in *Natural Gas Policy Issues, op. cit.,* Part Two, pp. 413-418.

24. *Natural Gas Policy Issues, op. cit.,* Part Two; pp. 456 ff; and FPC, Form No. 432 data, monthly reports.

25. *Oil and Gas Journal,* November 26, 1973; May 21, 1973, pp. 64-5 *inter alia.* Desulphurization costs are specific both to the individual processes and the different crude oils.

26. Federal Power Commission, Order No. 467-B, Docket R-469, March 2, 1973.

27. Based upon a twenty-year lifetime and a social discount rate of ten percent.

28. U.S. Senate, Committee on Interior and Insular Affairs, *Natural Gas Policy Issues* (1973), pp. 200-214, and Stauffer, *Journal of Petroleum Technology, op. cit.*

29. The productivity and cost figures themselves are alleged by the producers to be low, which would result in a further downward bias. On the other hand, inclusion of bonuses as part of "cost" biases the price upwards. The net impact of the latter two effects cannot be assessed, but it appears to be small, if positive, and may still be negative.

30. The volume of new reserves needed to support an increase in production equals that increase, multiplied by the minimum reserve-to-production ratio. For example, if production is 11 trillion cubic feet; if the year's growth in production is one TCF; and if the minimum reserve-to-production ratio—$(R/P)_0$—is ten, then $11 + 10 \times 1 = 21$ TCF of gas reserves must be added to sustain equilibrium growth in that year.

31. The price elasticity of demand for gas does not enter this calculus, since gas in most markets was priced well below parity with alternate fuels on a heating-value basis, quite aside from any consideration of its form value premium. Thus a considerable increase in the *average* price could occur before demand would be noticeably diminished.

32. Counsel for the Panhandle Eastern Pipeline Company devoted days of effort in one hearing in order to suppress even the presentation of economic evidence relating to rationing priorities; FPC Docket RP71-119, *in passim.*

33. See S.G. Breyer and P.W. MacAvoy, *Energy Regulation by the Federal Power Commission* (Washington, D.C.: Brookings Institution, 1974), especially pp. 56-88 and 122-34 for a more comprehensive, but somewhat different, interpretation.

34. Paul MacAvoy, *Price Formation in Natural Gas Fields: A Study in Competition, Monopsony and Regulation* (New Haven: Yale University Press, 1962).

Part Four

Regulation, Welfare and the Distribution of Products

Chapter Ten

Optimal Pricing and Income Distribution

Elisha A. Pazner

1. INTRODUCTION

Public discussion of regulated industries is now filled with concern for income distribution. As prices in various industries have risen in recent years, there have been many suggestions for altering rate structures for distributive purposes. Two examples are special low "life-line" rates for poor, elderly telephone subscribers, and inverting the traditional declining block-rate structure of electricity prices so that larger users pay higher, not lower, average prices. These proposed departures from marginal cost pricing cannot just be dismissed by the economist as "inefficient," since today it is well known that the traditional precept that prices should equal marginal costs is not necessarily applicable in imperfect, real-world situations. But posing the problem is not sufficient. Once we take distributional considerations into account, what should prices be?

As a response to these questions, this paper tries to develop some of the implications of a non-optimal distribution of income for departures from marginal cost pricing. While we will pose the discussion in terms of a public enterprise, a slight reinterpretation of the definitions would allow exactly the same analysis to be used for a regulated private firm whose prices are subject to public control. The plan of the paper is as follows: section 2 explains the general methodology followed throughout the paper; section 3 derives the optimal pricing rule for when a single private good is supplied to all consumers at a uniform price (and these consumers are homogeneous from a social welfare perspective). In section 4, the analysis of the previous section is extended to the case where the set of consumers may be heterogeneous and where price discrimination is an additional policy tool. In section 5, extensions of the analysis to any number of commodities, to consumption externalities and merit wants and to an exogenously imposed budget constraint are briefly discussed. Finally, section 6 concludes the paper.

2. METHODOLOGICAL PREAMBLE

The basic hypothesis underlying all of what follows is that the lump-sum taxes and subsidies necessary to achieve the blissful first-best optimum are infeasible. Hence the economy rests at a second-best optimum. The exact nature of the second-best solution depends, of course, on the imperfections and the policy instruments one assumes. One very general way to characterize such a second-best optimum, however, is to say that whatever the optimal solution turns out to be, the social marginal utility of income will not (save by "accident") be equalized across individuals. This indeed is the general approach adopted here.

Methodologically, I have tried to combine the cost-benefit approach initiated (independently) by Feldstein and Marglin and the explicit general equilibrium formulation developed (jointly) by Diamond and Mirrlees.[1] From the former I have adopted the useful and elegant devices of putting shadow prices on benefits and costs and presenting the maximand as some kind of "social surplus." From the latter I have borrowed the important notion that second-best optimization involves explicitly maximizing the social welfare function subject to constraints. These include the market equilibrium conditions, and the behavior patterns of all the private agents in the economy. As a consequence, the general formulation of the optimization problem resembles strongly that used by Feldstein and Marglin. Much of the underlying reasoning, however, is directly influenced by the work of Diamond and Mirrlees.

In the present paper, the economy is assumed to consist of a public sector, of a private production sector, and of N consumers whose utility indicators are denoted by $U^h (h=1, \ldots, N)$. This social welfare function is given by $W(U^1, \ldots, U^N)$. Suppose now that a public enterprise provides a purely private commodity x, x^h of which is bought (and consumed) by man h. At the margin, when the provision of x to man h is slightly increased, the social net benefits arising directly from the consumption of x are:

$$\frac{\partial W}{\partial U^h} \cdot \frac{\partial U^h}{\partial x^h} = \frac{\partial W}{\partial U^h} \cdot \alpha^h \cdot p = \lambda^h p \, ,$$

where α^h denotes the marginal utility of income of man h, p is the market price of x, and $\lambda^h = \dfrac{\partial W}{\partial U^h} \cdot \alpha^h$ is the social marginal utility of income of man h. Note that when all the demanders of x command the same social marginal utility of income denoted by λ^B it does not matter how the "marginal unit" of x is divided among the different buyers. In such a case, therefore, the social marginal benefits arising directly from the consumption of x will simply be $\lambda^B p$

independent of "who" gets "how much" of x at the margin. λ^B is our first shadow price.

Our second shadow price, denoted by λ^T, is associated with the government's budget constraint. The assumption that the economy rests at a second best optimum implies that at the margin a "dollar's worth" of resources (i.e., the resources equivalent in market value to one unit of our numeraire commodity) has the same implications for social welfare whether it is used in the private or public sector.[2] Withdrawing a marginal unit of resources from the private sector entails an opportunity cost equal to the social welfare "value" it would have generated if left in the private sector. We assume that the cost will be equal to the value of social welfare generated by the use of these resources in the public sector. This common social-welfare value is our second shadow price, λ^T.[3]

Our general approach is to formulate the (social) optimization problem relating to the prices of one enterprise under the assumption that all other economic variables are set at their (second-best) optimal values. In this sense we are dealing with "valid" partial-equilibrium analysis. Furthermore, relaxing the various assumptions (as we do in section 6) does not affect the basic nature of the optimal pricing rule, but would have prevented our "social surplus" exposition. Expository convenience and intuitive interpretation have thus been chosen at the cost of some rigor, but this is inconsequential so far as the conclusions are concerned.

3. THE SIMPLEST PRICING PROBLEM

In this section we deal with the simplest possible pricing problem faced by a public enterprise operating in a second-best environment. We assume that (i) the enterprise provides a single private good x, (ii) all consumers of which have the same social marginal utility of consumption λ^B, and (iii) it must charge a uniform price over all consumers. By relaxing each of these assumptions, we can extend these results to more complicated and interesting cases. It turns out, however, that the basic nature of the optimal pricing rule derived here remains unaltered by the various complications. To make the economic rationale intuitively more transparent, we will undertake a detailed examination of several simplified examples. This will enable us to deal more succinctly with the more complicated cases of the following sections.

In order to reach a second-best optimal outcome, the price we are concerned with should be set so as to maximize the difference between social benefits and social costs. As suggested earlier, in a public enterprise benefits arise from the consumption of x and from the revenue generated to the government. Costs arise because the resources devoted to the provision of x have alternative uses, whether these are paid for out of prices or government revenue.

The following notational conventions are adopted:

x quantity of the commodity provided by the public enterprise,

p price per unit of x,

$p(x)$ inverse demand function for x,

λ^B social marginal utility of income (of each) of the buyers of x,

λ^T social value of a "dollar" of government revenue,

$\lambda^c = \lambda^T$ social value of a "dollar's worth" of resources used in providing x,

$c(x)$ cost function derived from the production function of x.

To simplify the exposition, we shall proceed as if the "shadow prices" λ^B, λ^T, and λ^c were constants, independent of the value of x. Relaxing this assumption would *in no way* affect the pricing rule derived below, but would involve a slightly more cumbersome formulation of the objective function. The assumption $\lambda^T = \lambda^c$ as discussed above reflects the fact that what we are interested in is an optimal pricing rule for a world resting at a second-best optimum. We also assume the absence of income effects on the demand for x so that the consumption benefits of x are indeed given by the area under the demand curve.[4]

An additional assumption is that we can disregard the welfare effects of any changes in governmental revenue due to adjustments in other markets which are in turn caused by changes in the price-quantity configuration of x. This assumption would be validated for instance if x is "small" relative to the economy. In that case only marginal changes occur in other markets, implying that the induced changes in other tax revenues and their excess burden are negligible. Finally, we ignore the distributional implication arising from the payment of governmental revenue to the owners of the factors of production used in the provision of x. That is, we implicitly assume the latter's social marginal utility of income to be λ^T. The reason for the last two assumptions lies in our desire to focus attention on the "direct" distributional elements entering the optimal pricing rule.

Turning now to the identification of social benefits and costs in our stylized world, we have:

direct consumption benefits: $\int_0^x \lambda^B p(q)dq - \lambda^B p(x) \cdot x$,

government revenue benefits: $\lambda^T p(x) \cdot x$,

resource costs: $\lambda^T C(x)$.

The objective function can thus be written:

$$\text{Max:} \int_0^x \lambda^B p(q)dq + (\lambda^T - \lambda^B)p(x) \cdot x - \lambda^T C(x), \tag{1}$$

subject to: $x \geqslant 0, p(x) \geqslant 0$ (i.e., $0 \leqslant x \leqslant x_{\max}$, where $p(x_{\max}) = 0$);

from which we derive the first-order condition for an interior maximum:[5]

$$\lambda^B p + (\lambda^T - \lambda^B)(p + x\frac{dp}{dx}) - \lambda^T c' = 0 \; ; \tag{2}$$

where $c' = c'(x)$ is the "physical" marginal cost of producing x.
    For $p \neq 0$ we can rewrite (2) as:

$$\lambda^B p + (\lambda^T - \lambda^B)(p + p \cdot \frac{x}{p} \cdot \frac{dp}{dx}) - \lambda^T c' = 0 \; ; \qquad (p \neq 0)$$

or as:

$$[\lambda^B + (\lambda^T - \lambda^B) \; 1 + \frac{1}{\eta_x} \;] p - \lambda^T c' = 0; \qquad (p \neq 0) \tag{2'}$$

where η_x denotes the algebraic value of the elasticity of the demand for x, i.e.,
$\eta_x = \dfrac{dx/x}{dp/p}$.

    From (2') we can now derive the optimal pricing rule for $p \neq 0$:

$$p = \frac{\lambda^T}{\lambda^B + (\lambda^T - \lambda^B) \; 1 + \dfrac{1}{\eta_x}} \; c', \qquad \text{for } p \neq 0. \tag{3}$$

    The price, p, is thus seen to depend, at the optimum, upon four different variables: λ^B, λ^T, c' and η_x. Of these the last (η_x) deserves special mention because the dependence of p upon the shadow values, λ^B and λ^T, is expected on a priori grounds from the very formulation of the problem, and its dependence upon c' is expected from the familiar opportunity-cost principle. The role of η_x in the determination of p is in fact dictated by our objective function in a double manner: the desire to minimize excess burdens in our second-best environment and (as the other side of the same coin) the special objective or revenue.
    Now we can rewrite (2') in the form:

$$\lambda^B p + (\lambda^T - \lambda^B) MR = \lambda^T c'; \qquad (p \neq 0) \tag{4}$$

where $MR = 1 + \dfrac{1}{\eta_x} \; p$ is the marginal revenue of x.

Then by rewriting (4) as,

$$\lambda^B p + \lambda^T MR = \lambda^T c' + \lambda^B MR; \qquad (p \neq 0) \qquad (5)$$

we truly separate the benefits side from the costs side. We have converted the first-order condition into the optimality maxim: "social marginal benefits = social marginal costs." Thus our optimal pricing rule requires the balancing at the margin of the sum of the direct (social) marginal benefits to consumers of $x(\lambda^B p)$ and the (social) benefits induced by marginal governmental revenue $(\lambda^T MR)$, with the sum of the (social) marginal production costs, $(\lambda^T c')$, and of the (social) marginal cost incurred by the buyers of x, $\lambda^B MR$.

To get a better intuitive feeling for what is involved, it is useful to consider a number of specific cases.

(i) Suppose $\lambda^B = \lambda^T$. Then, as far as the public enterprise is concerned "a dollar is a dollar is a dollar," just as if it were operating in a first-best environment. And indeed, we see from (3) that the optimal pricing rule in this case reduces to marginal-cost pricing, namely, $p = c'$.

(ii) Suppose $\lambda^B = 0$, i.e., society finds itself indifferent with respect to changes in the income of the consumers of x. This could happen, for instance, if the marginal valuation placed by society on anyone's income is a decreasing function of that income, and if all the consumers of x are so rich that for them λ^B is zero for all practical purposes. In such a case we see from (3) that the optimal pricing rule reduces to

$$p = \frac{1}{1 + \dfrac{1}{\eta_x}} \, c',$$

i.e., to $MR = c'$, the monopoly outcome. Since $\lambda^B \cong 0$, the direct consumption benefits and the costs associated with raising the revenue disappear from the objective function. All that is left is to maximize socially valuable net revenue (i.e., profit).

(iii) Suppose $c' = 0$. This is the case of an uncongested facility for which there is excess capacity at $p = 0$. Traditionally, the application of the marginal-cost principle implies that the optimal price (or toll) should be $p = 0$. In a sense, x is a "noneconomic good," one for which there is no "scarcity" problem since at zero price there is excess supply. However, in our model, even though there is no (current) resource use involved in the provision of x, the effects of price on the distribution costs and benefits require that a positive price be charged.

Since all of the various forms in which we have expressed the basic optimality condition (2) hold only for $p \neq 0$, we have to go back to (2) and see what happens at $p = 0$, and $c' = 0$. Then (2) becomes:

$$(\lambda^T - \lambda^B) \, x \frac{dp}{dx} = 0$$

Thus (assuming $x \neq 0$), $p = 0$ can satisfy the necessary conditions for an optimum if either: (a) $\lambda^t = \lambda^v$; or (b) $\frac{dp}{dx} = 0$ at $p = 0$. In all other cases it seems that $p = 0$ cannot be optimal. This, however, is not true and results from our presenting the first-order conditions as satisfied with equality. We will see below that "corner conditions" imply $p = 0$ also when $\lambda^T < \lambda^B$.

Turning to case (a), we infer that $c' = 0$ and $\lambda^T = \lambda^B$ imply that at the optimum x should be provided free of charge. This is not surprising, since $\lambda^T = \lambda^B$ implies that society is indifferent between one dollar's worth of consumption of x and one dollar revenue to the government. Since marginal costs of production are assumed to be zero, society's objective is to maximize the *total* number of dollar benefits. Under uniform pricing, benefits from x (the area under the demand curve for x) will always be greater than the revenue collected from selling that amount. Hence, welfare will be maximized at that x for which the consumption benefits are largest, implying $p = 0$ at the optimum. Any positive price entails excess burden. Any dollar of revenue will entail more than a dollar foregone in consumption benefits! Finally (since $\lambda^T = \lambda^B$ as in case (ii)) this is a first-best type of situation, implying the first-best solution of marginal-cost pricing.

In contrast, in all cases where we know $p \neq 0$, we can use (2'), which when $c' = 0$, reduces to:

$$p \left[\lambda^B + (\lambda^T - \lambda^B) \left(1 + \frac{1}{\eta_x} \right) \right] = 0.$$

And since $p \neq 0$, we must have at the optimum:

$$\lambda^B + (\lambda^T - \lambda^B) \left(1 + \frac{1}{\eta_x} \right) = 0;$$

from which we find that at the optimum:

$$\eta_x = -1 + \frac{\lambda^B}{\lambda^T}, \text{ for } p \neq 0.$$

And of course, once we know η_x at the optimum, we know p (and x) as well. Yet p (and x) need not be uniquely determined in this way. So, in general, we will have to have recourse to global considerations in order to find the truly optimizing $p(x)$. A few special cases will be of help in understanding the above condition on η_x.

Suppose, again, $\lambda^B \cong 0$ and $c' = 0$. Then at the optimum we require $\eta_x \cong -1$. This means that the socially optimal policy for the public enterprise will be to maximize total revenue, like a private monopolist, equating $MR = c' = 0$. Since society attaches no value to the benefits accruing to the consumers of x ($\lambda^B \cong 0$), and since there is no resource use involved in the provision of x ($c' = 0$), the only remaining benefit is government revenue (assuming $\lambda^T > 0$). And since this benefit is "costless" (λ^B *and* $c' = 0$), we seek to maximize it.

Suppose $\lambda^B < \lambda^T$, $c' = 0$, and $\dfrac{dp}{dx} \neq 0$ at $p = 0$. In this case, $\eta_x < 0$ at the optimum, and this is compatible with the usually assumed downward sloping demand curve for x. That is, as long as $\lambda^B < \lambda^T$ a positive price (toll) is the rule, even though $c' = 0$. The reason is that $\lambda^T > \lambda^B$ means that the government's revenue objective is more socially important than the consumption-benefits objective. Thus, if only the "rich" use the uncongested facility, they should have to pay a positive price even though there is no resource cost involved. Note that if $\dfrac{dp}{dx} = 0$ at $p = 0$, one will have to make recourse to global considerations in order to determine whether $p = 0$ or (one of) the p's corresponding to $\eta_x = -1 + \dfrac{\lambda^B}{\lambda^T}$ is the optimal one. But anyhow, we can say that in general $\lambda^B < \lambda^T$ implies $p > 0$.

For $\lambda^B > \lambda^T$ and $c' = 0$ we should have $\eta_x > 0$ at the optimum. But this is impossible for a downward sloping demand curve. We can therefore rule out $p > 0$ when $\lambda^B > \lambda^T$. But can $p = 0$ be optimal in such a case? We might expect this on a priori grounds since $\lambda^B > \lambda^T$ means that both direct consumption benefits and costs of raising governmental revenue are socially more valuable, dollar per dollar, than the benefits from governmental revenue, while $c' = 0$ again means that "current" resource costs are zero.

If $p = 0$ turns out to be optimal, why is it that in our earlier discussion we did not have the condition $\lambda^B > \lambda^T$? The answer lies in the fact that so far we have neglected to take into account the fact that we might have a corner solution. When $p(x) = 0$ we do in fact have such a solution, which involves inequalities in the first-order conditions. Thus for $p = 0$ and $c' = 0$, the first-order condition (2) should be rewritten as:

$$\lambda^B p + (\lambda^T - \lambda^B)\ p + x\frac{dp}{dx} - \lambda^T c' = (\lambda^T - \lambda^B)\ x\frac{dp}{dx} \geqslant 0, \text{ since } x > 0. \qquad (2'')$$

Hence, in addition to our earlier conditions for $p = 0$, we find that for $\lambda^B > \lambda^T$ the inequality also holds ($\dfrac{dp}{dx} \leqslant 0$ and $x > 0$ by assumption), implying that $p = 0$ is optimal. What happens here is that consumer benefits are weighted more heavily than revenue ($\lambda^B > \lambda^T$), there are no resource costs ($c' = 0$), and the "worthy poor" are the users of the uncongested facility.

To sum up the discussion of an uncrowded bridge or uncongested road, we have found that in some instances the optimal charge should be zero (as conventional theorizing advocates) and in others should be positive. The correct price depends on who the users of the facility are. In general, we can say that for the case where the users satisfy the condition $\lambda^B \geqslant \lambda^T$ (the "poor"), the optimal price is zero; if the users are such that $\lambda^B < \lambda^T$ (the "rich"), a positive price is called for even if (current) resource costs are zero.

In a second-best environment, a good is not necessarily a "noneconomic" even when there is excess supply of it at zero price. In a second-best world, redistributive measures, being "scarce," entail "real" costs and benefits. Such considerations have to be taken explicitly into account when formulating an optimal price policy.

(iv) In the general case, as (3) makes clear, marginal cost pricing will not be optimal. The direction of departure from that rule will be unambiguously determined by the magnitude of λ^B relative to λ^T. In fact, as expected, it can easily be shown that as λ^B is greater than, equal to, or less than λ^T, price should be greater than, equal to, or less than marginal cost.[6] Because the proofs of these three assertions are essentially identical, we will prove here only the first one.

Suppose $\lambda^B > \lambda^T$. Observe first that the denominator of the right-hand side of (3) can be expressed as:

$$\lambda^B + (\lambda^T - \lambda^B) \left[1 + \frac{1}{\eta_x} \right] = \lambda^T + \frac{\lambda^T - \lambda^B}{\eta_x}$$

Now $\lambda^B > \lambda^T$ implies $\lambda^T + \dfrac{\lambda^T - \lambda^B}{\eta_x} > \lambda^T$ since $\eta_x < 0$ and $\lambda^T - \lambda^B < 0$. The denominator of the coefficient of c' in (3) is thus larger than the numerator, implying $p < c'$. It is equally easy to work backward to show that if $p < c'$ in equilibrium we must have $\lambda^B > \lambda^T$ This is what we set out to prove.

In general then, we have, for $p > 0$, the general rule:

$$\lambda^B \gtreqless \lambda^T \leftrightarrow p \lesseqgtr c'$$

Put in simple words, this rule says that whenever the balance of equity weighs in favor of the consumers of x $(\lambda^B > \lambda^T)$, its price should be below marginal production cost; and vice versa when the balance is tilted against them $(\lambda^B < \lambda^T)$ while, when equity becomes a matter of indifference $(\lambda^B = \lambda^T)$, marginal cost pricing is optimal. These are of course extremely intuitive results!

To give a concrete example of what the pricing rule may imply, consider the well-known problem of peak-load pricing. The standard solution of this problem involves the principle of charging marginal capacity costs in periods of peak demand (since capacity decisions are affected by peak periods only) while charging only marginal operating cost in off-peak periods.[7] In this model, however, if the demanders in peak periods are more socially worthy than those in off-peak periods, the pattern of optimal pricing could be reversed with lower prices in peak periods. Whether this is, in fact, optimal or not depends, of course, on the precise nature of the trade-off involved between equity and efficiency.

4. OPTIMAL DISCRIMINATORY PRICING

While retaining all our other previous assumptions, we wish to deal in the present section with the more realistic case where the various demanders of x belong to different "social welfare brackets." Instead of assuming λ^B to be uniform over all consumers, let λ^h denote the (generally unequal) social value of a dollar's worth of consumption of x by man h. Here $h=1, \ldots, H$ (H being the number of people demanding x). Now each λ^h is assumed constant throughout the analysis, so that all changes in individual circumstances do not affect the social value of an individual's consumption.

First we still assume that only one price can be charged to all customers, and investigate the nature of the optimal-pricing rule emerging from this case. Then we will investigate the case where the enterprise is able to charge different prices to different customers. In the sequel, we call this simply "discriminatory pricing." In addition we also examine what happens when the enterprise is not only able to engage in such discriminatory pricing but also can price discriminate among the different units of x sold to any given individual. This we will call "perfectly discriminatory pricing."

Since the basic features of the general pricing problem and its solution have been analyzed in depth in the previous section, and since the pricing rules derived below are essentially similar to rule (3) above, the exposition here has been reduced to a minimum.

Uniform Pricing

Denote by α^h the fraction of a "unit" of x sold in the market bought by man h. For the sake of simplicity assume α^h to be independent of x. Clearly, $0 < \alpha^h < 1$ and $\sum_{h=1}^{H} \alpha^h = 1$. Since we assume uniform pricing in this subsection, the social marginal benefit from consumption of x becomes now $\sum_{h=1}^{H} \alpha^h \lambda^h p(x)$ where $p(x)$ denotes the inverse of the market demand curve for x. Each man, equating his (private) marginal utility of x to the market price p derives a marginal benefit of $\alpha^h p$ (since from the "marginal" unit of x sold on the market he buys a fraction α^h). This carries a social value $\lambda^h \alpha^h p$. Similarly, on the revenue side of benefits, man h's contribution to total revenue is $\alpha^h px = px^h$, where x^h denotes the amount of x bought by man h, and the social evaluation of the cost borne by him in contributing this revenue is $\lambda^h \alpha^h px = \lambda^h px^h$. The total social costs of raising the revenue $p \cdot x$ are therefore $px \sum_{h=1}^{H} \alpha^h \lambda^h$. The remaining components of objective function (1) are unaffected by the removal of the assumption that λ^B is the same for all consumers of x.

The objective function can thus be written as:

$$\text{Max:} \quad \int_{0}^{x} \sum_{h=1}^{H} \alpha^h \lambda^h \, p\,(q)\, dq + \left(\lambda^T - \sum_{h=1}^{H} \alpha^h \lambda^h\right) p(x) \cdot x - \lambda^T C(x);$$

$$\text{subject to:} \quad 0 \leqslant x \leqslant x\,(0);$$

from which we derive the first-order condition for an interior maximum:[8]

$$\sum_{h=1}^{H} \alpha^h \lambda^h \cdot p(x) + \left(\lambda^T - \sum_{h=1}^{H} \alpha^h \lambda^h\right)\left[p(x) + x\frac{dp(x)}{dx}\right] - \lambda^T c'(x) = 0; \tag{7}$$

which, for $p \neq 0$, becomes:

$$p \sum_{h=1}^{H} \alpha^h \lambda^h + p\left[\lambda^T - \sum_{h=1}^{H} \alpha^h \lambda^h\right]\left[1 + \frac{1}{\eta_x}\right] - \lambda^T c' = 0; \qquad (p \neq 0). \tag{8}$$

From (8) we derive the optimal pricing rule:

$$p = \frac{\lambda^T}{\sum_{h=1}^{H} \alpha^h \lambda^h + \left[\lambda^T - \sum_{h=1}^{H} \alpha^h \lambda^h\right]\left[1 + \frac{1}{\eta_x}\right]} \, c', \text{ for } p \neq 0. \tag{9}$$

By comparing (9) to our earlier pricing rule, we observe that wherever we had λ^B before, we now have $\sum_{h=1}^{H} \alpha^h \lambda^h$, a weighted average of the social utility of income of the various consumers of x. In fact, (3) is a special case of (9), since for $\lambda^h = \lambda^B$ (all $h=1, \ldots ,H)$, $\sum_{h=1}^{H} \alpha^h \lambda^h = \lambda^B \sum_{h=1}^{H} \alpha^h = \lambda^B$.

Let us go briefly over the special cases dealt with in the previous section and note the difference in interpretation that this more general formulation requires.

(i) For marginal cost pricing ($p = c'$) to be optimal we no longer require that "a dollar be a dollar be a dollar . . ." for everybody involved, i.e., we do not need $\lambda^1 = \ldots = \lambda^H = \lambda^T$. Instead $\sum_{h=1}^{H} \alpha^h \lambda^h = \lambda^T$ is sufficient; that is if the

λ^h's happen to average out (at the weights α^h) to λ^T, a dollar of consumption spent on x "is a dollar" even though each dollar spent by each individual ". . . is not . . ."

(ii) If instead of $\lambda^B \simeq 0$ (previously) we now have $\lambda^1 \simeq \ldots \simeq \lambda^H \simeq 0$, exactly the same result as in the previous section will obtain here as well.

(iii) When $c' = 0$, every condition of the previous section involving λ^B remains unaffected except for the substitution of $\sum\limits_{h=1}^{H} \alpha^h \lambda^h$ for λ^B. The interpretation of the results parallels, then, the one given above. However, since people will differ in λ^h, some will wind up paying the "wrong" price. For example when $\sum\limits_{h=1}^{H} \alpha^h \lambda^h \geqslant \lambda^T$, everybody will enjoy the optimal zero price, and all the individuals for whom $\lambda^h < \lambda^T$ are "undeservingly subsidized" in accordance with our previous analysis. Similarly, in case that $\sum\limits_{h=1}^{H} \alpha^h \lambda^h < \lambda^T$, a positive toll will be charged to everybody, and all the individuals for whom $\lambda^h > \lambda^T$ are inappropriately taxed. The "fairness" of the pricing rule for any individual depends upon whether he finds himself in "good" or "bad" company in the market place. Social welfare could presumably be increased by allowing more flexibility in the pricing policy, for instance by enabling the public enterprise to apply discriminatory pricing across "social brackets" of individuals. To precisely this matter we now turn.

Discriminatory Pricing

Denote by x^h the amount of x bought (and consumed) by man h, and by $p^h(x^h)$ his inverse demand function for x. Retaining all the notations and assumptions of the previous subsection, the objective function now becomes:

$$\text{Max:} \ \sum_{h=1}^{H} \int_0^{x^h} \lambda^h p^h(q^h)\, dq^h + \sum_{h=1}^{H} (\lambda^T - \lambda^h) p^h(x^h) \cdot x^h - \lambda^T C \sum_{h=1}^{H} x^h \ ; \ (10)$$

$$\text{subject to: } 0 \leqslant x^h \leqslant x^h(0), \qquad\qquad h=1, \ldots, H,$$

where $\bar{x} = (x^1, \ldots, x^h, \ldots, x^H)$.

From (10) we derive the H first-order conditions for an interior maximum:

$$\lambda^h p^h(x^h) + (\lambda^T - \lambda^h)(p^h(x^h) + x^h \frac{dp^h(x^h)}{dx^h} - \lambda^T c' = 0; h=1, \ldots, H. \qquad (11)$$

From (11) we derive in the usual manner for $p^h \neq 0$:

$$\lambda^h p^h + (\lambda^T - \lambda^h) \left(1 + \frac{1}{\eta_x^h} \right) p^h - \lambda^T c' = 0, p^h \neq 0, h=1, \ldots, H. \qquad (12)$$

From (12) we derive the "individualistic" pricing rule for $p^h \neq 0$:

$$p^h = \frac{\lambda^T}{\lambda^h + (\lambda^T - \lambda^h)\left(1 + \dfrac{1}{\eta_x{}^h}\right)} c', \quad \text{for } p^h \neq 0, h=1, \ldots, H; \tag{13}$$

where $\eta_x{}^h$ denotes the elasticity of man h's demand function. We immediately notice that, apart from the h superscript, (13) is identical to our earlier pricing rule (3). Hence, all the analysis that we did earlier for all the buyers of x as a group applies now to each consumer individually—assuming that the sellers can distinguish among consumers with different values for λ^h

While there is no point in going over all the special cases, the general meaning of these results can be seen in the case of the uncrowded bridge or uncongested road. Then socially deserving individuals (i.e., those for whom $\lambda^h \geqslant \lambda^T$) will enjoy the services free of charge, while the socially undeserving (those for whom $\lambda^h < \lambda^T$) will have to pay a positive price. This illustrates nicely the "scarce" nature of policy instruments in a second-best environment: the introduction of the additional policy tool of price discrimination can be used to improve social welfare!

Even though varying λ^h's gives price discrimination a special role, social welfare maximization would be aided if this possibility were allowed wherever the demand functions differ in elasticities, even when all the λ^h's are equal. For example where $\lambda^h \cong 0$ for all h, and the $\eta_x{}^h$'s functions differ, the socially optimal policy of the enterprise is to act exactly like the classic discriminating monopolist, equating marginal revenue for each class of customers to marginal cost.

Another interesting illustration of the potential value of discriminatory pricing even with uniform λ^h's ($\lambda^h = \lambda^B$, $h=1, \ldots, H$) is provided by the case of an uncongested facility. Suppose $\lambda^B < \lambda^T$ and $\dfrac{dp^h}{dx^h} \neq 0$ at $p^h=0$ for all h. Then we know from our earlier analysis that $p^h > 0$, all h. Now, since for any h ($h=1, \ldots, H$) the first order condition implies $\lambda^T p^h = (\lambda^h - \lambda^T)\dfrac{x^h}{p^h}\dfrac{dp^h}{dx^h} \cdot p^h$ (since $c' = 0$), and because the change Δx^h in x^h induced by the imposition of $p^h > 0$ rather than $p^h = 0$ is approximately given by $\Delta x^h \cong \dfrac{dx^h}{dp^h} \cdot p^h$ (since $p^h = dp^h$), we obtain for any h the condition $\lambda^T p^h = (\lambda^h - \lambda^T)\dfrac{x^h}{\Delta x^h}p^h$, which reduces to $\lambda^T = (\lambda^h - \lambda^T)\dfrac{x^h}{\Delta x^h}$. Thus, at the optimum $\dfrac{\Delta x^h}{x^h} = \dfrac{\lambda^h - \lambda^T}{\lambda^T}$ for all $h=1, \ldots, H$. And since in the case of uniform λ^h's, $\dfrac{\Delta x^h}{x^h} = \dfrac{\lambda^B - \lambda^T}{\lambda^T}$ is *independent of h*, optimal discriminatory pricing implies setting, for each individual, a price such that he reduces his consumption of x (as compared with his demand for x at a price of zero) by the same proportion as everybody else.

This equiproportional-reduction rule parallels Ramsey's optimal excise taxation rule. This says that to minimize deadweight loss, tax rates, commodity by commodity, should reduce compensated demands in an equiproportional manner as compared to the no-tax situation. This in turn implies ad valorem excise tax rates that are inversely proportional to the elasticity of demand. In our problem, when all λ^h's are equal, distributional considerations are no longer a factor. The optimal pricing problem reduces to the minimization of (social) deadweight loss of imposing a positive price for the commodity. If we look then at each x^h as a separate commodity, the analytical analogy to the Ramsey problem is complete, which is why we get the same result.[9]

Perfectly Discriminatory Pricing

When the public utility is allowed to sell its devices (or goods) on an all-or-none basis to each individual, the first-order conditions (11) of the previous subsection remain unchanged. The quantities consumed by each person remain the same and the price charged for the "marginal" unit of x^h can be read from (13) if it is nonzero. The real question in this case is how should the inframarginal units of x^h be priced; that is to say, how should the enterprise implement its perfect discriminatory power?

Denote by $S^h(x^h)$ the consumer surplus enjoyed by man h when he buys the quantity x^h at the uniform price p^h. $S^h(x^h)$ is the maximal amount of revenue that the enterprise can extract from man h over and above the revenue obtained from selling all of x^h at a price of p^h. The value of this revenue to the government in social terms is $\lambda^T S^h(x^h)$ and the cost to man h is valued in social terms at $\lambda^h S^h(x^h)$. The net social benefits obtained by perfect discrimination are

therefore $\sum_{h=1}^{H} (\lambda^T - \lambda^h) S^h$. This implies that the power to discriminate across different units of consumption should be enforced only with respect to "undeserving" individuals for whom $\lambda^h > \lambda^T$. For individuals for whom $\lambda^h > \lambda^T$ the average price should never be higher than p^h as given by (13). By adding the policy tool of perfect discrimination to the set of instruments available, social welfare can be improved by means of squeezing more revenue out of the "rich"!

5. SOME EXTENSIONS

In this section we briefly discuss various extensions of the analysis and their implications for our basic pricing rule. In particular we consider the case where the public enterprise provides a number of different commodities with joint costs. We also explore how the presence of consumption externalities and merit wants would affect the optimal pricing rule. Then we go on to discuss the implications of imposing some kind of budget constraint on the enterprise.

The Multiple-Output Enterprise

Suppose that the enterprise provides n different pure private commodities $\bar{x} = (x_1, \ldots, x_n)$ produced under joint costs $C(\bar{x}) = C^*(x_1, \ldots, x_n)$. Retaining all the assumptions of earlier sections, it can be shown that in the case where the demand functions for $x_1, \ldots, x_n$ are mutually independent of one another, the general pricing rule (13) applies without modification, and for exactly the same reasons.

In the case where demands for $x_1, \ldots, x$ (by *any* individual) are interdependent, the rule is slightly complicated. Then, as we change one price, we affect the sales and revenues of other goods. In fact, these revenue implications are not really any different from the effects on the rest of the economy that would result from changes in price-output decisions about a single commodity. This complication does not arise specifically from our present case. So far in this paper we have assumed these to be negligible. Hence, what we are saying below applies equally to the cases discussed in sections 3 and 4 above.

When we do the formal analysis, for the case of interdependent demands and joint costs, we find that the first-order condition (11) for any good j and any consumer k now become:

$$\lambda^k p_j^k + (\lambda^T - \lambda^k) \; p_j^k + x_j^k \; \frac{\partial p_j^k}{\partial x_j^k} \; + (\lambda^T - \lambda^k)(\Delta T_{i/j}^k) - \lambda^T C_j = 0 \qquad (11')$$

where $C_j = \dfrac{\partial C}{\partial x_j}$ and $\Delta T_{i/j}^k$ is the (net) change in revenue obtained from man k due to his adjustments in the consumption of all the other commodities (indexed i) resulting from a marginal change in x_j^k (his consumption of good j). This new element $\Delta T_{i/j}^k$ depends in sign on whether the effects of commodities complementary to j or substitutes for j are "dominant."

The new term is multiplied by the coefficient $\lambda^T - \lambda^k$. When $\lambda^T > \lambda^k$, the discrepancy between P_j^k and the marginal cost of production C_j will be larger or smaller than when cross effects are neglected, depending on whether the sign of $\Delta T_{i/j}^k$ is negative or positive. As an example, consider that when $\Delta T_{i/j}^k$ is negative, a decline in man k's consumption of good j is accompanied by an increase in revenues from other goods. Those other goods are "predominantly" substitutes for good j. When $\lambda^T > \lambda^k$ the marginal social value of such revenues is greater than the marginal social value of the loss to individual k. Thus the price for good j should be higher than in the previous analysis because of cross-revenue effects. On the other hand if $\lambda^T < \lambda^k$, the effect on the discrepancy of p_j^k from C_j will be reversed in sign! Finally, if $\lambda^T = \lambda^k$, the additional revenue implications can just be neglected!

Consumption Externalities and
Merit Wants

The presence of consumption externalities or "merit wants" implies that marginal cost pricing is not optimal even in a first-best world.[10] In the present analysis these complications would just add another element to the general departure from marginal cost under optimal pricing in our imperfect environment. This indeed is precisely the case.

Let us denote by λ_j^{eh} the externality arising from man h's marginal consumption of commodity j. To develop this explicitly, we want to make every consumer's utility depend not only on his own consumption, but also on everyone else's consumption. Thus if there are N consumers, the utility of man k is $U^k(x^1, \ldots, x^N)$. Here x^h is the consumption bundle of man h, while x_j^h is his consumption of good j. Then social welfare, w, is:

$$w = w\,[U^1\,(x^1, \ldots, x^N), \ldots, U^N\,(x^1, \ldots, x^N)]\,.$$

This implies that the change in social welfare resulting from a marginal change in x_j^h is:

$$\sum_{k=1}^{H} \frac{\partial W}{\partial U^k} \cdot \frac{\partial U^k}{\partial x_j^h} = \lambda^h p_j + \sum_{k \neq h} \frac{\partial W}{\partial U^k} \cdot \frac{\partial U^k}{\partial x_j^h} = \lambda^h p_j + \lambda_j^{eh}\,,$$

where

$$\lambda_j^{eh} = \sum_{k \neq h} \frac{\partial W}{\partial U^k} \cdot \frac{\partial U^k}{\partial x_j^h}\,.$$

In the same way, we can write the social welfare function in the presence of merit wants as $W(U^1, \ldots, U^N; x_1^1, \ldots, x_j^h, \ldots, x_n^N)$. The merit-want considerations attached to the marginal consumption of good j by man h are:

$$\frac{\partial W}{\partial x_j^h} = \lambda_j^{mh}.$$

In either case we see that we simply have to add λ_j^{eh} or λ_j^{mh} to the left hand side of (11′) above in order to characterize the implications for optimal pricing of the presence of externalities or merit wants. Whether the inclusion of λ_j^{eh} and/or λ_j^{mh} in the pricing rule will cause greater discrepancies between marginal production cost and optimal price depends on whether their signs agree with the "original" discrepancy (i.e., the discrepancy arising only on distributional grounds).

Imposing a Budgetary Constraint

There is nothing in our pricing rule that prevents the public utility from having a profit or loss when charging optimal prices. Yet in practice such enterprises are required to break even or to earn no more than a "fair" rate of return. The optimization problem should then be stated with this condition as a side constraint. A number of modern writers have addressed themselves to this problem but they have all ignored the possibility of multipart tariffs advocated in the early literature of public utility pricing.[11] Instead these treatments implicitly assume that only one price can be charged and, as a consequence, end up with some form or another of Ramsey's optimal tax formula.

Suppose one wanted to use instead a two-part tariff, in which the price per unit is determined by the usual marginal calculus and in addition there is some sort of fixed fee levied to cover any deficit after the first part has been imposed. Even in such cases, it is clear that the optimal pricing rule will still dictate departures from marginal-cost pricing as far as the "user charge" is concerned.[12] After all, a "fixed" fee which took into account, and corrected, all distributional imperfections would be nothing other than a perfect lump-sum tax of the sort we have explicitly rejected from the beginning of the analysis as infeasible. Somewhat paradoxically, we are confined to applying distributional objectives at the margin and thus have to interfere with "efficiency," rather than applying them at the "efficiency-neutral" level of poll taxation.[13] But after all, that is precisely what a second-best situation is all about.

7. CONCLUSIONS

The basic pricing rule derived in this paper presents, in compact form, the distributional elements involved in the optimal price. The intuitive interpretation of the rule accords closely with common sense. As expected, distributional second-best optimality calls for optimal discrepancies between prices and marginal production costs.

Among the most interesting specific conclusions are the following:

(i) Excess supply at a zero price is no longer sufficient to characterize a free good when the distribution of income is not optimal. Thus, for instance, contrary to the usual analysis, a positive toll on the use of an uncongested road could be optimal as could a zero toll on a congested road. It all depends on who the users are.

(ii) If price discrimination is possible across consumers who vary with respect to the social marginal utility of their income, it should be practiced. Many public utilities provide services for which arbitrage problems that price discrimination sometimes produces will not arise (e.g., gas, electricity, telephone). In such cases our analyses suggests that price discrimination across groups of consumers, classified by income, is an appropriate policy.

(iii) Distributional considerations could reverse the pricing patterns in peak-load situations, i.e., charging lower prices under peak demands than under off-peak demands.

(iv) When a budget constaint is externally imposed, then even under a multipart tariff system, distributional considerations will be (partly) reflected in optimal discrepancies between prices and marginal production costs.

We conclude this paper by noting that the basic constraints of all of our pricing problems were that consumers ought to be on their demand curves and hence (implicitly) that prices should be set so as to clear markets. In other words, the possibility of rationing demands by means other than price exclusion has been ignored. Adding rationing as a policy tool could, doubtless, serve the purpose of improving social welfare, and this would seem to be the first direction to be taken in future research on the subject.

Notes to Chapter 10

1. See Martin S. Feldstein, "Financing in the Evaluation of Public Expenditure," *Essays in Public Finance and Stabilization Policy,* ed. W. Smith, *et al.* (Amsterdam: North-Holland Publishing Co., 1974), pp. 13-36, and references to Feldstein therein; S. A. Marglin, *Public Investment Criteria,* (Cambridge: M.I.T. Press, 1967), and references to Marglin therein; P. Diamond and J. Mirrlees, "Optimal Taxation and Public Production," *American Economic Review,* 61 (March 1971), 8-27; 61 (June 1971), 261-278.

2. See Diamond and Mirrlees.

3. If we were to reinterpret this model in the context of a regulated industry, this shadow price would reflect not the value of net additions to the government budget, but rather the value of increased revenue to the regulated firm. The assumption that the marginal social value of revenue is equal to the marginal cost of its use in private hands would become the postulate that we are indifferent at the margin between giving resources to the factors specialized in production in the regulated sector, and returning it to the economy generally. Thus the "balancing" we will do in the optimization analysis would become one of comparing the value of additional income to factors vs. buyers, not the government vs. buyers as in the public firm interpretation of the model.

4. Since we assume λ^B to be constant under changes in x, we do not really need this assumption at this point. However, in conjunction with the next assumption that prices affecting the demand for x do not ("markedly") change as we vary x, this assumption is important, e.g., for the subsection on perfectly discriminatory pricing and that on budgetary constraints below.

Let us also note here that relaxing the assumption $\lambda^c = \lambda^T$, while slightly affecting the form of the optimal pricing rule derived below, would impair neither the rationale used in its derivation nor the intuitive interpretation in its essentials.

5. Corner conditions are dealt with below. The second-order conditions

$$(2\lambda^T - \lambda^B)\frac{dp}{dx} + (\lambda^T - \lambda^B)x\frac{d^2p}{dx^2} - \lambda^T c'' < 0,$$

are assumed satisfied.

6. While $\eta_x = -\infty$ also implies $p=c$, this is not an interesting case and is thus disregarded in the sequel. Note therefore that throughout the paper we (implicitly) assume the public enterprise to have a monopoly in the market of x.

7. See M. Boiteux, "Peak Load Pricing," *Journal of Business,* 33 (April 1960) pp. 157–179; J. Dreze, "Some Postwar Contributions of French Economists," *American Economic Review,* 54 (June 1964), *Part 2* (a supplement); O. E. Williamson, "Peak Load Pricing and Optimal Capacity under Indivisibility Constraints," *American Economic Review,* 56 (September 1966), pp. 810–827.

8. We discussed earlier corner conditions and second-order and global conditions. Since no new principle is involved, we disregard these matters throughout the remainder of this paper.

9. Note that our assumptions about the demand for x^h effectively amount to ensuring that, for any x^h, "ordinary" and "compensated" demand curves coincide.

10. See my "Merits Wants and the Theory of Taxation," mimeo, 1970.

11. See, for instance, M. Boiteux, "Sur la Gestion des Monopoles Publics Astreints à l'Equilibre Budgétaire," *Econometrica,* 24 (January 1956), pp. 22–40. W. J. Baumol and D. F. Bradford, "Optimal Departures from Marginal Cost Pricing," *American Economic Review,* 60 (June 1970), pp. 265–283. In both of these works, however, the treatment of the distributional implications for optimal pricing is neglected, leading to inconsistent statements in the Baumol-Bradford paper. The work of Diamond and Mirrlees, mentioned in note 1 above, is, to the best of my knowledge, the only comprehensive analysis of this kind of problem to date.

Also disregarded by the various authors is the motivational problem under breakeven conditions and its implications for efficiency. This problem is briefly discussed in my "Effects of Taxes on a Regulated Monopoly," mimeo, December 1970.

12. While the departure from marginal cost pricing is still there, it should be noted that the optimal quantity-(user) price configuration will not, in general, be the same as that obtaining when there is no budget constraint.

13. This should not be taken too literally. Since distributional judgments enter the optimal quantity-(user) price determination, it is clear that the overall amount of "deficit" that will have to be financed by the "head fee" is a variable of the problem. This variable, of course, entails distributional judgments of its own. The point that I really want to make here is that, by means of contrast to a first-best world, the possibility of applying a two-part tariff does not remove the second-best reasons for departing from marginal cost pricing.

Chapter Eleven

Franchise Values, Merit Programming and Policy Options in Television Broadcasting

Harvey J. Levin

1. INTRODUCTION AND STATEMENT OF THE PROBLEM

In many regulated industries, public policy is clearly not concerned solely with allocative efficiency. Instead the variety or quality of the goods and services produced is often of major interest. Often neither the unregulated nor the regulated industry, subject only to rate-of-return controls, will produce what would-be regulators perceive as a socially desirable output mix. This is because the products or services involved are unprofitable, whether they be air service to small cities or public-service television programming.

A regulator then faces two interlinked dilemmas. First he has to get the regulated firm to alter its product mix. Second, he has to command funds to finance the provision of these outputs. The first problem has been handled in ways varying from expressions of hope or concern by members of regulatory bodies to explicit requirements to provide specified services. The second task has been approached via direct subsidy or cross-subsidy, with the latter usually linked to entry controls in order to preserve "super-normal" profits in the subsidy-generating sector.[1] Policies designed to promote competition among regulated firms often contravene product-mix goals because they reduce the profits available for cross-subsidy.

There results a tension between quantitative (restrictive) and qualitative (nonrestrictive) licensing. Qualitative licensing—doctors, accountants, lawyers, barbers, etc.—ostensibly safeguards standards of professional competence for the public. In theory, every qualified applicant can secure a grant, although qualitative licensing may be perverted *ex post* to restrict competition.[2]

*Preparation of this paper and the underlying research were funded entirely by National Science Foundation Grant GI-39845. Special thanks for extensive statistical help are due to Jacob Merriwether, Graduate School of Business, Columbia University, and Jefferson Latham, New College Research Associate, Hofstra University.

Outright quantitative restrictions are apparent in transportation, utilities, etc., often excused as reducing temptations to cut corners on product or service quality, reliability and diversity and providing the funds to support higher quality service.[3] In either case, the question is whether a regulator's stated *ex ante* commitment to product quality and diversity is in fact realized *ex post.*

Television broadcasting presents almost exactly this problem, with one major variation. There is only so much usable "room" in the electromagnetic spectrum. Thus, as is not the situation with taxicabs or liquor stores, we cannot distinguish the "natural" (hence "inevitable") entry barriers in TV from "artificial" ones due, say, to the imposition of external administrative signal standards.[4] Their interlinkage distinguishes the entry conditions in TV from those in many other licensed fields.

The rents generated in television are partly unavoidable. More of the spectrum could be assigned to television, or frequencies could be allocated to increase the number of stations any one home typically receives. However, these possibilities are quite limited—especially given the large stock of receivers that operate only in certain ranges.

Some questions about product quality persist, whether restrictions on entry are inevitable or contrived. They include the equity, social desirability and political feasibility of alternative ways to distribute the "rents." Some observers suggest that government's role in the creation of such rents legitimizes public control over their disposition; but recipients of the rents decry all attempts at diverting them as "unfair" or "expropriation," even if they resulted inadvertently from prior public actions. On a nonpartisan view, determining how much "socially valuable" output to provide is distinct from choosing whether to provide it at all.

To the extent that rent-yielding scarcities are deliberately contrived, these various questions become much more closely interconnected. The financing of public goods through diverted rents then results in (and capitalizes on) allocative inefficiency in the activities that provide the subsidy. The value of such goods has to be balanced against these indirect costs, as well as any direct ones.

This paper explores these policy questions in television broadcasting. At the end I will evaluate various techniques for accomplishing these public purposes. The next section analyzes the magnitude of "franchise value," i.e., the capital value of a television broadcast license that is due to the scarcity of licenses. The occurrence and magnitude of franchise values are essential information for choosing among the available policy options.

What was "really" intended by regulation may not be a question we can answer *ex post.* Different participants in the process that creates and controls regulatory policy will have different goals and use different rationales for their action. Both the intended and the unintended effects of regulation must, therefore, be taken carefully into account. After all, industry often does "buy" regulation with votes and resources for its own private ends.[6] Similarly, politically potent groups outside the industry may secure services to their liking, supported from rents extracted from other customers. Yet, in either case, government rarely institutes direct cash subsidies, restrictive licensing or the suppression of substitutes and promotion of complements baldly. Rather they are masked as essential to meritorious product and service quality. In such cases, probing the "real" goals of regulation can produce little more than an arid semantic wrangle.

Hence we shall take the regulator's professions of his aims at face value. When performance falls short of professed goals, a full explanation is called for. Do the political, strategic and institutional/organizational constraints on regulation preclude the officially sanctioned results? Or do regulators ignore their own professions?

The proximate goals of broadcast regulation appear to include both promoting competition and imposing public service responsibilities on all licenses. Both serve the ultimate goal of providing maximum program choice and diversity with merit service to all areas and all communities. One problem is that policies designed both to support and to limit competition are undertaken in the service of common ends.[6]

Diversity is strengthened by procompetitive rules limiting the numbers of stations that companies can own, both in the same and in different markets, and by a policy to discourage co-located newspaper-TV joint ownership. Similarly, by regulating the networks, the Federal Communications Commission has apparently sought to equalize the competitive position of network and non-network program suppliers, again increasing "diversity."

However, licensees are also expected to be professionally responsible, to follow a principle of only qualified profit maximization by providing some voluntary internal subsidization of relatively unprofitable merit service. Influences on their conduct include control of the length, frequency, loudness and propriety of commercials; restrictions on the portrayal of crime, sex and violence, particularly in children's programs; requirements as to fairness, political coverage, editorials, rural service, local live service, cultural-informational programs; etc. Last, the FCC claims to impose standards of program balance and diversity on individual licensees.[7]

What has been the effect of the procompetitive policies on the amount of funds available for diversity? Have these policies, or those on licensee conduct, effectively converted such funds *ex post* into diversity and merit service? What measures could attain the latter goal in fuller measure? These are the questions to which we now turn.

2. ORIGIN, MAGNITUDE AND SIGNIFICANCE OF TV FRANCHISE VALUES

We have to realize at the outset that once stations are sold, their franchise values might well be capitalized in the purchase price. The new owner then will earn only "normal" returns, limiting the funds available for subsidizing merit outputs. Both the equity and political issues involved in such diversion become significantly transformed once the current owners suffer uncompensated (undeserved? unjust?) capital losses. They can be expected to protest vigorously and, perhaps, to be heard sympathetically as well. Yet this capitalization process allows us to detect statistically the determinants of these franchise values.

We shall not be surprised to find them, because regulation has clearly not succeeded in forcing operators to devote all rents to "desirable" purposes. Conduct standards are vague and elusive; license renewals, until recently, were virtually automatic. The risk of revocation is still nil, and prices are completely unregulated, with licenses freely transferable in fact if not in legal theory. The net result is that TV franchises are extremely valuable and there is an active market for them.

The origin of these franchise values lies in the virtual inevitability of some government control on licensing of the electromagnetic spectrum. In the absence of any framework to limit or structure property rights, the spectrum as a common property resource is almost certain to be misused. In addition, the number of parties to potential market transactions is extremely large, so the costs of organizing such transactions may conceivably exceed the value of the "better" allocation that would result. A market system of allocation will then be inefficient and inappropriate. Indeed, it is not clear that such transactions could proceed at all unless unambiguous rights were first awarded to someone to serve as a basis for negotiation, no easy matter. Even if that were done, market-arrangement costs would be very high in the older, lower, more crowded and more accessible bands where radio first developed, and where communications is still plagued by intractable, farflung interference problems. Even in higher frequency, new technology bands where participants are fewer and interference less, many complex and costly multiparty transactions would be required.

Franchise values can probably best be studied by analyzing the sales prices of the licensed premises, incoporating the capitalized value of the income-earning opportunities the license confers. Franchise value is easier to segregate when the licensee's whole business is licensed (e.g., broadcasting, package stores) than where only a small segment is (the manufacturer's or taxicab's use of mobile radio, the restaurant's use of liquor, etc.). Even so, when sales typically include both license and facilities, it is hard to determine the precise portion of the spread between sales prices and replacement cost of physical assets properly allocable to the license itself.

By limiting the number of stations in leading television markets, the FCC's allocation plan—which assigns frequencies to specific locations—has virtually guaranteed a rise in license values in the face of sustained economic growth. Consider the following data on percentage increases per station:[8]

	Median Revenues	Income	Time Sales
55 markets, 1956–1971	264%	204%	126%
84 markets, 1961–1971	187%	226%	119%

In both periods the median number of stations changed little. Over a still longer period, 1950-1970, median revenues per station for eleven identical markets actually rose over tenfold.

What determines franchise values? Have public service obligations or other procompetitive policies fully absorbed those rents? Television stations derive their revenue from selling advertising time, generally on the basis of a price that recognizes audience size—i.e., in terms of "cost per thousand." Thus the potential value of a station should depend upon the number of homes in its market area, while its revenues in the short run will depend on how many people actually watch its programs. If franchise values had been fully "competed" away, profit rates would decline as the number of stations in a market increases. But that is not the case, as table 11-1 indicates. The data clearly suggest that the number of stations in large markets is smaller, relative to viewing audiences, than in small markets. Hence franchise values generally are likely to be higher. Note too that the averages for markets with many stations include more of the relatively unprofitable independents, especially those on UHF.

Table 11-1.   TV Station Revenues, Net Income and Profit Rates, 1971, in Relation to Number of Stations Per Market.

	Number of Stations in Market						
	1 and 2	*3*	*4*	*5*	*6*	*7*	*8*
Broadcast revenues per station ($ millions)	0.6	1.7	2.9	4.6	6.9	11.9	17.5
Broadcast income per station ($ millions)	.06	.2	.5	1.3	1.6	2.7	3.9
Profit on sales (percent)	10	15	20	29	22	23	23
Number of markets	154	83	26	13	4	1	1

Source: U.S. Federal Communications Commission, *Television Broadcast Financial Data for 1971.*

To explore these questions more directly, a regression analysis was undertaken in three stages. First, we analyzed variations in TV station sales prices in relation to market size, number of stations, channel type, network tie, group and newspaper ownership (table 11-2). Then we explored the influence of similar structural parameters on selected market averages, particularly on station average-time sales, revenue, income and program diversity (table 11-3). Here the independent variables were TV homes, number of stations and proportion of stations in each market affiliated with a national network, with a group owner, a newspaper enterprise or operating with a VHF license. Similar independent variables were related to individual station data on audience size, on station time devoted to news, public affairs, local programming, and on station diversity, etc. (table 11-4).

The estimated $\bar{R}^2$s in table 11-2 suggest we have at least captured some of the relevant factors. My published studies have established the decisive

Table 11-2. Regression Analysis of Television Station Sales Prices, 1949-1965 (Standardized Regression Coefficients and their Standard Errors)*

Equa-tion	Sample	N	TV Homes	Age of Stations	Group Affil-iation	News-paper Affil-iation	No. of VHF in Market
1	All Markets	174	.5671[a] (.0894)	.2318[a] (.06898)	.0986 (.0632)	.0390 (.0634)	−.0599 (.0895)
2	Top 50 Markets	55	.5592[a] (.2020)	.3068[c] (.1547)	.1702 (.1180)	.0200 (.1222)	−.3027 (.1903)
3	Top 100 Markets	91	.5285[a] (.1339)	.3039[a] (.1034)	.1060 (.0897)	−.0077 (.0978)	−.1542 (.1335)
4	Type A Sales	53	.7493[a] (.1596)	.1468 (.1299)	.2021[c] (.1098)	.1267 (.0986)	−.0791 (.1573
5	Type B Sales	42	.9680[a] (.2855)	.1045 (.1708)	.1038 (.1437)	.0163 (.1658)	−.1446 (.3091)
6	Type C Sales	79	.5459[a] (.0840)	.2752[a] (.0874)	.0381 (.0815)	−.0419 (.0827)	.1041 (.0911)

Network Affiliation

Equa-tion	CBS	NBC	ABC	CBS-ABC	NBC-ABC	CBS-NBC	CBS-NBC-ABC	Adj. R^2
1	.3812[a] (.1180)	.3908[a] (.1061)	.2775[b] (.1119)	.1895[c] (.1116)	.1391 (.0971)	.2635[b] (.1140)	.0581 (.0675)	.3769

Joint Affiliation

Equa-tion	CBS	NBC	ABC	Joint Affiliation		Adj. R^2
2	.3499[b] (.1591)	.4242[b] (.1721)	.2216 (.1843)	.0858 (.1537)		.3180
3	.3731[b] (.1472)	.3732[b] (.1433)	.2615[c] (.1498)	.2006 (.1566)		.3346
4	.1231 (.1375)	.0755 (.1377)	−.0362 (.1440)	.0962 (.1864)		.5441
5	1.0030[a] (.3602)	.9745[a] (.3218)	1.1915[a] (.3743)	1.1549[b] (.4555)		.2839
6	−.0950 (.3245)	.0156 (.2708)	−.1269 (.2481)	−.1945 (.3570)		.5317

*Dependent variable is TV station sales price, as reported in *Television Factbook* for 1967. The 174 sale prices (equation 1) include 55 in the top 50 markets (equation 2) and 91 in the top 100 (equation 3). The 174 are also subdivided in equations 4-6 into:

Type A sales: 100 percent ownership transfer, with all cash and noncash elements combined to secure a total price.

Type B sales: transfer of less than 100 percent but more than 50 percent interest, with calculated price (including all cash and non-cash items) adjusted to project a 100 percent ownership transfer price.

Type C sales: sales including an AM and/or FM station with a TV station and only a combined price for the package was available, but where TV proportion of package is presumed to account for the bulk of the combined price.

The independent variables (columns) are defined as follows:

TV homes: number of homes with TV sets in market (as defined by American Research Bureau of station at time of sale).

Age of station: number of months station had been on air when sold.

Group affiliation: 2 if group owned, 1 otherwise.

Newspaper affiliation: 2 if newspaper owned, 1 otherwise.

Network affiliation: 1 if affiliated with the network or combination of networks shown, 0 otherwise (in equations 2-6, 1 if mixed affiliation, 0 otherwise).

Levels of statistical significance (one-tailed test) are: a = 1 percent, b = 5 percent, c = 10 percent.

Table 11-3. Regression Analysis of TV Station Income, Net Revenue, and Program Diversity in Relation to Rent-Yielding Market Variables

Independent Variables	Income per Station	Revenue per Station	Time Sales per Station	Commercial Choices	
				Per Station	Total
Number of commercial units	-1.676^b 2.06	$-.891^c$ 1.97	-1.396^b 3.63	$-.311^a$ 9.00	$.670^a$ 16.81
10,000's of TV homes	1.200^a 9.87	$.835^a$ 12.40	$.639^a$ 10.97	$.027^a$ 3.52	.010 1.16
Network proportion	-2.186^a 1.73	-1.870^a 2.65	-1.232^a 2.07	$-.135^c$ 1.90	-.115 1.41
VHF proportion	.329 1.46	$.297^a$ 2.36	.172 1.62	.026 1.43	.014 .66
Group proportion	3.40^c 1.88	$.171^c$ 1.68	$.180^b$ 2.11	.0014 .12	.0084 .64
Newspaper proportion	.057 .46	.025 .36	.026 .45	.0025 .34	.010 1.17
Adjusted R^2	.6708	.7893	.6755	.4752	.8806
Number of observations	101	101	101	143	143

Upper number in each cell is an elasticity calculated at the mean: percentage change in the dependent variable per 1 percent change in the independent variable. Lower number is the t-value of the regression coefficient; superscripts indicate statistical significance (two-tailed test), a = 1 percent, b = 5 percent, c = 10 percent. The variables are defined as follows:

Income per station: Net broadcast income before tax in market divided by number of commercial stations reporting.

Revenues per station: Broadcast revenues in market divided by number of stations reporting.

Time sales per station: Time sales in market divided by number of stations reporting.

Commercial choices: Number of prime time program type differences across all commercial stations in market, during sample week, among 20 program classes—adventure, cartoons, other children's, situation comedy, drama, quiz or game, popular music, fine arts, sports events, serials, variety, feature film, news, instructional (heavy), instructional (light), interview, discussion and debate, political, documentary and news specials, religious. Calculated for all markets with two or more commercial stations only.

Commercial choices per station: Commercial choices divided by number of stations in market.

Number of commercial units: Number of prime-time quarter-hour units broadcast over all commercial stations in market (140 units maximum per station per week).

TV homes: Number of homes with one or more TV set within sample ARB markets.

Network proportion: Proportion of stations in market affiliated with a national TV network.

VHF proportion: Proportion of stations in market with VHF licenses.

Group proportion: Proportion of stations in market affiliated with group owner.

Newspaper proportion: Proportion of stations in market affiliated with a newspaper.

Table 11–4. Sensitivity of Station's Share of Viewers, Advertising Rates, Prime-Time Program Diversity, and Composition of Prime-Time Programs to Changes in Rent-Yielding Market Variables*

Change in Independent Variable	Station's Share of Viewers		20-sec. Prime Rate	Prime-Time Program Diversity	Type of Prime-Time Programming				Entertainment		Feature Film
	ADI Ratings	Metro Ratings			Local	All Non-Network	News	Public Affairs	High Brow	Low Brow	
Add 1 commercial station	-10.58[a]	-8.67[a]	13.08[a]	-1.17[c]	2.95	1.72	-.14	-1.27	-2.83	.0034	2.15
	4.60	4.88	3.26	1.85	1.13	1.16	.06	.37	.55	.00	.81
Add 100,000 TV homes	-.16	.18	9.14[a]	.14[c]	-.58[c]	-.25	-.26	-.01	.15	-.17[b]	-.22
	.61	.95	17.50	1.80	1.75	1.33	.93	.02	.23	2.10	.64
Switch from UHF to VHF	21.37[a]	23.85[a]	47.45[a]	2.96[b]	-3.27	.45	5.24	-11.68	-17.17	3.12[b]	3.66
	4.55	7.09	5.51	2.22	.59	.14	1.11	1.62	1.59	2.36	.65
Switch nongroup to network group	24.90[b]	10.59	220.87[a]	-3.96	10.75	-11.42	32.14[a]	31.16[c]	10.70	-8.66[b]	12.02
	2.18	1.33	9.75	1.13	.74	1.39	2.59	1.64	.38	2.49	.82
Switch nongroup to nonnetwork group	6.24[c]	2.22	7.03	.19	3.60	12.39	8.66[b]	6.55	-6.83	-.15	1.43
	1.72	.83	1.01	.18	.80	2.25	2.25	1.11	.78	.14	.31
Switch nonnewspaper to outside newspaper	-.48	-1.46	-5.12	-1.18	-5.48	-.97	-4.03	3.88	2.54	1.17	.44
	.10	.41	.54	.78	.87	.27	.75	.47	.21	.77	.07
Switch nonnewspaper in-town newspaper	8.06[c]	9.34[a]	9.74	3.57[b]	-1.94	.94	4.40	20.77[a]	-3.89	-2.72	-7.82
	1.75	2.78	1.10	2.52	.33	.29	.88	2.72	.34	1.23	1.32
Switch independent to CBS	39.14[a]	63.40[a]	109.45[a]	7.19[a]	-131.03[a]	-208.63[a]	60.04[a]	-55.87[a]	-127.53[a]	5.78[b]	-38.81[a]
	4.58	10.89	7.17	2.99	13.20	37.02	7.06	4.30	6.56	2.43	3.85
NBC	33.47[a]	60.26[a]	111.38[a]	-4.79[b]	-142.20[a]	-223.54[a]	70.73[a]	106.51[a]	26.50	2.82	-58.66[a]
	3.88	10.23	7.37	1.99	14.34	39.68	8.32	8.19	1.36	1.18	5.82
ABC	16.69[c]	43.67[a]	100.08[a]	-7.52[a]	-130.88[a]	-198.83[a]	5.99	-71.86[a]	-11.61	12.94[a]	-13.38
	1.90	7.49	6.61	3.13	13.19	35.30	.70	5.53	.60	5.44	1.33
CBS-ABC	60.41[a]	87.10[a]	98.47	4.54	-133.18[a]	-219.71[a]	40.96[a]	-59.31[a]	-98.99[a]	7.33[b]	-42.95[a]
	5.31	10.82	4.89	1.47	10.43	30.00	3.74	3.55	3.96	2.39	3.31
NBC-ABC	49.18[a]	74.55[a]	86.86[a]	-4.44	-140.55[a]	-225.77[a]	55.75[a]	-94.83[a]	7.89	4.27	-60.37[a]
	4.50	9.39	4.52	1.44	11.08	31.34	5.13	5.70	.32	1.40	4.76

Table 11-4. Cont.-

Change in Independent Variable	Station's Share of Viewers		20-sec. Prime Rate	Prime-Time Program Diversity	Type of Prime-Time Programming						
	ADI Rating	Metro Ratings			Local	All Non-Network	News	Public Affairs	Entertainment High Brow	Entertainment Low Brow	Feature Film
CBS-NBC	40.63ᵃ	65.64ᵃ	86.46ᵃ	-3.68	-121.77ᵃ	-211.59ᵃ	59.70ᵃ	-103.52ᵃ	-87.62ᵇ	7.51ᶜ	-52.37ᵃ
	2.68	6.16	3.19	.86	6.94	21.25	3.97	4.50	2.55	1.78	2.94
CBS-NBC-ABC	75.53ᵃ	79.61ᵃ	101.30ᵃ	2.33	-147.26ᵃ	-226.62ᵃ	44.72ᵃ	-93.05ᵃ	-38.32	8.95ᵃ	-50.48ᵃ
	6.43	8.82	4.98	.71	10.94	29.65	3.88	5.27	1.45	2.77	3.69
Adjusted R²	.4321	.6362	.7694	.2261	.3934	.8393	.3456	.1854	.3024	.1215	.1578

*The upper number in each cell is a response elasticity showing the percentage change in the dependent variable (column heading) due to the change specified in the independent variable. Lower value is the t-value of the underlying regression coefficient. Statistical significance (two-tailed test) is: a = 1 percent; b = 5 percent; c = 10 percent. The variables are defined as follows:

Dependent variables (columns):

ADI ratings: Percentage of TV homes in areas of dominant influence (ADI) which tune in a station some minimum amount of time per week, as estimated by American Research Bureau.

Metro ratings: Percentage of TV homes in metropolitan market areas (narrower than ADI markets) which tune in a station some minimum amount of time per week, as estimated by American Research Bureau.

20-second prime rate: Station advertising rate for one 20-second "spot" announcement per week in prime time.

Program diversity: Average number of prime-time program types available daily on the station during the sample week.

Types of prime-time program: In the sample week each 15-minute unit of a station's prime-time programming was allocated to one of these categories: the respective variables are the numbers of these 15-minute units in each class. (For discussion of the classification system see footnote 13.)

Independent variables (rows):

Commercial stations: Number of commercial stations in the metropolitan area market.

TV homes: Number of homes with one or more TV sets within the American Research Bureau market area.

Network affiliation: Same dummy variables used in table 11-2.

Network-owned group station: 1 if owned by network, 0 otherwise.

Nonnetwork group station: 1 if group-owned but not network-owned, 0 otherwise.

Out-of-town newspaper station: 1 if owned by out-of-town newspaper, 0 otherwise.

Co-located newspaper station: 1 if owned by co-located newspaper, 0 otherwise.

impact of license limitation on income-earning capabilities.[9] The enjoyment of rents by local stations is revealed both by the significant impact of network affiliation on sales price and the statistical insignificance of the original cost of assets in that price. The significant effects of the age of license (relative to the FCC's moratorium on all new grants, 1948-1952), and of the number of TV homes confirms this view. These conclusions were based mainly on a study of 68 VHF network affiliates sold between 1956 and 1959.

To corroborate further, and to investigate whether the restrictions on newspaper and group ownership have any economic significance, I have now analyzed a much larger sample of 174 TV transfers, about 58 percent of all such transactions during the 1949-1965 period. The principal findings are shown in table 11-2. In equations 4 through 6, the observations are subdivided to minimize any distortion due to composite radio-TV sales, sales of less than 100 percent stock, etc.[10] For all markets, the price of a station is mainly a function of TV homes in the market and, to a lesser extent, age of license and network ties (group and newspaper ties are insignificant at the .10 level). The results for the top 50 and top 100 markets are very similar. Only when sales are grouped according to differences in heterogeneity (equations 4-6), do we discern even the weakest evidence that group or newspaper ownership may affect sales price. Thus, parallel to my initial studies, TV homes appear as the principal determinant of franchise value and are an effective proxy for license limitation. At the same time, there is evidence that network affiliates sell their stations for significantly more than do comparable independents. This presumably reflects the former's more popular programming and the low risk of disaffiliation after sale (even in markets with independents, where the networks could clearly switch).

These findings are consistent with studies of TV advertising rates by both Peterman and United Research Inc., which revealed comparable advertising rates for group and non-group stations.[11] The URI study also reached similar conclusions with respect to station sales prices. Coefficients reported in table 11-4 below further confirm Peterman's findings for rates charged by group-affiliated stations not owned by networks. Table 11-4's results are also consistent with Peterman's finding the newspaper ownership does not influence advertising rates. However, that finding disagrees with a study by Owen, whose contrary result is due to the different assumptions of his model.[12]

Next we study the programming and economic variables, to determine how far franchise values have been converted into merit programming, local service and diversity. The dependent variables of interest are broadcast revenues and net pretax income per station, time sales per station, and "commercial choices"—a measure of the number of unduplicated program-types available (among 20 classes). These were regressed on independent variables outlined in the notes to table 11-3, differing only slightly from those used in table 11-2. Table 11-3 displays not the regression coefficients but rather the corresponding elasticities calculated at the means of the variables, along with the *t*-values of the underlying regression coefficients. Table 11-3 clearly shows that rent-yielding market attributes increase actual sales and profits but not average program diversity. For every 1 percent reduction in quarter-hour broadcast units, income, revenue and time sales per station rise 1.7 percent, 0.9 percent and 1.4 percent respectively, diversity per station by only 0.3 percent, whereas overall diversity actually declines by 0.7 percent. In contrast, the proportion of stations with newspaper ties affects neither economic performance nor market diversity, whereas group and VHF proportions affect some economic indicators though, again, not program diversity. These results prevail after we have controlled for market size—the prime determinant of potential profit and diversity.

      The negative coefficient of the network proportion on income per station shows the effect noted previously of higher average revenue in markets with more stations; the network proportion seldom falls below 100 percent unless the number of stations exceeds three. This result clearly suggests that the viewing audience per station is larger in larger markets so that franchise values should also increase with market size. (Our revenue and profit averages in markets with many stations include more of the relatively unprofitable independents, especially those on UHF, and thus tend to conceal this effect.) In contrast, the network proportion has but negligible if any effect on program diversity.

      Table 11-4 extends the analysis of table 11-3 while retaining its form (i.e., response elasticities and *t*-values relating to the underlying regression coefficients). The dependent variables shown in the column headings include four types: two measures of average share of TV homes viewing a station; one type of advertising rate; one measure of prime-time program type-diversity of individual stations; and seven measures of the amount of prime-time programs in various categories.[13] The coefficients in table 11-4 show the percentage response of these dependent variables at the sample mean to the specified unit changes in the independent variables. Thus, removing one commercial station from the market raises the others' effective audiences by at least 9 percent but leaves most classes of program unaffected. Local programs actually fall by 3 percent when a station is removed. Indeed, adding 100,000 more TV homes to the market—a good proxy for license limitation—raises station advertising rates 9 percent with few if any significant effects on programming, and none supportive of FCC goals.[14]

      The effects of other independent variables are less clear-cut. In line with FCC goals network affiliation raises not only audiences and rates but also the amount of news carried, while reducing the amount of feature film. Contrary to the commission's goals, however, affiliation reduces local service, public affairs and high-brow entertainment while raising low-brow. Even the prosperous network-owned stations generate notable dividends only for some FCC program policies: rates, audiences, news and possibly public affairs are significantly higher than for nongroup stations and low-brow entertainment lower, but high-brow programs and prime-time program diversity are no different. Similarly, non-network group ownership raises news and (with weak significance) audience size but leaves other program variables unaffected. Co-located newspaper ownership raises audiences more and contributes significantly to public affairs and diversity but has no other significant effects.[15]

In sum, FCC's procompetitive efforts aimed at limiting group and newspaper ownership do not seem to be dealing with the really significant factors that generate franchise value, with program diversity or with the merit programming the commission has sought to encourage. My earlier exploratory study of production economies of cross-media ownership also concluded that these are not obviously significant.[16] Yet the TV allocation plan, the embodiment of FCC licensing policy, appears to favor old versus new stations and those with VHF grants in the largest markets. Especially for those stations, but for most stations as well, this regulatory system creates significant franchise values.

The magnitude of monopoly rents in TV broadcasting can be derived and interpreted as follows. First, a study of the 174 station sales analyzed in table 11-2 reveals an average sale price of $3.1 million. A rough estimate of the upper bound of the rents can be derived from the $1.6 million spread between that price and average original cost of physical plant in those years. In one sense at least, virtually this *whole* sum can be ascribed to the TV license. For the fewer the stations in any market, the greater the market shares of licensees competing therein, and the greater the income-earning capabilities, even taking account of different station characteristics.

This is presumably an upper-bound estimate because TV station intangibles also reflect going-concern value, good will and working capital. A lower-bound estimate can be derived along somewhat different lines. The FCC publishes data on the distribution of pre-tax TV profits and revenues. We also have an estimate of the profit margin on sales (pre-tax) for all leading manufacturing corporations (from the First National City Bank Letter). All income above that needed to produce the average profit margin for these leading companies is assumed to comprise dollar economic rents in each revenue class of station.

For the 332 profitable VHF stations in 1972 which enjoyed excess margins, I estimate that $309,000,000 out of a pretax income of $433,250,000 and revenues of $1,244,600,000 was such economic rent. This amounts to $930,000 per station. Comparable figures for 308 profitable VHF stations in 1965 implied excess returns of about $887,000 per station. Rents were essentially stable, then, rising about 5 percent with a 23 percent rise in income and 62 percent rise in revenue between 1965 and 1972. These estimates imply that almost 60 percent of the total intangible investment in the 174 stations studied in table 11-2 (some $1.6 million per station) represents pure franchise value.[17]

By the same token, annual expenditures by the three national TV networks on news and public affairs averaged some $115,000,000 from 1969 to 1971, less than one-half of estimated monopoly rents in 1971. From another viewpoint, 1972 rents were over seven times greater than the whole 1974 FCC budget. Even the $10 million spent on TV broadcast regulation in 1972 was only 3 percent of economic rents in that year, and less than one-half of one percent of gross TV revenues. Indeed my 1972 estimate of rent comes modestly close to the Carnegie Commission's estimated annualized capital and operating costs (in 1972 prices) for the whole of a full-bodied public television system.

3. POLICY OPTIONS IN BROADCASTING

From the evidence thus far reviewed, FCC licensing policies appear to bolster industry rents and profits rather than channel them into diversity and merit service generally. The choice we confront is therefore twofold. We should either organize broadcasting so that monopolistic competition will dissipate more of the rents or else try to divert them towards priority activities.

Trying to eliminate the rents "solves" the regulatory problem by avoiding it. Given the real scarcity of advertising time within the current spectrum allocations, clearing the market for broadcast advertising time by price will continue to generate substantial revenues. Thus "eliminating" the rents really involves transferring them to someone else, most obviously the public. Once in public hands, they become a candidate for subsidizing meritorious activities, because equity does not call loudly for their collection once many of the original owners have liquidated their initial franchise values.

There are at least three major strategies in the short to medium run: (1) have the commercial system itself spend the rents more meritoriously; (2) collect them and transfer them to *another* programming entity, and (3) cross-subsidize such an alternate programming source via below-cost access to interconnection. In addition there is (4) the longer-run question of how one might proceed in a cable as opposed to broadcast system. We shall consider each of these alternatives in turn.

Better Performance from
the Commercial System

Can we improve "qualitative" regulation and use the rents to obtain better product performance from the commercial system? The basic obstacle to such efforts is the short-run economic self-interest of stations and networks, which makes them very concerned with maximizing audience size and hence sales revenue. Of course, even now broadcasters accept some internal subsidization of public service to forestall expanded government action. Both the radio and TV broadcast codes represent such defensive strategies.

One way the industry might be induced to convert additional rents into public service is suggested by an earlier FCC-sanctioned collaborative market-sharing scheme called the Doerfer Plan.[18] Each TV network agreed to schedule one hour of public service shows in prime time once every three weeks, leaving an hour of prime time open every fourth week to allow affiliates the opportunity to provide local public service programs. If it had broader regulatory authority, the FCC might actually impose such requirements on networks—although first-amendment concerns about government control of program content would no doubt arise. If implemented through cooperation and not regulation, some relaxation or reinterpretation of the antitrust laws might be required.[19] In either case, the industry's rents would be left largely undisturbed, although there might be some redistribution from networks and network affiliates to independents unless the latter faced comparable requirements.

Given the political and legal difficulties of the cooperative approach, critics more often call for tighter regulation. Such proposals include licensing TV networks directly, the exclusion of advertisers from decisions on program content and scheduling and subjecting licensees to mandatory renewal hearings (wherein precise ratios of program types may be imposed and program promises enforced). Concomitantly the critics also urge that licensees be required to carry public service programming in prime time and that an independent citizen's council be created to audit industry performance annually.

Such proposals tacitly sanction rents but devise new ways to insure their use for public purposes. The difficulty is that these tactics would probably intensify the commission's propensity to protect broadcast investments, even by retarding the introduction of new procompetitive technologies like cable TV, satellites, videocassettes, etc. Unless the kind of service expected from licensees were specified in far greater detail than today and rigorous steps taken to secure it, it is not clear that the performance gains would be worth the costs. Furthermore, tighter entry controls could have adverse effects on program innovation and impair the industry's creative-experimental capacities. They could also raise to dangerous levels the influence of government over content. Since something akin to this approach has had only limited success in the past, anyway, the time seems ripe to consider other alternatives, including techniques to eliminate or recapture the rents directly and divert them (perhaps automatically) into merit programs and diversity.

Collecting and Transferring Rents

Numerous proposals aim to collect rents either *ex ante* by auctions or *ex post* by taxation and to divert the proceeds through some intermediary mechanism into merit goods. I will argue that these rents can and ought to be recaptured and devoted to communications purposes on both equity and administrative grounds. However, there is no single ideal technique for doing so, which means that a combined approach is best. I will also argue that there are advantages to linking rents and public service internal to a single entity, which leads to proposals in the next subsection.

Auctioning broadcast licenses is an oft-repeated proposal usually made by economists who believe that the current "giveaway" does not encourage efficient spectrum utilization. There are two major options: perpetual rights and periodic resale. It is hard to see how auctioning perpetual rights would lead to very different program behavior or station prices from today's, for licenses now are effectively perpetual when renewal and transfer are so little constrained. The fact that the initial owners got licenses very inexpensively would be irrelevant to a rational profit-maximizer's operation in the present.

The main difference between today's market for stations (and licenses) and a scheme to auction off new FCC grants lies neither in the level to which transfer prices will rise nor in their resultant impact on program quality and diversity. The difference derives rather from the ultimate disposition of the franchise values in question. Today, TV transfers redistribute rents among the participating buyers and sellers over time, except for token amounts now converted into merit service and diversity. An auction scheme would at least permit a separate decision to redirect more rents directly into public service.

Nevertheless, to limit the auctions to new grants restricts the share of rents collected. The scheme could indeed put such a premium on buying *existing* stations and merging applications for quick uncontested *new* grants as to circumvent the goal of converting rents into merit service.

A scheme to reauction periodically faces objections no less serious. On the one hand, if it worked effectively it would expropriate too much—all the franchise value—and thus sharply limit merit programming on commercial channels. Therefore, to insure a *net* social gain, such a scheme would require more intensive qualitative regulation and a willingness to disqualify owners who fail to measure up. Also the transfer price of physical assets from the old broadcaster to the new would require regulation in case of a change in ownership (this might be handled by public ownership of such facilities as in the case of roads, airports, etc.).

Yet there are significant political impediments to such a reform. Any proposal that the FCC set a price on the replacement value of physical assets would fly in the face of the Congress's longstanding reluctance to permit any direct regulation of broadcast station sales prices. In addition, broadcasters who are very influential politically and have been working to make their licenses more secure, could be expected to oppose the proposal (and its implied renewal uncertainties) very vigorously.[20] Periodic license terms could hardly be long enough to avoid creating uncertainty for long-term program investments. Any proposed lengthening could well founder on the continued reluctance in American broadcast regulation to grant legal property rights in spectrum; consider the recent defeats of two massive political attempts towards that end.

As an alternative to auctions, a tax for spectrum use on broadcasters' gross receipts offers a number of special attrations as a way to fund public service programming. Its three-way incidence represents a potentially equitable apportionment of the tax burden for public television. Insofar as it is shifted forward, the tax raises the price of advertised products and is widely diffused among the general population. It will, in fact, fall on the main beneficiaries of public television, because even non-viewers benefit from the latter's contribution to an informed electorate, expanded political dialogue, the resolution of group conflicts and improvement of cultural values generally.

To the extent that television rates do not rise, however, backward shifting would mean that programmers, talent and network companies that now share in the licensee's quasi-monopolistic position would also tend to share in some of his obligations through reduced income. Also the licensee will himself probably have to pay something out of rents in return for privileged access to the spectrum. Thus such a tax would have some of the equity advantages of a tax on net income (or excess profits), while being no more regressive than an excise on TV sets or a household TV license fee. Yet the gross receipts tax's partial shiftability will presumably reduce the hostility vested interests normally display toward a tax on rents alone.

The alternative to such specialized taxes is use of the general revenue. Yet the normally attractive, traditional case for a general levy seems less persuasive for merit programs in broadcasting. True, the nominal progressiveness of general revenue funding rates high on equity grounds, especially since the precise consumers of "merit" programs are not known and therefore cannot be charged. Nor does general taxation distort relative prices or otherwise impair efficiency. By not imposing special burdens, use of the general revenue may also be less likely to antagonize powerful interests who would oppose dedicated funding. Even the oft-discussed dangers of undue intrusions into broadcaster decision-making could be reduced by distributing general revenue funds by statutory formula, with predetermined appropriations.

Yet the ease of insulating the broadcaster against unwanted federal intrusions via general funding must not be exaggerated. The repeated failures of recent proposals for ten-, five-, or even two-year general appropriations give one pause, notwithstanding the latest White House endorsement of a new long-run funding scheme. In contrast, a dedicated tax is more insulated. It requires a major congressional effort to alter its use.

Can we rationalize recovering the rents not simply on general equity, but on the spectrum's unique characteristics and the government's recognized role in developing it? That is the really critical question that differentiates the case for recovering rents between broadcast and public utility regulation. Television programs are free once the viewer has his set, whereas in public utilities and transport the goal has been to reduce price and increase output (or improve service) until monopoly profits disappear. Common carrier status and rate control have indeed been accompanied by very concrete service standards. In contrast, continued spectrum scarcities and the absence of rate regulation in broadcasting have made a far vaguer goal of merit service and diversity the fundamental regulatory priority.

The rationale for linking rents to expanded public service thus derives from the government's decisive role in creating the industry's rents and from the FCC's longstanding commitment (still unattained) to negotiating back commensurate merit service and diversity. The broadcast spectrum is valuable to competing broadcast users, and licensees have long enjoyed rents from their access to this spectrum gratis, despite the extra costs thereby imposed on non-broadcast services. The community has a right to recover a fair return in educational-cultural service for valuable privileges granted. After all, those who drill for oil, graze cattle or build dams on public land all pay for the privilege. Yet today TV license fees ($10 million in 1972) just cover the administrative costs of TV regulation and constitute less than one-half of one percent of pretax TV broadcast revenues!

In the search for an optimal package of special funding arrangements, however, proposals to convert rents into public service through internal linkage (within a single communications entity) merit special review. Aside from admitted limitations on the probable sums they can be expected to divert, they do offer a chance to explore mechanisms at once automatic, dedicated and less vulnerable to the tensions generated by the clash of separate agencies or the political exigencies of the Congress. Two such devices are the so-called Ford satellite proposal and reduced rate interconnection for public television networks, to which we now turn.

Subsidy in Kind for
Alternate Programming

The idea of facilitating merit programming via cross-subsidy was given vivid expression in the 1966 Ford Foundation proposal on the operation of the domestic television satellite system.[21] By charging the commercial networks more than the cost of serving them (but less than the costs of alternative arrangements), funds would be generated for free interconnection circuits for public networks, as well as to support cultural-informational programming. Essentially the plan sought to recapture for educational purposes part of the increased value of the radio spectrum due to new satellite technology. That was the difference between the annual interconnection costs through AT&T landlines and the cost of comparable interconnection through relay satellites.

The assumption behind this approach is that the increased rents created by the government R&D should not accrue as windfall gains to the communications industries. With the TV stations unmotivated to use the larger rents from satellite cost-savings for merit service, we must follow an alternative strategy: either devise new techniques to induce the licensees to use their rents for more merit service *ex post,* or adopt something like the Ford plan to divert any new rents at the source, *ex ante.* The Ford plan proceeds from the view that any lowering of interconnection charges to commercial networks would have less effect on program diversity (via new network entry or internal subsidies by licensees who enjoyed the larger rents) than would a scheme to divert the cost savings into public television directly. Of course, one result of this plan would be to raise the price of using the satellite facility above its marginal cost and hence interfere with efficient resource allocation. But this efficiency cost does not seem likely to be very large, given the inelasticity of demand by the networks for such interconnection.[22]

The whole virtue of the plan turns on its relatively automatic operation, freer from political pressures and the strains of an external linkage of fund sources to fund uses. It is perhaps ironic that some of the public support for the plan hinged on the appropriateness of the government's recovering a part of its massive investment in satellite development. In fact there would be no necessary relationship between the rents collected by the proposed discriminatory pricing, and the total costs of satellite development. Yet the plan has withered on the vine, presumably because of the meager satellite economies then estimated and to industry opposition to being taxed to support public television.[23]

In any case, exclusive funding derived from this source seems inappropriate for a public service of such importance. Such income could be quite uncertain, because the level of AT&T landline or microwave charges would limit the possible spread between satellite circuit costs and the circuit prices charged the commercial networks. That income might decline substantially if technological improvements should continue to reduce land circuit costs, as they have in the past. It would be the height of folly to have the FCC trying to stave off technical advances in microwave or cable transmission merely to protect this funding source.

Today, about $21 million annually would seem to be available under such a proposal, since each network's costs could be lowered from $20 million to $13 million.[24] Such a sum would have covered almost all of the Corporation for Public Broadcasting's outlays for both interconnection and programming in 1971 (albeit only 13 percent of total expenditures by all public television licensees that year). Obviously also by not charging quite so much, some of the cost savings could be returned to the commercial system in the hope of better programming from that source.

Once we recognize that some relatively automatic diversion of funds, especially for highly sensitive news and public affairs programming is in order, there is no reason to confine our attention only to satellite interconnection.[25] The linkage of rents and public service could be located within the current AT&T-Bell complex by means of different interconnection rates for public and private networks. This arrangement also could recapture the rents *ex ante* and avoid the difficult problems of acting *ex post*. Presumably the higher charges for commercial interconnection partly would be passed on to advertisers (and hence consumers), partly would be shifted backward and partly would be borne by licensees.

Such reduced-rate interconnection for public television could indeed be realized by setting its rates near long-run incremental costs as presently calculated. Because this calculation excludes spectrum costs, it would permit public television to enjoy the economic rents associated with the frequencies used to serve it. Assuming a dedicated and self-sustaining interconnection facility, Bell would have to charge the private commercial users for the common costs of servicing the public users too, so that these commercial users would pay more than the fully distributed cost of servicing them alone.

We must make more specific the meaning of interconnection rates for public television. One might use several different standards. The ambiguity arises because of joint costs of providing these services. Thus long-run marginal (incremental) costs are below long-run average costs (so-called fully distributed costs). However, a rational, profit-maximizing, discriminating monopolist would not rely on either of these as a basis for prices but would also take different demand elasticities into account. Under such "value-of-service" pricing, customers with less-elastic demand get charged more, those with more-elastic demand, less. Such prices could be above or below long-run average costs (or long-run marginal costs, if the supplier was not in long-run equilibrium). The rational monopolist would never price below short-run marginal costs however.

In addition there is obviously a limit to such cross-subsidy. First, as we increase the flow, the "cost" of resource misallocation rises. And from a practical viewpoint, at some price the demand for interconnection from the commercial networks will become elastic, so that further price increases would actually lower the amount of subsidy funds available. That level will depend upon the value of simultaneity to the networks and the value and costs of various alternatives. For example, what would the "bicycling" of videotapes or delayed program transmission cost, and what audiences (and hence advertiser revenue) be lost as a result? What are the comparative costs of the other major TV network interconnection alternatives, such as various private, joint network or specialized carriers?[26]

What effect would this proposal have on possible entry into the business of providing such interconnection? Cross-subsidy would make it more difficult for new firms to secure the interconnection business of public television stations. On the other hand, entry into the commercial business would become more attractive. However, if such entry were to occur, it appears that some element of cross-subsidy to the public network would have to be maintained. Hence the price structure of the would-be entrant would have to be regulated, lowering the attractiveness of specialized carrier entry as a result. There is some evidence that even today the Bell System is pricing television interconnection, and services generally, to deter potential entry.[27]

Note that spectrum costs are even now explicitly excluded from the estimated long-run incremental costs the Bell System uses in setting prices for servicing the public network. Yet any would-be specialized entrant into the interconnection business is likely to have even higher spectrum costs than the existing common carriers (from lower use of his frequency allocation). Thus, not including spectrum costs does seem appropriate because if they were included in all prices, that would serve as a deterrent to new entry just at a time when the threat of that event is a powerful inducement to the existing carriers to provide cost-reducing innovations.

Some of the possible consequences of this differential proposal are suggested by Microwave Communications Inc.'s abortive plan for a special nonprofit interconnection system (EDUCOM). ETV stations were to be permitted to hang their own radio transmission equipment gratis on microwave towers operated for other purposes by CATV systems or specialized carriers. The initial annualized comparative costs estimated for EDUCOM were considerably lower than even for Bell's then newly proposed part-time, daytime rates for ETV stations.[28] However Bell subsequently set rates interconnecting a 110-point CPB network still lower, down near the then estimate of long-run incremental cost, and the MCI plan doubtless suffered as a consequence.[29] Afer all, similarly specialized carriers like United Video and Western Telecommunications have for some time interconnected local CATV systems by terrestrial microwave hook-ups, and the American Broadcasting Companies still operate their own private system for partial interconnection of certain affiliates. Thus the structural effects and regulatory burdens of this proposal are not necessarily trivial.

Insofar as public television would be helped by such schemes, two sorts of benefits would result. Some viewers would get to see programs they valued that would otherwise be unavailable. In addition, as the political history of the Public Broadcasting Act (and subsequent appropriations hearings) reveals, there is widespread belief in the "merit" nature of some programming. This amounts to a value in having certain programs available for others to see, even if few choose to take advantage of them. This merit justification goes to the heart of this proposal, for increased diversity could also be provided by pay TV or other technical options. In evaluating this tactic, public TV's flexibility and adventuresomeness must be balanced against the commercial networks' skill in attracting large audiences, even for some "meritorious" fare. Numbers of viewers, as well as what is viewed, should enter into our judgments.

Nevertheless, the proposed rate structure will probably not be adopted without far more research than anyone has so far conducted to provide a rigorous definition and measurement of benefits so as to justify the departure from conventional cost criteria. Without such systematic work, many may continue to question the economist's competence qua economist to make the value judgments required to justify reduced rates as an appropriate policy.

Cable Television and Cross-Subsidy
in the Long Run

The discussion so far has focused primarily on the possibilities for supporting "merit" programming over a moderate time horizon of five to ten years. In the longer run, the possibility that much of the nation might be connected into systems of cable transmission has to be considered seriously. We have to explore both the expanded possibilities for supporting socially desirable programming, as well as the possible impact of such policies on existing broadcast offerings.

Various studies predict that cable's main adverse impact will not be on independent UHF stations, either generally or those in the largest markets. Instead, the greatest revenue losses (over half) will be suffered by VHF affiliates in the smallest markets.[30] VHF affiliates in large cities will be less affected, especially since cable could serve to extend their audiences.[31]

In analyzing these effects, we have to remedy the failure of economists to consider what could be a protracted interim coexistence of cable and broadcasting and the likely accommodations of the two in programming, rates and spectrum.[32] Thus far, the FCC has deliberately slowed the growth of cable TV to safeguard the monopoly rents that make it possible to subsidize news and public affairs. They also claim to want to protect UHF broadcasting, local live service and the wide geographic dispersion of broadcast facilities characteristic of current channel allocations. For these reasons, the FCC continues to exclude the entry of cable into the top fifty markets, where major VHF rents exist. If cable did threaten those rents (as broadcasters and FCC allege), this would mean that penetration ratios would be high and the cable system itself would be generating a potentially divertible "cable surplus." Whereas, if cable does not seriously threaten the rents because broadcasting is sufficiently distinctive, the penetration ratios and the surplus would be much smaller.

Where cable does succeed, it is worth considering the remedy of mandated special-purpose cable channels as an alternative to broadcast regulation by "raised eyebrow." The potential gains from such a move depend on the magnitude of the potential "cable surplus," that is, how much expected profits exceed the minimum necessary to induce cable investment. Clearly the magnitude of such a "surplus" will depend on what the regulators do to subscriber rates, lease charges, non-exclusive franchises, access to the municipality's subterranean ducts, etc. It will also depend on advertising revenue which will in turn depend upon cable penetration, and in turn on the availability of attractive programming.[33]

Can mandatory provision of special purpose channels convert any economic rents in cable into public service products without risking government regulation of program content?[34] To answer this question fully would require a more extensive argument than we can really present here. To an extent the issue turns on what will happen if we do not provide such "dedicated" channels. Profit maximizing cable system owners, unable to price discriminate, might well be reluctant to expand channel capacity or to sell the rights to use all available capacity at what would be the very low marginal cost of such use. Furthermore additional channels could make it more difficult to maximize advertiser revenue for the cable system by fractionalizing audiences. On the other hand, abundant channels, pay-TV systems and low-cost interconnection could make what are now "merit" programs into marketable commodities.[35] But surely a long transitional period is in store before that situation develops, if it ever does.

Another argument for such dedication is the likelihood that cable systems too will potentially earn rents whose disposal raises similar issues to the broadcasting case. It is likely but perhaps not inevitable that the cost structure of cable distribution will lead to local geographic monopolies. If the cities grant only non-exclusive licenses and guarantee non-discriminatory access to both underground ducts and subscriber terminals, this effect could be minimized.[36] Yet even then potential entry might not be a sufficiently credible threat to control profit levels.

The case for special purpose channels is also strengthened if we make an effort to insure that such signals will be available to low income families. Unless there is some cross-subsidy for such expansion, however, we face the prospect that "merit programs" on the cable will be supported in part by advertising and higher product prices. In that situation, low income families would pay some of the costs and gain few of the benefits, an obviously unattractive outcome.

As this review makes clear, the issue is not just whether "room" is made available on the cable, but also how much is spent (i.e., diverted from rents) to support the programming put on to fill that space. In one respect, the mere existence of cable makes matters easier. Substantial time and hardware are simply not needed to activate the education channels, unlike the broadcast case where program investments alone will not suffice. On the other hand reserving space for public broadcasts on the cable, with no programming support, could turn out to be a mere "paper" promise.

It seems worth considering a gross receipts charge on the whole cable system, paid by all lessees and earmarked to a new nonprofit program subsidiary. This would be a local (not centrally controlled) program resource that would give substance to the notion of local educational and public access channels.[37] Some such arrangement seems essential if we are to avoid the repetition of past broadcast regulatory myths that have been trotted out over and over to justify local channel allocations, unused UHF, ETV, etc. By tapping cable users to contribute to a local system-wide programming capability, we might not only justify the opportunity costs of public access and educational cable channels, but also begin to provide the merit programming so often promised and so seldom produced.

Notes to Chapter Eleven

1. Richard A. Posner, "Taxation by Regulation," *Bell Journal of Economics and Management Science,* 2 (Spring 1971), p. 22, n.1.

2. See generally Fritz Machlup, *The Political Economy of Monopoly* (Baltimore: The Johns Hopkins Press, 1952), pp. 289-94; Thomas G.

Moore, "The Purpose of Licensing," *Journal of Law and Economics,* 4 (October 1961), pp. 93–117.

3. This is obviously not always successful. See Richard E. Caves, "Direct Regulation and Market Performance in the American Economy," *American Economic Review,* 54 (May 1964), pp. 172–75.

4. See Edward W. Kitch *et al.,* "The Regulation of Taxicabs in Chicago," *Journal of Law and Economics,* 14 (October 1971), pp. 321–22; Harvey J. Levin, "Economic and Regulatory Aspects of Liquor Licensing," *University of Pennsylvania Law Review,* 112 (April 1964), pp. 813–14, 819–21.

5. George J. Stigler, "The Theory of Economic Regulation," *Bell Journal of Economics and Management Science,* 2 (Spring 1971), pp. 3–9. Compare with the two-pronged approach suggested in George W. Hilton, "The Basic Behavior of Regulatory Commissions," *American Economic Review,* 62 (May 1972), pp. 50–52; and Lucille S. Keyes, "The Protective Functions of Commission Regulation," *American Economic Review,* 48 (May 1958), pp. 544–47.

6. These divergent elements are set forth at length in *Report of Network Broadcasting,* H. Rept. 1297, 85 Cong. 2 sess. (1958), chap. 3 (passim.). See further discussion in Harvey J. Levin, *The Invisible Resource: Use and Regulation of the Radio Spectrum* (Baltimore: The Johns Hopkins Press, 1971), pp. 53–55.

7. Some preliminary results of an ongoing analysis of diversity appear in Harvey J. Levin, "Program Duplication, Diversity and Effective Viewer Choices: Some Empirical Findings," *American Economic Review,* 61 (May 1971), pp. 81–88.

8. See U.S. Federal Communications Commission, *Television Broadcast Financial Data for 1956* (1957); idem *1961* (1962); idem *1971* (1972).

9. See Levin, *The Invisible Resource,* pp. 369–74, 93–97; and Levin, "Economic Effects of Broadcast Licensing," *Journal of Political Economy,* 72 (April 1964), pp. 151–62.

10. The sales price data used in this latest analysis are described in Levin, *The Invisible Resource,* pp. 397–98.

11. See John L. Peterman, "Concentration of Control and the Price of Television Time," *American Economic Review,* 61 (May 1971), pp. 74–80; United Research Inc., "The Implications of Limiting Multiple Ownership of Television Stations," transmitted on October 1, 1966 to FCC docket no. 16068, vol. 2, appendix H. They found only insignificant differences (at the .05 level) in the purchase prices paid, irrespective of type of seller or buyer, market size or network affiliation. This held true for the top 50, top 100, as well as for all markets, and separately for three types of sales transactions. Of further interest are additional URI studies.

12. Bruce Owen, "Newspaper and Television Station Joint Ownership," *Antitrust Bulletin,* 18 (Winter 1973), pp. 787–807. There are some technical econometric arguments over whether Owen or other researchers have used the correct specification. See J. N. Rosse, "Credible and Incredible Economic Evidence," Memorandum no. 109, Research Center in Economic Growth, Stanford University, April 1971.

13. The program categories are adapted from Gary E. Steiner, *The People Look at Television* (New York: Knopf, 1963). The data are compiled from logs in *TV Guide*, February 25–March 3, 1967, and reflect industry self-classifications. The "high brow entertainment" types, for example, are defined as the number of 15-minute units of prime-time programming self-classified as "drama" and "fine arts"; ten "low brow entertainment" types include dramatic adventure, situation comedy, quiz, serial melodrama, variety, etc.; the eight public-affairs categories include interviews, discussion and debate, political, documentary and news specials, instructional, etc. The program typology is summarized in Levin, "Program Duplication, Diversity, and Effective Viewer Choices," pp. 81–88. Also see Herman W. Land Associates, *Television and the Wired City* (Washington D.C.: National Association of Broadcasters, 1968), esp. chapter 2.

14. The 20-second rate for one prime-time commercial weekly is widely viewed as a good index of a station's viability. The unexpected sign of the coefficient for the number of stations seems due to the sharply increased levels of income, revenue and time sales per station in markets where stations exceed 3 (see table 11-1). In the larger markets those economic indicators grow much more rapidly than does the number of operating stations, constrained by the limitist allocation plan.

15. Inclusion of a dummy for educational television (commercial station = 1, ETV = 0) into the station regressions reported in table 11–4 raises the $\bar{R}^2$ values often substantially: for high-brow entertainment from .3024 to .6643; for news from .3456 to .4507; for public affairs from .1884 to .4533; for feature film from .1518 to .3778; and for prime-time program diversity from .2288 to .2292. However, many of the newspaper, group and network coefficients are relatively unaffected.

16. See Harvey J. Levin, *Broadcast Regulation and Joint Ownership of Media* (New York: New York University Press, 1960), pp. 89–102; and Reply Comments of Harvey J. Levin, FCC Docket no. 18110, August 1971, at pp. 9–14.

17. These two separate estimates of rents are indeed close to the $300,000,000 estimate for 1970 of Roger G. Noll, M. J. Peck and John J. McGowan, *Economic Aspects of Television Regulation* (Washington, D.C.: Brookings Institution, 1973), p. 17.

18. See *Broadcasting*, March 27, 1961, pp. 64–74.

19. See, e.g., John E. Coons, "Non-Commercial Purpose as a Sherman Act Defense," *Northwestern University Law Review*, 56 (January-February 1962), pp. 705–13; Note, "Concerted Refusals to Deal under the Federal Antitrust Laws," *Harvard Law Review*, 71 (June 1958), pp. 1531–41. Compare Note, "Trade Association Exclusionary Practices: An Affirmative Role for the Rule of Reason," *Columbia Law Review*, 66 (December 1966), pp. 1503–10.

20. Broadcasters are especially upset by the intensifying struggle between incumbents and challengers at license renewal time, as is readily apparent in the trade press. Of special interest is the imbroglio over Commissioner Nicholas Johnson's explicit guidance to potential challengers. In

part this is because petitions to deny renewal applications have risen dramatically since the 1971 Appeals Court decision confirming the rights to challenge even if forfeiture of licenses would result. As a partial response, the now defunct Whitehead Bill sought to extend the license term to five years and to raise important barriers to challengers at renewal time. These matters were discussed almost weekly in *Broadcasting* throughout 1973, in instances too numerous to list individually. The intricacies of the most recent struggles are described in Friendly, "The Campaign to Politicize Broadcasting," *Columbia Journalism Review,* March/April 1973, pp. 9-18.

21. The Ford satellite plan was originally filed in FCC Docket no. 16495, Comments of Ford Foundation, vol. 1, August 1, 1966, pp. 7-23; Reply Comments vol. 1, Dec. 12, 1966, pp. 1-11, 48-59. See also Joel B. Dirlan and Alfred E. Kahn, "The Merits of Reserving the Cost-Savings from Communications Satellites for Support of Education Television," *Yale Law Journal,* 77 (January 1968), pp. 494-519; and Dick Netzer, *Long Range Financing of Public Broadcasting* (National Citizens' Committee for Broadcasting, 1970).

22. "Even a tax of as much as 40% on satellite services is unlikely to deter their use," whereas the "amount of a tax could be as high as $25 to $30 million without making satellites more expensive than [terrestrial] . . . interconnection." (Noll, Peck and McGowan, p. 232.)

23. See critique of Ford plan in Comments of AT&T in Docket no. 16495, December 15, 1966, Attachment #1, #3.

24. The estimates cited in this paragraph and the next appear in Noll, Peck and McGowan, pp. 231-32, 149-51.

25. This point was driven home in testimony before the Senate Commerce Committee, *Hearings on S.1160-The Public Television Act of 1967,* 90 Cong. 1 sess. (1967), pp. 173-76 (Fred Friendly). An automatic diversion of BNSC cost savings was viewed as guaranteeing even more "insulation" than would dedicated tax revenues in a federal trust fund.

26. For some evidence that the networks are considering turning elsewhere, if only as a useful bargaining strategy in dealing with Bell and FCC, see Docket no. 18684, Networks Ex. no. P10, May 28, 1971, Proposed Testimony of David M. Blank on Behalf of ABC, CBS, and NBC, and Attachment A thereto—Joint Statement of ABC, CBS and NBC in Docket no. 16495, March 29, 1971.

27. Melody, "Market Structure and Public Policy in Communications," unpublished paper presented at 82d Annual Meetings of American Economic Association, December 28, 1969, pp. 7-18; Roger G. Noll and Lewis A. Rivlin, "Regulating Prices in Competitive Markets," *Yale Law Journal,* 82 (June 1973), pp. 1426-34. There is some evidence that the television tariff adjustments Bell has offered are normally consistent with a strategy to preclude new system entry. See, *Hearings on S.1160,* pp. 411-15.

28. See FCC, RM-1418, Microwave Communications Inc., a Proposal to the Corporation for Public Broadcasting and the Interuniversity Communications Council (EDUCOM), December 13, 1968, transmitted as petition to FCC; letter from Goeken, MCI, to Waple, FCC, March 10, 1969 (RM 1418) and attached Report, MCI's Proposal to Establish a Nationwide Network

to Interconnect Non-Commercial Educational Broadcast Stations, February 10, 1969 (RM-1).

29. During the long negotiating period with CPB, Bell did successively reduce its public TV offer of 50 percent of commercial rates (letter from Emerson, AT&T to FCC Chairman Hyde, April 29, 1969), to 40 percent (letter from Delley, AT&T to Griffith, FCC, September 25, 1969), to 33 percent (FCC Memorandum and Order in Docket no. 18316, June 3, 1971, paragraphs 4, 6–7, 18–19).

30. See Johnson, *Cable Television and the Question of Protecting Local Broadcasting,* Rand Memo R-595-MF, October 1970, pp. 5–6; Rolla Edward Park, "The Growth of Cable TV and its Probable Impact on Over-the-Air Broadcasting," *American Economic Review,* 61 (May 1971), pp. 69–73.

31. See Noll, Peck and McGowan, pp. 166–69.

32. A highly suggestive approach for analysis of potential long-run program adjustments appears in Johnson, *Future of Cable Television: Some Problems of Federal Regulation,* Rand Memo RM-6199-FF, January 1970, pp. 66–72. See also Noll, Peck and McGowan, pp. 169–70.

33. See Noll, Peck and McGowan, esp. pp. 194–97, and more generally, pp. 153–62.

34. "Mandated" channels designate the uses to which some proportion of given channels shall be put. In one proposal, one-half of a 20-channel system would be "mandated," with six channels for network and local signals, two channels for government and nongovernment services, and one channel for experimental and education. Of the ten remaining channels, eight would be open for leasing on a first-come, first-served basis to any or all bidders. See *On the Cable: Report of the Sloan Commission on Cable Communications* (New York: McGraw-Hill, 1971), pp. 141–46.

35. The full possibilities in this regard are not clear; see Chayes, *Impact of Satellites on Cable Communications,* prepared for Sloan Cable Commission (May 1971), pp. 15–24.

36. See Barton, Dunn, Parker and Rosse, *Nondiscriminatory Access to Cable Television Channels,* Stanford Institute for Public Policy Analysis, May 1972, pp. 37–40. Nondiscriminatory access to terminals and rate regulatory issues to one side, public divulgence of all detailed contract terms between conduit owners, leasees and subscribers might operate to help. check pricing excesses or preclusive, discriminatory practices. Yet under oligopoly, secret price cutting may be needed to generate open generalized price cuts, except where products are differentiated. Open public records and full divulgence of contract provisions could eliminate the needed degree of secrecy and discrimination. Either way, dissipation of the rents would be imperfect, and the case for their recovery stands.

37. See Frederiksen, *Community Access Video* (Berkeley, Calif.: Book People, 1972), pp. 17–28. A more limited approach would require the conduit owner to provide studios, other production facilities, training and publicity, with the financial burden shared with commercial lessees, and drawing

where possible on underutilized educational facilities in the community. (See Massachusetts CATV Commission, Discussion of Policy and Ojectives, Draft 5, July 9, 1973, pt. I, sec. M.) Daily management of the public access channels might be located in a community board, again funded jointly. This approach contrasts with the Public Dividend Plan to use similar revenues to support the Corporation for Public Broadcasting.

Chapter Twelve

Value of Options, Value of Time and Local Airline Subsidy

Richard E. Caves and Elisha A. Pazner

Local air service to and from small cities has been actively promoted by public policy in the United States. The local service airlines have received direct subsidies that ran as high as $67 million (in 1963). Additional indirect subsidies are provided through public funding of airport construction and navigation aids. Finally, the regulatory policies of the Civil Aeronautics Board have long been heavily weighted by the objective of generating commercial profits that could be used to cross-subsidize unprofitable service to small cities.

Although most observers agree that these policies have incurred heavy real costs in resource misallocation, hard evidence has generally been lacking. Given this lack, the purpose of this paper is to make an admittedly crude attempt at quantitatively evaluating those subsidies.

As a measure of benefit, we propose to use the value of the travel time saved by the existence of the air service. However, in doing so, we must first respond to the argument (frequently made by defenders of these subsidies) that such actual use does not fully capture the social value of the policies. The people served, it is suggested, would be willing to pay something to have the option available *ex ante,* that is not fully reflected in the value they ultimately turn out to derive from the service *ex post.* Given large numbers, we will assume that benefits actually enjoyed closely approach benefits expected *ex ante.* Thus the theoretical issue becomes: does the "option value" to potential travelers of having air service available differ systematically from the consumer surplus they expect to enjoy when they actually use it? We argue that there is no general theoretical presumption about the direction in which option value differs from consumer surplus. Given that, we turn to the empirical evidence, employing recent research on the value of time saved by air travel to estimate the net benefits that it generates. We conclude that a case may exist for a small flow of subsidy, under different institutional arrangements, to provide air service that is not commercially viable but warranted by option value. The present relation between total net benefits and the cost of subsidy, however, is decidedly unfavorable.

1. CONSUMER SURPLUS:
PROBLEMS OF UNCERTAIN BENEFIT

In trying to evaluate airline subsidies, we need at least to acknowledge the many complexities involved in all social policy judgments. We have *not* posed the problem as the search for some criteria for the overall "optimum" outcome, or even for the "second-best" optimum under explicit constraints. Rather—as in most "cost-benefit" analysis—we simply seek to identify what changes in economic arrangements are desirable; that is, which policies will, in some sense, make us "better off." The "consumer surplus" measures we employ do not really respect the logic of utilitarian "social welfare functions," which emphasizes changes in an individual's subjective experience. And they provide at best a necessary, not a sufficient condition, for making policy changes. We neglect these difficulties in what follows.

A complexity which we cannot ignore, however, because it has been held central to the case for subsidizing local air service, is the effect of uncertainty on our benefit measures. The particular kind of uncertainty we are interested in is not like that associated with, say, a dam, whose flood control and hydroelectric benefits are uncertain because they depend on uncertain rainfall.[1] Rather, the key uncertainty in demand for local air service is that consumers cannot predict in advance exactly how much of the good they will want. Instead, this depends on what will happen to them, on what "state of nature" will prevail. This trait of air transportation is shared with health facilities, fire protection and so on. A citizen of Hazleton, Pa., might be willing to pay something for the assurance that for the coming year daily air service to New York and back will be available (at a set fare). He is uncertain when or how often he will, in fact, want to make the trip. Does the value of this option to him differ in any way from the (discounted) consumer's surplus he expects to derive from air journeys to New York? Would the (estimated) surpluses of all travelers using this service provide an unbiased test of the social justification of any subsidy needed to keep the service going?

For the problem to be an important one for economic policy, the activity in question must entail inflated costs of expanding output once it has been curtailed. Airline service clearly has these characteristics. An efficient airline can hardly be organized on the spot every time a citizen of Hazleton wishes to fly to New York.

The existing literature hardly resolves this problem satisfactorily. In the paper which first raised this issue, Weisbrod argued that an unprofitable public facility (e.g., a park) might be economically justified even though consumers at any one time might or might not visit it.[2] The maximum payment potential users would make for the option of visiting the park, should they so desire (over and above any user charges), should appear explicitly in the list of the park's benefits. In contrast, Long claimed that Weisbrod's option value is no other than expected consumer surplus.[3] Thus, to use both in measuring benefits would be double counting. Lindsay then criticized Long for failing to take into account Weisbrod's explicit condition of uncertainty and suggested that option value must include a risk-premium and is therefore greater than expected consumer's surplus.[4] At the same time, Byerlee purported to show that, under certain conditions, option value is less than expected consumer surplus for a risk-averse individual and equal to expected surplus for a risk-neutral one.[5]

Cicchetti and Freeman, by contrast, assume that the final level of utility attained by the consumer, whether or not he demands the good, is always the same.[6] They then proceed to show that for a risk-averse individual, option value is higher than expected consumer surplus. Their result, however, depends critically on the assumption of comparable utility levels.

A somewhat similar point must be made about the most recent treatment of this issue by Schmalensee.[7] His four major "theorems" all adduce special cases in which utility levels (and hence marginal utilities) can be set equal under all potential states of nature. He finds that, in some cases, option value is above, and in other cases below, expected consumer surplus.

These contradictory views are easy enough to understand once we review a little background. The general assumption has been that decision-makers are risk-averse, that is they will refuse a fair gamble. This in turn implies that the marginal utility of additional income declines with income, and that decision-makers will, under the right circumstances, purchase insurance to avoid uncertain outcomes. This accounts for Byerlee's result, because an uncertain service is worth *less* than a certain one consumed in the same expected quantity.

On the other hand, when it is preferences that are uncertain, the desire to consume a given service may be correlated with changes in a decision-maker's *overall welfare.* For example, he might want/need airline service only in a disaster or only on some special, happy occasion. In the former case, having the service available acts as insurance (i.e., it raises his welfare under an adverse contingency). Under such circumstances, a risk-averse decision-maker might pay something just for the option value. On the other hand, if someone only demands the service under prosperous circumstances, paying an option price has the effect of increasing the riskiness of his future. He becomes better off when better off, and worse off when worse off because he pays for the service whether he uses it or not. In a sense, our decision-maker now faces a *portfolio* problem. Hence the covariance between the returns from the service, and his overall welfare level is relevant to the decision.[8]

As this review makes clear, the relationship between option value and expected consumer surplus is still an open question. The model presented in the next section generates many of the results previously obtained in the literature. The conclusion is that no necessary relation holds between expected consumer surplus and option value. The attempt to look for general rules for the single consumer is futile.

2. A SIMPLE MODEL OF OPTION VALUE

Even though the essence of the option value problem has to do with consumption in the future, we follow the previous literature in compressing all of the future into a single period and assume that the marginal rate of time preference is zero. Introducing discounted values would only unduly complicate the presentation, without adding any new insight to the problem. Consider then a consumer whose utility function is $U = (X, Y, \epsilon)$ where X is the commodity with respect to which we seek to determine option value, Y ("income") is the composite good formed from all other commodities, and ϵ is a random variable that indicates which state of nature occurs. The demand for X (and hence Y) is dependent on that state; that is, on the particular value assumed by ϵ. To be parallel to the earlier literature we shall postulate that ϵ can only assume two values, ϵ_0 and ϵ_1. When the state of nature indicated by ϵ_0 occurs, the consumer will not wish to consume X at all. On the other hand, if state ϵ_1 prevails, the consumer will choose to consume some positive amount of X, depending on its price.

 The problem we have posed is: how does a consumer's expected consumer surplus ($\overline{CS}$) compare to the maximum amount he would be willing to pay to have the good available (call that OP^*). We shall proceed somewhat indirectly by noting that the consumer's expected utility under payment of an option price goes down as that price goes up. Thus we will seek to compare the expected utility of a consumer who pays $\overline{CS}$ as an option price, call that $E[U_{\overline{CS}}]$, with that of one who pays the maximum option price, $E[U_{OP^*}]$. If the first expected utility level is higher than the second, we will know that the maximum option price is larger than expected consumer surplus and vice versa.

 Furthermore, note that the consumer's expected utility when he must pay OP^* will be equal to the expected utility level he would receive if he paid no option price and received none of the good, call that $E[U_{NO}]$. As an expected utility maximizer, he would never agree to pay an option price that would reduce his expected utility below the latter level, and until he reached that level, he would always be willing to pay a higher option price. Thus we are able to substitute $E[U_{NO}]$ for $E[U_{OP^*}]$ in the comparison with $E[U_{\overline{CS}}]$.

 To make this comparison, we begin by noting that the consumer will only derive a consumer surplus from X if state ϵ_0 will prevail with probability α and state ϵ_1 with probability $1 - \alpha$. Furthermore, we will fix the consumer's income at Y_0 and the price of X at some value P_x. Under these assumptions, the consumer faces some positive consumer surplus, say CS, out of X with probability $1 - \alpha$ (when ϵ_1 occurs) and a zero consumer surplus out of X with probability α (when ϵ_0 occurs). Expected consumer surplus is thus

$$\overline{CS} = \alpha \cdot 0 + (1 - \alpha)\, CS = (1 - \alpha)\, CS. \tag{1}$$

 As the next step, note that if the consumer pays no option price, he always receives income Y_0, and consumes $X = 0$. So,

$$E[U_{NO}] = \alpha U(0, Y_0, \epsilon_0) + (1 - \alpha)U(0, Y_0, \epsilon_1). \tag{2}$$

It will be helpful to be able to rewrite the second term of this expression. To do this note that in state ϵ_1, the definition of consumer surplus means that when our subject consumes no X he must derive the same utility as he would if he (i) consumed a freely chosen amount of X and, (ii) gave up in return both the cost of that purchase and his consumer surplus. Thus we have

$$U(0, Y_0, \epsilon_1) = U(X, Y_0 - CS - P_x X, \epsilon_1), \tag{3}$$

and substituting back into (2) we have,

$$E[U_{NO}] = \alpha U(0, Y_0, \epsilon_0) + (1-\alpha)(X, Y_0 - CS - P_x X, \epsilon_1); \tag{4}$$

where X denotes the amount chosen by the consumer when all his consumer surplus is extracted from him.[9]

Next we must determine the expected utility $E[U_{\overline{CS}}]$ of the consumer when he is charged an option price equal to his expected consumer surplus of $\overline{CS} = (1-\alpha)CS$. Let $\overline{X}$ be the amount of X demanded by the consumer under state of nature ϵ_1 when he is paying an option price of $\overline{CS}$. Since his income available for other commodities in both states is $Y_0 - \overline{CS}$, we have

$$E[U_{\overline{CS}}] = \alpha U(0, Y_0 - \overline{CS}, \epsilon_0) + (1 - \alpha) U(\overline{X}, Y_0 - \overline{CS} - P_x X, \epsilon_1). \tag{5}$$

In comparing (4) with (5), to find if $\overline{CS}$ is greater or less than OP^*, we find in each expression one magnitude which is larger and one which is smaller than in the other equation. Specifically, $U(0, Y_0, \epsilon_0) > U(0, Y_0 - \overline{CS}, \epsilon_0)$ since Y_0 is obviously greater than $Y_0 - \overline{CS}$. Yet $U(X, Y_0 - CS - P_x X, \epsilon_1) < U(\overline{X}, Y_0 - \overline{CS} - P_x \overline{X}, \epsilon_1)$ since $CS > \overline{CS}$. Thus, without further restrictions it is impossible to determine whether $E[U_{\overline{CS}}] \gtreqless E[U_{NO}]$ and hence whether $\overline{CS} \gtreqless OP^*$.

To proceed further we shall make the reasonable assumption that U is a strictly concave function in both X and Y. Our consumer is assumed to have declining marginal utility, that is to be risk-averse, with respect to both income and the consumption of X. In addition, we must make some explicit assumption about the nature of the events ϵ_0 and ϵ_1 and the demand for X, related to the consumer's overall utility levels. There are then three major possibilities in this regard.

(I) The utility level reached by the consumer at the respective equilibria is the same regardless of whether ϵ_0 or ϵ_1 obtains. This means that for given income Y and price P_e, the following obtains

$$U(0, Y, \epsilon_0) = U(X^e, Y - P_e X^e, \epsilon_1), \tag{6}$$

where X^e is the quantity of X demanded by the consumer under ϵ_1, when his income is Y and the price of X is P_e. The consumer is indifferent between events ϵ_0 and ϵ_1 for after adjusting his consumption pattern according to the state of nature which actually prevails, he enjoys the same level of utility in either case.

(II) An alternative is that the event ϵ_1 is preferred by the customer to the event ϵ_0. For a given income, Y, and price, P_e, we would therefore have

$$U(0, Y, \epsilon_0) < U(X^e, Y - P_e X^e, \epsilon_1). \tag{7}$$

(III) Finally the event ϵ_0 could be preferred by the consumer to the event ϵ_1. For given income Y and price P_e we therefore would have

$$U(0, Y, \epsilon_0) > U(X^e, Y - P_e X^e, \epsilon_1). \tag{8}$$

We show now that under Case I—where utility levels are the same in both states—it follows that $OP^* > \overline{CS}$, i.e., that the consumer will be willing to pay a maximal option price which is higher than his expected consumer surplus. First, in this case, the utility the consumer derives, in either state of nature, when he pays GS as an option price, must be equal to the utility in the other state. That is,

$$U(X, Y_0 - CS - P_e X, \epsilon_1) = U(0, Y_0 - CS, \epsilon_0).$$

From (3) we know that the left hand side is simply equal to $U(0, Y_0, \epsilon_1)$, which implies,

$$U(0, Y_0, \epsilon_1) = U(0, Y_0 - CS, \epsilon_0).$$

Substituting the second expression for the first in (2) yields

$$E[U_{NO}] = \alpha U(0, Y_0, \epsilon_0) + (1 - \alpha) U(0, Y_0 - CS, \epsilon_0). \tag{9}$$

Now the concavity of $U(\cdot)$ with respect to Y means that the weighted average of two values of the function, generated by two different values of Y, will be less than the value of $U(\cdot)$ taken at the comparably weighted average value of Y. Thus, since $CS = (1 - \alpha)CS$, we have from (9)

$$E[U_{NO}] < U(0, Y_0 - \overline{CS}, \epsilon_0). \tag{10}$$

On the other hand, we know that *in this case*

$$E[U_{\overline{CS}}] = U(0, Y_0 - \overline{CS}, \epsilon_0). \tag{11}$$

This follows from (5) because when the terminal utility level is the same under either state, the expected utility must be equal to the utility level which will prevail in either state.

Together (10) and (11) imply for Case I that:

$$E[U_{\overline{CS}}] > E[U_{NO}] \to OP^* > \overline{CS} \tag{12}$$

which is what we set out to prove.[10] Intuitively, what is happening is that in Case I, the man is actually worse off under ϵ_1 than ϵ_0, if no X is available, since only when he can consume X and earn some consumer surplus on it in state ϵ_1 will his utility level be equal to that in ϵ_0. Thus the option has a risk-reducing feature and is worth more than its expected consumer surplus. For some other quite special cases, where utility in state ϵ_1, with no consumption of X, is higher than under ϵ_0, Schmalensee has shown that the reverse is true: expected consumer surplus is greater than or equal to maximum option value.[11]

We should be clear that the assumptions of Case I are very specialized. Even if they are correct for a consumer for some income and some price of X, it cannot in general be correct for a whole set of prices. If it were so for any two prices $P_e \neq P_f$ we would have

$$U(0, Y. \epsilon_0) = U(X^e, Y - P_e X^e, \epsilon_1) = U(X^f, Y - P_f X^f, \epsilon_1),$$

which violates the basic convexity property of consistent utility functions.

Despite its limitations, the assumption of Case I, that utility is the same under both outcomes, is necessary to secure any determinate result at all. In general as the reader can readily verify, the relationship between $\overline{CS}$ and OP^* in Cases II and III cannot be determined on *a priori* grounds. The assumptions needed in order to reach determinate results are of such a specialized nature that there is no point in elaborating on them.

The preceding analysis does not seem to leave us with very much. In one rather special case we have found that option value exceeds expected consumer surplus. But this is only a special case. The components of total consumer surplus will be too low for some consumers and too high for others. One could invoke the law of large numbers, together with the notion that lacking other information overestimates are equally as likely as underestimates, to argue that observed consumer surplus will approximately equal previously expected surplus. Thus, in all, we might conclude, observed consumer surplus will come close to estimating *ex ante* option demand, and the neglect of uncertainty does not impose a devastating qualification on the use of consumer surplus analysis. In any case, local air travel entails a large amount of routine and predictable demand and (as we shall see) relatively little superiority over alternatives, even for the emergency traveler, making it most unlikely that option value diverges greatly from *ex post* consumer surplus.

The available data would support quite an elaborate and sophisticated study of the value of local air service. The calculations shown here aspire to less; they could be described as back-of-envelope scribblings, with the caveat that a large envelope was used. But they do suggest important conclusions about the order of magnitude of consumer surplus and thus the worth of the subsidy payments now made to the local-service carriers and other public policies that are associated with their subsidized status. The findings seem sufficiently clearcut that, even given all the difficulties we have encountered, the burden of proof is now clearly shifted to subsidy advocates. As we will see, it is quite hard to justify current policies in terms of the analysis to be presented.

3. CONSUMER SURPLUS FROM LOCAL AIR SERVICE

The local-service carriers—now numbering eight—have been heavily subsidized since their birth for the avowed purpose of providing socially valuable air service to cities able to generate a minimum volume of passenger traffic but not enough to be commercially profitable. In the mid 1950s, direct subsidy payments ran about $20 million annually, rose to $67 million in 1963, and then declined to $36 million by 1969.[12] The figures are not large compared, say, to maritime or farm subsidies, and the fiction of public policy has always been that they would disappear as the growth of air traffic renders these services commercially profitable. But they remain and, indeed, are supplemented by indirect subsidies from other sources. Furthermore, as Eads and others have argued, the subsidy payments have, in fact, been buying less and less service to points with marginal traffic-generating capacity, and have instead supported the enlargement of the local-service carriers into weak regional trunks.[13] At the same time, unsubsidized commuter airlines have appeared, flying smaller aircraft than the local service carriers but outperforming them in frequency and convenience of schedules.

Thus, subsidy to local air service presents us with several intersecting questions. Have the benefits from service actually provided by the local airlines been justified by the subsidy paid? Have the subsidy payments bought as much extra local service as they could? How much subsidy would be justified by the value of an air-service option if the service were indeed provided in a cost-minimizing way?

To answer these questions, we need to know how much consumer surplus has been generated by the services in question. Given the stochastic element in demand, we could use actual demand as an estimate of expected demand. But even on this assumption, deriving the demand curve for the relevant class of air services has proved very difficult. A major reason for this failure is the trouble researchers have in finding any economically relevant variation of the price of trips by air. Fares have tended to change little over time in individual markets. Any comparison of different markets poses thorny problems of holding all their important differences constant—and then casts up nothing more than a single price elasticity of very dubious significance.[14]

It does seem feasible, though, to construct a synthetic estimate of this surplus. We do this by hypothesizing that the traveler by air chooses this mode over competing forms of surface transport whenever the time it saves him is worth the extra money cost that air travel entails for relatively short distances.[15] Our basic strategy thus will be to measure the value of the time that travelers save by having local air service available. We will calculate that time saving and its value by assuming a traveler is randomly drawn from a distribution of the traveling public who could be expected to choose air service. Total surplus will then be estimated by multiplying the amount of time saved per traveler by the applicable mean value of time and number of persons traveling.

This approach is reasonable because the typical traveler on a local-service airline moves a relatively short distance between a small city and a metropolitan hub, where he either transacts business or connects for long-haul air transportation. In 1966—the year on which our calculations will focus—the mean length of on-line passenger trips for the local-service carriers was 223 miles, and the mean stage-length of flight (i.e., distance flown between landings) was 112 miles.[16] For a substantial portion of these travelers, surface transport—and especially the private automobile—is a relatively good substitute. The growth of the interstate highway network has sharply reduced automobile travel times between cities—often by 50 percent—and rendered air travel between many points served by local airlines only marginally faster than driving. Thus, for many travelers the choice is indeed time vs. money, flying vs. driving.

We confirmed this widely-acknowledged substitutability by an analysis of data from a Civil Aeronautics Board study of cities served unprofitably by four of the local airlines.[17] The CAB's calculations simulate the financial effects of deleting air service at these marginal points, in the process giving data on driving distance to the nearest point retaining air service by trunk or local airlines. We would expect a city's traffic-generating ability (measured by passengers originated per annum relative to population) to increase with such distance. In the sample these range from zero—in cases where the point is served by another airline—to 206 miles. Mean traffic generating capacity for cities in various subgroups of the sample was as follows:

Distance to nearest airport	Ratio of originations to population	Number of cities
0	.11	17
1 to 50 miles	.17	26
51 to 100 miles	.26	42
over 100 miles	.48	25

Thus the use of local air service seems quite responsive to the presence of alternative airports nearby—which might serve either as natural business destinations or specifically as places where competing air service could be secured.[18] Other studies have shown similar effects on a city's traffic generation of its distance from a major commercial center.[19]

Other evidence also supports this value-of-time approach. Many local air travelers are businessmen, more conscious than personal travelers of the value of their time and less likely to thrill to air travel for its own sake. Their alternative for short journeys is in most cases probably a trip by car rather than no trip at all. Similarly the volume of local air travel has been found to be highly sensitive to the frequency with which flights are offered and to the convenience of their timing in relation to the business day.[20] In addition, the pleas for local air service periodically voiced before Congress invariably stress the frequency and convenience of air service and eschew the mention of its price.[21] All this suggests a "time sensitivity" which makes our methods that much more reasonable.

4. ESTIMATION OF VALUE OF TIME SAVED

To estimate the value of time saved by the provision of local air service we need, first, information on the values that travelers place on their time. The evidence collected in various surveys is not completely consistent, but it generally supports the proposition that business travelers value their time at the equivalent of their average hourly wage. If profit-maximizing entrepreneurs determined their employees' travel activities, it is hard to see why time lost in travel would be valued at anything but the employee's wage, presuming that measured the marginal value product of his time in other activities.[22] Gronau's results are consistent with this valuation for business travelers, although his evidence does not establish that people making nonbusiness trips place a positive shadow price on their time.[23]

The assumption that travelers value their time at their average hourly wage can be combined with information on the incomes of air travelers in the United States to derive a distribution of the values placed on time saved by air travel. In table 12-1 the first two columns show the distribution of incomes reported by air travelers in the National Travel Survey for 1967. Column 3 indicates the range of hourly wages (and thus values placed on time) for individuals in each annual income class. Column 4 presents an estimate of the mean value for individuals in each class; it is nothing but the midpoint for each class, with rough guesses for the top and bottom classes to smooth the underlying distribution. Finally, column 5 contains estimates of the weighted average value of time for all travelers with incomes above the lower bound for the class in question. For example, suppose that we think some population of

**Table 12-1.   Distribution of Air Travelers by Income Class and
Implied Cumulative Distribution of Average Values of Time**

Annual Income ($000)	Percent of Respondents[a]	Range of Hourly Wages[b]	Mean Value of Time[c]	Cumulative Mean Value of Time[d]
(1)	(2)	(3)	(4)	(5)
0 – 2	1.6%	$ 0 – 1.00	$ 0.75	$ 6.84
2 – 3	1.4	1.00 – 1.50	1.25	6.93
3 – 4	2.6	1.50 – 2.00	1.75	7.01
4 – 5	2.4	2.00 – 2.50	2.25	7.16
5 – 6	5.0	2.50 – 3.00	2.75	7.29
6 – 7.5	9.1	3.00 – 3.75	3.38	7.55
7.5 – 10	16.2	3.75 – 5.00	4.38	8.04
10 – 15	30.4	5.00 – 7.50	6.25	9.00
15 – 25	20.9	7.50 – 12.50	10.00	11.66
over 25	10.4	over 12.50	15.00	15.00

[a]From U.S. Bureau of the Census, *1967 Census of Transportation, vol. I, National Travel Survey* (Washington: Government Printing Office, 1969), p. 23. Nonrespondents were assumed to have incomes distributed the same as respondents.

[b]Individuals are assumed to work 2000 hours annually (50 40–hour weeks).

[c]Assumed to equal midpoint of the range, but with arbitrary adjustments to the top and bottom classes to smooth the distribution.

[d]Weighted average value of time for all travelers with incomes above the minimum for each income class.

travelers is randomly drawn from all those who report incomes of $10,000 a year or more, corresponding to a minimum time-value of $5 an hour; the expected mean value of time for this population would be $9.00 an hour, a figure derived by multiplying the assumed mean value for each over–$10,000 income class by its corresponding percentage in the distribution.

The significance of column 5 becomes apparent when we consider the choice of travel mode by people who place a well-defined value on their time. When one mode is faster *and* cheaper, it should always be chosen. When one mode (air travel) is faster but dearer than another (private auto), it will be chosen by those who value their time higher than the time-cost trade-off between the two modes. Thus, if air travel between two points saves 30 minutes over travel by private auto but costs $2.50 more, it will (typically) be chosen by all travelers who value their time at more than $5 an hour. If those who fly between these points are randomly drawn from the distribution of all air travelers by income class, they would value their time on the average at $9.00 an hour. They would enjoy an *aggregate* surplus of $4.00 ($9.00 minus $5.00) times one-half (hour saved) times the number of travelers.

It is best to make explicit several possible sources of bias in this approach. In one respect our procedure underestimates potential total benefits. If the airline fares used in these calculations exceed marginal cost, a deadweight loss is being incurred; the lowering of fares to marginal cost would increase total benefits by more than it increases costs. In another respect also we are misestimating benefits. Some travelers might get psychic income out of air travel, or do so in relation to driving. Of course, some of that psychic income is negative—for those who fear flying. Furthermore, the assumptions of the table are quite conservative relative to wage rates. If higher-income people work longer hours, our assumption that everyone works 2000 hours per year assigns too high a time cost to such travelers. Finally, for some people, automobile transport is not an option, but bus travel often will be for those few, and cost of the latter will not be so different from car travel. Like the other factors just reviewed, this should not imply any major errors in this analysis.

It is worth noting that our value-of-time calculations imply synthetic price-elasticities of demand for air service. They vary with the distance of the flight and the size of the price change assumed, but can be rather high. Using the data that underlie case 4 in table 12-2 below, an increase of 10 percent in the fare for a 100-mile journey should provoke a quantity response indicating an elasticity of −3. This is perhaps a bit high, but not enough to be too worrisome, since it is for local service only, not all air transport.

Table 12-2. **Minimum Value of Time (Dollars per Hour) Needed for Traveler to Choose Air over Private Automobile, in Relation to Distance Traveled and Assumptions About Price and Speed of Travel Modes**

		Distance (miles)				
Case	Assumptions	75	100	150	200	250
1.	Drivers price auto services at marginal cost; air fares heavily tapered with distance[a]	36.83	13.79	6.88	4.98	4.08
2.	Drivers price at marginal cost; air fares typical of local airlines[b]	25.41	10.10	5.51	4.25	3.65
3.	Drivers price at average cost; air fares heavily tapered with distance[c]	25.94	8.77	3.62	2.20	1.53
4.	Drivers price at average cost; air fares typical of local airlines	14.64	5.13	2.29	1.50	1.13
5.	Drivers price at average cost; air fares typical of local airlines; non-stop air service offered in all markets[d]	14.14	4.62	2.02	1.32	0.99

[a]Gronau's (1963) figure for the marginal cost of auto travel is 3.7¢ per mile. The structure of air fares is that given for the domestic airlines' light-density routes in general (from U.S. Civil Aeronautics Board, *A Study of the Domestic Passenger Air Fare Structure*, table 2): Fare = $6.75 + $0.0663 miles.

[b]Median fare equation for local airlines: Fare = $3.41 + $0.0741 miles.

[c]Gronau's average-cost figure for highway travel, 7.2¢ a mile, he suggests, describes both private motorists' average costs and rental car rates as of 1963.

[d]Cases 1–4 use our equation for the time-cost of air travel assuming the typical number of intermediate stops; case 5 employs the equation calculated from nonstop segments only.

Besides this method of estimating benefits, we also need information on the travel time and the money cost to the traveler of air travel and competing surface modes. We will work mainly with Gronau's estimates, which provide such separate time and money cost functions for each transport mode. He employed the simple functional form

(Time or money) Cost = constant + *b* (miles traveled),

in all cases. His data pertain to city pairs anchored on New York City, but his estimates of average and marginal money costs of travel by private auto look reasonable for application to moderate-length journeys in the United States generally. His time- and money-cost functions for air travel are not applicable to local airlines, however, and his equation for the time cost of private auto travel seems somewhat questionable.[24]

In particular, for automobile travel, his equation for travel time contains a constant of 0.89 hours and implies a line-haul speed of 35 m.p.h., perhaps appropriate for a highly congested metropolitan region but probably slow for smaller hubs well served by interstate highways. We arbitrarily substituted the following: time = 0.25 hours + 0.025 miles. This is a "constant" of 15 minutes plus 40 m.p.h. By being conservative on automobile speeds, we tend to overestimate air service benefits.

For local airlines a travel-time function was estimated by taking a sample of cities classified as marginal in the CAB's study, *Service to Small Communities.* The *Official Airline Guide* yielded scheduled elapsed times for city pairs involving these points.[25] For a city pair to be included, it had to be served by the turboprop Convair and Fairchild aircraft that were typically used on these routes in 1966. Time-cost functions of Gronau's type were estimated both from nonstop flights only and from times calculated by using the weighted average of nonstop and intermediate-stop flights actually offered. After an arbitrary allowance for surface travel time to and from airports, this procedure yields the following functions:

Time = 1.59 hours plus 0.00373 miles (nonstop only)
Time = 1.39 hours plus 0.00655 miles (all flights).[26]

An equation describing the fare structure for local airlines could be taken from a study of 1966 data by the Civil Aeronautics Board.[27] It gives Gronau-type functions for individual local airlines and for light-density domestic routes generally (including those of the trunks), although not for the local airlines as a group. We used the overall light-density function and also the "median" equation among those for the individual local carriers.[28]

Following Gronau's procedure, these ingredients yield a functional relation between intercity distance and the minimum valuation of time needed to lure the traveler to the swifter and more costly mode. Table 12-2 shows these minimum values under various combinations of assumptions. The combinations are arrayed from the assumptions least favorable to air travel down to those most favorable. Our calculations (fortuitously) agree with Gronau's in making travel by private auto quicker as well as cheaper for journeys up to about 64 miles, when the air service entails an average number of intermediate stops. In the following calculations we make use of the assumptions underlying case 4 in the table, which seems to rest on the most defensible combination of assumptions. The variation from case to case is obviously large, and table 12-2 will thus serve as a cautionary sensitivity analysis for the conclusions that follow.

To conduct our analysis, ideally we would employ data on the length of trips taken by passengers enplaning and deplaning at traffic generation points too small to be profitable. This, together with our other estimates, would enable us to calculate the gross value-of-time surplus enjoyed by all passengers making trips of each (discrete) trip-length class. We could then cumulate these surpluses into an overall benefit measure. However, the necessary data on the joint distribution of trip lengths and size of origin/destination points are not readily available, and we must employ less direct and accurate methods.

CAB data do provide the distribution by trip length of all passengers enplaning on scheduled domestic trunk and local-service flights. These data are given by 50-mile ranges. They tell us, for example, that in 1966, 10.9 million (14.5 percent) of the 75.1 million air travelers flew less than 200 miles, and 22.5 million (30.0 percent) took trips shorter than 300 miles. Suppose what is clearly not true: that *all* short-haul passengers used local airlines and enjoyed value-of-time surpluses that would have been foregone without local-airline subsidies. Starting with the shortest surplus-yielding flights, one must cumulate imputed surpluses for all trips shorter than 182 miles to "justify" the 1966 allocated subsidy of $56.4 million.[29] Since this includes both local and trunk passengers, the prospects are not good for comparably justifying the subsidy bill by travel on the local airlines alone.

Let us go at the same question somewhat differently. Suppose what again is not true: that all passengers who used local airlines would have lost their service, and thus their value-of-time surpluses, in the absence of subsidies. Of the 75.1 million domestic air trips taken in 1966, 15.6 million originated on the local-service airlines. Their distribution by trip length is not at hand, but we do know the mean on-line trip length—223 miles. The necessary skewness of the distribution tells us that the median was less—perhaps 200 miles.[30] A rough distribution of local-service trip lengths was estimated that satisfies these assumptions and is consistent with the assumption that the local airlines' share of aggregate domestic scheduled traffic falls steadily as trip length increases. Starting from the shortest air trips, one must cumulate all trips by this estimated flow of local-service passengers out to lengths slightly over 200 miles to justify the 1966 subsidy payment.[31]

But we are still overstating substantially the number of travelers who necessarily benefited from subsidies. Even these last numbers are for *all* local service travelers. But not all such service would disappear absent subsidy. More likely, the absence of subsidies would have denied local-airline service only to those enplaning or deplaning at points generating too little traffic to yield an operating profit. The CAB's study, *Service to Small Communities,* puts this margin (as of 1969) at around 40 passengers originating daily, or 14,600 annually. Assume that on-line trip lengths for passengers enplaning or deplaning at these marginal points are the same as for all travelers on local-service airlines. Then value-of-time surpluses accruing to such travelers, who flew less than 200 miles, cumulates to $13 million, only one-quarter of the 1966 subsidy bill. Allowance for the surpluses of those taking longer trips cannot be reasonably calculated using our methodology, but they could hardly boost the total to the actual subsidy figure of $56.4 million.[32]

Finally, the value-of-time surplus of travelers to and from marginal points served by the local airlines is still overestimated, because we have neglected the possible substitution of aircraft smaller than the 44-53 seat turboprops that represent the smallest equipment in common use by the subsidized local-service carriers. Smaller turboprops seating 15 to 20 passengers are available, and indeed widely used by the commuter airlines that have sprung into existence since the latter 1960s. Although their seat-mile costs exceed those of the larger turboprops, their plane-mile direct operating costs appear no more than half as high. It seems likely that they can earn a commercial profit serving a significant number of smaller cities that would require subsidy if served by larger aircraft.

5. CONCLUSIONS

What conclusions can be drawn from this evidence? Despite all the difficulties and ambiguities, we find strong presumptive evidence that measured benefits fall short of (applicable) total costs. Furthermore, it seems difficult to argue that a more complex reckoning of option values could, say, double the benefit figure reported above. After all, the option of air service merely assures the traveler of the choice of a faster over a slower mode of travel. No doubt some potential travelers can contemplate emergency situations in which their subjective value of time would rise to levels much above their wages. Yet only relatively modest gross savings of time can be effected through using local air service in most cases. This makes one doubt that many potential travelers would willingly surrender an option premium much in excess of their expected consumer surplus. Thus, we would bet against a surplus of net benefits, correctly measured and inclusive of option values, over direct subsidy.

The reasonableness of this bet increases when we relate our results to certain features of regulation and market behavior in the local airline industry. The local airlines were heavily influenced during the last decade by their own efforts, fostered by the Civil Aeronautics Board, to enter into competition with the trunk airlines on short, regional routes appropriately served by small jet aircraft. The Board's interest in this development was spurred by the hope that cross-subsidy with profits from these routes could ultimately replace public subsidy in supporting service to small cities. The local airlines themselves may well have been motivated more by the realization that strictly local air service, supported by an impermanent subsidy, would at best yield them a normal rate of profit.

In any case, the considerable expansion of the local airlines into short-haul jet routes has clearly been dysfunctional for the support of unprofitable service, at least in the short run. The carriers faced severe capital-rationing constraints as they invested in expensive jet fleets in order to enter these new markets. Such constraints in turn constitute a sufficient reason for their lack of interest in small, short-haul turboprops that would have minimized the costs of serving the unprofitable small cities.[34] In fact, the local-service airlines showed no interest in buying small turboprops when they finally became available in the late 1960s. Simultaneously, new commuter airlines, unsubsidized and largely unregulated, sprang into existence to provide just the service that heavy subsidy failed to coax from the local airlines. The commuter airlines have experienced heavy turnover and obviously have not been highly profitable in the aggregate, but their proliferation strongly suggests that at best subsidy to the local airlines has bought a service produced at higher than minimum cost.[35] Public subsidy is hardly warranted if the same service can be provided more efficiently without subsidy.[36]

Indeed, the actual subsidy bill was higher than we have been discussing because of the large indirect subsidies associated with the public provision of airports and navigation aids. The enlargement of the aircraft used by the local airlines, from DC–3s to turboprop conversions to small jets, has entailed large public outlays to expand small cities' airports to receive them. In 1964, the Federal Aviation Agency found that introducing the turboprops would require modifications at 180 of 309 airports served exclusively by local airlines, at a total cost of $75 to $100 million. If all of the 309 were to receive service by two-engine turbojets, the bill would go to $300 million.[37] Outlays of this magnitude, when annualized and properly allocated, would yield a much higher figure for true annual subsidy to local airlines than that quoted above.

Our position, then, is that total costs of local airline service to small cities have probably exceeded the total benefits, including option values. On the other hand, in *some* markets an otherwise marginal commuter-airline service might yield total benefits exceeding its costs, yet not be able to cover those costs from profit-maximizing commercial revenues. Can a more efficient policy of public subsidy be contrived to deal with this class of market failure? The issue is a live one, for it has been urged in some quarters that the commuter airlines be certified into monopolistic authorized routes and given subsidies, like their regulated airline predecessors. The affinity between subsidy and monopoly is not hard to understand; if the public is to support a minimum service, it does not wish to finance any excess capacity associated with oligopolistic rivalry. Yet the apparently widespread evidence that commuter airlines are commercially viable where it was once thought that only subsidized local-service carriers would operate make us dubious about accepting this package for broad application.

Can the cases of *bona fide* market failure be somehow selected, and "chosen instruments" subsidized only in these markets? We note that the benefits of local air service are in large measure confined to local businesses, institutions, and wealthy individuals. Even if we show a healthy respect for the impeding force of transactions costs, we find not wildly unlikely a market solution in which these beneficiaries would join a club and pay sums up to expected net benefits in order to insure a guaranteed level of air service. Local governments provide an obvious mechanism for forming such clubs. If they present their own threats of socially unwarranted cross-subsidy between taxpayer groups, they nonetheless localize the decision to subsidize much more closely to the local beneficiaries of the subsidy than does action by a higher level of government. Such a procedure seems at least worth a try.

Notes to Chapter Twelve

1. This is the sort of problem discussed in K. J. Arrow, and R. C. Lind, "Uncertainty and the Evaluation of Public Investment Decisions," *American Economic Review*, 60 (June 1970), pp. 364–78.

2. Burton W. Weisbrod, "Collective-Consumption Services of Individual-Consumption Goods: Comment," *Quarterly Journal of Economics*, 78 (August 1964), pp. 471–77.

3. Millard F. Long, "Collective-Consumption Services of Individual-Consumption Goods: Comment," *Quarterly Journal of Economics*, 81 (May 1967), pp. 351–52.

4. Cotton M. Lindsay, "Option Demand and Consumer's Surplus," *Quarterly Journal of Economics*, 83 (May 1969), pp. 344–46.

5. D. R. Byerlee, "Option Demand and Consumer Surplus: Comment," *Quarterly Journal of Economics*, 85 (August 1971), pp. 523–27. The problem with his analysis, however, is that he treated the *good* as stochastic, when in fact it is the consumer's preferences which should be considered uncertain.

6. See Charles C. Cicchetti and A. Myrick Freeman III, "Option Demand and Consumer Surplus: Further Comment," *Quarterly Journal of Economics*, 85 (August 1971), pp. 528–39.

7. Richard Schmalensee, "Option Demand and Consumer's Surplus: Valuing Price Changes under Uncertainty," *American Economic Review*, 62 (December 1972), pp. 813–23. This paper was published after the current work was largely completed and resembles the treatment below to some extent.

8. M. C. Jensen, "Capital Markets: Theory and Evidence," *Bell Journal of Economics and Management Science*, 3 (Autumn 1972), pp. 357–98.

9. If we knew the utility function, using the fact that $E[U_{OP*}] = E[U_{NO}]$ we could write out the first expression and then use equation (2) and solve for $OP*$. But that is not possible in the empirical problem at hand.

10. Note that if U,while still strictly concave in X, is linear in Y, then the maximum option price that the consumer would be willing to pay in this case would be exactly equal to the expected consumer surplus. This is so because, in this case, the right side of (9) equals $U(O,Y_0 - \overline{CS},\epsilon_0)$ so that (10) becomes an equality, and both inequalities in (12) likewise become equalities.

11. Schmalensee, "Option Demand," pp. 817-18.

12. For a thorough general discussion of the local service airlines and their subsidization, see George C. Eads, *The Local Service Airline Experiment* (Washington, D.C.: Brookings Institution, 1972); figures for subsidy payments adjusted to the period in which they were earned appear at p. 142. Also see U.S. Civil Aeronautics Board, *Handbook of Airline Statistics, 1971 Edition* (Washington: Government Printing Office, 1972), p. 59-62.

13. Their emergence as significant competitors in some dense short- and medium-haul routes with the established trunk airlines is not without its social value, given the fact that airline regulation, as administered by the Civil Aeronautics Board, has blockaded the entry of *de novo* trunkline carriers without curbing all the distortions introduced by the fewness of sellers in the domestic air travel market. See Richard E. Caves, *Air Transport and Its Regulators: An Industry Study* (Cambridge: Harvard University Press, 1962), esp. chapters 4, 8, 16, and 18. In what follows, however, we shall neglect this possible "second-best" justification for subsidy to the local carriers.

14. See Eads, chapter 2, and Philip K. Verleger Jr., "Models of the Demand for Air Transportation," *Bell Journal of Economics and Management Science*, 3 (Autumn 1972), pp. 437-57.

15. The behavioral significance of the value of traveler's time has been developed by Bjorn J. Elle, *Issues and Prospects in Interurban Air Transport* (Stockholm: Almqvist & Wiksell, 1968); and Reuben Gronau, "The Effect of Traveling Time on the Demand for Passenger Transportation," *Journal of Political Economy*, 78 (March/April 1970), 377-394, and *The Value of Time in Passenger Transportation: the Demand for Air Travel*, National Bureau of Economic Research, Occasional Paper 109 (New York: Columbia University Press, 1970); James R. Nelson, "The Value of Travel Time," in Samuel B. Chase Jr. (ed.), *Problems in Public Expenditure Analysis* (Washington, D.C.: Brookings Institution 1968); Peter L. Watson, *The Value of Time: Behavioral Models of Modal Choice* (Lexington, Mass.: D. C. Heath and Co., Lexington Books, 1974); Arthur De Vany, "The Revealed Value of Time in Air Travel," *Review of Economics and Statistics*, 56 (February 1974), pp. 77-82.

16. Standard deviations of means for the individual airlines are respectively 40.1 miles and 18.7 miles. Figures are taken from U.S. Civil Aeronautics Board, *Handbook of Airline Statistics, 1967 Edition* (Washington: Government Printing Office, 1968), pp. 135, 156-168.

17. U.S. Civil Aeronautics Board, Bureau of Operating Rights, *Service to Small Communities* (Washington: Civil Aeronautics Board, 1972), Part 1 "Local Service Carrier Costs and Subsidy Need Requirements to Serve Marginal Routes." Traffic data are for 1969, population for the most recent year available (often 1960).

18. We tested the significance of the difference between mean values of the measure of traffic generating capacity, for various bifurcated

subsamples, on the assumption that the variances of the sampled subpopulations are identical. The difference between the zero group and all others is not significant (t = 1.4); that between cities under and over 50 miles is marginally significant (t = 2.0), and that between cities under and over 100 miles is quite significant (t = 2.4). It is worth noting that the sample heavily overrepresents cities west of the Mississippi River.

19. For example, R. Dixon Speas Associates, *Regional Air Transportation Study: The Demand for Scheduled Air Carrier Service, 1971–1990* (Manhasset, N.Y.: Speas Associates, 1971), especially p. 58.

20. See Eads, chapter 1. Verleger (pp. 455–56) reports price-elasticity estimates that are more scattered for the short routes than for the long routes in his sample and concludes that the price elasticities for the former are quite small.

21. For example, U.S. Senate, Committee on Commerce, Aviation Subcommittee, *Review of the Local Air Carrier Industry,* Hearings, 89 Cong., 2 sess. (Washington: Government Printing Office, 1966); *idem, Local Air Service to Small Communities,* Hearings, 91 Cong., 2 sess. (Washington: Government Printing Office, 1970).

22. Of course, different forms of travel might have differential impact on the employee's ability to perform his work *after* arrival. But for journeys of the sort being considered here, this does not seem likely to be a major effect.

23. Gronau, *The Value of Time,* chapter 5.

24. See Gronau, "The Effect of Traveling Time," p. 387. His equation for travel time by air implies a line-haul speed of 476 m.p.h., and thus pertains only to nonstop jet service. Correspondingly, the equation for money cost of air service obviously describes the structure of trunk rather than local-service fares, as is shown below.

25. Chicago: Reuben H. Donnelly Corp.

26. We assumed that the typical local-airline journey is between a small city and a major hub. The destination to/from airport journey takes 40 minutes in the hub, 20 minutes in the small city. The average wait at the airport is 30 minutes at the hub, 20 minutes at the small city. In selecting the city-pair sample for the regression analysis, we sought to make it representative as between small city to hub and other journeys.

27. U.S. Civil Aeronautics Board, Bureau of Economics, Rates Division, *A Study of the Domestic Passenger Air Fare Structure* (Washington: Civil Aeronautics Board, 1968), table 2.

28. The equations for the individual airlines neatly array themselves in increasing order of constant term *and* decreasing order of slope coefficient, making one of them the unambiguous median of these two-parameter measures.

29. Data in the C.A.B. *Handbook of Airline Statistics, 1967 Edition,* p. 396, are given only for the mileage ranges 0–49, 50–99, 100–149, etc. Passenger trips falling in these 50–mile blocks were subdivided into 10–mile blocks by a process no more precise than fitting a smooth curve by hand to the 50-mile-block data. Using the relations underlying case 4 of table 12-2, a minimum value of time was then calculated for travelers falling into each 10–mile block. Using data from column 5 of table 12-1, a mean and a total

value-of-time saving could then be calculated for each 10-mile block

30. For *all* domestic air journeys in 1966, the mean trip length was 728 miles, the median 546 miles.

31. The surplus becomes overestimated in one important respect as trip length increases. If air service at city *A* were deleted, the traveled from *A* to *B* can either drive the whole distance or instead drive to nearer city *C* that retains air service and fly from *C* to *B*. For the sample of marginal points taken from the CAB study, *Service to Small Communities,* the mean distance to the nearest city sustaining commercially viable service is 68 miles. As *A*-to-*B* journeys approach 200 miles, it would certainly pay some travelers to drive to nearer points *C,* and so the calculation procedure begins seriously to over-estimate the value-of-time surplus.

32. The reason is given in the preceding footnote. Suppose that access to alternative airports limits the average time saving for the local-airline traveler to two hours, no matter what the length of his actual air journey. We would then impute a value-of-time surplus of $28.4 million to all travelers enplaning or deplaning at marginal points in 1966, about half of the actual subsidy bill.

33. This matter has been examined extensively by Eads, especially chapter 3 and pp. 187-90; and U.S. Civil Aeronautics Board, *Service to Small Communities* (Washington: Civil Aeronautics Board, 1972), Part 2, "Small Aircraft and Small Communities: A History and Economic Analysis."

34. See Eads, especially chapters 5 and 6.

35. The commuter lines have often charged high fares but offered frequent service and generated more traffic than local airlines which previously offered limited or poorly-timed schedules in the same markets. In a general way this experience supports the importance of an analysis of the benefits of local air service based on the value of time saved for the traveler. See Eads, pp. 24-29 and 166-169; Civil Aeronautics Board, *Service to Small Communities,* Part 2, chapters 4, 5, 7, 8.

36. This statement needs two qualifications. First, a significant component of the difference between reported local-service airline and commuter airline costs lies in pilot's wages, reflecting in large part union bargaining power. Yet it is not obvious that public subsidy should support any quasi rents that are changing hands. Second, the "quality of service" provided by the commuter airlines is in some ways inferior (bouncier airplanes, no stewardess); and allowance should be made for lower levels of travelers' benefit due to the absence of these ancillary utilities.

37. U.S. Senate, *Review of the Local Air Carrier Industry,* pp. 70-71. Also Jeremy J. Warford, *Public Policy toward General Aviation* (Washington, D.C.: Brookings Institution, 1971).

About the Authors

Richard E. Caves is Professor of Economics at Harvard University. He was born in Akron, Ohio in 1931. He received his B.A. degree from Oberlin College and his Ph.D. degree from Harvard University. From 1957 to 1962 he taught at the University of California (Berkeley) before coming to Harvard. At Harvard he teaches in the fields of industrial organization and international trade. He is the author or co-author of numerous books and articles in these areas. His books include: *The Canadian Economy: Prospect and Retrospect, Trade and Economic Structure, Air Transport and Its Regulators, American Industry: Structure, Conduct, Performance, Britain's Economic Prospects, Capital Transfers and Economic Policy: Canada, 1951-1962,* and *World Trade and Payments.*

Marc J. Roberts is an Associate Professor of Economics at Harvard University. He was born in 1943 in Bayonne, New Jersey. He received his B.A. degree from Harvard in 1964 and his Ph.D. degree in 1969. He has taught industrial organization and environmental economics at Harvard. He is the author of a number of articles on the problems of public policy, including, "River Basin Authorities: A National Solution to Water Pollution," *Harvard Law Review;* "On Reforming Economic Growth," *Daedalus;* "Is there an Energy Crisis?" *Public Interest;* as well as a forthcoming book on environmental decision-making by electric utilities.

27